Sounds of Change

A HISTORY OF

Sounds of Change))))))

CHRISTOPHER H. STERLING &

MICHAEL C. KEITH

Foreword by LYNN CHRISTIAN &

BILL SIEMERING

THE UNIVERSITY OF

NORTH CAROLINA PRESS

CHAPEL HILL

The University of North Carolina Press
Designed by Eric M. Brooks
Typeset in Quadraat, Quadraat Sans, and Quartz
Bold by Tseng Information Systems, Inc.
Manufactured in the United States of America

The paper in this book meets the guidelines for
permanence and durability of the Committee on
Production Guidelines for Book Longevity of the
Council on Library Resources.

The University of North Carolina Press has been a
member of the Green Press Initiative since 2003.

Library of Congress Cataloging-in-Publication Data
Sterling, Christopher H., 1943–
Sounds of change: a history of FM broadcasting in
America / Christopher H. Sterling and Michael C.
Keith.
    p. cm.
Includes bibliographical references and index.
ISBN 978-0-8078-3215-8 (cloth: alk. paper)
ISBN 978-0-8078-5888-2 (pbk.: alk. paper)
1. Radio broadcasting—United States—History.
2. FM broadcasting—United States—History.
I. Keith, Michael C., 1945– II. Title.
PN1991.3.U6S78   2008
384.540973—dc22   2007046716

cloth   12 11 10 09 08   5 4 3 2 1
paper   12 11 10 09 08   5 4 3 2 1

Contents

Tables, Diagrams, and Maps

Foreword

BUILDING COMMERCIAL FM

Having begun a career in FM broadcasting between what this book describes as the "dismal" and "dominance" eras, I now look back on the early
years of FM radio with great pride. With this short preamble to this outstanding record of FM's trials and tribulations, I salute that diverse group
of people, with varying agendas and marketplaces, who came together and
developed FM into its current position as America's leading commercial
radio choice.

Early commercial FM radio operators—those in the late 1950s and early
1960s—were unsure whether FM's rather esoteric programming could
effectively compete for AM radio's advertising dollars. The few FM radios
in use throughout the country made time and program sales extremely
difficult. Fortunately, the advent of stereo FM in 1961 accelerated set sales
for both the home and the all-important car-radio market, which in turn
boosted the growth of FM advertising dollars by the late 1960s.

So how did FM's position change over those two decades? As witnessed
so effectively in the following chapters, between 1960 and 1980 consumers
of radio advertising time discovered the effectiveness of the "new and improved" radio medium. Stereo FM radio's commercial success rewarded the
longtime investment by its independent entrepreneurs and group owners.
These were men and women who recognized FM's potential and invested
heavily in making it a viable entertainment and advertising medium.

A case in point, which this writer personally witnessed in Houston,
Texas, involved pioneer TV broadcaster Paul Taft. In November 1958 he
convinced me to leave television in Denver to join him in a great new venture managing his Class C FM radio station, which he had just purchased
from the Houston Post Company for $10,000—including studio, transmit-
ter, antenna, and extensive program library. As was the case with some
other early FM operators, Taft's primary reason for buying this facility
was to utilize its subcarrier to transmit Muzak background music to business customers, eliminating costly telephone-line charges. He was a great
entrepreneur and reinvested all Muzak profits into "main channel" devel-

opment of his over-the-air station, KHGM—which he soon dubbed "The Home of Good Music." Recognizing the potential of FM's quality sound, he was willing to underwrite the expense of hiring professional people, making technical improvements, and creating America's first twenty-four-hour FM stereo station in the early 1960s. By 1980 KODA-FM (its new call sign) became one of the market's top three stations, consistently leading all Houston stations among audiences age twenty-five to fifty-four—the demographic most desired by advertisers. This is but one of hundreds of cases in which independent-operator belief in the high-fidelity medium led to its eventual commercial success. With thousands of new FM stations going on the air after 1960, property values in the 1980s and 1990s accelerated explosively, handsomely rewarding its supporters and advocates.

Those difficult early days of commercial FM radio are now far behind us. As radio executives search for successful programming platforms for the twenty-first century, there are countless sales and marketing professionals successfully selling FM radio time across the United States. Their work is being ably assisted by the efforts of a revitalized Radio Advertising Bureau.

The big question today appears to be whether FM radio will retain its position as the major distribution source of music programming in the United States during the twenty-first century. This writer's short but considered reply is that three things are required to make this happen: (1) creative programming; (2) brave management; and (3) successful marketing of high-definition, digital FM receivers.

In this book, Chris Sterling and Mike Keith provide a cogent and fascinating history of FM. It is an excellent resource on the growth and nurturing of FM radio in America, a period that many of us so proudly remember. As for the future of FM, a still-apt opinion was voiced by FCC commissioner Robert Bartley at the 1963 annual convention of the National Association of FM Broadcasters in Chicago. Bartley, who had worked in FM earlier in his career, ended his keynote address with these words:

> During about a two-decade history of FM broadcasting, many knowledgeable and influential broadcasters and manufacturers have earnestly predicted that FM would die on the vine. Many of these same people have subtly fought FM, . . . but FM did not die on the vine. It has had some setbacks and close calls, but it has survived like a cat with nine lives. It has survived because it's too good a thing to kill off. . . . It is good for

the listener because the signal is reliable and its quality of reception is infinitely better. FM radio has survived and progressed because it has offered a service which has become a symbol of quality. I urge you to keep it a symbol of quality.

Long live FM radio, and may its early pioneers' dedication to quality service continue to inspire it in the twenty-first century.

Lynn Christian

FM AND THE RISE OF PUBLIC RADIO

Would public radio exist without FM? The answer to this question is probably not, certainly not with over 2,600 noncommercial or public radio stations on the air. There just would not be enough AM frequencies to handle this many stations. Given the importance of public radio in America today, its growth alone would be reason enough for a book on FM's long history.

My own career coincides with the development of FM radio. As a college freshman in 1952, I started working for WHA, the University of Wisconsin station in Madison. H. B. McCarty, the longtime station manager, was directing the completion of the first statewide educational radio network. As the "oldest station in the nation" (a claim often aired and as often argued about), the network helped to realize this land-grant university's motto, "The boundaries of the campus are the boundaries of the state."

While what is now public radio began on university campuses and was regarded as an extraordinary educational tool, (I remember listening to "Wisconsin School of the Air" broadcasts in the two-room country school I attended), commercial interests soon moved in to take over the increasingly valuable AM frequencies. Learning from this, educational broadcasters like McCarty lobbied the FCC in the late 1930s to set aside frequencies for noncommercial use when FM was introduced. This would assure a place for education, for without dedicated frequencies, educational (later public) radio would be elbowed out again. The FCC eventually agreed, and the first dedicated noncommercial channels were the result.

As Chris Sterling and Mike Keith document in this history, however, FM was slow to catch on. Those farsighted enough to get a license capitalized on the high-quality sound, and many stations used FM to define themselves as fine-music stations. News and information was left to AM for the most part. Early educational radio outlets sought to offer a full range of programs, from radio plays to college lectures, farm and homemaker programs, reading books on the air, and jazz and classical music.

With the 1967 creation of the Corporation for Public Broadcasting, federal support for noncommercial radio and television grew. More funds and the name change from "educational" to "public" radio expanded the mission and the number of licensees of—and the audience for—noncommercial radio. When National Public Radio began producing programs in May 1971, fewer than 100 stations were affiliates or "members." Many only went on the air after noon, which is one reason *All Things Considered* was an afternoon news and information program.

With plenty of frequencies and the relatively low cost to start a station, FM radio soon expanded from a fine-music service for the elite to a medium serving varied listener interests from all news to all country, as well as stations serving specific ethnic groups. Yet, as the formats became more specialized, they often became more rigid and less connected to the community. Genres such as documentaries, radio plays, local-personality DJs, and local musicians disappeared. Some argued that FM radio had come full circle and now suffered many of AM's problems—albeit with better sound quality.

Today, we often need to look overseas to find FM radio with more colors in its palate and more connections to its locale. With the opening of a more independent radio sector in many nations, FM has expanded in both industrial nations and the developing world. Community radio (both abroad and in the United States) reflects the varied uniqueness of place. Since radio can be a wonderful storytelling medium, radio plays are often the most popular programs overseas. I regularly visit stations in developing regions to research how they are evolving and to apply lessons from one country to others.

Here are just two examples from Africa. One radio station in rural Mozambique produces radio plays to convince husbands that their wives can and should go to school and to educate listeners on how to prevent contracting HIV. Sixty percent of the music played on this station is performed by local musicians. Radio Friendship Clubs meet twice a month as a link between the community and the radio station. Public officials appear regularly on the station to answer questions from listeners. Listeners call it "our station"—indeed, community engagement is so pronounced that people come to the station with their problems before going to the government. In Kabala, Sierra Leone, the monthly stipend for station volunteers is less than the price of a bag of rice. Yet programming is central to the community. The local district councilman is on the air every week and is held accountable for expenses. Youth sponsored a peace festival with local musicians to raise money, and radio programs are credited for increasing the number of girls attending school from 40 to 60 percent.

We can learn from such stations just how successful radio can be at giving voice to people to air and solve their own problems, hold public officials accountable, and celebrate local culture. Most of these stations operate on 100 watts of power, enough to reach out ten to twelve miles and cover a regional trading center. FM makes it possible.

With the growth of satellite radio and other digital services, this is a good time to reflect on how FM has opened so many possibilities for so many—and to reaffirm the importance of local radio, the most accessible and democratic medium worldwide.

Bill Siemering

Acknowledgments

Few histories are solely the work of their authors, and this one fits that pattern. We have had a great deal of help along the way—and in one sense, it has been a *very* long way. While this specific team-authored study was hatched in 2004, its inquiry stems from Chris Sterling's long interest in the subject matter. Some of the research and interviews (many with pioneers no longer with us) undertaken for his earlier research substantially inform our initial chapters. Lawrence W. Lichty and Richard G. Lawson played central roles in guiding Sterling's earlier study of commercial FM's story into the late 1960s. Others who have helped us with specific information and advice along the way include Allen Myers of the FCC's Media Bureau; Tom Taylor, onetime editor of *Inside Radio*; David Pearlman; and Chip Morgan, who created the 2005 FM-coverage map used here.

As will be evident in the chapter notes, several important repositories of FM documentation have been valuable in researching this history. The staff of the Library of American Broadcasting at the University of Maryland, especially curator Chuck Howell, provided access to a number of resource materials used here. Also important were the NBC archives, different parts of which reside in both the Library of Congress and the State Historical Society of Wisconsin. The Radio Advertising Bureau, then located in New York City, was a prime source of material when the first research for what became this book took place in the late 1960s, and the bureau's Kenneth Costa was invaluable.

We are especially grateful to Bill Siemering and Lynn Christian for contributing the perceptive two-part foreword to this book. Bill has spent his career in noncommercial FM broadcasting, authoring the original National Public Radio mission statement and serving as founding producer of *All Things Considered*, among other achievements. Lynn's thirty-five-year career in television and radio—which included a stint as a pioneering FM-station manager in the 1960s in Houston and New York City—was followed by ten years with the National Association of Broadcasters and the Radio Advertising Bureau. Lynn also read some parts of this manuscript twice and provided invaluable memories of the turnaround of the 1960s and 1970s.

We are also very grateful to the other accommodating readers who went through some or all of the manuscript and made valuable suggestions. Michael Brown (who knows radio history), Donna Halper (whose seemingly bottomless archive turned up wonderful treasures), and Ed Shane (who provided early feedback despite a hurricane displacing his office) all helped us greatly improve the manuscript. David Layer of the National Association of Broadcasters was very helpful with the preparation of appendix A. To each of them, we are indebted. We appreciate as well the comments and suggestions of the two anonymous reviewers.

At the University of North Carolina Press, Sian Hunter was in our corner from the beginning, making insightful scholarly suggestions and providing calm guidance to sometimes frazzled authors. And Jay Mazzocchi did a fine editing job to make your reading easier. Jillian Saltpaw did the computer artwork for our diagrams and maps—and demonstrated considerable patience in the process. We very much appreciate the financial assistance of the Shiers Memorial Fund in underwriting the preparation of graphic material and other aspects of getting this book into print.

Last but by no means least, we each benefit enormously from the support of our respective spouses, Ellen and Susanne, both of whom have already suffered through the writing of many books and yet remain interested in and supportive of the process that leads to them.

CHS & MCK
Washington, D.C.,
& Boston

Sounds of Change

FM in Radio's History

The change was so minor, it easily could have been overlooked. By early 1958 scattered indications suggested that radio broadcasting was poised for a transformation. For one thing, the frenetic burst of early television expansion had run its course; nearly 500 stations were on the air, up five-fold since 1950. At the same time, AM radio continued growing; more than 3,000 stations were broadcasting in 1958, as new stations opened in small towns and suburbs. AM's middle-of-the-road programming and Top 40 formats were hugely popular. Almost forgotten amidst this growth of AM and television, some 530 FM radio stations continued to attract tiny audiences, although the number of these stations had been in decline. Few listened to FM because receivers were expensive and hard to come by, and most stations merely duplicated AM programming anyway. What had seemed a promising service when introduced on the eve of America's entry into World War II had in the years since declined to unimportance. Indeed, FM service seemed to be fading into oblivion.

Or was it? By early 1958 a few indicators suggested that radio's second service might be turning around. More applications for new FM stations were arriving at the Federal Communications Commission (FCC), especially in cities lacking channels for more AM or television outlets. For a growing number of urban communities, the only way to add a new broadcast voice was by resorting to FM. In 1958, for the first time in nearly a decade, there were a few more FM stations on the air than a year earlier. Other trends were also encouraging. Marketing of new stereo records was fueling interest in high-fidelity listening — and thus to better-sounding FM. Trade-press stories suggested that both broadcasters and advertisers should re-examine FM's potential. The stories noted that a few major-market FM outlets were building loyal audiences and some were even selling advertising time, offering models of what others might accomplish. Having long ignored FM as radio's perennial money loser, some broadcasters were beginning to reconsider that view.

Now, jump ahead a half century. FM is the predominant American radio service in terms of both audience and advertising. Three-quarters of all radio listening is to FM outlets. American public radio is almost entirely FM based and serves a growing audience. What happened? How did FM change from a tiny elite service to become the heart of American radio?

This book answers that question, telling the story of FM's transformation—from its innovation in the 1930s, through its dismal era of decline in the 1950s, to the medium's eventual turnaround and growth after 1960. Threatening FM's success, however, are the digital storm clouds gathering on the horizon, promising further change.

The story we tell here is a distinctly American one. FM broadcasting was invented and first developed in the United States. Only after World War II did FM begin to play a part in western Europe, helping to resolve two problems at once. Most European radio had been devastated by six years of war. Furthermore, there never had been sufficient AM frequencies available in Europe to allow the multiplicity of programming that American cities took for granted.[1] New FM channels gave Europeans a chance to rebuild their radio systems with more stations and greater program diversity, and, as in America, the ability to create a system with vastly improved sound quality. Occupied parts of western Germany were among the first regions to place FM on the air. Into the 1950s and 1960s, many more FM outlets began to air in other nations. In at least one case, ironically, FM radio was introduced to limit radio diversity rather than to expand it: in the 1960s the white-dominated government of South Africa introduced FM service to limit black tuning to the AM or shortwave signals available from other nations. FM thus helped reinforce the policy of apartheid.

The chapters that follow, describing and assessing the reasons behind American FM radio's constantly changing story, have been written with several goals in mind. First, this story has not fully been told before now. Within today's radio business, few have any sense of the fascinating tale of what FM had to overcome to succeed. This is a tale of innovation and success, followed by dismal failure and, ultimately, survival and growth. Many factors contributed to that up-and-down FM story, and some of them are still around today.

Second, we hope that FM's story may be useful in clarifying past mistakes in electronic media so we might better avoid future ones. As American philosopher George Santayana famously stated, "Those who cannot remember the past are condemned to repeat it."[2] As the first "new technology" to face policy makers and broadcasters, FM's story includes many wrong roads taken, some of them avoidable.

Finally—and this is a central rationale for studying the development of any business (or biography of an individual, for that matter)—we have undertaken this project to update and fill in the story from its checkered telling in the past. Well-considered historical narrative and analysis can and should elevate historical events and trends from what Thomas Carlyle dubbed a mere "distillation of rumor."[3] And there have been plenty of FM rumors to go around.

Our analysis of FM's place in American culture appears amidst growing historical interest in media generally and in radio more specifically. For several decades, radio was dismissed as a mere background medium of escape and entertainment, not worthy of scholarly attention. Indeed, as historian Susan Brinson describes: "Radio and television lurked among the 'inconsequential' subjects of study, dismissed by the cultural elite as simply the opiate of the masses and cultural pollution."[4] American radio is largely a commercial business, or industry,[5] based on entertainment and selling, with but a thin frosting of public service and news (these days, this aspect is very thin outside of public radio). Radio lacked much art or literature (other than a few playwrights in the 1940s)—certainly nothing like that feeding the thriving academic field of film studies[6]—and thus was not deemed worthy of academic research.

Yet as early as the 1930s' heyday of commercial network radio, some scholarly attention was already being paid to radio's developing relationship with its listeners. One analysis of radio audience research methods appeared as early as 1934,[7] and another study incorporated empirical work a year later.[8] Better known is a now-classic study of the impact of Orson Welles's infamous 1938 *Invasion from Mars* broadcast on its frightened listeners.[9] Further evidence of radio's importance was found in two foundation-based radio study centers established at Princeton (later Columbia) and Harvard Universities, which began to turn out cultural and policy studies, respectively. Two examples of the former include a pioneering analysis of radio-audience social stratification[10] and a study of how radio compared to newspapers.[11]

With the dominance of television beginning in the late 1940s, however, academic interest in radio all but disappeared for decades. The lack of a substantial documentary record of much of what happened on the air is one key problem that prospective radio researchers face. Another part of radio's long-running scholarly image problem has been the relative dearth, until quite recently, of much theoretical framing or context. Some seventy years ago, Rudolph Arnheim offered the first English-language conceptualization of radio as an important cultural experience.[12] But almost no one built on his themes, let alone developed others. Preoccupied first by a global war and then by expanding television, radio disappeared into the mists of academic neglect. Research funding and priorities did not begin to change significantly until the late 1980s.

What led to that change? For one thing, renewed interest in radio has grown out of the political and social controversies engendered by conservative talk radio. Scholars reawakened to what had first been noted in that landmark study of the 1938 Orson Welles drama: radio has the potential to effect society. An influx of scholars from many different academic fields (including those focused on media studies) helped push the study of radio. Contributions by researchers in anthropology, business, law, political science, and even literature laid ground for further contextual analysis of radio as each discipline perceived viable topics for analysis. Thanks to these and other researchers, historical writing about radio has grown more in the past two decades or so than in the previous half century.[13] As but one measure, no less than two scholarly journals focusing on radio's history and larger cultural impact now further encourage and shape radio studies in both the United States and Europe.[14] All of these changes have helped diminish radio's academic inferiority complex. While one aspect of the interest in radio is the development of more media theory in recent decades, research has also been inspired by some of radio's past and present program and business trends.

An excellent example is Susan Douglas's study of the first two decades of American radio,[15] which is in many ways a landmark. Hers was the first modern scholarly assessment of a brief but vitally important period of technological awakening and early policy struggles: essentially the two decades up to 1922 that laid the foundation for mass broadcasting.[16] Douglas argues that her seemingly distant historical analysis provides a "social construction" of radio that leads to a better understanding of the business today. She utilizes contemporary press reports about radio as one measure of understanding what those in and out of the business thought about it. She compares and contrasts that coverage to the behind-the-scenes struggles of inventors and companies to build, centralize, and control the new medium. We use her effort as a commendable model, though FM got its start later than her period of focus.

Considerable theoretically based historical effort is found within the "critical studies" movement, which has expanded into a variety of fields. Often applying Marxist theoretical approaches and based on the pioneering economic work of Dallas Smythe in the 1950s[17] —and the sometimes slashing attacks on the Establishment by Herbert Schiller a decade later[18] —critical studies scholars have plumbed media history by questioning corporate control and its impact. Who owns the media, and how does that matter? Vincent Mosco,[19] Janet Wasko,[20] and others continue to shape some of these approaches. While some disagree with the ideological bugles of critical researchers, they have posed valuable questions about the establishment generally not considered by others. While our study is not "critical" in the same sense, we have readily adopted their practice of questioning accepted versions of history.

Other historians focus on artifacts as a physical means of measuring progress and diffusion of innovation. Technology historians, for example, have developed interesting theoretical constructs. Perhaps the most widely known exemplar was Canadian theorist Marshall McLuhan,[21] who drew upon the work of, among several others, Harold Innis.[22] In a host of books and popular articles published in the 1960s, when he was a hot cultural commodity, McLuhan argued that old media do not disappear but become the content for newer services (as with AM programs carried on FM outlets). While criticized for raising ideas and then skittering away from any in-depth consideration of them (turning on the light but then leaving the room, as it were), McLuhan enlivened scholarly and critical media debate that continues a quarter century after his death. More recently, Carolyn Marvin reviewed the innovation of electric light, power, and communications in the late nineteenth century as social phenomena.[23] Her work underlines a point important in our own study: that so-called new technologies appear among a continuing string of developments and will, in time, be supplemented or superceded by others. But she also makes clear the public excitement over what new systems might accomplish—an excitement that is, as we shall see, exactly what greeted FM on its unveiling in the late 1930s.

Daniel Czitrom contributed greatly to this reawakening of media history.[24] His analysis melded theory (with chapters on early theorists as well as on both Innis and McLuhan) within a broad view of American life, including a chapter each on the rise of the nineteenth-century telegraph, early twentieth-century motion pictures, and radio up to 1940. His integrated assessment cut quite an academic swath when it appeared. In his quite different approach, Michael Schiffer's history of the portable radio provides what the author describes as an "archaeology" (his own profession) of the small radio receiver, one of the many "common, unglamorous items of everyday existence."[25] But he sees the portable (which he argues first appeared in its modern form in 1939, just as FM was gaining public attention) as a means to more clearly understanding radio's changing roles. As with the hulking consoles that preceded it, the cheap little radio becomes a kind of archaeological potsherd through which more profound things about the medium may be perceived. Unlike many earlier technical histories, Schiffer usefully places his story within larger contexts of social taste and public desires, just as we provide in this book. More recently, Jonathan Sterne focused on the changing sounds of modern life,[26] and especially on how the growing technical ability to reproduce and record voice, music, and other sounds reflects changing social needs and interests. While he does not mention FM or the high-fidelity movement specifically, we would argue that both are relevant examples.

As might be expected, scholarly program history focused first on radio's important news and public affairs role, with a focus on the 1930s and 1940s, an era before the transformations forced by television. David Culbert was one of the first to analyze radio and foreign affairs before 1940,[27] though he offers limited theoretical context. Douglas Craig covers the same period with different content choices and, writing a quarter century later, makes clear how much theory had caught up with narrative history.[28] He frames his material in the domestic political context of the time, assessing the growing political power of radio as the medium became essential to politicians and citizens alike. More recently, Edward Miller set his narrative within a theoretical nest,[29] arguing that the disembodied "voice" of radio was (we would argue it still is) a vital part of its appeal and impact. He underlines the point with such examples as Roosevelt's Fireside Chats, Herb Morrison's coverage of the loss of the *Hindenburg*, and the radio thrillers *The Shadow* and *War of the Worlds*, all of which predate FM but set useful analytic parameters.

Entertainment has been harder for scholars to assess, both because we have only a partial record of what has been broadcast (and what exists is at the network level—we have precious little from the local radio scene) and the radio "opiate of the masses" thinking already noted. This is a serious issue with FM radio in particular since so little survives of the medium's early decades, forcing a reliance on printed station schedules and program descriptions. Further, most program historians write for a popular-collector audience rather than for scholars, and they focus on collectible network programs and stars rather than the local scene.[30] Serious program-genre research has begun to develop, however, to some degree growing out of the much larger cinema literature as well as that about television. Given FM's traditional emphasis on music programming, much of the research concerning drama and comedy is of limited relevance here. Studies of popular music tend to focus on the rock and country formats, which well into the 1980s were primarily AM-station fare. As we discuss later, FM emphasized its vastly improved sound, hoping (though with only limited success) that a better listening experience would attract audiences. Those planning digital radio today would do well to review what actually happened with FM in the 1940s and 1950s.

Two books describing the 1920-to-1950 era appeared within a year of each other in the 1990s and helped herald the rebirth of academic interest in radio. Ray Barfield provides an oral history,[31] calling on both academics and practitioners to describe how people listened as well as what they heard during network radio's great days. Michele Hilmes's first radio book offered an excellent overall study of radio's content prior to the incursions of television.[32] She notes that she gave little thought to radio as a film student (nor did her professors)—a useful individual example of radio's scholarly image problem. She underlines the many problems already mentioned, noting that there has been more focus on national networks simply because more of their records survive. Both Barfield and Hilmes provide a solid AM context for better understanding the development of FM.

Hilmes also argues for a broad cultural-studies framework when considering radio's role, including the study of marginal programs, segments of the business, and its audience. One perhaps unexpected result of such research, she notes, is that the industry's view of its own inevitable (that is, advertiser-supported) rise and role comes apart under careful examination of the historical record. More recently, Jason Loviglio examined how network radio helped—or hindered—the democratic process.[33] He argues perceptively that radio helped promote nationalism and a degree of populism and walked a varied line between what was private (the listening process for one) and public (anybody could listen).

Michael Keith (coauthor of this volume) has produced several analyses of radio culture that substantially inform this book's later chapters. A number of his books speak to FM radio fare, including the almost invisible (to most listeners) role of radio by and for Native Americans,[34] the brief underground radio boom of the 1960s (virtually all of it on FM outlets),[35] an oral history of radio after the arrival of television (from FM's worst years to its slow turnaround) as seen through the memories and commentary of dozens of participants and observers,[36] the unique role of all-night radio in American life (often on FM given many AM station's limited hours or nighttime power),[37] the story of gay and lesbian radio (another service found largely on FM stations),[38] the hot (in every sense of the word) world of sex and indecency in radio (almost exclusively found on FM due to AM's greater conservatism),[39] and, most recently, the long rise and almost total decline of local programming on both AM and FM.[40]

The importance of radio in American life—defined, among many other ways, by how much time people spend listening—is evident in three recent anthologies of scholarly papers, most of which frame their narrative against theoretical foundations. Hilmes and Loviglio focus on a number of specific aspects of radio,[41] drawing larger comments about its changing social role, some of which we address further here. Susan Squier speaks equally to technology (including some foreclosed options), culture (radio and alternative or minority groups), and ideology (specifically feminist theory about radio).[42] Finally, Emmett Winn and Susan Brinson assemble two approaches to broadcast history—the traditional objective assessment and the more-nuanced cultural study—placing several topics in the broader perspective of media and American life.[43] We have drawn here from each of these precedents, placing FM within changing technology, industry structure, programming, the audience's changing use of radio, and policy questions posed by the new service.

Radio-policy studies have closely adhered to the legal-precedent paradigm. Historical writing about radio regulation was fairly cut-and-dried for decades—here's what happened (and perhaps why) and here's what it (probably) means. Few authors questioned what had happened or posited other possibilities. Robert McChesney's critical history of the early radio-policy debate encouraged scholars to take a more independent role and

question the state of the emperor's clothes.[44] Reexamining the same formative period (to 1935), but focusing on freedom-of-speech issues, Louise
Benjamin posits that the most important decisions about radio speech
were essentially in place even before passage of the Communications Act
of 1934.[45] In her analysis of the interplay between corporate and government leaders, she disagrees with some of McChesney's conclusions. Both
studies demonstrate that many long-accepted versions of radio's presumed
development are giving way to more consideration of alternative views,
minority positions, and might-have-beens (the "what-ifs" of history) that
shed new light both on the period in question and broadcasting today. A
careful telling of FM's story fits readily into this questioning mode, as the
chapters that follow make clear.

Susan Smulyan ranges over the 1930s and 1940s, centering on the deri-
vation of (and the fight over) radio's advertising support.[46] Combining
technology, cultural studies, politics, and economics, she paints a more
complex picture than is commonly perceived. Or, put more simply: since
nobody knew how to make money from radio broadcasting when it began,
how did the notion of advertising support arise and thrive? She describes
the impact of lobbying, which as we will see was of vital importance in
shaping FM's role as well. Kathy Newman carries the advertising story
through the next dozen years and finds that despite its wide acceptance,
some still fought its excesses.[47] Indeed, early FM operators built on their
limited advertiser appeal by promoting FM as a "sales-free" zone for peace-
ful listening. Thomas Streeter covers the whole story, critically assessing
the interplay among the various forces that have created the present American broadcasting system.[48]

Numerous critical moments of choice present themselves in the development of any social, economic, or political institution — including, as will
be seen, FM radio — where a perfectly rational decision to "go the other
way" by making an alternative choice (to the decision actually made) would
have dramatic impact later. Alternative or counter history is a movement
that has not yet penetrated media studies but offers interesting options,
some of which we suggest in these pages.

A rarity among radio-policy researchers in his focus on a single issue,
James Foust reviews the long argument over "clear-channel" radio stations
(not to be confused with today's radio owner of the same name).[49] Created
in 1928 by the new Federal Radio Commission, AM clear channels were
high-powered (50 kw) outlets that initially were the only users of their

frequencies at night; thus, operating on "clear" channels, they could serve the vast rural countryside then lacking local stations. As radio expanded, these stations became increasingly controversial because listeners wanted local stations more than (or at least in addition to) distant signals, no matter how good their programming. The argument between clear-channel station owners and the rest of the radio business as well as the FCC largely defined radio policy for decades, not being finally resolved until the early 1980s, though by then all AM frequencies featured competing signals. As with arguments between AM and FM from the 1940s into the 1970s, the clear-channel debate saw radio's haves and have-nots arguing the basics of the business.

Hugh Slotten offers six case studies of how the federal government (chiefly the FCC) dealt with changing technology, one of which focuses specifically on the struggle in the 1940s over FM's spectrum allocation.[50] Noting that regulators seldom demonstrate much institutional memory, he argues that early broadcast policy—such as the 1945 decision to move FM radio to its present spectrum allocation—remains important over time. He also explores the reliance on technical experts by the nontechnical policy community, again citing the FM story as a key example. Our discussion of FM builds on the version Slotten provides, extending it over a longer period.

Radio research has in recent years demonstrated a scholarly maturity on which further work will continue to build. Among the themes evident in the research reviewed here is increased questioning of the long-accepted sense of how American radio developed. This volume is a part of that questioning as we seek to define the real story of FM, a medium in the shadows for so much of its history. Growing archival evidence of the business and policy arguments that lie behind America's commercial radio illustrates that struggles between the broadcasting establishment and government created a system defined by compromise. Radio's development makes clear the difficult path any new system will face in obtaining support and achieving success—a lesson made abundantly clear with FM's own development.

Given this growing radio literature, where does FM's segment of the story fit? As noted, there has been no overall study of FM's specific path and contribution. There are studies on some aspects,[51] especially concerning public radio, which is predominantly FM based. But FM's larger story is important because of what the medium has been, has become, and shall be in the not-too-distant future. While FM began in the 1930s as a new interloper to an established radio business, since 1980 it has increasingly dominated and defined that business. Yet the thousands of FM stations that collectively reach more than 80 percent of the American radio audience are facing digital competition that will soon dethrone them in turn. Put another way, only now does the FM story have a clearly discernable beginning, a long and eventually successful middle, and a seeming end (as an analog medium in reality if not in name).

When inventor Edwin Howard Armstrong first unveiled his system of FM in 1935 (described in chapter 1), it was perceived as a cutting-edge technical marvel, all but eliminating the static that plagued existing AM service and providing far better quality sound (frequency response). The new service was touted as broadcasting's "better mousetrap." After the forced wartime hiatus in expanding domestic radio (see chapter 2), new FM stations appeared poised to lead the radio business to new heights. But instead, from the late 1940s to the late 1950s (as recorded in chapter 3), FM declined in the face of both television's competition and the clear lack of FM interest by radio owners focused on placing more AM outlets on the air. Faced with little audience or advertiser interest, hundreds of FM stations closed down. FM declined to, at best, a secondary service, and one seemingly destined to stay that way. In 1954 FM inventor Armstrong took his own life, despairing that his innovation was a market failure.

Only in the late 1950s, as major market channels for AM and television were taken up, did FM slowly turn the corner (related in chapter 4). Great excitement again surrounded FM in the 1960s (with FCC decisions allowing stereo transmission and then requiring programs to be different from those on co-owned AM stations) and the 1970s (as FM outlets began to lead major market ratings).

Another significant aspect of the FM story, though one less clearly understood, has been the medium's unique and varied cultural role (related in chapter 5). In the late 1960s, a swelling counterculture movement co-opted many FM outlets (both commercial and noncommercial) to convey its antiestablishment message. The rise of public radio in the 1970s was almost entirely built on FM stations, as was the parallel development of smaller community stations. At the same time, Native Americans employed FM frequencies to help preserve their languages and culture, while alternative lifestyle groups (such as gays and lesbians) used FM airwaves to help overcome bias and ignorance directed toward them. By 1979 mainstream commercial FM was for the first time serving larger audiences than was the far-older AM. The story of FM since 1980 (chapters 6 and 7) is increasingly of the medium as an integral definer of radio, especially in its many music formats, as most talk transferred to lower-fidelity AM stations. In the 1980s and 1990s, as media conglomerates bought up most FM outlets, illegal low-power FM (micro) stations surfaced as an antidote for the resulting decline in local service and programming diversity—and led to the creation of Low Power FM, albeit limited by incumbent broadcaster competitive concerns. As is outlined in appendix B, by the early twenty-first century there were far more FM than AM stations, and the gap continues to widen.

This study is arranged in the chronological order we feel is most conducive to providing insight into FM's long and sometimes convoluted development. Each chapter stands alone while building on the developments and trends that took place earlier. We have strived to provide a balanced story, combining and integrating the important elements of FM development—technology, stations and networks, economic issues, programming, audience, and policy. This introduction and a brief epilogue place the FM story in broader perspective—radio's historiography in the former, and useful theoretical insights in the latter. Naturally, such an assessment is built on hindsight, as the patterns observable now were rarely clear at the time they were being made. There may be some useful lessons for current technologies in the FM story.

FM's development is filled with elements of striking innovation (by one of radio's most important inventors), excitement (as audiences first heard radio lacking any static noise), seeming opportunity (for many more to participate in broadcasting), experimentation (with a variety of changing music formats), eventual success (as FM came to dominate the radio business over the past quarter century), and impending replacement with digital satellite and terrestrial services as well as the Internet. Today youthful listeners are departing analog radio in droves in favor of new commercial-free digital audio music services. Growing numbers of MP3 players (iPods being the best-known brand), satellite radio services, and other options are sowing the seeds of FM's eventual disappearance.

Creating a New System

(Before 1941)))))

The first high-powered, staticless radio station in the world, employing a "frequency-modulation" system of transmission and reception, will be put into scheduled operation early this year, with the call letters W2XMN, it is announced by Major Edwin H. Armstrong, professor of electrical engineering in Columbia University, who designed and built the broadcasting equipment. The new system will use an invention of Major Armstrong's which wipes out static, tube noises, and interference. It will greatly relieve the danger of the airwaves being monopolized, which has given so much concern to Congress, by making possible a service on the ultra-high frequency channels that are comparatively unused at present.[1]

While countless people and organizations eventually contributed to the development of this new form of broadcasting, FM's core technology largely resulted from the inventive work and innovative drive of one man: Howard Armstrong. As will be seen, Armstrong was central to FM's innovation in a way difficult to imagine in the very different world of the early twenty-first century. FM's early development before World War II began with experimentation in the laboratory and then on the air, combined with vital persuasion about FM's value to a skeptical industry and its regulator. FM's innovation involved marketing a new type of radio, first to station operators and then to their listeners, both against a context of the continuing Depression and a growing international tension.

These early events resonate today, for in many ways FM was the first of what would become a flood of new electronic technologies that competed with—and sometimes threatened—established media. One can see in FM radio's initial innovation during the 1930s many of the same problems that would face UHF television two decades later, cable TV in the 1960s, and more recently (as just one example) the Internet streaming of audio or video signals.

While the basic steps in successfully innovating any consumer technology—seeking industry support, gaining regulator approval, and then marketing to the public—are essentially the same today, the financial pressure is greater as the risk is higher. The pace of technological change and financial risk now combine to narrow the time window within which any new service must either achieve success or fail. FM was different in that it began with a single inventor working largely alone for several years. The strength and focus of Armstrong's drive to perfect his invention were vital to FM's innovation—as was the context of the time in which he worked.

AM EMPIRE

It is hard now to comprehend the paucity of media available in most American households in the expansive 1920s or Depression-ridden 1930s. Even by 1935 (a decade and a half after the inception of regular broadcasting), a third of American homes did not yet own a radio receiver, and only 10 percent of cars were equipped with a radio.[2] Less than a third of all households leased (one could not then *own*) a telephone, and that meant using a heavy device hard-wired to the wall.[3] Facsimile in offices operated only in a crude experimental form,[4] and today's multichannel world of audio, video, and data then existed only as science fiction.

For those who could build, borrow, or buy a radio receiver, however, radio was the exciting medium of the day. Indeed, the desire to listen to radio drove many to build their own receivers, whether simple crystal sets or more complex vacuum tube–driven devices. From the first stations in

1920 to the development of the NBC network in late 1926 (and CBS just months later), radio quickly expanded into a recreational panacea for those facing Depression job losses and little income. Radio was different from the widely popular movies because once you had a receiver, listening was free, while you had to pay every time you visited a theater. Further, by the mid-1930s, radio was expanding its program variety to attract more listeners. Families gathered around the living room console radio with its glowing dial, tuning in prime-time comedy and drama programs night after night. Millions followed the adventures of radio stars both on and off the air.[5] Numerous fan magazines helped stoke public interest in and adulation of top stars. Daytime listening was expanding, too, and by the early 1930s, the first network-radio news programs were on the air. By the middle of the decade, daily radio serial, or soap opera, was telling its endless tales in fifteen-minute episodes that moved slowly but attracted millions. Radio seemed to offer something for everybody.[6]

From the White House, President Franklin Roosevelt developed radio's political potential with his reassuring "fireside chats" about the state of the country, broadcast directly to the people without any of the editorial interface that accompanied newspaper reports. His calm and informal demeanor came over well on radio and helped his listeners believe that the nation was emerging from the worst of the Depression. On the other hand, demagogues such as Senator Huey Long and Father Charles Coughlin demonstrated a darker side of radio with their often harsh on-air harangues against Roosevelt and the New Deal.[7] The national networks (there were four of them by 1935, two operated by NBC and one each by CBS and Mutual) were beginning to develop a news-reporting capability and already had a few correspondents stationed in Europe.

Given this growing popularity, it is not surprising that radio broadcasting networks and stations already earned 7 percent of all the country's advertising expenditures in 1935, up from virtually nothing a decade before— a remarkable feat considering the nation's dire economic circumstances.[8] The four networks absorbed more than half of that total, underlining both the powerful listener appeal of their programs and advertisers' eagerness to reach that audience. Individual radio stations offered a new option for local advertisers as competition for daily newspapers.

Early commercial research into the nature and habits of radio's audience (composed of virtually everyone in the course of a typical week) was only beginning to provide a sense of who was listening to which programs at what times. For example, the importance of women in the audience became clearer when one analyzed the numbers of who was listening. Both the Cooperative Analysis of Broadcasting and the Hooper Company were developing methods of rating programs to help advertisers better plan their purchase of radio time. Listening to radio while on the move or driving (in the few cars with radios) was an expanding pastime as well.[9] Even staid academics were beginning to examine the growing radio business. While radio was clearly popular rather than "serious" in most of its content, any cultural phenomenon this widespread was presumed to have a substantial impact—and thus be important enough to study.[10]

AN ACHILLES' HEEL

On the surface all seemed well, given radio's rapid rise to success over fifteen years. Naturally some were unhappy with one aspect or another of the increasingly commercial service, but one consistent complaint stood out: all too often, static interference or electrical noise would make radio listening nearly impossible. Electrical storms (those that produced lightning) could create crashing blasts of noise that all but wiped out any ability to appreciate radio's talk and music. In the semitropical southern states, static interference with radio signals was a chronic problem for much of the year. All radio receivers suffered from the problem, and there seemed to be no solution. How to overcome static was radio's chief technical dilemma.

There were plenty of theories about what *might* work—applying more station transmitter power, for example, though that seemed only to make the unwanted static even louder. Engineers suggested using a narrower radio channel through which to "squeeze" the desired signal—maybe even combining that with an increase in power to simply overpower static. David Sarnoff, head of the Radio Corporation of America (RCA), the dominant radio manufacturer, pleaded with his engineers for a "black box" fix that would do the trick.[11] Because RCA owned a number of stations and NBC's two networks, Sarnoff had strong impetus for seeking a solution. But despite numerous attempts, nothing worked. By 1930 most of radio's technical people despaired of ever finding an answer.

Among the many methods explored to diminish or completely eliminate static was changing the way a radio signal was modulated before it was transmitted (see appendix A). "Standard" or amplitude-modulation (AM) radio could not seem to overcome either natural or man-made static because most static was amplitude modulated itself, making the wanted and unwanted signals electrically indivisible.[12]

Though it eventually proved to be unsuccessful, the first attempt to modulate the *frequency* of a wireless signal (rather than its amplitude) was Vladimir Poulson's 1903 "arc generator" wireless transmitter.[13] Two years later, Cornelius Ehret of Philadelphia received two American patents for a "means of transmitting intelligence" that appear to have been the first granted anywhere that make reference to "frequency modulation"—or more specifically, operating a receiver by "changes in frequency of the transmitted energy."[14] While occasional later references to FM appeared in radio's technical literature, they were usually disparaging.[15] One 1918 radio textbook, for example, noted that FM transmission would radiate radio waves in a manner likely to cause interference with other sending and receiving devices.[16] In 1922 John Carson, a scientist at the American Telephone and Telegraph Company (AT&T), applied mathematical theory to conclude that "this type of modulation [FM] inherently distorts without any compensating advantages whatever."[17]

Despite these seemingly dismal results, and faced with growing demand to resolve the interference problem, a few persistent researchers continued to probe FM's potential. Most were engineers who worked for one of the receiver-manufacturing companies that supported such ventures with the needed laboratory facilities (and had the impetus to do so). Westinghouse engineers, for example, had applied for nearly thirty FM patents by 1928.[18] A number of RCA engineers also worked with FM during the same period and applied the technique to key the company's telegraph circuits in 1925. By 1928 RCA began a three-year test of FM's potential application to transmit clear wireless (though not broadcast) signals across the country.[19]

Most of these experiments seemed only to confirm Carson's depressing conclusion that FM caused more harm than good. FM remained an interesting technological curiosity, little more than a bothersome side effect of regular (AM) radio transmissions. Seeing little likely return from any further FM effort, most researchers by 1930 reluctantly had moved on to other pursuits. One exception was a well-accomplished radio engineer working on his own in New York.

ARMSTRONG'S CONCEPT

Born in New York City in 1890, Edwin Howard Armstrong grew up there and in Yonkers, tinkering with mechanical and electrical devices while finding special joy in climbing towers and other high places.[20] As with many well-off boys of the early twentieth century, he had an early fascination with model trains. Soon he became even more intrigued with wireless technologies, building and experimenting with his own receivers and putting up high antennas. Within a few years he was pulling in signals from transmitters thousands of miles away while constantly perfecting his own reception devices. In 1909 Armstrong entered Columbia University to earn a degree in electrical engineering.

In 1912, when he was but twenty-two years old and still working toward his undergraduate degree, Armstrong developed the first of his three landmark radio innovations: the regenerative, or feedback, circuit.[21] This device showed that the vacuum tube, then relatively new, could be an effective amplifier as well as a generator of radio waves. With the new circuit, Armstrong demonstrated a far broader understanding of the technology than had others—including the tube's best-known developer, Lee de Forest. Armstrong became an almost overnight sensation in the radio field. Though later subject to a bitter two-decade patent battle that he eventually lost to de Forest on legal technicalities, radio engineers never wavered in granting Armstrong primacy for this fundamental innovation.[22]

By April 1917, when the United States entered World War I, Armstrong was a graduate assistant to Columbia University physics professor and electrical inventor Michael Pupin.[23] As would happen with many of Armstrong's generation, his education was interrupted by the war. Thanks to his growing reputation as a radio wizard, he entered the Army Signal Corps as an officer and shipped out to France in late 1917. There, Captain Armstrong in 1918 developed his second important radio innovation: a "superheterodyne" circuit that made a radio receiver more stable and selective, greatly improving the process of tuning and listening to a desired signal.[24] Early in 1919 he was promoted to major, a title that remained with him in later life.[25] Armstrong returned to New York as a civilian late that summer and resumed his work with Pupin. With his new patent in hand, he began to actively promote his superheterodyne innovation.

Within five years, Armstrong had become a wealthy young man. This was largely the result of RCA's purchase of patent rights to both of his radio innovations. RCA was the central player in receiver manufacturing and needed those vital Armstrong circuits to perfect their radio sets. With the patent rights payment, Armstrong became the largest individual shareholder in that growing company. Freed of the need to earn a regular income, and by now a member of the electrical engineering faculty at Columbia, he was able to focus full-time on research. This ability to conduct research as he liked became vitally important, for his third radio innovation took a good deal longer to come to fruition than did the first two.

Armstrong had by the late 1920s become intrigued by the seeming failure of the many FM experiments undertaken by others. Not yet ready to dismiss FM (especially after his earlier contrary thinking had led to both his feedback and superheterodyne innovations), Armstrong decided to focus his own research efforts on frequency modulation. He soon confirmed what others had discovered: trying to use FM in the narrow spectrum channels (10 kilohertz [kHz]) then assigned to radio stations was nearly worthless. With that finding, he very nearly gave up on FM as well. However, instead of joining the other naysayers, he made an intuitive leap that so characterized the man: what about combining FM transmission and a *wider* transmission channel? What might result with a channel perhaps ten or even twenty times wider than that used for AM? While such channels would occupy more spectrum (not as crucial an issue in the 1920s and 1930s as it would be today), the results might be worth it.

Initial experimental results in his Columbia University laboratory suggested that Armstrong was on the right course. With his test apparatus soon filling more than one large room in the basement of the university's Philosophy Hall (home of the physics department), Armstrong worked virtually full-time for six years to perfect his wideband FM system (he eventually settled on 200 kHz–wide channels), conducting what he estimated to be more than 100,000 experiments between 1928 and 1933. Emerging success allowed him to apply for his first FM patent in July 1930 and the last of the four basic system patents by January 1933. All were granted on December 26, 1933.

With those applications safely filed, sometime late in 1933 Armstrong first approached RCA chief Sarnoff to demonstrate his latest innovation. RCA was an obvious first point of contact because the inventor had often worked closely with RCA engineers. He and Sarnoff were longtime friends and had agreed years earlier to share their technical findings.[26] Armstrong was not only the largest stockholder in the company, he also had married Sarnoff's secretary. But what Sarnoff first saw spread out on tables in that Columbia University basement laboratory was far from his long-desired "black box." Rather, Armstrong's apparatus was a wholly new radio system. Adopting it could at least threaten and might even totally replace the existing AM radio system on which much of RCA's broadcasting and manufacturing success had been built.

Playing for time to consider what RCA should do about this latest Armstrong innovation, Sarnoff assigned several RCA engineers to further evaluate FM. Soon armed with their enthusiastic recommendation of FM's capabilities, he invited Armstrong to use RCA's experimental laboratory on the eighty-fifth floor of the new Empire State Building so that the FM system could be tested in realistic field conditions.[27] Working with RCA and NBC engineers, Armstrong installed his FM equipment as a series of "breadboards" (equipment laid out without any concern about design or space efficiency) next to RCA's existing experimental television transmitter W2XF.[28] Beginning on June 2, 1934, he used it to transmit test signals, broadcasting as experimental station W2XDG, the world's first FM transmitter.[29] A reception site was set up about eighty miles away at NBC engineer Harry Saddenwater's home in Haddenfield, New Jersey, and many system demonstrations took place there. Saddenwater and other engineers were duly impressed with what they witnessed. These initial FM experiments continued through July but were then interrupted to address antenna problems that persisted until October. Then, over a space of several weeks, Armstrong tested means of "multiplexing," or transmitting two separate programs at the same time. Into the early months of 1935, a series of comparative AM and FM transmission tests were run, some experimenting with different frequencies to determine those best for FM signals. But despite progress and positive results, there seemed to be markedly little RCA publicity about what was going on, and Armstrong began to wonder about the company's level of commitment to his new radio system.

He had every reason to worry. While the successful testing confirmed Armstrong's belief in his latest innovation, RCA's interest seemed to lag. This was confirmed in May 1935, when Sarnoff announced with considerable fanfare RCA's plan to focus corporate research efforts on development of a viable electronic system of television. In October, to create more room for the company's expanding television work, NBC managers asked Armstrong to remove his FM equipment. Bitterly disappointed at this turn of events, Armstrong dismantled the breadboards and trucked them back to Columbia University within a few days.

Despite several RCA engineering reports favorable to FM's capabilities (some of which were not made public for years), Sarnoff and others in the RCA leadership concluded that to adopt FM would call for a huge expenditure by both the radio industry and consumers—and that a second (though vastly improved) radio system made little sense in light of the huge promise of even more exciting television a few years hence.[30] RCA demonstrated little further interest in FM, instead touting the coming wonders of television. While perfectly understandable from the company's point of view, this change in direction marked the inception of an increasingly bitter conflict between Armstrong and Sarnoff that would soon destroy their friendship and last even beyond Armstrong's death two decades later.

GOING PUBLIC

Faced with RCA's lack of interest in FM, the frustrated Armstrong saw the need to take his latest innovation public in order to build radio industry and popular support for its commercial introduction. The first step was to reach out to his fellow radio engineers and convince them of what FM could accomplish, which he did with a spectacular demonstration.[31]

During the summer of 1935, in preparation for unveiling FM to the engineering community, Armstrong worked with his longtime friend Carmine R. "Randy" Runyon to rebuild Runyon's amateur transmitter to operate with FM technology on 110 megahertz (MHz). A makeshift studio was built in Runyon's living room. On the evening of November 5, 1935, Armstrong made his technical presentation to a session of the New York chapter of the Institute of Radio Engineers (IRE), meeting in downtown Manhattan. After Armstrong carefully described his new FM system, he turned on a receiver next to him onstage.

> For a moment the receiver groped . . . until the new station was tuned in with a dead unearthly silence, as if the whole apparatus had been abruptly turned off. Suddenly out of the silence came Runyon's supernaturally clear voice: "This is amateur station W2AG in Yonkers, New York, operating on frequency modulation at two and a half meters." A hush fell over the large audience. Waves of two and a half meters [approximately 110 MHz] were waves so short that up until then they had been regarded as too weak to carry a message across a street. Moreover, W2AG's announced transmitter power [100 watts] was barely enough to light one good-sized electric bulb. Yet these shortwaves and weak power were not only carrying a message over the seventeen miles from Yonkers, but carrying it by a method of modulation which the textbooks still held to be of no value. And doing it with a life-like clarity never heard on

even the best clear-channel stations in the regular broadcast band. . . . A paper was crumpled and torn; it sounded like the paper and not like a crackling forest fire. An oriental gong was softly struck and its overtones hung shimmering in the meeting hall's arrested air. . . . The absence of background noise and the lack of distortion in FM circuits made music stand out against the velvety silence with a presence that was something new in auditory experiences.[32]

Most of the listening engineers were astounded by what they heard. FM had long been considered useless, and yet here was a low-power FM transmitter operating on what was for the time a very high frequency—and coming through loud and clear.

"Clear" was the operative term, for what the assembled technical audience heard was an amazing clarity of sound without the crackle of the usual AM static or background noise to interfere with the intended signal. The various sound effects that Runyon broadcast (which included pouring water and lighting matches) also sounded far more realistic than the same sounds transmitted over AM radio. The desired signal-to-noise ratio with the FM transmitter was on the order of 1 to 100, compared to perhaps 1 to 30 with AM—meaning there was almost no background noise on the FM signal (appendix A). The demonstration also demonstrated a far greater frequency response than was possible with narrow-band AM signals. In plain terms, this meant that FM could broadcast far more realistic, or "fuller," sound and music.[33]

Despite his sterling reputation for solid work, Armstrong had for once outdone himself. Many of the engineers present for that historic demonstration found what they were hearing hard to believe. Despite Armstrong's record of innovation, FM skeptics abounded. It soon became clear that continuing demonstrations using real (even if still experimental) station transmitters would be required to gain the broadcast industry support that was essential if the new radio system was to succeed. In the meantime, Armstrong's IRE presentation appeared in print in May 1936, making more details of his patented invention available to all.[34]

Armstrong was well aware that he would now have to persuade radio manufacturers and commercial broadcasters that they stood to profit by adopting his system. This would be more difficult than dealing with engineers, since business leaders cared less about technical bells and whistles and far more about revenue potential. Here, Armstrong faced the classic "chicken-and-egg" problem: how could potential listeners be persuaded to purchase initially expensive receivers if there were no FM programs on the air? On the other hand, why should hard-nosed broadcast owners and managers spend money to build and program stations if there were no listeners? Someone had to make the risky first move.

PIONEERING STATIONS

To get FM's ball rolling, Armstrong decided that he would construct the world's first continuing FM station himself, using money gained by selling a block of his RCA stock. Receiving an experimental transmitter license from the FCC, Armstrong began to convert his FM plans into action. He selected a site high above the western shore of the Hudson River palisades at Alpine, New Jersey, which would allow the transmission of a strong signal over the New York City metropolitan market. Soon neighbors could see a substantial self-supporting steel tower rising up 400 feet, to which soon were added three broad cross arms stretching out about 100 feet each.[35] On April 10, 1938, operating as experimental station W2XMN, Armstrong's FM transmitter took to the air with low-power (600 watts) program tests. By July 1939 the station was operating with its FCC-authorized full power of 35,000 watts, transmitting an FM signal (usually transcribed music)[36] over much of the Northeast. At first, of course, listeners were almost non-existent, given the lack of FM receivers.

To begin the long process of developing those listeners, Armstrong late in 1937 ordered twenty-five FM receivers—at a cost of $400 each, or $4,000 in 2007 figures—from General Electric (GE). Expensive because they would be virtually handmade, the receivers would be used to demonstrate FM reception around New York City. They were also the first FM production receivers, as well as the first built outside of Armstrong's own lab. GE became the first manufacturer to obtain an Armstrong license to make FM receivers under his patents. They presented him with his first FM royalty check (worth $22.66) in December 1937.[37] The next year the Radio Engineering Laboratories (REL), a specialized firm founded and managed by Carmine Runyon, also began to manufacture professional FM monitors with high-quality speakers for station use.[38]

By this point, the first important commercial broadcaster had joined the small FM bandwagon. Armstrong demonstrated his FM system for the chief engineer of the regional Yankee Network, Paul A. deMars, who was quickly convinced of FM's potential. Another early wireless tinkerer, deMars had also sought methods to reduce static. Working with deMars, Armstrong soon persuaded network owner John Shepard III to build several experimental FM transmitters for his New England–based radio operation. This was a vital step: obtaining a broadcaster of Shepard's stature that others in the industry admired and listened to was to go a long way toward moving FM into a commercial reality.

Shepard is a good example of the right man being in the right place at the right time. In late July 1922 his interest in the growing radio hobby led him to install station WNAC on the fifth floor of the family-owned Shepard department store in Boston, following the inception of another station two months earlier, WEAN, at the store's Providence, Rhode Island, branch. While both stations initially were intended to promote the retail stores, fifteen years later Shepard would sell his flagship Boston store in order to focus his full-time efforts on further developing radio. He was elected the first vice president of the National Association of Broadcasters when the trade group was founded in 1923. After experimentally interconnecting his stations with telephone lines in 1928, he began to operate as the "Yankee Network" by 1930, providing shared regional programs. In 1934 Shepard started a news service for his stations (one of the earliest in the country),[39] and he also played an active part in organizing the Mutual Broadcasting System, which first aired that year. By the time deMars and Armstrong talked with him about FM's potential, Shepard was a widely respected broadcaster whose decisions were watched closely by other station managers.[40]

Quickly persuaded of FM's potential for extending the audience reach of his existing four AM stations, Shepard eventually committed a quarter of a million dollars ($2.5 million in 2007 values) just to construct what local papers referred to as the "static-less radio" venture.[41] Yankee Network station WIXOJ, built on top of Mount Asnebumskit near Paxton, Massachusetts, became the first to go on the air on May 27, 1939, with 2,000 watts, operating on 43.0 MHz. By July it was operating sixteen hours a day (from 8:00 A.M. to midnight) and was soon transmitting with 50 kw of power, spreading its signal out 100 miles and more. To relay programs from the Boston-based network studios out to Paxton, Yankee engineers installed a low-power FM transmitter of 250 watts.[42] This was far less expensive than leasing traditional telephone-wire links and demonstrated the new radio service's ability to relay signals from one station to others.

A second high-power Yankee Network FM transmitter, WIXER, began to operate late in 1940 from atop New Hampshire's windswept Mount Washington. This was an especially difficult construction task given mountaintop weather conditions most of the year.

The brutally cold temperatures and frequent high winds the engineers encountered while building WIXER delayed the project, such that it took three years to complete. At times, the engineers were stranded at the site, with only the provisions they had brought with them, until the bad weather diminished. One wonders if Shepard had realized that the new station would be so difficult for his engineers to build. They persevered, and their efforts finally paid off—but it was not exactly a camping trip. [Engineer Paul] deMars recalled, "During the last two months of the construction and testing period at WIXER, it was necessary for the Yankee engineers . . . to either ski or walk the eight miles of mountain road to the Summit, because snow made the road impassible even to a tractor. Some of the equipment was taken half way up the mountain by ski-mobile. . . . It was back-packed by men the remainder of the way."[43]

Plans were made for a third large transmitter to be located somewhere in Vermont. With these three FM transmitters, Shepard's network planned to cover New England without recourse to the telephone connections then required to link multiple AM stations.[44] Indeed, Shepard soon dreamed of a national FM-based network to rival the existing CBS and NBC webs. Due to a change in network ownership and the onset of war, however, the Vermont transmitter was never built.

SEEKING ACCEPTANCE

Observing these pioneering efforts by the astute and respected Yankee Network managers, several other broadcasters began to actively consider building their own FM stations. General Electric, which had long operated several AM outlets, built two low-power experimental FM transmitters in New York by mid-1939, one in Albany and the other at company headquarters in Schenectady. Interested primarily in the potential to manufacture FM transmitters and receivers, GE managers hoped these stations would provide essential information to support that role. Franklin Doolittle, another longtime radio-station owner, placed an experimental transmitter on the air in Meriden, Connecticut, in May. Westinghouse (the pioneering AM-station operator) added an FM station in Springfield, Massachusetts, in August, and the nation's capital got its first FM station when W3XO aired

TABLE I.I. Pioneering Experimental FM Stations, 1934–1940

Date	Call letters	Owner/Licensee	Location	Power	Frequency (in MHz)
Through 1938					
9 June 1934	W2XF[a]	Armstrong/NBC Labs	NY City	2 kw	40.0
6 Nov. 1935	W2AG[b]	C. R. Runyon	Yonkers	500 watts	110.0
10 Apr. 1938	W2XMN[c]	Edwin H. Armstrong	Alpine, NJ	600 watts	41.6
N/A	W2XOY[d]	General Electric	Albany	150 watts	43.2
N/A	W2XDA	General Electric	Schenectady	500 watts	43.2
1939					
13 May	WIXPW	F. M. Doolittle (WRDC)	Meriden, CT	1 kw	43.4
May	WIXOK[e]	Yankee Network	Boston	250 watts	133.0
June	WIXOJ	Yankee Network	Paxton, MA	50 kw	44.3
29 Aug.	WIXSN	Westinghouse	Springfield, MA	1 kw	48.0
Sept.	W3XO	Jansky & Bailey	Washington, DC	1 kw	43.2
1 Nov.	W8XVB	Stromberg-Carlson	Rochester, NY	1 kw	43.2
8 Nov.	W2XQR	John V. L. Hogan	NY City	1 kW	43.2
N/A	WIXCS[f]	Prof. Daniel E. Noble	Storrs, CT	250 watts	39.5
Dec.	WIXER[g]	Yankee Network	Mt. Washington	1 kw	N/A
1940					
11 Jan.	W2XWG[h]	NBC Network	NY City	1 kw	42.6
15 Jan.	W9XAO[i]	Journal Co.	Milwaukee	1 kw	42.6
1 Feb.	W9XAD	WHEC, Inc.	Rochester	1 kw	42.6
2 Feb.	W9XEN	Zenith Radio	Chicago	1 kw	42.8
1 Mar.	W2XOR[j]	Bamberger Broadcasting	Newark, NJ	1 kw	43.4
15 Mar.	W9XYH	WEBC, Inc.	Superior, WI	1 kw	43.0
Mar.	WIXSO	Travelers Insurance	Hartford, CT	1 kw	43.2
29 Mar.	W8XVH	WBNS, Inc.	Columbus, OH	250 watts	43.0
17 June	WIXTG	Telegram Publishing	Worchester, MA	1 kw	43.4
N/A	W2XWF[k]	Finch Laboratories	NY City	1 kw	42.1
N/A	W3XMC	McNary & Chambers	Bethesda, MD	100 watts	42.6
N/A	WIXK	Westinghouse (WBZ)	Boston	1 kw	42.6
N/A	W8XFM[l]	Crosley Corp (WLW)	Cincinnati	1 kw	43.2

Sources: *Broadcasting* (1939–40) and *Broadcasting Yearbook* 1940, p. 374; *Frequency Modulation Business* (February 1946), pp. 22, 24; *Radio and Television Retailing* (January–September 1940); Orrin E. Dunlap, *Dunlap's Radio and Television Almanac* (New York: Harper, 1951); and Lawrence Lessing, *Man of High Fidelity: Edwin Howard Armstrong* (Philadelphia: J. B. Lippincott, 1956).

TABLE I.I. (*continued*)

These FM transmitters went on the air prior to December 31, 1940, which marked the end of FM's experimental period. Stations are listed by initial air date, though a few specific dates are now lost. The initial air date was often earlier than the inception of regular program schedules. These call letters were used until the end of 1940, when, for most, commercial call letters were assigned. As will be seen, most stations used 1,000 watts (1 kw) of power since that was the most allowed under the FCC rules (only the Yankee stations and Armstrong's outlet were allowed greater power for FM-coverage research). Most of these stations became commercial operations during or after 1941.

a. This transmitter left the air in mid-1935.

b. Runyon's amateur transmitter was subsequently licensed for operation on 117.9 MHz with 5kw of power (October 1939).

c. Armstrong's big operation began a regular program schedule with full power (40kw) on July 18, 1939.

d. These two low-power GE transmitters were used in experiments with both AM and FM, the results of which were published early in 1939; but other than the fact that the Albany outlet is listed first in contemporary sources, no actual air date is known for either transmitter. The Schenectady station later operated with 3 kw of power on 48.5 MHz.

e. Relay transmitter used to send programs from Boston studios to the Paxton transmitter, forty-two air miles to the west. Exact air date not known. This outlet later used WEOD call letters.

f. This was a purely experimental transmitter that also used 139.5 and 300–400 MHz for research undertaken at what was then Connecticut State College.

g. No actual air date is listed in available contemporary sources; this is taken from Lessing, *Man of High Fidelity*, p. 238.

h. The first network-owned FM transmitter, it was located in the Empire State Building in space vacated five years earlier by Howard Armstrong.

i. First FM outlet owned by a newspaper (the *Milwaukee Journal*) and the first FM transmitter west of the Alleghenies. See C. H. Sterling, "WTMJ-FM: A Case Study in the Development of FM Broadcasting," *Journal of Broadcasting* 12 (Fall 1968): 341–52. This experimental station became W55M in 1942 and WTMJ-FM after the war; it left the air in 1949.

j. Regular program service began August 1, with service from 9:00 A.M. to midnight.

k. This transmitter was used primarily for facsimile experimentation, not voice broadcasting.

l. There is doubt about whether this station actually aired, especially as WLW-FM did not go on the air until 1946.

in September. Radio engineer and innovator John V. L. Hogan placed his New York City W2XQR on the air in early November.[45] Thus nearly a dozen FM outlets were licensed for experimental operation by the FCC and were on the air by the end of 1939,[46] and many more followed the next year (Table I.I). Several began to share programs by utilizing over-the-air relays, demonstrating what a fuller network of FM stations might accomplish.

Transmitters for these and other pioneering stations were manufactured by REL and Western Electric (an arm of AT&T), as well as by GE. Each company agreed to pay Armstrong a patent royalty on each transmitter they sold. The first consumer FM radio receivers soon appeared, made by GE, Stromberg-Carlson, and a handful of other firms—though at $100 or more each (about $1,000 in 2007 values), sales were understandably limited and were made primarily to high-income households. Perhaps 3,000 FM receivers had been sold by April 1940. Many were handsome multi-band console sets that included AM- and shortwave-tuning capabilities; they often featured a phonograph as well. At the same time, the manufacturers of these and other sets began the first promotional campaigns to inform listeners about FM and persuade them to buy the new receivers.[47] Given that several stations already were on the air in New York, Macy's department store devoted part of its radio department to explaining how FM worked and what it offered, displaying several console receivers for sale.[48] The store's combination of banners, explanatory signs, and promotion was one of the first retail FM-receiver displays designed to catch shoppers' eyes and interest, and it was soon copied in other cities. All this activity carried an element of risk, however, as the FCC had yet to approve regular commercial FM operation, only licensing experimental transmitters.

Early in 1940, the first network-owned FM station took to the air when NBC began operating W2XWG from atop the Empire State Building.[49] Just four days later, W9XAO aired as the first FM outlet located west of the Alleghenies and the first owned by a newspaper (the *Milwaukee Journal*).[50] Radio manufacturer Zenith placed W9XEN on the air in Chicago shortly thereafter.[51] Runyon's REL manufactured transmitters for most of these stations. This steadily expanding FM activity made clear to the FCC that the new medium seemed to be developing critical mass and the potential to become a viable commercial service. Indeed, pressure now began to build for the commission to authorize such broadcasting.

Three years earlier (in 1936), the FCC had conducted extensive spectrum allocation hearings for a variety of experimental services, including fledgling television. At that time, only Armstrong and deMars testified on behalf of FM's needs.[52] On the other hand, a number of RCA and other engineers testified about the extensive spectrum needs of developing television. As part of a larger October 1937 decision, the FCC allocated three widely spaced channels that could accommodate up to about a dozen experimental FM stations.[53] Licenses would be granted for a six-month period, renewable only with clearly demonstrated experimental goals in mind. Faced with increasing FM interest early in 1939, the FCC greatly expanded FM's spectrum allocation to seventy-five channels, all between 41 and 44 MHz.[54] This new allocation, though still restricted to experimental operations, made possible the growing number of transmitters—and, of course, added still more pressure for commercial authorization so that stations could sell advertising and begin to recoup their investment.

At the same time, stations and receiver manufacturers undertook what would become an extensive public-relations campaign to build popular support for the new radio service. At an organizational meeting in New York City in January 1940, Yankee Network chief John Shepard was elected the first president of FM Broadcasters, Inc. (FMBI), a trade association dedicated to rapid approval of FM's commercial status.[55] FMBI soon issued *Broadcasting's Better Mousetrap*, perhaps the first general-interest promotional booklet describing FM. More than 30,000 copies were widely distributed. In plain language, the booklet explained FM's potential.

> First of all, the programs are clearer than the proverbial bell. Each sound, each note of music comes over the air with the identical clarity it would have if produced right in the same room with you. The announcer whispers, and you start at his nearness. A match strike; you can hear its crackle, then the intake of breath as a cigarette is lit. Water is poured from one class to another with a clear, liquid slosh. Try these things in front of the microphone of a regular amplitude modulated station and you'll find your listeners tuning away from an ear-splitting galaxy of misshapen sounds. But FM is so lifelike you can practically reach out and shake hands with the announcer![56]

FMBI also announced plans for a New York office to be headed by public-relations expert and writer Dick Dorrance, author of the *Broadcasting's Better Mousetrap*. He soon began issuing a mimeographed biweekly newsletter to keep a growing list of readers current on all aspects of the expanding FM scene.

In support of this promotional process, Armstrong took on a heavy schedule of speaking about FM, touting and demonstrating what FM service could accomplish. At one such demonstration in Washington, D.C., he and others suggested how use of FM could allow far more broadcast stations than AM alone, thus greatly expanding the radio business—perhaps not what incumbent AM operators wanted to hear.[57] Articles touting FM also began to appear in the popular-science press,[58] as well as in business periodicals.[59] Those well outside of the range of the few stations on the air began to hear and read more about this new and improved radio service. How to handle conflicting views concerning FM's future became a matter of rising priority in Washington's policy-making circles, portending similar situations in later years as new technologies became viable and threatened those already operating.

BEFORE THE FCC

More than 400 observers and participants crowded into the Interstate Commerce Commission's auditorium in Washington, D.C., on March 18, 1940, as the FCC began the first day of nearly two weeks of intensive hearings about the status of FM.[60] Many others who wanted to be present could not squeeze in and lined nearby hallways. All branches of the American broadcast business were present, as were engineer representatives from Canada and even the Soviet Union. After the first session, the hearing was transferred to a larger room at the Department of Labor.[61]

Armstrong's opening testimony fittingly took up the first day and much of the second. He outlined the background and development of FM, his own patent situation (rather than selling his patent rights as with his first two innovations, he told the FCC he planned to issue royalty-paying licenses to help fund further research), and his reasons for choosing the wide 200 kHz channel for the service. Among other benefits, he noted, was the fact that stations would be able to multiplex (or transmit supplementary signals to the main broadcast channel) as a result of the wide channel. Though not perceived at the time, that ability would become hugely important two decades later with supplementary and stereo broadcasting (see chapter 3). Economics had played a part in his choice of the wide-channel, because, as Armstrong told the commissioners, use of a channel half as wide would have required a transmitter four times as powerful (an even narrower 30 kHz channel would mandate a transmitter with twenty-five times more power to achieve the same quality of service). Receivers would also be harder to design for a narrower band. With the broader channel, a mere 1,000 watts would suffice for a station to cover a radius of thirty miles. Armstrong argued for two types of FM outlets: a limited number of large stations serving substantial regions and many smaller stations for more specific market areas—a model not unlike that defining the existing AM service. FM outlets could inexpensively link up simply by relaying their signals over the air rather than leasing expensive AT&T telephone lines, as was the AM practice. Armstrong wrapped up his more than eight hours of testimony and responses to questions from the commissioners and FCC staff by concluding that FM radio was ready to go while television was not, and thus a decision allowing commercial FM should be made now.

Following a couple of other witnesses, Shepard spoke strongly in favor of FM based on the Yankee Network experience. He focused on Yankee's use of high-power FM stations to facilitate relay networks. He also argued that at least some FM-only programs should be required to encourage potential listeners to purchase receivers—thus touching on an issue that would remain contentious for three decades. Several engineers (including Yankee's deMars) spoke on the third and fourth days of the hearing, testifying about what had been learned regarding FM from the various experimental stations on the air, and especially how the new service was superior to AM stations. Officials of GE and several other companies also testified in support of FM's readiness for commercial service.

Given RCA's strong investment in and promotion of television, the one real surprise of the hearing came on the second-to-last day, when the company's counsel, Frank W. Wozencraft, rose to agree with much of what had already been said—that FM *was* ready for commercial operation. But RCA's representatives made clear they felt that FM would likely never serve the whole country, and thus AM would continue to play an important role. They also argued that the high-power relay idea touted by Armstrong and others was not feasible on a larger scale (of course it could also be seen as potentially competitive with the existing networks, including RCA's NBC). Wozencraft called on several RCA engineers to testify in favor of a 40 kHz–wide channel rather than Armstrong's 200 kHz standard because RCA was concerned about preserving sufficient spectrum space for television. A Zenith witness suggested that both FM and television should be tested for another year before any final decision was made on regular allocations for either.

The final day of the FCC hearing focused on possible FM allocations for commercial service. Armstrong and the fledgling FMBI organization pushed for FM to use the whole 41–50 MHz band, which would necessitate shifting one television channel (probably higher) in the spectrum.[62] RCA countered with a somewhat confusing alternative that would enable both FM and television to use different parts of the VHF spectrum while preserving television's existing position. The testimonies of both RCA and

CBS officials were aimed at limiting FM's encroachment on channels they hoped to use for television.

As the FCC commissioners and staff withdrew to consider their options and draw up a decision, applications to construct new FM stations continued to flow into the FCC's Washington headquarters. Given the complexity of the issues—and the desired use of the same VHF frequencies by both television and FM—the allocation decision was not going to be an easy task. All agreed that the spectrum issue had to be resolved so both new services could progress.[63] At the same time, the decision would also define parameters for the growing number of receiver manufacturers interested in entering the new market.

On May 20, 1940, the FCC issued its landmark "Report on Frequency Modulation" decision, approving commercial FM operation beginning at the start of the new year. The commission summarized its long hearings by concluding:

> Frequency modulation is highly developed. It is ready to move forward on a broad scale and on a full commercial basis. On this point there is complete agreement amongst the engineers of both the manufacturing and the broadcasting industries. A substantial demand for FM . . . transmitting stations for full operation exists today. A comparable public demand for receiving sets is predicted. It can be expected, therefore, that this advancement in the broadcast art will create employment for thousands of persons in the manufacturing, installation, and maintenance of transmitting and receiving equipment and the programming of such stations.[64]

Though a few radio observers were already suggesting that FM would likely replace AM entirely, the FCC concluded, "The extent to which in future years listeners will be attracted away from the standard [AM] band cannot be predicted."[65] Indeed, only four decades later would that issue be fully resolved in FM's favor.

The commission decided that all existing experimental FM stations would have to apply for commercial licenses. The commission also accepted Armstrong's wide-channel (200 kHz) technical standard and the growing industry research data demonstrating FM's superiority over AM transmission. This was a huge victory for Armstrong and something of a defeat for RCA, which (despite the FCC comment quoted above suggesting broad industry agreement) had sought to limit FM to narrower channels.[66]

The commission allocated FM forty channels in the 42–50 MHZ VHF-frequency band, to be used by both commercial and educational stations. Indeed, this decision marked the inception of a new FCC policy to reserve or set aside some (in this case, five) channels of new services for use by noncommercial operators. The new allocation would allow up to eighteen FM outlets in virtually any community without any of them interfering with the others. With an antenna mounted atop a 1,000-foot tower, FM stations were expected to transmit usable signals up to a 100-mile radius.[67] The FCC classified FM stations to broadcast to either "basic" or "limited" trade areas (defined by how much ground each one covered). Twenty-two of the channels were intended for communities of more than 25,000 people (the limited area) and six for more rural regions, while only seven were intended to serve extensive regions as large as 15,000 square miles (the basic area).[68] Unlike many AM outlets that had to leave the air at night to reduce interference with others, FM stations would operate day and night.[69] As was then the case with AM, only one FM station could be owned by any entity in any given market, and no owner could have more than six nationally. This was the first time the FCC issued a rule limiting station ownership in any service.[70]

For a transitional period while FM was being introduced, the commission required stations to program for at least three hours before 6:00 P.M. plus another three hours later in the evening. At least one of those hours was to be devoted to providing programming not otherwise available in the same market (this was another early indication of what would become the hotly contested debate over the degree to which FM outlets could duplicate programs of co-owned AM stations).

The broadcast business seemed to take FCC approval of the new service in stride; indeed, many broadcasters were laying plans to play a big if not controlling part in FM. As *Broadcasting*, the main industry biweekly, editorialized after the decision had been released:

It is logical to assume that when the shakedown period is over, all but a few FM licensees will be standard [AM] broadcasters of today. The real test of FM will be public acceptance. Will the public buy high-fidelity for the sake of better reception alone? That is doubtful. But if FM provides the proverbial better mousetrap, with programs equaling or eclipsing present high standards, plus the static-free inducement, it should attract plenty of combination receiver purchasers. Henceforth it's a merchandising-programming job. And FM is certainly worth the gambler's chance for every present-day broadcast licensee.[71]

Clearly, a lot was at stake. The public already had some $3 billion invested in 40 million AM receivers, broadcasters had expended about $75 million in the more than 800 AM stations then on the air, and radio advertisers were spending some $170 million annually to advertise over those stations.[72] FM raised the threat that some of this AM infrastructure might have to be supplemented or even replaced. Much more would have to be spent by the industry and its listeners before FM radio became a widespread reality.

One receiver manufacturer made clear it was ready to serve the new medium and help build its audience.

When we say that Stromberg-Carlson is *ready* with a *complete* line of FM receivers, we mean this in the full sense of the words. Ready with a complete selection of radio and radio-phonograph models in a wide price range! . . . The very fact that Stromberg-Carlson FM receivers have been repeatedly selected to demonstrate Frequency Modulation reception before [the FCC and other] such critical and authoritative groups is indisputable evidence of Stromberg-Carlson's leadership in this new field. . . . No other manufacturer can match Stromberg-Carlson's months of successful manufacture of FM receivers. *All Stromberg-Carlson FM equipment is licensed under Armstrong Wide-Swing Frequency Modulation patents.*[73]

Armstrong made clear in June that there were already 7,000 to 8,000 FM receivers in use.[74] Based on the FCC decision, about a dozen manufacturers announced plans to be in full production of many more FM sets by the fall.

The FCC's report and order also contained a warning, however, which in light of future events was prophetic. The commission expressed concern about possible atmospheric interference in the 42–50 MHz frequency band and noted that as more was learned, a later shift in FM's allocation might prove necessary. Largely ignored amid the celebrations of FM's arrival as a commercial service, this cautionary note would come back to haunt the fledgling business just five years later.[75]

HOPE

The period to the end of 1940 was one of rising excitement and hope among the growing coterie of FM devotees. From Armstrong's lone laboratory experiments to the early field tests and persuasion of a sometimes skeptical industry and regulator, FM began to pick up speed. With a number of experimental stations on the air, by late 1940 progress was being made in marketing this new concept of radio listening to radio retailers and potential listeners. To those able to tune in, FM marked a clear advance in radio listening. The bugaboo of static seemed finally conquered, though by using a different system from AM. Those living outside the few cities served by FM, however, could only read about the promise of this new type of radio.

FM's potential to allow many more stations and possibly new broadcasters fueled the enthusiasm many felt about the medium's future. While a few proponents were predicting that FM would replace AM, most expected that the two would coexist in an expanded and popular radio service.

92.5 MHz

War and Evolution (1941–1945))))))

A radical change in the FM band will introduce several aspects of the chicken-and-egg stalemate. . . . High-power tubes for the [new] band have not been developed at this time. That work must be completed and production samples must be available before transmitters can be designed. . . . Past experience shows that new types of transmitters cannot be put into commercial operation without extensive tests and alterations. . . . Final determination of receiver design and performance . . . cannot be made in the laboratory. Actual field testing is required. . . . Therefore receiver production cannot start until sometime after there are transmitters on the air.[1]

These worrisome concerns lay in the future when the start of 1941 brought the inception of commercial FM-station operation. Portending more change was the growing buzz about television, which would begin commercial operation, though only in a few cities, by midyear. There was already concern among FM proponents that the video medium could become a serious spectrum competitor for FM.

Amidst these broadcasting events, much of the country was devouring the increasingly grim news from overseas. President Franklin Roosevelt had just been elected to an unprecedented third term. World War II was into its third year in Europe, and fighting had been going on even longer in China. Radio reflected these crises with more network and station news broadcasts from both home and abroad. On a more positive note, more people were working, as the dregs of the Depression faded amidst rising production and business.

COMMERCIAL AT LAST

Regular FM broadcasting got off to a somewhat subdued and confusing start on January 1, 1941, with few among the general public even aware of the event. Experimental outlets on the air continued their existing programming—generally orchestral music—with little change. Most signed on at noon or in the afternoon and programmed into the early evening hours. Few penetrated morning-listening time due to a lack of personnel to maintain longer hours in a service not yet earning any revenue. The chief difference from the experimental period seemed that stations could now sell time, though most announced they would delay doing so until they were operating at their full technical capacity and had plenty of program material on hand.[2]

In Milwaukee, for example, the Journal Company's station W9XAO had been on the air experimentally since April, broadcasting from 1:00 P.M. to 10:15 P.M. each day. Programs mixed various kinds of popular and light concert music (some performed live in the studio and simulcast from WTMJ [AM], but several others by transcription recordings) with periodic news highlights. Several of the music programs were only fifteen minutes long. Perhaps inadvertently, a half hour of "slumber music" preceded the evening newscast just before sign-off! The station had eight dedicated employees and reported it was already serving about 1,000 FM-owning households.[3]

While the FCC intended that such FM experimental operations leave the air at the end of 1940, it was apparent well before Christmas that doing so would cut off service in a number of markets just as stations were trying to build public interest in tuning to FM radio. So the FCC allowed the experimental stations to continue operating into the new year, though sometimes on a different frequency and with new call letters. They were extended on two further occasions to maintain continuity of FM service.[4]

The chief problem facing commercial FM operation was not a lack of broadcaster interest but a backlog of station applications at the commission's offices. The FCC had issued construction permits (the last step before a formal grant of license) to fifteen stations in as many cities at the end of October 1940, noting that there were "more than 27 million people embraced in the 110,000 square miles of potential service area of these stations."[5] These new outlets ranged from four in New York City to one each in Los Angeles and Chicago; there was even one in comparatively tiny Evansville, Indiana (which in 1942 claimed FM's only mobile-transmitting unit for special broadcasts).[6] Among the first batch were commercial applications from five licensees already operating experimental stations.[7] More new FM applications came in daily.

One indication of FM's commercial arrival—and its presumed future—was the appearance of the first FM-focused periodical. Founded by publisher Milton Sleeper, FM appeared as a monthly in November 1940 and under changing titles would continue through the war. By its second year (beginning just before U.S. entry into World War II), the magazine was presenting business and technical articles as well as illustrated features on new FM stations.[8] Daily newspapers in a dozen cities ran special sections on FM radio as local stations took to the air. These included articles explaining FM as well as ads for the first FM receivers and schedules of programs for the new FM stations.[9] General-press coverage of FM continued (at least early in the war) at a good pace—the FMBI clipping count suggested some 3,000 mentions in New York dailies (there were nearly a dozen papers in New York City at the time) and in trade magazines from 1940 to early 1942.

The continuing need to educate both the public and broadcasters brought forth more promotional booklets explaining to consumers in straightforward fashion just what FM was and how it worked. Several receiver manufacturers, including both GE and Stromberg-Carlson, issued booklets to promote the service. Both used two-color illustrations and, not unexpectedly, touted their own receivers. Receivers from GE were in handsome but pricy wooden consoles featuring AM and FM (and often shortwave) and a record changer, clearly marketed to an upscale audience.[10]

GE went a step further and released a brief color (still uncommon at that time) promotional film called Listen—It's FM!, which described the new system and demonstrated how it worked. Using the story line of a Mr. Morrison visiting his local radio shop, the film depicts a radio salesman describing how FM differed from (and was better than) the AM service the customer was used to. Using diagrams and examples, he shows Morrison what FM promises. In the end Morrison calls his wife, and they arrange for a special evening demonstration back in the shop, promising there "will be an FM set in his home or his name isn't Morrison!"[11] The film was used in a number of school districts during the war to explain FM to students.[12]

Identifying the new service over the air so that listeners would not confuse AM and FM stations was an issue resolved only a short time before commercial operations began. In early December 1940, the FCC announced plans to identify FM outlets using a combination of letters and numbers to denote both the station's frequency and the city in which it operated (AM stations had always been identified with three or four letters). FMBI officials suggested a variation, which the commission quickly accepted. Thus, the new stations would receive calls like W44B (an FM station operating on 44.4 MHz in Boston) or W55M (the Journal Company outlet on 45.5 MHz in Milwaukee). As with AM stations, an initial letter K would usually indicate a station operating west of the Mississippi River, with W denoting stations east of that line. The addition of the letter E would indicate an educational FM station, of which there were at first only a handful.[13]

By mid-1943, after two years of experience using the system, many FM broadcasters and their trade association concluded that the number-letter combinations were not really helping the medium and were hard to clearly announce on the air. Thus they petitioned the FCC to allow FM stations to use four-letter calls just like AM stations.[14] The commission agreed, announcing that as of November 1, 1943, FM stations would be so identified (those on the air could be relabeled). FM outlets owned by AM stations could use the same call letters, adding the suffix "-FM" for clarity. The FCC reported there were about 1,100 W and 2,900 K sets of call letters still available for use—seemingly plenty for years to come.[15]

The first full operating license for a commercial FM station, W47NV, affiliated with AM station WSM in Nashville, Tennessee, was issued on March 1, 1941.[16] In September the first West Coast FM took to the air as the Don Lee regional network placed its Los Angeles station into service. By mid-October, seventeen commercial FM stations were broadcasting, all but two of them owned by colocated AM outlets. More than forty additional stations held construction permits but were not yet on the air, and fourteen experimental FM transmitters continued in operation. Philadelphia received its first FM outlet in November, a fourth construction permit was granted to Detroit, and the first Ohio FM station went on the air the next month, as W45CM began broadcasting from Columbus.[17] The relatively slow expansion of the new business was largely due to difficulty in obtaining transmitters and other parts because of the country's growing national-defense contracting. Prewar military priorities were already diverting materials from the civilian market.

Amazingly, not even six weeks after the beginning of commercial operations, fears were already being expressed that major cities were quickly going to run out of FM assignments. The FCC's FM rules allowed for no more than eleven stations in even the largest city. And in New York, ten applications were pending for the last four remaining channels, demonstrating growing interest in the medium but also requiring a comparative hearing at the FCC. As *Broadcasting* editorialized with some alarm: "What exists in New York today is destined to happen perhaps in a dozen major markets. Thus, it is evident that the supply will not equal the demand even before FM has been accorded a real trial."[18]

This rapid urban saturation arose because of the FCC's policy of granting licenses on a first-come, first-served basis without any obvious planning for the limited number of channels in any one area. With only eleven channels to assign for New York, it seems odd that five were granted over a period of months before the commission awoke to the fact (as still more applications came in) that even if half of the city's AM stations applied for FM licenses, there would not be enough channels. One result of this approach, of course, was to shut out many potential new broadcasters — despite the fact that the FCC and industry critics had hoped FM would expand the number of first-time station owners. But newcomers rarely had the experience or funds to undertake building an FM station as readily as did existing AM operators. The slowly growing number of applications in major markets also demonstrated that a protectionist feeling was taking hold among AM licensees as they sought FM outlets to protect against the possibility that FM just might replace AM.

NEWSPAPERS' QUANDARY

Protectionism also arose in an even older medium: the nation's daily newspapers. Many publishers felt the pressure of this newer technology on their existing AM stations, let alone their newspapers. Applying for and operating an FM station seemed a reasonable insurance policy to avoid being shut out.

FM was cheaper to build and operate than all but the smallest standard-broadcast stations. Furthermore, the choice facing would-be publisher-broadcasters was really between *building* an FM outlet or *buying* older broadcast properties *at bloated prices* in the crowded standard (AM) band. . . . It was easier to enter FM without costly competitive hearings. . . . Lastly, FM's . . . channel . . . enhanced the technical possibility of entering choice markets where standard-broadcast outlets were all pre-empted or where . . . sales prices were exorbitant.[19]

Clearly a number of publishers came to the same conclusion at about the same time. By March 1941 the FCC noted that twenty-seven of the nearly 100 pending FM commercial-station applications had been filed by newspaper publishers. This proportion concerned commissioners already deeply involved in an ongoing investigation of radio networks and about to recommend sweeping changes to limit their monopoly power.[20]

On March 20, 1941, the commission released Order No. 79, which called for "an immediate investigation to determine what statement of policy or rules, if any, should be issued concerning applications for high frequency broadcast stations (FM) with which are associated persons also associated with the publication of one or more newspapers."[21] The investigation would begin with an open hearing, clearly triggered by the FM application situation. The immediate effect was to stop application processing for and construction activities of any broadcast facilities owned by newspapers until after the FCC study.[22] An exception was made for one North Carolina station so that region could receive its first FM service.[23]

Hearings began in a hot and sticky Washington, D.C., on July 23, 1941.[24] One business magazine suggested that the hearings would be brief since FCC chairman James Lawrence Fly hated the heat (and air-conditioning in the city was rare at that point), and since little could be done other than banning newspaper ownership entirely, which seemed unlikely.[25] FM came up early in the proceedings, with FMBI officials arguing that any limit on newspaper participation would slow down FM growth.[26] The hearings turned out to be anything but brief; indeed, occasional sessions were held into early 1943. After another year, the record was closed as the FCC decided (as many had predicted) not to pursue the issue.[27] The proceedings' impact on FM was largely one of delay, with some station construction postponed or outlets operating for extended periods on temporary permits.

By the end of 1941 (with the United States now in the war), the FCC reported that sixty-seven commercial FM outlets had been authorized, nearly thirty were on the air, and forty-three more had pending applications.[28] Further permits were issued into early 1942, though defense priorities made obtaining building material, personnel, and electronic equipment more difficult by the day. On the plus side for FM was the January news that two Yankee Network stations would begin operating on a twenty-four-hour basis — the first FM outlets to do so.[29] Two of six New York FM outlets also extended their time on the air, to about fifteen hours daily.

Early in March, some forty managers representing most of the FM outlets on the air (or those about to be) gathered in a New York hotel for the third annual FMBI convention. Due to wartime travel restrictions and the growing realization that FM was going to be largely frozen in place for the duration, they reluctantly agreed to close their New York office and "hunker down" at a lower pace until the war's end. The *Milwaukee Journal*'s Walter Damm took the organization's helm, relieving founding president John Shepard III, who was by then heavily involved in several wartime organizations. The mimeographed FMBI FM *Bulletin*, edited by sprightly writer and publicist Dick Dorrance, would remain as the chief means of keeping everyone in touch with developments around the country (nearly 100 issues had appeared since 1940, and the publication was soon appearing biweekly from Dorrance's Washington, D.C., office).[30] Naturally, no one could project how long this state of suspended animation might last.

Some answers appeared fairly quickly. On April 27, 1942, further FCC processing of FM-station applications was frozen under orders from the War Production Board, as it had been for AM stations three weeks earlier. No one was surprised; there was simply too much demand by the military for just the sort of equipment and personnel that broadcast stations required. By the time the freeze began, forty-nine FM applications were pending, sixty-three construction permits were granted, and twenty-seven stations were on the air.[31] By July several construction permits were canceled as potential stations gave up the struggle to get on the air.[32] The FCC announced several policies intended to keep stations on the air, including the ability to broadcast using temporary facilities (almost always lower power than originally intended) and providing fewer broadcast hours per day.[33] About fifty stations (some pending, others on the air under terms of a construction permit) were affected by the changed rules.[34]

By late October 1942, thirty-seven commercial FM stations were operating, with eight additional experimental outlets still on the air under extended authority. Nine of these were using less than full power and thus serving only part of their assigned coverage area, chiefly due to the growing difficulty in obtaining replacement parts.[35] But despite seemingly total bans on civilian construction, some work progressed, albeit slowly and sporadically. As before the war, weather sometimes intervened; engineers at the transmitter of W41MM on Clingman's Peak in North Carolina were marooned by forty-three hours of steady snow piling up four feet (not counting drifts) in mid-March 1942. The foreman and one assistant hiked nearly thirty miles to the nearest town to get the access road ploughed clear.[36] By late 1943 operating FM stations had crept up to an even fifty, counting commercial, a few experimental, and four noncommercial outlets.[37]

As Zenith discovered in a survey of on-air stations, the typical FM outlet was on the air for more than eleven hours a day, though most operated with only about half of their authorized power. Few stations sold commercial time, although they were authorized to do so (all planned to at sometime in the future).[38] Thus, virtually no FM station was making money. Finding personnel was one factor limiting non-air hours; many FM outlets programmed only from the afternoon into the evening. But operators agreed that they wanted to retain their frequency assignment in the hope of postwar growth and financial success.

As more men were absorbed into the armed forces or other wartime jobs, women began to move into broadcasting and related positions—some of them not heretofore known as "women's work." For example, Marjorie E. Allen served as a transmitter engineer—said to be the first such posting for a female anywhere in commercial broadcasting—at W47NY, the Muzak FM station in New York City (the city's only station operating with close to a full-time schedule). Already holding a number of FCC certificates, Allen was studying for her First Class Operator License.[39] Beth Muir was a busy sound-effects engineer for a Schenectady, New York, FM outlet.[40] By late 1942, both FM stations in Pittsburgh had female program directors, and several stations employed female staff announcers (at a time when few women were heard, save as singers).[41] The Fort Wayne, Indiana, FM station had a woman station manager (even rarer) as of early 1943.[42] By early 1943, Westinghouse-owned station W67B in Boston was reported as being operated entirely by women—perhaps another first in broadcasting.[43] Shortly thereafter, an experimental FM station in Worcester, Massachusetts, also had an all-female staff.[44] The once-uncommon hiring of women was, under wartime manpower pressures, becoming commonplace.

In an effort to stretch personnel and equipment (especially hard-to-replace transmitter tubes) for the duration of the war, four Philadelphia stations developed a plan to rotate time on the air so that an estimated 17,000 FM listeners would be provided with eight hours of programs a day. In March 1943 the FCC approved a ninety-day trial of the process, which saw each station broadcast eight hours one day a week, with the remaining days taken in rotation. The plan called for pooling all spare parts as well as transcription libraries.[45] A fifth station joined the pool in July, and the FCC continued the operation with successive ninety-day authorizations.

As the tide turned on battlefields abroad, broadcasters regained some of their prewar optimism, as was evident, among other indicators, in the growing number of new station construction applications received at the FCC. The January 1944 two-day convention (the fifth) of FMBI, held at New York City's Commodore Hotel, attracted some 750 people (despite wartime travel restrictions), some of them potential advertisers—a huge increase over earlier meetings. By mid-February 1944, seventy-eight applications for new FM stations were awaiting action by the FCC, and by late April that number had doubled.[46] About sixty of those were submitted by firms with both newspaper and AM-station holdings, thanks in part to the termination of the FCC newspaper-ownership study. By the end of 1944, forty-eight stations were on the air (see Table 2.1), and more than 250 FM-station applications awaited lifting of the wartime construction ban.

NETWORK DREAMS

For the few stations on the air, programming was expensive. AM radio proved that sharing costs through networking could work wonders. FM proponents knew that to succeed commercially, individual stations (and especially those outside of the major metropolitan areas) would need a network affiliation. The first FM station to affiliate with an existing radio network appears to have been WBCA (once W47A) in Schenectady, which in the fall of 1943 affiliated with the Mutual Broadcasting System.[47]

NBC management struggled with how best to handle FM. Watching FM expansion, and specifically noting a special FM section in one of New York's daily papers, one senior network official wondered shortly before Pearl Harbor whether it was time "to review our present policy . . . to decide whether we are going to continue playing FM down, or to do some-

TABLE 2.1. Commercial FM Stations Operating by Late 1944

State and City	Station	Licensee	Year on Air	Power (in kw)	Frequency (in MHz)
California					
Los Angeles	KHJ-FM	Don Lee Network	1941	1	44.5
Connecticut					
Hartford	WDRC-FM	WDRC, Inc.	1939	1	46.5
Hartford	WTIC-FM	Travelers Insurance	1940	1	45.3
Illinois					
Chicago	WBBM-FM	CBS Network	1941	10	46.7
Chicago	WDLM	Moody Bible Institute	1943	1	47.5
Chicago	WGNB	Chicago Tribune (N)	1941	3	45.9
Chicago	WWZR	Zenith Radio	1940	50	45.1
Indiana					
Evansville	WMLL	On the Air, Inc.	1941	10	44.5
Ft. Wayne	WOWO-FM	Westinghouse	1942	1	44.9
South Bend	WSBF	South Bend Tribune (N)	1943	.5	47.1
Louisiana					
Baton Rouge	WBRL	Baton Rouge Broadcasting	1944	1	44.5
Massachusetts					
Boston	WBZ-FM	Westinghouse	1941	10	46.7
Paxton	WTGR	Yankee Network	1939	50	44.3
Springfield	WBZA-FM	Westinghouse	1939	1	48.0
Worchester	WTAG-FM	Worchester Telegram (N)	1940	1	46.1
Michigan					
Detroit	WENA	Evening News Assoc. (N)	1941	50	44.5
Detroit	WLOU	John L. Booth	N/A	10	44.9
Minnesota					
Duluth	WDUL	Head of Lakes Broadcasting	1940	1	44.5
Missouri					
Kansas City	KOZY	Commercial Radio Equip.*	1942	.4	44.9
Kansas City	KMBC-FM	Midland Broadcasting Co.	1944	1.5	46.5
New Hampshire					
Mt. Washington	WMTW	Yankee Network	1939	5	43.9
New Jersey					
Alpine	WFMN	Edwin H. Armstrong*	1938	55	43.1
New York					
Binghampton	WNBF-FM	Jones Advertising Agency	1942	3	44.9
New York	WABC-FM	CBS Network	1941	3	46.7
New York	WABF	Metropolitan Television, Inc.*	1942	1	47.5
New York	WBAM	Bamberger Broadcasting	1940	10	47.1
New York	WEAF-FM	NBC Network	1940	1	45.1
New York	WGYN	Muzak Radio Broadcast*	1941	3	44.7

TABLE 2.1. (continued)

State and City	Station	Licensee	Year on Air	Power (in kw)	Frequency (in MHz)
New York	WHNF	Marcus Loew Agency	1941	10	46.3
New York	WNYC-FM	City of New York	1943	1	43.9
New York	WQXQ	John V. L. Hogan	1939	1	45.9
Rochester	WHEF	WHEC, Inc.	1940	3	44.7
Rochester	WHFM	Stromberg-Carlson	1939	3	45.1
Schenectady	WBCA	Capitol Broadcasting*	1941	1	44.7
Schenectady	WGFM	General Electric	1940	3	48.5
North Carolina					
Winston-Salem	WMIT	Gordon Grey	1942	3	44.1
Ohio					
Columbus	WELD	RadiOhio, Inc.	1940	5	44.5
Pennsylvania					
Philadelphia	KYW-FM	Westinghouse	1942	10	45.7
Philadelphia	WCAU-FM	WCAU Broadcasting Co.	1941	10	46.9
Philadelphia	WFIL-FM	WFIL Broadcasting Co.	1941	10	45.3
Philadelphia	WIP-FM	Pennsylvania Broadcasting Co.	1942	3	44.9
Philadelphia	WPEN-FM	William Penn Broadcasting Co.	1942	3	47.3
Pittsburgh	KDKA-FM	Westinghouse	1942	3	47.5
Pittsburgh	WMOT	Pittsburgh Post Gazette (N)	1941	3	47.3
Tennessee					
Nashville	WSM-FM	National Life Insurance Co.	1941	20	44.7
Wisconsin					
Milwaukee	WMFM	Milwaukee Journal (N)	1940	50	45.5
Superior	WDUL	Head of Lakes Broadcasting	1940	1	44.5

Sources: *Broadcasting*, April 24, 1944, p. 18; *Journal of Frequency Modulation*, February 1946, pp. 22, 24.

Stations are listed by state (notice how many states are missing, meaning that they lacked local FM service). Only five of the forty-eight outlets were not owned by colocated AM stations and are indicated with an asterisk. N indicates a newspaper-owned station. Year first on the air includes experimental operation for those showing earlier than 1941. Many stations used less power than is shown here due to wartime restrictions. The call letters are those granted after the 1943 change in FM nomenclature.

thing more progressive about it."[48] Under a directive from RCA president David Sarnoff, the network had already received FCC permits for high-powered FM stations in New York and Chicago and was seeking construction permits for FM outlets in Washington, Cleveland, Denver, and San Francisco—all of which would provide a strong foundation for any possible FM network.[49]

Many aspiring FM broadcasters sought to develop a network of their own. Plans for just such a linkup had been announced in mid-1940, even before the inception of commercial operation. Given the ongoing FCC network inquiry and likely rule changes, a cooperative venture became attractive, somewhat along the lines of the Mutual Broadcasting System. There would be a limited central operation and no owned-and-operated stations like the CBS and NBC networks. Instead, following the Mutual Broadcasting example, stations would share their programs. By 1941 the project anticipated linking forty stations in markets reaching a potential total of 55 million listeners.[50] Confusing the picture were rumors that Mutual Broadcasting was considering setting up a parallel FM network. CBS and NBC polled their AM affiliates about such an idea.[51]

One part-time regional network demonstrated what could be accomplished. A seven-station hookup relied upon the on-air relay of programs rather than renting pricy telephone lines (which were not up to carrying FM's full frequency response anyway). The occasional network began operating just a week before the Pearl Harbor attack. Four commercial programs relayed programs from Armstrong's W2XMN in Alpine, New Jersey, as far north as the Yankee station in New Hampshire, and as far south as Washington, D.C. Programs included the popular *Burns and Allen* comedy half hour, a music program, the dedication of a New York FM outlet, and news (all of which was sponsored). The two-hour block of programs was said to reach about one-sixth of the country and some 60,000 FM receivers.[52]

A new American Network, Inc. (ANI), applied to the FCC for a New York flagship FM outlet and laid plans for linking stations across the country. In December 1941 an experimental linkup of seven stations in the Northeast carried a *Burns and Allen* comedy episode.[53] But the ANI was to go no further after the country declared war. With few FM stations on the air, network plans were shelved. Late in 1943, however, ANI began to revive with a renewed application for a New York flagship station. Stations in twenty-three markets were said to be interested, which was about half of the prewar plan for a forty-five-station chain.[54] Still, noting the growing number of station applications, network proponents bought a full-page advertisement in *Broadcasting*, claiming that "the American Network will be a network with a definite programming policy . . . of bringing you the kind of programs you want to hear—at a time of day or night you want to hear them. . . . [It will be] a *quality* network, . . . each station reflecting the character and policies of the network. . . . A new era in radio broadcasting will soon begin.[55] By May network organizers claimed to possess signed agreements with stations in half of the intended fifty-one-market chain.[56] But this optimism could not survive continued wartime restrictions. Stations were reluctant to invest in a network that would not begin operations until after the war, and no one could foretell when that might be. NBC and CBS revived talk of their own FM networks, which had the effect (perhaps intended) of squelching the potential new chain. In August 1944 ANI officials met in Chicago and agreed to dissolve, selling their name to the newly independent Blue Network (which would become ABC the following year) for $10,000.[57] FM stations were resigned to signing up with the existing networks or developing further regional linkups.

CREATING CONTENT

Wartime FM programming consisted of either music or duplicate AM programs (especially among the outlets that were owned by AM licensees).[58] New stations often would provide long informational "programs" demonstrating what FM could do with various sound effects (typically segments of different types of music, the striking of matches, thunder and rain, and other sounds), but the novelty of that quickly wore off.[59] The national networks, both worried by and somewhat confused about the future of FM, had instructed their AM affiliates not to share or "simulcast" programs on their FM outlets. The result was that for much of the war, FM stations programmed separately from their AM owners—a situation that would not recur for another three decades.

Armstrong's pioneering station in Alpine, New Jersey, had simulcast CBS programs until 1941. When CBS began to plan for its own New York outlet, Armstrong's station turned to programming high-fidelity light classical music provided by a transcription service.[60] Transcription companies proved very useful to early FM operations, providing recorded music with the frequency response necessary to really show off what FM could do. Milwaukee's W55M subscribed to several such services, supplementing them with occasional remote broadcasts (often local dance bands from city hotels) and in-studio live orchestra performances. Only newscasts were simulcast on FM from the parent AM station. Both stations were located by 1942 in a handsome new Art Deco building on Capital Drive on the north side of Milwaukee's downtown, combining offices and studios and earmarking space for postwar television expansion.[61]

Even during the war, however, a shift was evident in management thinking, as many broadcasters began to perceive FM as being "different" from AM because the new service catered to a "better quality" audience interested in public affairs and fine music. To a considerable extent, this was a face-saving way of explaining FM's small audiences, limited in part by the high retail prices of receiving sets (when any sets were available at all). In turn, costly receivers defined a presumably highbrow audience with discriminating taste. Catering to the needs of these refined listeners, stations generally began broadcasting at noon or in early afternoon hours, usually programming until about 10:00 P.M. When one New York station sought to conserve transmitter tubes by eliminating morning hours, a host of listeners complained and the morning broadcasts remained. But few FM outlets made any attempt to compete with AM in the morning hours. FM's evening programs were almost entirely music, providing an alternative to the network-originated, prime-time comedy and drama carried on AM affiliates. This foreshadowed FM's potential as an alternative to AM's established programming. By late 1942, however, nearly three-quarters of FM programs were original (not heard on AM outlets), most of them music.

Behind the scenes, a debate over the pros and cons of simulcasting programs on AM and FM was taking place. As the FCC relaxed operating rules for FM in light of wartime personnel and equipment shortages, some AM stations began additional simulcasting over their colocated FM stations—which were not making money anyway. Simulcasting saved money because both outlets offered the same programs. By 1944 the networks changed their policy and allowed duplication by affiliates, though only if FM stations carried the entire schedule "so as to be fair" to all advertisers, which certainly made their priorities clear. NBC went so far as to actively promote simulcasting as the best way to build FM: "If FM is required to create and maintain a separate program service in competition with well-established and highly popular [AM and network] programs, its development will be greatly retarded."[62] NBC vice president John Royal suggested in an internal memo that the demise of vaudeville made a useful example: overexpansion of that stage business without enough talent to make it viable had killed the business. Royal argued that forcing FM to develop its own programs might well achieve similar results.[63] CBS quickly followed suit, as did the Blue Network, soon to become ABC. They all argued that simulcasting would promote FM listening and receiver sales.[64]

Faced with continuing wartime shortages, few FM-station operators had any reason to oppose simulcasting. The issue was to become hugely divisive in the years to come, however, as it became clearer that, despite the rhetoric of support, simulcasting did little to help FM create its own image (or "brand" in early 2000s terminology), making it impossible to sell air time to advertisers who were already being carried free on simulcasting FM outlets. As will be seen (chapters 4 and 5), only two decades later the FCC would finally move to disallow simulcasting on most AM-FM combinations, both to make more effective use of spectrum and to enhance FM's ability to attract an audience. The question lingers, however, as to just why the broadcasting establishment promoted simulcasting in the first place. With the passage of time it seems clear that shared programming accomplished two goals at once: it helped limit FM competition with AM while occupying frequencies that might otherwise be sought by new and independent entrants to actively compete with AM. The rhetoric about promoting FM with AM's popular programs seems to have been just that— words to hide the real purpose of sharing.

The first FM station to issue a rate card for advertisers appears to have been W39B, the Yankee Network outlet on Mount Washington, New Hampshire, in April 1941. Rates started at $25 an hour during the day and $50 at night—a fraction of AM-station rates for major markets at the time.[65] Station W2XOR in Newark, New Jersey, just across the Hudson River from New York City, claimed the very first FM advertiser when the Longine-Wittenauer watch company signed up to provide a year's worth of time signals on the station in 1941.[66] A Nashville station made the same claim, and an outlet in Evansville, Indiana, claimed to be the first to publish commercial rates for selling time.[67] The first sponsored FM news program appeared on Yankee Network stations in mid-1941.[68] By early 1942, a Zenith survey showed that though perhaps 40 percent of FM outlets had attempted to sell advertising time, few sold very much if any.[69] On the other hand, Milwaukee's W55M claimed more than twenty commercial programs and a dozen spot-advertising campaigns running each week (said to be an FM record).[70] Most FM outlets were financially supported by their AM owners, or, for the few independent stations, by funds coming from their owner's pockets.

Facing this dismal revenue situation, one New York FM station proposed something quite different. Muzak petitioned the FCC to set aside a number of channels across the country for a network of subscription-radio outlets that would provide three transcription-based channels (classical or "mood" music, popular songs, and educational-cultural talk programs).

None would carry advertising, supported instead by direct audience payment. The plan would require three stations in a market to provide the three channels of programming—thus the application to the FCC for a rules change.[71] Though the FCC briefly considered the idea, no action was taken and the pay-radio plan was stillborn, although it anticipated listener-supported public and subscription satellite radio decades later.

In 1943 the Zenith station in Chicago (W51C, soon known as WWZR) and the Bamberger Broadcasting New York station (W47NY, soon to become WBAM) appear to have been the first FM outlets to publish regular program guides, sold to listeners on a subscription basis. This sort of promotion would become a useful revenue source for many stations in years to come. W47NY's effort included program listings with details on the music played. Both stations published background articles on music, performers, and general plans for the future. The FMBI newsletter suggested that stations in different markets might issue such guides on a cooperative basis.[72]

WEE SMALL VOICE

The application of FM to education was widely discussed if not quickly implemented. By late 1941, seven educational stations had been approved or were on the air on channels set aside for them; stations run by the Cleveland (WBOE) and New York City (WNYE) boards of education were among the first. Both utilized call letters ending in E as per FCC practice for noncommercial stations, a practice soon dropped.[73] The New York station began to provide programs to over 700 city schools by early 1943. The Cleveland station aired eight hours daily to all 150 schools in that city. The Moody Bible Institute of Chicago and the New York municipal station WNYC-FM were on the air by late 1944. Soon licenses had been granted for educational outlets in Chicago, at the University of Illinois, in Memphis, and in Buffalo, though these were slowed due to wartime priorities or funding issues. By 1945 there were a dozen educational stations on the air, with twenty-two more applications awaiting processing after the end of hostilities.[74] Construction of educational outlets had not been formally restricted during the war years, but the same lack of materials and personnel that affected commercial operators had held up their development.[75]

School districts in several cities experimented with placing FM receivers in schools for use with selected programs. KALW in San Francisco was soon broadcasting educational programs on a daily basis. In Milwaukee,

W55M placed sets in thirteen schools to allow use of its *Meet the Orchestra* program in classes. Noncommercial FM thus played a very small part in the medium's development during the war. Nonetheless, encouraged by the FCC's reservation of channels for noncommercial operations, many institutions actively planned to file postwar applications for new stations and — in a few cases — for statewide FM networks (see chapter 3).[76]

These initial wartime successes prompted requests for further channels as more educational organizations began to apply for FM stations. At a 1943 meeting of one educational group, however, FCC chairman Fly made clear that the FM reservations were not "set aside for absentees."[77] His warning would resonate strongly in coming years. The channel requests resulted in a fourfold increase to twenty reservations in the mid-1945 reallocation discussed below. One reason for the educators' success was at least informal support from commercial FM operators and applicants. Rather than provide public-service programming on their own channels, it was more effective to support set-aside channels for educators who would undertake the job full-time.[78] To help move things along, the federal Office of Education issued FM for Education, with nearly sixty pages suggesting numerous "best practices" based on what both AM and FM noncommercial licensees had already accomplished. Illustrated with charts and photos, the booklet began with Fly's admonition about utilizing the reserved frequencies, then went on to outline how and why FM might be applied to educational needs, name the schools and other audiences that could be served, and explain how to go about getting such a station on the air. The twenty-page FCC form for applying for a noncommercial station was included.[79]

BUILDING AN AUDIENCE

Looking at FM's wartime problems, it is easy to conclude that the service got started at just the wrong time — less than a year before the country entered the war and began to experience all the resulting shortages and governmental delays. None of that was yet on the horizon during the initial excitement of getting stations on the air and receivers into stores and then homes. Estimates suggest about 15,000 receivers were being used by listeners when commercial FM operations began in January 1941. As the business got started in earnest, it appeared that a dozen or more manufacturers would soon be selling FM receivers.

Stromberg-Carlson, for example, offered nine different receiver models and even touted FM in its AM advertising.[80] Some expensive console models featuring AM, FM, and shortwave bands and a phonograph cost as much as $500 (about $5,000 in 2007 values). Lower-priced sets could be bought for $100 or less—still a serious expenditure, considering that an AM table radio cost one-fifth as much. The least-expensive option was a "translator" device attached to an AM receiver, which allowed it to pick up FM signals and provide fidelity sound (albeit of relatively poor quality) through the AM speaker. GE made one for $50, recognizing it as merely a transitional product.[81] Manufacturers provided thousands of booklets explaining FM because, to sell receivers, dealers first had to sell the concept and make clear what the listener would gain by purchasing a receiver.

By the fall of 1941, some 1,500 FM sets (in more than 100 different models) were being produced on a daily basis. One Chicago newspaper reported that given multiple listeners to each receiver, FM's audience was "believed to be increasing at the rate of 5,000 or more each day."[82] That was probably overstating it, but dealers reported that demand was running 20 to 50 percent higher than that, especially as FM stations began to serve new markets. The FMBI estimated that New York had the most sets in actual use—about 25,000 to 30,000—and another 15,000 were in Chicago. By the end of the year (just as war was declared), Radio Engineering Laboratories installed the world's first FM car radio in Walter Damm's automobile (he managed stations WTMJ and W55M in Milwaukee) and suggested they might put the specially built set into general production.[83]

U.S. entry into the war had little immediate FM impact, and some 50,000 new FM receivers were sold in January 1942 alone. Set totals in most cities had doubled, thanks in large part to Christmas gift giving. Broadcasters looked forward to a rapidly growing FM audience. But by April, production was winding down in the face of wartime priority needs, and the last new sets were shipped to dealers by midyear, when the industry estimated there were perhaps 400,000 FM receivers in use.[84] Surveys and manufacturer information indicated that 80,000 of those were in the greater New York area—which was understandable, given that six FM stations were on the air there. Chicago was the second-largest FM market with about 42,000 receivers. Another 35,000 were in New England, about a third of those in Boston alone. Cities like Philadelphia, Detroit, Milwaukee, and Los Angeles each had about 15,000 receivers.[85] Researchers projected three or four listeners per FM set to reach estimates of the medium's total audience.

Unable to make new receivers after mid-1942, manufacturers instead undertook profuse advertising and promotional campaigns suggesting what they *planned* to do after the war ended. This was common with most other consumer products, especially automobiles. But in FM's case, of course, the new service had barely gotten off the ground. Still, companies promised to take up active FM manufacture as soon as production controls were lifted. A number of manufacturers planned to make AM-FM dual-service receivers. Indeed, judging from the promises, it appeared that millions of FM receivers might be made available in the first year or so after the war.

There were a few bad eggs in this process. FM publications highlighted problems with low-cost FM receivers from at least one manufacturer (not named) that lacked the vital limiter or discriminator circuits central to the Armstrong FM system. While less expensive (the manufacturer did not have to pay royalties to Armstrong), these sets provided poor sound and gave the new medium a bad name.[86] RCA touted its projected "Super FM" that would include circuits developed by their own engineers rather than those based on Armstrong's patents. Though few in the general public knew or cared, the announcement underlined the developing bad blood between Armstrong and RCA. Unlike GE, Zenith, Stromberg-Carlson, and others, RCA was unwilling to sign one of the inventor's licenses to manufacture FM receivers and equipment.[87] (Indeed, most wartime RCA publications make no reference to Armstrong at all, another indication of the rising trouble between the company and its onetime largest stockholder.)[88]

ALLOCATION HEARINGS

Beyond the hoopla about FM stations, programs, and receivers, the most important development during the war occurred with little public notice. This was understandable, as a good deal of what transpired was highly technical, and much of it was classified. A series of FCC hearings in 1944–45 were designed as a fundamental review of FM and television spectrum allocations—what and how much each service would likely need after the war and where best to locate them in the spectrum. The hearings were based in part on new knowledge gained from military experience and research. Given increasing indications of rising postwar demand for all broadcast services, the FCC sought to define the best possible spectrum allocations before wartime restrictions on station and receiver construction were lifted, thus making spectrum changes difficult if not impossible to make. And evidence was mounting that changes would, indeed, have to be made.

The FCC's complex analysis of FM- and television-allocation needs in the VHF spectrum was colored by differing viewpoints of industry "haves" and "have-nots." The "haves" included AM licensees (many worried about what FM might do to their investment) and the few FM broadcasters already on the air. On the other side were "have-nots" — RCA, which lacked a central patent position in FM and was promoting television, and the handful of television broadcasters, then lagging behind FM in development. With the FCC's prewar allocation decisions, fledgling FM broadcasters had unwittingly developed dangerous competitors if not actual enemies in RCA and the television business. The FCC was caught in the middle, as each side mustered a host of distinguished engineers and consultants to show that their arguments were correct and that the other side was merely trying to cloud the issue with short-term economic gains not in the public interest. Controversy was rife and would remain so for years to come.

At issue during the FCC proceedings were the fundamental questions of how much spectrum space each new broadcasting service would need in order to expand in a postwar world and where best to locate both FM and TV with the least danger of interference. By 1943 some trade-press reports were suggesting a possible strategy that was merely hinted at in the FCC hearings of 1940: the commission was considering shifting both services up to 100 MHz in the VHF spectrum so that more channels could be provided than was possible in the more-crowded lower frequencies.[89]

Late in 1943, the FCC called upon broadcasters and radio manufacturers to form a Radio Technical Planning Board (RTPB) to evaluate the new spectrum information and recommend possible adjustments in postwar allocations.[90] By September, nine broadcast organizations contributed to the membership of what became thirteen different RTPB panels, each assigned to investigate a specific part of the overall allocation question. RTPB chairman W. R. G. Baker of GE suggested it might take five or six years to fully evaluate the mass of new information, though few figured the FCC would have that much time before having to make its decisions.[91] FM issues were assigned to Panel 5, whose thirty-six members, most of them engineers with FM stations or manufacturers, operated under the chairmanship of respected broadcast engineer C. M. Jansky. They first met at New York's Roosevelt Hotel in mid-September 1943.

There was general agreement that the excitement over FM would require making additional channels available to adequately serve expected postwar growth. The FMBI recommended expanding the existing 42–50 MHz

FM band up to 56 MHz—which had been assigned to television channel 1 in 1940. Such an expanded FM band would then have seventy channels, thirty more than the original allocation. Both CBS and NBC voiced their concerns over potential "skywave" interference (see appendix A) in FM's existing spectrum, suggesting a shift of FM service up to around 100 MHz. Dr. J. H. Dellinger of the National Bureau of Standards (NBS), an authority on spectrum propagation, concluded that fears about interference problems with the existing FM band were unfounded. Taking all this in, by mid-1944 Panel 5 recommended an increase of FM channels in the 50 MHz band.[92]

All through October, RTPB panel members participated in extensive FCC hearings on postwar allocations.[93] While most agreed FM would be a major postwar service, engineering opinion was still divided on where best to place it in the spectrum. Questions from commissioners seemed to suggest "support for movement of FM to the 100 [MHz] band in lieu of the lower portion of the spectrum heretofore strongly favored by FM advocates."[94] But Jansky reported for RTPB Panel 5 that the 42–50 MHz band remained more suitable for FM.[95]

When questioned by the FCC's chief engineer about *when* to make any possible spectrum shift, FMBI president Walter Damm replied, "If you're going to have a change, it ought to be made now to save the public."[96] A spokesman for one of the receiver manufacturers warned, however, that any FM shift to a higher band would probably make receivers more expensive. Another firm added that any shift would delay postwar FM due to the needed retooling needed to make receivers. Still another manufacturing expert agreed that a shift would delay FM at least a year and would greatly increase transmitter costs because it would take more power to cover the same areas that stations reached in the existing band. Several witnesses added that only a final decision could allow manufacturers to begin planning postwar equipment.[97] All of these predictions would prove to be true.

A number of participants favored shifting FM upward. T. A. M. Craven, an engineer and commissioner recently retired from the FCC, argued that the 88–108 MHz band (which turned out to be the FM channels that were eventually chosen) would better reject interference than FM's existing band.[98] CBS senior official Paul Keston spoke in favor of 100 FM channels and of his network's "single market coverage" plan for all FM stations in the same area to have similar characteristics to equally compete within that market. CBS was against larger stations serving whole regions, as several existing FM outlets were then doing (for example, the Yankee Network's stations in New England). Surely this position was taken in part to preserve network radio, which might otherwise face strong competition from FM outlets with large coverage areas. Keston suggested that adoption of the CBS approach would make space for as many as 4,000 to 5,000 stations across the nation and perhaps ten new national networks. He revealed that CBS was making plans for just such a network, which, with about 175 affiliate FM stations, could reach 80 percent of the nation's listeners.[99]

As had happened in 1940, the surprise came near the end of the 1944 hearings. A week after other FM testimony had been heard, the FCC called on former FCC engineer Kenneth A. Norton, then working with the military. Making use of still-secret propagation data, Norton concluded that FM should be moved to higher frequencies (he advocated at least to 120 MHz) to eliminate most likely interference. His testimony placed him in sharp disagreement with both the NBS's Dellinger and Armstrong, who had reported little likelihood of interference in FM's existing band. Though Norton called for further atmospheric tests to make sure of his suggestion to shift the service higher, FM proponents were taken off guard.[100] It was at this point that the FCC wrapped up its hearings and began to draft a decision.

DECISION TO SHIFT

Nine weeks later, on January 16, 1945, the FCC released its proposed allocations for services using spectrum above 25 MHz.[101] Requesting comments and scheduling still another hearing, the commission proposed shifting FM up to 84–102 MHz, gaining an additional fifty channels over the forty then allocated. The 102–108 MHz band would be held open for possible further FM expansion. The FCC made clear in its unanimous report that any shift would have to be made soon, before the public or industry made any further investment in FM's existing spectrum location. The commission concluded that an FM shift was necessary to avoid feared interference in the existing 42–50 MHz band. At the same time, commissioners reinforced their support of Armstrong's 200 kHz, wide-band channels, although some experts again had testified that they should be narrowed. The FCC also planned to continue reserving some FM channels (in the new allocation, 84–88 MHz) for noncommercial users. Realizing that it would take some time for receivers for the new band to appear, the FCC said it would allow the fifty or so existing stations (all then operating in the 42–44 MHz band) to continue service on their existing frequencies for a short transitional period—probably a year or so—so that FM-set owners would have programming options.

Reaction to the FCC proposal varied. Most applauded the additional FM channels, but opinion on lower- versus higher-band service was divided pretty much as it had during the 1944 hearings. Most also agreed, as *Broadcasting* put it in an editorial, "This is radio's last frontier. Mistakes made now will be visited upon future radio generations. . . . The slower starts which may be entailed, and which seem all-important now, will be forgotten a few years hence."[102] With so much at stake, debate grew sharper as the next scheduled hearings drew closer. Among the points made were that the FCC had too few facts to support its interpretation and that too much attention had been paid to problems of the existing band, with little research devoted to possible drawbacks of the proposed FM spectrum.[103] The FMBI reiterated its recommendation to expand the existing FM band rather than initiate a wholesale shift upwards. Several broadcasting entities with investments in television lauded the FCC decision, as did the networks and the National Association of Broadcasters, the main industry trade organization.

Oral arguments before the commission, scheduled to last four days, began on February 28, 1945, and quickly focused more on FM than on television or other services. Several witnesses, including Jansky, speaking for RTPB Panel 5, and Armstrong, testified again that FM should remain where it was—perhaps extended, but not totally shifted as the FCC proposed. Both argued that Norton's fears over interference in the existing band were not matched by any available research on potential interference problems with the proposed higher band. Manufacturers warned again about delays that such a shift would cause.[104] But others agreed with the FCC's tentative decision. On March 12–13, the FCC met in closed session to hear some of the still-secret military data on which Kenneth Norton had based his concerns. Only at that point did FM's proponents and opponents hear, for the first time, the specific concerns that had prompted his 1944 testimony that seemed to underpin the new FCC decision. The commission also demonstrated an inexpensive FM converter and urged manufacturers to make them available when wartime controls were lifted.[105]

The FCC now had taken extensive testimony in November 1944 and in February and March 1945, and from all of that input the commission had distilled an initial allocations proposal. Once again it retired to consider the massive pile of technical and economic evidence that had accumulated along with the testimony. As everyone waited for final FCC action, some sent messages to Congress urging retention and expansion of the existing FM band rather than a wholesale shift. But members of Congress decided not to enter the fray while the FCC's final decision was pending.[106] In mid-May the commission released final decisions on all frequencies and services above 25 MHz *except* for the 44–108 MHz band and FM. It made clear it was still reviewing three different options for FM —50–68 MHz, 68–86 MHz, or 84–102 MHz, the latter as had been proposed in January. An additional 2 MHz would be given to the developing wireless facsimile service but might be used for FM in the long run.[107]

The FCC was caught in a serious bind. The best engineering advice agreed that the next period of substantial solar spectrum interference would not come until 1948, and the war would be over long before then (it had ended in Europe in early May). The War Production Board was likely to lift wartime manufacturing restrictions at any time. A decision was needed before that happened, and thus, as often is the case, the FCC would have to decide without all the information it might need. Playing for time (since the best guesses were that full civilian production would not begin until 1946 at the earliest), the FCC planned a series of comparative tests to determine summer levels of interference on the existing (low) and projected (high) FM bands. In the end, however, only one such study was completed, and its results appeared only after the FCC decided the matter.[108]

Struggling with the need to resolve the FM question, the commission called for yet another hearing in mid-June under pressure from receiver manufacturers, who needed a final allocation decision before they could begin tooling for postwar production. Adding pressure, the War Production Board advised the FCC that lifting of construction restrictions might indeed come sooner than expected. Nearly all the witnesses reiterated their earlier positions during the two-day hearing. Summing up all the hearings (not all of which had focused on FM) since November, *Broadcasting* found that they had "consumed a total of 35 hearing days, at which 5,992 pages of testimony were taken and 659 exhibits were received. More than 250 witnesses testified."[109]

On June 27, 1945, the FCC by unanimous decision reallocated FM up to 88–106 MHz. Future use of the 106–108 MHz band was also allocated to FM after a temporary period of use by the newer radio facsimile service.

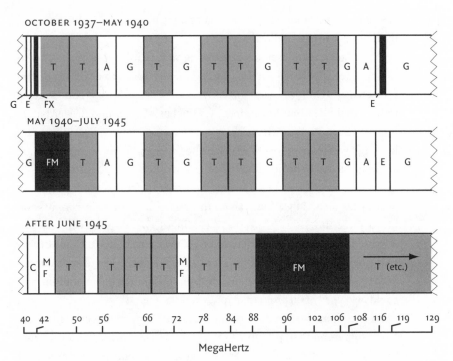

OCTOBER 1937–MAY 1940

MAY 1940–JULY 1945

AFTER JUNE 1945

MegaHertz

DIAGRAM 2.1. Changing FM Allocations, 1937–1945 (Sources: The first two bars are based on those submitted with testimony of Howard Armstrong before U.S. Congress [Senate Committee on Interstate and Foreign Commerce, *Hearings on S. 814 to Amend the Communications Act of 1934*, 78th Cong., 1st sess., 1943, p. 680]. The third bar is based on the first two, with 1945 data drawn from FCC allocations decisions.)

The FCC's reasoning for deviating from its earlier options for FM was to retain sufficient room in the VHF band to operate thirteen television channels. Educational FM operators were to have sole access to the 88–92 MHz portion of the new FM band. No new FM stations would be allowed to use the old FM band, but shared use of the existing and new bands would be allowed for a period of a year or so to serve the approximately 400,000 owners of existing FM receivers.

A summary of the FCC changes appears in Diagram 2.1. These bar charts represent the 40–129 MHz portion of the VHF radio spectrum. The first shows the initial experimental FM allocation from 1937 to 1940, the second shows the initial commercial allocation from 1940 to 1945, and the third illustrates FM's allocation since 1945. FM channels are shown by dark shading. Allocations for other services include T for television; FX for facsimile; G for various government services (including the military); A for amateur ("ham") radio; E for experimental stations; and MF for mobile and fixed point-to-point radio services.

While some congressional spluttering was heard, most opposition to the FCC decision faded within a week. The FCC noted that what had been projected as a two-year delay in making receivers for the new band seemed to have dwindled to a few months on the basis of testimony heard at its June hearings.[110] Even then, however, the seemingly endless allocation hearings were not yet over. Specific rules and regulations governing FM stations needed to be updated to fit the new frequency allocation, and before doing that, the FCC again sought further advice. An implementation hearing began on July 30 and ran for three days. This time, the commission heard some thirty-five witnesses, including network spokespersons who admitted that FM "might well become the dominant if not the only broadcast service."[111] Not surprisingly, the networks and other representatives of the AM business argued for no limits on the number of FM stations that could be owned or on program duplication (simulcasting) between AM and FM. FM proponents, on the other hand, called for more independent (from AM) programming to promote FM's development. Former commissioner Craven and former chairman Fly appeared, now representing broadcast clients, and critiqued their FCC colleagues for various shortcomings in their FM plans. One of the last witnesses was Armstrong, who, as FM's inventor, admitted to having created all the difficulty. He agreed with other witnesses that special problems in New England (potentially too many stations crammed into a small area) should not dictate plans for other parts of the country. When the commission issued its final regulations, they agreed: New England would operate under a separate set of rules.

On September 12, 1945, just ten days after the formal signing of the Japanese surrender in Tokyo Bay, the FCC issued definitive rules for the new FM-spectrum band. In what would be only the first of several FM-station classification schemes over the years, the commission established three types of FM stations: community, metropolitan, and rural. These would be allotted into the more-crowded Area I (only New England at first, but later including the Midwest and all of the Northeast) and the much-larger remainder of the nation, Area II (the South and states west of the Mississippi), with some differences in what type of station could serve each.[112]

Small community stations would be allowed no more than 250 watts of power on twenty of the eighty commercial FM channels available. They would use the highest frequencies in the band. Metropolitan outlets would be the most common (sixty channels) and could use up to 20 kw of power in Area I, with more flexibility as needed in Area II. Rural FM stations (very roughly analogous to AM's "clear-channel" outlets) would be licensed only in Area II and would share the same channels as metropolitan outlets.[113] There was a good deal of variance within these categories, but the idea was to have stations of similar characteristics competing directly with each other, an echo of arguments that CBS had made earlier.

Owners were limited to no more than six FM stations nationally, and no two could serve substantially the same market. While stations would be licensed for unlimited airtime,[114] they would have to broadcast at least three hours before and after 6:00 P.M. every day. After considerable discussion, the commission decided not to limit FM duplication of AM programs. FCC commissioner Clifford Durr dissented on that point, arguing that at least two hours a day of original programming ought to be required. He also wanted to reserve twenty FM channels for postwar newcomers to broadcasting.[115]

APPEALING REALITY

FM proponents, led by Armstrong and a few broadcasters and manufacturers, made several attempts to roll back or at least modify the FCC's final decision to shift FM "upstairs." Despite considerable rhetoric and even two congressional hearings in 1948, their effort was unsuccessful and may well have had the unintended effect of further delaying investment in the medium while confusing potential receiver buyers.

The first appeal—a petition from Zenith—came early in January 1946, leading the commission to call for yet another hearing just two weeks later.[116] Some of the trade press expressed surprise at the FCC's quick response and suggested it might indicate second thoughts about the FM decision among the commissioners.[117] The proceedings focused on how much, if any, of the old lower band should be used for FM service, what types of stations would be allowed, and the likely added cost of the two-band receivers that would be required. FM proponents sought to hold some of the lower channels for use in relay networking, as these had proved very valuable during the experimental period. It was clear the hearing would be largely a battle among conflicting engineering findings in various tests the FCC and others had conducted on the high band. Also clear was that any FM use of the lower frequencies would have to somehow accommodate television's expanding needs. Manufacturers testified that one-band receivers were simpler and thus cheaper to make and sell, and they spoke against a divided allocation for FM. Little new data was offered one way or the other. The FCC decided quickly (on January 24) against the Zenith petition. FM's reallocation would stand, in part because nonbroadcast services newly assigned to the former FM band were already beginning to move into it. The formal and confirming printed FCC opinion was released early in March.[118]

Lengthier and more revealing appeals came two years later, though by that time changes in the FCC allocation decision were even less likely given the development of all services in their new frequency allocations. This time, attention focused on Congress, where in 1948 hearings took place in both the House and Senate, though no legislation resulted in either case. Proceedings in the House began in February, with witnesses appearing before members of the commerce committee.[119] A South Dakota representative had introduced a resolution calling for at least some FM service to remain in the 50 MHz band to better serve his rural constituents. The testimony of and questions to Howard Armstrong took up the first of four days. The inventor reviewed the whole development of FM and supported retention of some 50 MHz channels for FM to allow long-distance relaying of signals. Witnesses from set manufacturers Zenith and Stromberg-Carlson supported Armstrong, though they were generally favorable to the added space FM had gained in the 100 MHz–spectrum range. Others focused on the controversial Norton interference data. The last two days of House hearings concentrated on witnesses from the FCC and RCA, who offered their view of the events of the past decade, especially the wartime spectrum hearings. In the end, the committee recommended no further House action.

On the other side of Capitol Hill, the Senate commerce committee took up the same issues in hearings over five days scattered from March to May.[120] There, however, the tone and focus was different, as proceedings centered more on the actions of RCA and whether or not the FCC was working with the communications manufacturer to retard FM development. Committee chairman Charles Tobey (R-N.H.) had been for some time sympathetic to Armstrong and FM. His hearing roasted RCA witnesses and, in questions to Armstrong, reviewed RCA engineering tests concerning FM dating back a dozen years. In effect, the hearings provided a final opportunity for FM proponents, some of whom had worked to promote the service for a decade or more, to air their frustrations with the FCC and RCA as major players (especially as the latter had hired a number of key personnel from the government agency) that were more invested in television and thus sought to delay FM expansion. The hearing seemed so obviously one-sided that one committee member protested.[121] But again, despite all the heat, no legislative action resulted.

While both hearings placed useful historical information on the record, they accomplished little else, as nothing the FCC had decided was changed. The high-band FM allocation remained unmodified and no longer effectively challenged. Armstrong filed a patent suit against RCA that summer that would reveal the bitterness between the inventor and the corporation, dragging on unresolved until after Armstrong's death six years later.[122]

WAITING

The war years had been a period of worrisome waiting for FM operators and proponents. After a brief growth surge in 1941 before American entry into the war, FM—as with the rest of broadcasting—was forced to spend nearly four years in a holding pattern as both personnel and equipment became harder to come by. FM backers suffered from a barely formed infrastructure and tiny audiences. Then, beginning with rumors about a shift in frequency band in 1943, FM backers had to wait again—this time for momentous FCC decisions that would define the structure of the postwar FM business. It was hard to maintain momentum in such circumstances, and several developments, including the first attempt to form a national FM network, the boosting of receiver sales necessary to build an audience, and the creation of original programming, fell by the wayside.

Aided by the wartime hiatus, a paternalistic pattern developed in which the FM outlets owned by AM stations (the majority by the end of the war) relied upon their radio elders to support the newer service's costs, given the inability to sell FM advertising time. Radio's network-dominated AM establishment quickly gained control of the newer technology, first promoting and then mandating total program duplication. While the establishment argued that this would help promote the new service, in fact, as events would prove, simulcasting had just the opposite effect—which may have been the intention all along.

The biggest loss for FM was its inability to quickly develop a distinct image or brand. Most Americans lived far outside the coverage area of the relative handful of operating stations; indeed, entire states had no FM reception at all. While people might read about this new radio service, too often they were far from existing outlets and thus could not fully appreciate its benefits. The few who could enjoy FM heard AM programs for the most part, thus diminishing any sense of independent identity for the newer medium. Now with a spectrum allocation that would in a short time make existing receivers obsolete, FM would have to begin anew. And on the horizon lay a new competitor of great appeal: television.

FM 93.5 MHz

The Dismal Years (1945–1957))))))

Is FM a dead duck? Or is it merely emerging from a state of shock as a result of early . . . station deaths, poised to start a new career that conceivably could end in the oft-promised supplanting of AM radio? There's no denying that most of the 686 operating FM stations are having a rough going. Some are making a little money and some are breaking even. But the percentage of profitable stations is small and few owners can back their brave enthusiasm with supporting CPA statements. Worst of all, FM's life is still blighted by its bad luck in having been commercially born at the same time as its glamorous twin sister—TV.[1]

These editorial words encapsulate why, after an exciting burst of initial euphoria in the first postwar year or two, the late 1940s and early 1950s would become the most depressing era in FM's development. FM was in decline, no matter how one measured the business. Hundreds of stations simply gave up the struggle to survive and left the air. Audiences remained tiny and advertising revenue all but nonexistent. Almost nobody made money—FM was an expenditure rather than a revenue producer. This was a dark era for the few optimists who persevered. Indeed, even Howard Armstrong was losing heart.

After the fight over the shift in FM's spectrum, Armstrong faced a growing conflict with RCA, which was unwilling to take out a royalty contract as most other radio manufacturers had. Convinced they could make FM receivers without infringing on Armstrong's patents, RCA offered a settlement that did not match what other firms paid, and thus Armstrong felt it was unfair. The endless wrangling led to his obtaining legal counsel and filing a patent infringement suit against RCA in July 1948.[2] By this time, his longtime friendship with RCA chief David Sarnoff had worn thin. Sarnoff—fresh from his wartime Signal Corps service and proud of his rank of brigadier general (he would be known as General Sarnoff for the rest of his life, while Armstrong was a mere "major" from the previous war)—focused completely on getting television commercially launched. FM was a trivial issue to him. Armstrong, on the other hand, was obsessed with the fact that RCA (and its NBC network) refused to recognize the value of FM. He had fought long and hard to make FM broadcasting a viable commercial reality. Within a few years, however, he was running out of money and could no longer carry on the fight. As his key FM patents expired in 1950–51, his last royalty income source disappeared. And as the patent battle dragged on, FM itself seemed to be on the ropes.

Early in 1954, a despairing Armstrong took his own life, leaping from the thirteenth-story window of his apartment building in New York City. Those who knew him well, including Sarnoff, surely noted the sad irony in his method of self-destruction: all of his life, Armstrong derived great joy from climbing radio antenna towers, once even dangling upside down from atop one of RCA's tall Manhattan antennas—to the chagrin of Sarnoff, who banned him from the site. Armstrong's suicide, reported in a front-page *New York Times* obituary, seemed only to underline the decline of his FM creation.[3]

CHANGING CONTEXT

With the end of World War II in 1945, multitudes of veterans returned home to pick up their lives. Many entered broadcasting, which promised excitement as well as considerable economic expansion. Hundreds of new AM stations took to the air all over the country, including many initial outlets in smaller towns. After 1948 television became widespread, prompting audience excitement, tremendous investment of industry time and effort, and, soon, substantial disruption to the existing radio business. The intimate prewar radio club was clearly becoming a far larger and more complex postwar industry.

AM stations totaled just over 900 as the war ended in 1945, and that number more than tripled (to just over 3,000) by 1957.[4] Returning military personnel (from World War II and the subsequent 1950–53 Korean War) found it easier, cheaper, and more prudent to apply for an AM station in a high-demand area rather than an FM outlet, given FM service's new frequencies, limited audience, and uncertain future. Indeed, continuing pressure to build AM stations led the FCC to weaken its own technical standards in 1946 to allow more outlets to be squeezed on the air in coming years — to the eventual detriment all AM operations, which suffered growing interference. To meet the pent-up demand for AM receivers after years with few repair or replacement options, as well as transmitters for the growing number of AM stations, manufacturers quickly shifted from wartime needs to AM manufacture, putting aside most FM receivers and transmitters, which required extensive new engineering.

Even more apparent as a factor limiting FM's ability to restart, however, was the explosive postwar growth of television. Many radio trade publications in 1945–48 continued to underestimate just how quickly television would expand. They stressed the medium's high cost, and thus likely very limited schedules, rather than consider the potential effect video might have on consumers when they finally got to see it (only a handful of stations were on the air in 1945–47). Real television growth began in 1948–49 with the inception of regular network service to the East and Midwest. Though live network interconnection only stretched from New York to the Mississippi (coast-to-coast live networking first became possible in 1951), publicity fed public demand for rapid television expansion.

Despite a 1948–52 FCC freeze on the granting of new station applications, the number of television stations grew to nearly 110, while (much more tellingly) the percentage of homes owning a TV receiver rose from less than .5 percent in 1948 to 34 percent in 1952 and nearly 79 percent by 1957.[5] With the end of the license freeze, a veritable feeding frenzy put hundreds of TV stations on the air over the next five years. Television rapidly took up "all the air in the room," absorbing industry revenues, personnel, and management attention as it rapidly filled out to assume national scope. The complex television business required substantial infusions of engineering time and talent, capital investment, and program creativity, all vital for the video medium to flourish. Rising audience and advertiser interest helped push television's growth.

As a result of television's expansion, the radio business was plunged into turmoil. This was already apparent by 1950, as the radio networks began to falter, providing fewer programs each season and beginning to force affiliates onto their own program resources. Facing a crisis, many stations tried to replicate network style with what became known as "middle-of-the-road" programming, offering a little bit of everything to different audience segments, from children to retirees. A varied mixture of talk and music was scheduled, often in formal programs of an hour or half hour, following the longtime network pattern. Some argued that radio's real answer lay — as it always had — with popular music, a programming staple since the medium's inception. But there was little agreement among radio managers on *what* music to play or how best to present it to retain, let alone rebuild, their once-loyal audiences.

Seeking survival in a more complex market, an increasing number of AM stations began to turn away from distinct programs to experiment instead with "formats" — nearly always some type of popular music — broadcast through the day and night and targeting particular audience groups. Music, advertising, and announcements were all tailored to the format, which became central to the station's identity (or, to again use the twenty-first century term, its "brand"). The idea was not new, as classical/arts AM (and a few FM) stations had already done much of this, but desperation now fed the quest as radio sought some continuing role in an increasingly television-dominated world. Two different AM-station owners finally developed the combination that would infuse new life into radio during the mid-1950s.

Todd Storz in Omaha and Gordon McLendon in Dallas independently developed aspects of what would soon be called "formula" or "Top 40" radio.[6] Simple in concept, Top 40 was often fairly complex in execution. The basic idea was to play a limited list of the most popular songs (often no more than a dozen and rarely exceeding forty), mixed in with announcer chatter, weather, short newscasts — and, of course, commercials. The announcers, who became known as "disc jockeys" or "DJs," spewed out a constant patter of call-letter repetition to attract and hold listeners, played endless promotional jingles, and strived to eliminate any silence or "dead air." This was very fast-paced (exhausting and barely comprehensible to older listeners) and tightly controlled, though it was subject to some variation. Only boredom was anathema. In the early 1950s, Storz developed the format to fit larger markets, while McLendon focused his efforts on smaller stations. Both men succeeded because Top 40 was something new, relatively inexpensive (the records were provided free by manufacturers), and hugely popular with young listeners. From only twenty stations in 1955 to hundreds of them a few years later, these formula AM stations soon dominated radio's audience ratings.[7] But much of AM's fabled success with Top 40 was due to fortuitous timing and three concurrent trends.

As formula radio took hold, rock music was also developing; some suggest that the release of Bill Haley and the Comets' hit song "Rock Around the Clock" in 1955 marked the format's coming of age. The appearance a year later of the first big Elvis Presley hits ("Hound Dog" and "Don't Be Cruel") built up further appeal as he combined rock with country and what had been dubbed "race" music (meaning black rhythm and blues).[8] Presley's success quickly prompted a host of other rock groups and singers.

At the same time, audience listening patterns were changing. While radio's largest audiences had tuned into network evening prime time through the late 1940s, the subsequent decline of network schedules and rise of television prime time soon shifted most radio listening into the early morning "drive-time" commuting period of 7:00 A.M. to 9:00 A.M., with declining numbers later in the day.[9] Aiding this shift and boosting radio's turnaround (as well as the spread of rock music) was the appearance in late 1954 of the first easily portable transistor radios. While portable receivers were not new, the tiny transistor-receiver sets allowed young listeners to more easily combine rock music with their increasingly mobile lives. Though at first expensive and of poor quality, the transistor set's easy mobility ("shirt-pocket" radio) soon made them hugely popular despite their initial expense. Now radio could accompany teens to school, the beach, and anywhere else in addition to home and car. But these early transistors could only tune AM signals—yet another sign of trouble for FM.

INITIAL EUPHORIA

Ironically, given how the story would play out in the 1950s, FM had begun the postwar years with considerable promise. One indicator was the appearance late in 1945 of FM for You from the U.S. Department of Agriculture, designed as a primer for those considering applying for a new FM station.[10] Another was the inception of the monthly Frequency Modulation Business in early 1946, aimed at the "FM broadcaster, advertiser and technician."[11] Founded by Martin Codel (who had cofounded *Broadcasting* fifteen years earlier), it would last only until late 1947, a victim of inadequate advertiser and reader support. In April 1946 a Senate committee released a report extolling *Small Business Opportunities in FM Broadcasting* in an attempt to encourage new entrants into the business while criticizing some FCC policies that got in their way.[12] A few months later came publication of Milton Sleeper's *FM Radio Handbook*, first issue of an intended annual directory.[13] And the title of a new book, otherwise sharply critical of AM commercial radio, touted FM as being "radio's second chance."[14] Articles about FM were increasingly common in the business press. Lots of authorities in both government and industry were predicting that FM would replace AM; the only question seemed to be how soon.

Adding to FM's euphoria was support from the FCC—indeed, right from the top. As Chairman James Lawrence Fly had made clear toward the end of the war, "Frequency modulation is of age and it has come to stay. Without a doubt, it will have a place of ever-increasing importance in American broadcasting. No one of us can stop it. FM is another radio service. It may be said to be a supplementary service, or an alternative service, but much more important, it is a higher quality radio service."[15] Just two years later, his successor Paul Porter agreed that "no one who has heard the interference-free, full-bodied, crystal-clear tone of FM can ever again be quite content with the limitations [of] AM. . . . FM should be one of the earliest and brightest boons of the reconstruction era."[16] Charles Denny, who followed Porter, told a group of FM broadcasters just a year later that "it is the American way of life to seek the best there is. And the best there is in aural radio is FM. The American people will insist on having FM in their new radios once they have had an opportunity to hear it."[17] Finally, Wayne Coy, who served as chair for the longest part of this period (1947–52), chimed in early in 1948 by confirming that "the Federal Communications Commission is highly enthusiastic over FM as the new system in broadcasting. Every new station that goes on the air is another step in speeding the establishment of this new system. We want the American people to have this superior service just as quickly as possible. We are doing everything possible to hasten the growth of this new type of broadcasting."[18] With such support, it seemed that FM was well on track for success, though all agreed its development was going to take considerable effort.

The handful of wartime FM stations began plans to shift up to their new frequencies and ramp up program hours to encourage people to buy the receivers that would soon become available. New station applications continued flowing into the FCC — more than 400 were pending even before the Japanese surrender in August 1945. Now that the spectrum-shift decision was final, the commission needed to "process the paper" to get those stations on the air. After all, more than thirty states still lacked even one FM station.

Manufacturers of FM transmitters and receivers met in New York City early in July 1945 to coordinate plans for developing equipment for FM's higher frequencies.[19] Companies began developing pilot models of new designs intended for commercial production in order to retain their trained personnel as military contracts wound down or were canceled. Postwar labor unrest often delayed plans. Strikes, or the threat of them, at Western Electric and GE, for example, made a hash of production schedules.[20]

In the meantime, Howard Armstrong had been doing his best to assure advocates that FM's new spectrum allocation would work out. He noted that "the original FM work [of the mid-1930s] was on 110 and 117 megacycles and it was on this band that the superiority of FM over AM was [first] demonstrated."[21] He also announced that a relatively inexpensive method had been developed to allow for temporary dual-band transmission during the transition period, and that his own Alpine station would soon begin to transmit on the new high band in addition to its original frequency.

Several other FM broadcasters announced similar plans for the transition. Station WDUL (FM) in Superior, Wisconsin, claimed (despite its uninspiring call letters, chosen because the station was close to Duluth, Minnesota) to be the first outlet operating on the new band (September 5, 1945) and ceased transmitting on the old.[22] This was highly risky, as their audience on the new frequency was as yet nonexistent. Ever hopeful, however, other stations chose to follow a similar course, though some retained low-power transmissions to serve existing receivers. Stromberg-Carlson station WHFM in Rochester, New York, was the first to begin such dual-band operation, followed shortly thereafter by WMFM in Milwaukee.[23]

By the beginning of 1946, however, very few stations were transmitting on the new band (including only one of the eight FM stations in New York City), in most cases simply for lack of equipment or personnel to get the job done. An FM station in Iowa announced it would switch and also build a 1,530-foot antenna tower, which it touted as the highest man-made object on earth.[24] Some outlets ceased broadcasting entirely in order to make the transition (including the CBS and Bamberger outlets in New York) and were often delayed in returning to the air by the lack of transmitter parts. Most FM stations operated with temporary facilities and often relatively low power. FM seemed to be going through a Band-Aid transition.

On October 25, 1945, the FCC announced its first "conditional grants" for sixty-four new FM licenses from what was now a pool of 600 accumulated station applications. All but ten were granted to those already holding AM licensees. These were the first new FM-station grants in nearly four years and were seen as evidence of the FCC's desire "to get the service started as soon as possible."[25] The grants were "conditioned" to allow the grantee to proceed with studio, program, and personnel planning, but they did not permit purchase of a transmitter or actual station construction. Specific channel and power assignments, as well as precise areas of station coverage, were to be assigned only when full engineering data had been submitted and analyzed. But receipt of such a grant at least told an applicant it would receive an FM channel.

The increase in FM-station authorizations over the next two years was phenomenal—indeed, the numbers exceeded those of AM during the latter's first two decades of development. Temporary FM conditional grants exploded to more than 400 by early 1947 and then declined as regular construction permits (CPs) were issued instead. The number of CPs grew from fewer than twenty in April 1946 to more than 400 at the end of that year, more than doubling again (to 978) by the end of 1947. Everybody seemingly wanted to climb on board the FM bandwagon. The director of the newly formed FM Association (FMA) predicted there would be thousands of new FM jobs at upwards of 2,000 stations before 1950.[26] Just months later, the FMA rather grandly projected that FM would soon be a half-billion-dollar business.[27] Stations actually on the air did grow threefold by early 1947 and more than doubled just a year later (see appendix Table B.1). Many more applicants still awaited permits to operate. All the FM growth signs seemed positive.

Behind the scenes, however, problems were already appearing. Most of the new applications were for the midsize "metropolitan" facilities with larger coverage areas (and thus potentially more audience and advertiser revenue), and their greater potential for overlap and interference forced the FCC to proceed carefully. Multiple applications for the same facilities and market required comparative hearings and further delay. As *Broadcasting* summarized the problem:

The FCC faces many baffling problems in breaking this new ground. One has been the dearth of applications for "community" stations. All seem to want "metropolitan" or rural stations because they connote larger operations corresponding to regional and perhaps high-power assignments in AM. The "community" station, however, seems to be an untouchable waif which carries the stigma of being simply a precinct operation. Engineers tell us the average FM community station will have coverage and signal intensity far superior to the average Class IV AM station, commonly called a local.[28]

Because of the increasing number of applications for the bigger metropolitan and rural stations, the FCC moved to establish a table of "allotments" (placing channels in specific locations for which applicants could then apply) for those two types of FM service.

In December 1945 the commission issued a detailed plan allotting more than 1,500 FM channels to specific cities and towns across the country, warning that there already appeared to be insufficient channels to meet likely demand in many urban areas. The commission's announced goal was to have 50 to 100 percent more FM channels than operating AM stations in any given area.[29] If too many applications were received for metropolitan or rural stations, FCC officials tried to persuade applicants to use the undervalued community channels instead. To that end, one commissioner touted the smaller stations as being far more effective than many people thought.[30]

In mid-1946 the FCC tried some psychology to lift the stigma from the underused community stations by changing how FM stations were labeled. The lower-power community stations were now to be termed Class A channels (and, more importantly, to have their maximum power increased fourfold to 1,000 watts), while the higher-powered metropolitan and rural channels would be known as Class B.[31] A year later came an indicator that the name change may have worked—but also of FM's growing pains. On April 10, 1947, the FCC announced a revised allocation plan for FM, increasing from one to four the number of channels that separated FM stations operating in the same market. There had been a growing number of complaints about interference with the old one-channel separation. About 90 percent of the 200 stations then on the air would have to shift frequencies, but no community would lose channels and a few areas gained some.

An increase in applications for the smaller Class A channels was a prime factor prompting commission action, which suggests that the FCC renaming of channels had worked.[32]

There were also signs that some new entrants to the broadcasting business were applying for FM stations, as many critics had hoped. For many years, for example, organized labor had a difficult time getting its views on the air. By late 1945 several different labor unions had applied for and later received licenses for sixteen FM stations. Clothing, automobile, electrical, and maritime unions were among the applicants for stations in larger urban markets.[33] At the same time, an FCC survey determined that equipment costs for an FM station were lower than many presumed and "well within reach of small business, farm, labor and other groups."[34] A suggestion that some FM channels be held back for perhaps six months to give veterans and other newcomers a chance to apply—introduced by veterans' groups and supported by FCC commissioner Clifford Durr—was adopted despite fierce opposition from AM broadcasters, who argued that such a reservation would merely retard FM expansion. Starting in mid-1946, the FCC withheld action on selected unused Class B channels across the country, intending to give small businesses, farmers, and veterans a better chance to get into the FM game.[35] What impact the year-long reservation had, however, is now difficult to discern. Surely, fewer stations got on the air by 1948 than might have been the case without the reservation, though ironically this saved a lot of would-be applicants grief when FM's light began to dim in 1949.

Nearly 70 percent of new FM applications came from AM owners, continuing the prewar pattern.[36] This was no surprise, since experienced broadcasters already knew the business, as well as how to "play" the FCC's application process. Most FM applications came from the Northeast and Midwest; even in 1947, over half of all applications were from markets east of the Mississippi.[37] There was evidence, however, that once AM owners received an FM construction permit, some of them dawdled at actually building their facilities, hoping that in the meantime, receiver sales would increase FM's small audience.[38] The first postwar commercial licenses (as opposed to mere CPs) were granted in mid-1947 to stations in Syracuse, New York; Winchester, Virginia; Topeka, Kansas; and Bristol, Tennessee.[39]

By late 1948 the FCC mandated the shutdown of the last transmitters still sending out FM signals on the old prewar FM band.[40] Howard Armstrong sought permission to continue relay experiments on his Alpine station over its original frequency but was turned down; when his operation switched to its new assigned channel in late 1949, it was the last of the prewar FM stations to do so.

Just before midcentury, FM service was available to about two-thirds of the country's population (see appendix Map C.1)—presuming, of course, that they owned FM receivers. Most of the Northeast and South was well covered with at least one signal and often several, though gaps existed. But much of the country west of the Mississippi (including all of Montana, Wyoming, Arizona, and New Mexico) still received no FM service at all.

NEW NETWORKS

The dream of separate FM networks, epitomized by the projected American Network in 1940, had not died with the end of that operation in 1944. As applications for more FM stations continued to pour in, some estimated that as many as 5,000 commercial FM stations might soon be on the air (a number actually reached only a half century later), and they could support the creation of up to ten new national networks. There was mixed opinion as to whether such chains might be linked with station-to-station broadcast relays as had occurred before the war, or whether more traditional wire links would be required. Over-the-air relays seemed less likely, as FM's higher frequencies did not lend themselves to the transmission distances required. Yet any wire connection would either suffer from the limited frequency response of the links provided by AT&T (which were engineered for the narrower frequency response of AM networks) or would require new higher-quality, and thus more costly, lines.[41]

Because of these limitations (among such others as limited finances and operators' focus on the station level), early experience with FM networking remained on a regional level. One early effort linked three stations in Indiana and Illinois.[42] In 1948 six New York stations set up the Rural Network, covering 80 percent of the state's population. It was funded by ten farmers' cooperatives and operated on a commercial basis.[43] More than a dozen FM outlets in the Carolinas formed the Dixie Network at about the same time to present "special features in the popular and concert music fields, special events, and complete coverage of the Carolina sports picture."[44] By the end of 1948 there were about a dozen of these regional hookups, most of them operating with over-the-air relay since distances separating the stations were not great.[45] In 1949 one powerful FM station in Birmingham,

Alabama, was used to feed, again by over-the-air relay, programs to twenty-four small AM outlets in Alabama and Tennessee.[46]

The first postwar national FM network proposal came from CBS. Following up on the network's previous promises, early in 1946 CBS's newly named president, Frank Stanton, proposed to the FCC a national linkup of some 200 FM outlets that would cover most of the country and 90 percent of its population (see Map 3.1). But this was not a "pure" FM proposal, as two huge AM transmitters in Kentucky and Colorado, each transmitting with 1 million watts (50 kw was the AM limit then and now) would be required to provide adequate rural coverage. Later the number of these fill-in AM stations increased to five, three of them in the West and all utilizing the normal 50 kw AM power limit. Stanton noted it might take a decade before such a network was economically feasible, as it would cost about $11 million to establish and another $4 million to operate each year. But his planners had already earmarked the 200 specific communities, going so far as to project specific power and antenna conditions for each. Presenting his plan, Stanton added that "we believe that aural broadcasting of the future will be identified, almost entirely, with FM broadcasting."[47] CBS was clearly hedging its bets by seeking a strong role in helping to define the FM service of the future. But skeptics saw the whole proposal as merely gift wrapping around the five powerful new AM stations that would be hugely attractive to national advertisers.

Just a few months later, the relatively new ABC network produced another plan for linked-up FM outlets that would duplicate its AM programming (CBS had not been clear about its own program plans). ABC proposed use of 243 stations, nearly eighty of which already were licenses or held CPs. Network officials admitted that their FM project—already being actively pursued—might be the only way for the third network to approach the importance and reach of CBS and NBC.[48]

Early in 1947 the first FM network designed as such began operation, though only with four affiliates and less than 130 miles of radio relay to connect them. This was to be the first live-program FM network and would survive until 1954. It was primarily the brainchild of Everett Dillard, an important postwar FM-station operator.

Like so many others, Dillard had first gotten into radio as an amateur ("ham") operator in the 1920s. He began broadcasting with WLBF in his hometown of Kansas City before 1930. Then he shifted away from broadcasting and supplied radio equipment for several years. His interest in FM

MAP 3.1. Projected CBS FM Network, 1946

was sparked by the FCC's first hearings into the service in 1936, and two years later he applied for an experimental FM license. He converted his Washington, D.C.–based high-frequency experimental AM outlet W9XA to operate on FM and kept it going during the war. He also began W49KC (later KOZY) as the first FM outlet in Kansas City. The Washington outlet became commercial WASH in 1947.[49] Years later, Dillard recalled how he next moved into FM networking. "It basically came out of a discussion with Major Armstrong. . . . One time we were talking and he mentioned the fact that if we could only get some live shows on FM that it would be quite a feather in his cap, and that also he'd like to establish that relay broadcasting was practicable—well, it had been established, but to establish it technically and to prove it to the public and to the industry was another thing."[50]

The first demonstration of what the Continental Network (Dillard had picked the name) might become was heard on the evening of March 26, 1947. An Army Air Forces band concert at a Washington auditorium was transmitted to Armstrong's W2XMN in Alpine, New Jersey, by means of an 8 kHz wire relay. The first of seven scheduled broadcasts of the army band, it was carried on four stations: WASH, which originated it, Armstrong's station, and outlets in Baltimore and Schenectady (which were linked using a radio relay). The process required 220 miles of wired circuits from AT&T and nearly 130 miles of radio relay.[51] Within a month,

MAP 3.2. Continental Network, 1947

thirteen stations were linked up and more had asked to participate.[52] By the end of July, some 570 miles of wire circuits and nearly 1,000 miles of radio links were providing Continental service to much of the Northeast (see Map 3.2).[53] The radio relays provided vastly better sound fidelity at a far lower cost than the wire relays, which could not carry the full range of FM sound. Dillard noted that the network had been formed "not as a nationwide venture . . . but to demonstrate the flexibility of FM network transmission, and to answer the complaint that there are no good live FM programs."[54]

After six months of operation, the network had grown to serve twenty-seven stations in the Northeast, with some sixty more stations expressing interest. On Friday, September 12, the first commercially sponsored program was transmitted when set manufacturer Stromberg-Carlson began a weekly half-hour live concert program from its Rochester, New York, station.[55] By February 1948 the network was using the first 15 kHz wire connections, which provided vastly improved sound fidelity. With occasional connections to the Dixie Network in the Carolinas, Continental served upwards of forty-one stations along the eastern seaboard, which collectively could reach 25 million people. More than a third of all on-air FM stations played a part—or wanted to become a part—of the growing network.[56]

Continental also became one of the first radio networks, AM or FM, to record many of its programs on audiotape. Taped programs served stations in the Midwest, where the chain linked to regional networks in Michigan, Indiana, and Ohio—most of which operated on Central Time, an hour earlier than the East Coast outlets.[57] Late in September 1948 came a test of the first coast-to-coast FM link, using a combination of wire and radio connections. Counting its live and delayed-tape services, the network was serving more than fifty stations by year's end, and line charges of some $1,500 a month (perhaps $15,000 in 2007 values) were being borne by Howard Armstrong.[58] Fuller development of the network was stymied not by money or technology but because of the labor dispute described below.

At its peak, Continental probably reached fifty or sixty stations, though it expanded very little after the late 1940s. With Armstrong's suicide early in 1954, however, the tenuous financial basis of its operation became all too evident when nobody else could afford to take up the monthly wire interconnection charges. The network ceased operation within a month of the inventor's death.[59] FM was left with no major multistate network for another fourteen years, though several small state or regional hook-ups continued.

REALITY SETS IN

Stymied networks reflected the larger FM decline after 1950. Indeed, the FM business in the 1950s was one defined by shrinking numbers (see appendix Table B.1). Though on the surface things looked solid for the medium—the number of stations on the air was rising annually to 1949—closer analysis of the official FCC figures suggested a different story. While educational FM stations slowly but steadily increased (being subject to different priorities than their commercial brethren, as discussed below), the commercial portion of the business was rapidly becoming a depressing sight indeed. The number of pending FM-station applications dropped in 1948, the total number of authorizations began to decline the next year, and stations actually on the air began to drop a year after that. Tellingly, some of the medium's pioneers began to give up.

Milwaukee's WTMJ-FM, which had aired in 1940 as the first FM west of the Alleghenies and broadcast with 50 kw of power, had dropped its extensive original programming to fully simulcast AM-station programs. Early in 1950, when managers conducted a three-month broadcast and print campaign (including ads in the *Milwaukee Journal*) to ascertain interest in FM, the station received only 173 replies. They began to cut back on-air hours (from nineteen to just over seven hours a day), yet they still garnered few complaints. In April 1950 the Journal Company gave up, returning its license to the FCC:

> Much to our regret FM has not lived up to the bright promise of ten years ago. The radio listeners in Wisconsin have not seen fit to invest in a sufficient number of FM receivers to make the continued operation of WTMJ-FM . . . a worthwhile undertaking. . . . The only justification for underwriting the cost of continued FM service would be a body of listeners far larger than the very limited one our research has shown to be in existence at the present time and which shows no sign of material growth.[60]

This letter clearly blames the station's failure on a lack of listeners. It seems not to have occurred to Journal Company management that carrying only simulcast AM programs gave people precious little reason to buy FM receivers. Within a few months, the tower and antenna and transmitter were sold (at virtually giveaway prices) to the University of Illinois.

Just a week after the Milwaukee station closed down, WMIT in Charlotte, North Carolina, which had been the first station in the South, also left the air. Managers of both stations had been key players in FM promotional activities all through the 1940s. The next month a second New York station left the air. If an FM outlet could not make it in the nation's largest city, then clearly the medium was in deep trouble. Indeed, when WMCA-FM turned in its license in late 1949, management noted they had been unable to give the station away.[61]

The FCC took note of these closing stations with concern and tried to do something about it. On several occasions in the early 1950s, the FCC eased various requirements to help FM licensees lower their costs. In 1951, for example, it allowed stations to automate operations of transmitters and even programming (not an easy thing to manage in an era before widespread use of computers). Eight FM outlets took up this option by early the next year. Most FM stations trimmed staff, some shortened their hours on the air, and a good deal of live programming disappeared in cost-cutting moves. One indication of the depths of financial concern in FM came in 1955, when a conference of broadcasters nearly adopted a resolution favoring toll or pay broadcast operations over FM outlets.[62]

By 1956–57, FM stations on the air had dropped to their lowest point since early 1948. Total authorizations had declined by half. Something heretofore unheard of was happening in an American broadcast service: unable to make money or even sell their operations, stations were voluntarily closing down and returning their licenses. And this was happening across markets large and small. FM stations were all but impossible to sell— or even give away—to other potential owners. A few departing licensees donated their equipment to educational institutions. FM was seemingly fading away, having become at best a "third service" behind still-growing AM and burgeoning television. And few people in or out of broadcasting seemed to care.

Indeed, as more FM stations turned in their licenses, spectrum poachers began to eye the large number of underutilized frequencies allocated to FM. *Broadcasting* reflected a good deal of industry thinking in no less than three editorials in the summer of 1951 calling on the FCC to reexamine FM's allocation for possible better uses of much of it—probably by television.[63] While *Broadcasting*'s letters column soon resounded with angry FM broadcaster responses at the suggested spectrum raids, the point had been made that the increasingly television-centric broadcast business had little use for an also-ran radio service. Two years later an FCC commissioner made much the same point in remarks to a broadcaster group.[64]

The greatest pressure for taking FM's spectrum was soon coming not from television (to which the FCC had added a large number of UHF channels in 1952), but from such nonbroadcast users as land mobile-radio services. In 1955 the National Association of Manufacturers petitioned the FCC for shared use of part of the FM band for industrial communication needs.[65] Though nothing came of this idea either, it underlined that concern over efficient use of spectrum remained not far from the surface. Two years later, technical papers for the FCC (then preparing for an international conference) suggested that underused FM and UHF television channels might be put to better use.[66] Again, though nothing transpired, FM fears remained, given the relatively few stations clinging to their spectrum assignments.

FM's troubles were mirrored in the changing status of the trade groups that promoted the medium. FM Broadcasters, Inc., the pioneering organization, by 1946 argued that its basic "let people know about FM" work was done and voted to merge with the FM department of the far larger National Association of Broadcasters (NAB). At that point, FM's future looked fairly rosy. Even so, and at almost the same time, a second attempt at a trade group, the FM Association (FMA) began to organize under broadcasters Roy Hofheintz of Houston (years later he would become mayor) and Everett Dillard of Washington, D.C.[67] The new organization demonstrated an important split among FM owners, as the FMA was founded by independent station owners, while most AM-owned FM outlets generally felt the larger NAB could handle FM issues.[68] FMA focused on getting permit holders to actually build the stations they had authority to construct.[69] Indeed, FMA pressure on the FCC led to the termination of a number of "warehoused" construction permits with which nothing was being done. But after two years of promoting FM to the public, the FMA followed the FMBI example and voted to merge with the NAB.[70]

FM broadcasters thus lost their focused promotional trade association that independent stations felt was still strongly needed. Indeed, a number of independents considered forming their own group, of which AM-owned stations could only be nonvoting members.[71] The NAB's FM department or office did help coordinate industry positions on the medium, but it was affected, of course, by the predominance of AM-station membership in the organization. In 1956 a third attempt was made through the organization of the FM Development Association (FMDA), which was designed to focus on getting better programs for listeners and more revenue for station owners.[72] The FMDA worked with a number of FM stations during 1957 to help promote the medium.[73] Part of their problem was FM's perceived lack of a clear purpose among potential listeners.

WHAT TO AIR?

Indeed, the sound of FM in the 1950s *was* somewhat inchoate, though there is little consistent information on independent FM program trends during this dozen-year period. The business was too small to attract research efforts, especially since most FM outlets (some 600 of the nearly 700 stations on the air in 1948) merely simulcast AM programs.

Independent stations generally provided background music, usually rejecting anything perceived as too up-tempo, loud, or "pop-culture" in feel and flavor. By inspiring something of an upscale image, they positioned FM as a counterpoint to AM's teen-appeal formulaic sound. Everything was clearly directed toward adult listeners and sounded relatively soft-edged so as not to alienate refugees from AM. Commercials were few and simple in format. Indeed, FM ads were minimalist by design, with few of AM's raucous jingles and promotions. WABF in New York, for example, noted that it was "banning theme songs, jingles, singing commercials, high pressure selling and exaggerated claims" as it "set a new course in radio."[74]

Music tended to rely either on classics (creating what some dubbed "Three B Band"—Beethoven, Brahms, and Bach) or popular standards (by orchestras such as those headed by Count Basie or Percy Faith, or singers like Frank Sinatra, the Ames Brothers, Ella Fitzgerald, Nat King Cole, and Perry Como). Some experimentation in genre (including jazz, folk, country, or ethnic) was evident in larger markets. There was usually little news and less sports on most FM outlets, though discussion and culturally oriented features on the fine arts appeared on many schedules. *Music for the Connoisseur* and *Speaking of Music* on New York's WNYC-FM are typical examples. New York's WQXR became the prototype classical music FM operation. By 1951 the station, owned by the *New York Times*, enjoyed a 25,000-record library and ready access to New York musical figures. Several other New York stations programmed much the same way, as did about fifty other independent FM stations nationally. All of them built upon a growing national interest in better sound.

That trend was underlined in 1953, when Milton Sleeper began publishing the bimonthly *Hi-Fi Music at Home* to provide a "complete guide to hi-fi reproduction from records, tape, and FM radio."[75] (The "hi-fi" term had been used at least as early as 1936.[76] As audio technologies improved, "high," or "hi," came to mean something better each year.) That FM came last in the magazine subtitle said something about the priority of most hi-fi fans as they bought and built complex home systems. Their focus was on long-playing record changers (CBS had introduced the LP record format in 1948) and tape-recording equipment, feeding often very complex speaker systems. Little of this equipment came cheaply, and thus upscale hi-fi "addicts" became intensely loyal to those few FM stations that fed their habit. Fine-arts stations (as they became known) in New York, Washington, Chicago, Philadelphia, and elsewhere survived these dismal years largely thanks to that loyalty. Sleeper contracted with such independents to include their program schedules as an insert in front of each issue. Everett Dillard's WASH-FM in Washington, D.C., was one of these. Eight pages provided details for two months of programming, followed by the glossy-paper main magazine featuring articles and ads aimed at hi-fi aficionados. Over the next decade, such program guides would become a standard feature at many of the larger independent stations.

Reliance on hi-fi's highbrow appeal worked best in the larger markets that had enough potential listeners. But some independent FM stations argued it was time to broaden their scope from classical music fare to appeal to more of a mass audience. Some even called for a broad middle-of-the-road approach melding music, news, and features throughout the day—very much as non-network AM stations were doing. All agreed that people had to be given some reason to listen. It was no longer sufficient simply to say that FM sound was better and suffered less interference. Who cared how good the sound was if there wasn't something interesting or appealing to tune to? This fundamental question of program and purpose was not immediately resolved, to the continuing detriment of FM development.

Throughout this period, AM broadcasters continued to argue that duplication of their popular programs was the best way to promote FM growth. For any existing broadcaster, it seemed nonsensical to develop an FM facility in order to provide separate programming to compete with their existing AM operation. Why divide radio's audience?

In response to broadcast lobbying pressure, the FCC's FM rules did not require separate programming. Charles Siepmann's 1946 book *Radio's Second Chance* expressed the fear that while FM might add "hundreds of new highways . . . the program traffic will be virtually the same as now."[77] Yet a mid-1947 survey showed that even independent FM operators agreed duplication would probably help FM grow (only 20 percent of all FM stations reported no duplication).[78] Though NBC claimed credit for prompting an AM-FM duplication policy,[79] the real reasons were already evident: defending AM's investment and servicing advertisers. The network's requirement that if an FM station duplicated any program it would have to duplicate *all* programs made abundantly clear that the policy was intended to serve advertisers rather than create variety for listeners.

TROUBLES WITH MUSIC

A difficult labor episode contributed to FM's music headache. The brief central role of James Caesar Petrillo in the radio industry is almost forgotten today, save in some American Federation of Musicians (AFM) meeting halls.[80] The president of the AFM beginning in 1940, Petrillo had already made a name for himself as a powerful union figure who was fiercely supportive of musicians. His critics argued that his short stature and pugnacious nature merited his middle name. His joking response was that had he been a better trumpet player, he might never have become a union organizer. Having taken up the union flag, however, he was unwavering in supporting his members' needs.

On October 17, 1945, Petrillo demanded that the radio networks either employ separate musicians for use on AM and FM broadcasts or pay the same players twice their normal rate for simulcasts (or, alternatively, not to duplicate programming). A few weeks later, Petrillo extended his ban to individual pairs of simulcasting stations, whether or not they were co-owned. He contended that musicians were providing twice the service (due to broadcasts over both AM and FM) for only one wage.[81] After negotiations for a compromise failed, the networks ceased allowing simulcasting. It appeared Petrillo's "featherbedding" demands were having an effect.[82]

Network and independent FM proponents noted that FM stations, lacking much revenue at this point, would have a hard time paying for live performances and would thus have to rely more on recordings. The argument was again made that lack of simulcasting was likely to limit FM growth and receiver sales. The New York Times (by then licensee of its own FM station in New York) editorialized that "the only result [of the ban] can be to retard the development of FM and deprive the public of better reception."[83]

The Washington Post and others urged Congress to do something about controlling such union featherbedding practices, as the FCC then lacked power to counter the AFM ban. Remedial congressional action was not long in coming. Already angered by the intransigence of Petrillo's AFM during the war (when he had banned any recording for more than a year), both houses passed legislation amending the Communications Act to prevent any private organization from coercing broadcasters into hiring personnel or requiring them to conduct specific practices. President Truman signed it into law in April 1946.[84] After a long legal appeals process upheld the law, Petrillo, in early 1948, finally allowed AM-FM program duplication to resume.

It is hard to pin down the effect of this brief and bitter battle over music performance. Some argued the fight hurt FM-receiver sales and may have kept some potential FM-station applicants out of the market. After all, network musical programming was denied to FM stations for more than two crucial years. Others, not enamored of what program duplication was doing to (rather than for) FM radio, felt that the ban was a mixed blessing: while it caused some economic hardship, it also forced stations to consider other programming—most of which turned out to be recorded music.

SUPPLEMENTARY SIGNALS

In their continuing search for revenue, a growing number of FM stations sought additional ways to use their facilities. One promising early option was the first of several so-called functional-music services, providing music aboard public transit systems.[85] While the earliest experiments may have taken place a year or so earlier, 1948 marked the real start of the move to use FM as an entertainment source in big-city buses and trolley cars. The first daily operation began in the Cincinnati area using the signal of WCTS (FM) on board about 100 busses in suburban Covington, Kentucky. Similar services soon appeared in Houston, Wilkes-Barre, Pennsylvania, and a trial operation in St. Louis.[86]

By October 1948, nearly 3,000 transit vehicles in these cities had speakers providing FM-station signals for the straphangers. Two years later, eighteen cities were offering transit radio (see Table 3.1), and the FM stations involved appeared to have found a new and very researchable audience to sell to advertisers at no added cost.[87] Polls of transit users suggested that most appreciated the service. At its peak, transit radio, or "transitcasting," served more than 4,500 vehicles in twenty-one cities.[88] But rising opposition would soon spell an early end to transit radio.

Two organizations representing users of public transit argued that such service invaded the personal space of riders, who had no choice but to listen. One, the Transit Riders Association, claimed that transitcasting in Washington, D.C., buses and trolleys was an "abuse of the broadcasting privilege."[89] Failing with petitions to the city public utility commission and the FCC, the group appealed to the courts. In June 1951 a federal appeals court held that the service was unconstitutional, only to be overturned a year later by the Supreme Court.[90] But by that point, growing adverse public opinion had killed transitcasting, despite the legal approval.

Another and eventually far more successful application of the functional-

TABLE 3.1. Transit-Radio Markets as of Mid-1950

Market and State (Alphabetical by Community)	FM Station Providing Transit Radio
Bradbury Heights, Maryland (and other Washington, D.C., suburbs)	WBUZ
Cincinnati, Ohio (including Covington, Kentucky)	WCTS
Des Moines, Iowa	KCBC-FM
Evansville, Indiana	WMLL
Flint, Michigan	WAJL-FM
Houston, Texas	KPRC-FM
Huntington, West Virginia	WPLH-FM
Jacksonville, Florida	WJHP
Kansas City, Missouri	KCMO-FM
Minneapolis/St. Paul, Minnesota	N/A
Omaha, Nebraska	KBON-FM
Pittsburgh, Pennsylvania (suburbs)	WJKF
St. Louis, Missouri	KXOK-FM
Tacoma, Washington	KTNT
Trenton, New Jersey	WTOA
Washington, D.C.	WWDC-FM
Wilkes-Barre, Pennsylvania	WIZZ
Worchester, Massachusetts	WGTR-FM

Source: Transit Radio, Inc., advertisement in *Broadcasting*, June 19, 1950 (reissued as promotional material by Transit Radio).

music idea was "storecasting" — providing music in stores or offices, as firms such as Muzak had long done using other means. FM offered a cheaper way to provide music than the traditional telephone line–delivered music systems. In mid-1948 a Chicago FM station's signal was beamed to a receiver and speakers in a grocery-store chain. The station charged a rental fee for the receivers. But the FCC argued in 1952 that this was not a proper use of the broadcasting signal (for signals were not being "broad" cast), and such "simplex" (single-signal) systems were closed down.[91] With the end of revenue from both transit and store services, more FM stations left the air in 1953.

Bowing to pleas from stations starving for revenues, however, the FCC approved a more complex industry suggestion to achieve the same end. On the last day of 1953, the commission issued a proposed ruling to allow such subsidiary uses of FM transmitter capacity by multiplexing.[92] In essence, multiplexing used one segment of the FM channel separate from the main (broadcast) carrier wave, allowing a subsidiary service without impact on the main broadcasting signal (see also appendix A). Multiplexing technology had first been demonstrated by Armstrong in 1934 and was perfected after 1948, when the inventor worked with John Bose. The improved version was announced late in 1953, shortly before Armstrong took his own life.[93] On March 22, 1955, the FCC adopted multiplexing rules that allowed functional-music services using what they termed a Subsidiary Communications Authorization (SCA).[94]

Though not widely apparent at first, the revenue potential of the SCA would become a substantial shot in the arm for FM stations struggling to survive. Twenty were providing such service on an experimental basis at the time, and soon many more were. The first new grants were made to Philadelphia and Washington, D.C., stations in October. The necessary equipment was fairly inexpensive (a few thousand dollars), and revenue from leasing the special receiver and speakers needed to tune the new service could be substantial. Because the music played was separate and different from the station's on-air signal, stores had to lease receivers rather than just turning on an ordinary radio. Such storecasting would become an important factor in the later turnaround of FM's fortunes.

SMALL AUDIENCE, SCARCE ADVERTISERS

But storecasting could not address FM's fundamental problem in the late 1940s (which only worsened in the 1950s): few FM stations offered anything to attract listeners or advertisers. Given that the vast majority of FM stations carried AM programs (and their advertisers) at no extra charge to sponsors, the task facing the few independent FM operators—trying to sell time that others were giving away—was often futile. The small size of FM's audience in the late 1940s just exacerbated their problems. This combination of negative factors kept most advertising agencies away and FM in radio's poorhouse.

A key issue was the general perception of FM radio. As a McCann-Erickson time buyer put it in 1947, "Paradoxically, the well-known high-fidelity of FM has become something of a liability commercially. This is because FM has become associated in the minds of many time-buyers with long-haired music. And long-haired music gets low Hoopers [ratings]." He called for more of a mixture of popular music with the classical to broaden FM's appeal.[95] Agencies also noted surveys such as one carried out in Chicago in early 1947, which reported that 90 percent of FM listeners wanted no advertising on the air at all.[96] Given the minuscule size of FM's listener pool anyway, agencies quickly concluded that trying to place advertising on FM was not worth the bother. The medium lacked "the numbers" (audience size and data about it) that agencies and advertisers craved.

Amidst the depressing numbers, however, were exceptional success stories. In June 1953 it was reported that "May Co., [the] large Baltimore department store, has started one of radio's largest campaigns—an all-day Sunday musical program on WITH-FM, Baltimore. The program is designed to bring 'a still larger share of the higher-income family purchasing dollar,' according to Sam Kravetz, WITH-FM manager. The 52-week contract involves an estimated $20,000 in time costs and carries a renewal option."[97] At the time, there were about 125,000 FM receivers in Baltimore. Other FM stations also were marketing their prime liability—small audiences—as an asset. Words in station advertisements directed to time buyers began to reference FM's "class" listeners rather than mere "mass" audience. FM's small audiences were loyal and enjoyed a higher income level than average radio listeners. They were touted as bigger spenders for high-tone brands and could be effectively sold that way to advertisers. The same "class" appeal promised fewer advertising interruptions, which appealed to advertisers who felt their message might better stand out given growing clutter on AM stations. Here again, FM converted the liability of too few advertisements into a sales pitch.

But nothing could diminish FM's failure to build a viable audience— a huge disappointment and surprise to those in the business. Frustrated broadcasters looked first to the sales of FM receivers. The low volume of FM-receiver production was initially due to the need to satisfy the huge pent-up demand for AM (and then television) sets. Manufacturers argued that the 1945 frequency shift had forced them to reengineer sets, and that took more time than predicted—indeed, well into 1946. The FCC had listened to Philco and some other firms that had said the job would only take four months, though several other manufacturers made clear it might take the better part of two years.[98] Given the existing demand for AM and television sets, any interest in focusing on manufacture of FM receivers for a problematic market quickly faded. Additionally, the classic "chicken-and-egg" problem cropped up again, as manufacturers said they would make FM receivers only if and when there were plenty of stations for people to tune.

FM audience surveys were common in the late 1940s. One conducted by Sylvania claimed that 60 percent of radio-set buyers wanted FM in their receivers, and most were willing to pay more to get it.[99] Yet a survey of *Colliers* magazine readers in early 1947 found that a third had no idea what FM even was, and another third either did not want it or were not sure.[100]

By 1948 the first relatively inexpensive FM table models were appearing on the market, priced at about $30 (roughly $300 in 2007 dollars). Zenith continued to be a major FM-receiver provider and heavily promoted the medium through the early 1950s. By 1951 the firm held about a third of the FM-receiver market and planned to ramp up production to 5,000 table-model receivers a week—until Korean War–driven government manufacturing limitations intervened.[101] As the FM marketplace declined, many other firms dropped out—Motorola in 1952, RCA in 1953, and Admiral a year later. They claimed it was not economically viable to remain in production with such small receiver runs, especially when compared to ample and growing AM- and TV-set demand. Doubtless this dismal outlook did not help Armstrong's frame of mind in the weeks before he ended his life.

A small firm owned by T. Mitchell Hastings developed the first production FM radios for automobiles in 1952. He had manufactured radar and other electrical components during the war. The FM car radio was built in a basement, having been suggested by a Philadelphia FM-station owner wanting to reach the growing car-radio market. Eventually the Hastings car radio was sold in two versions: a tuner for use with an existing car radio (and costing $109) and a complete FM radio installation (for $190). As nobody else then made FM car radios, Hastings hoped to build a business. But once again, FM results fell far short of expectations: "We sold about 500 of them. We shipped them abroad to Germany and we shipped them to all the radio companies in [that] country because they were interested. . . . And as a result [they] began to produce the FM car radio. Then Motorola finally went into production in 1959. We gave it up because we found that there were, well, there really wasn't going to be a big demand for FM radios [until] there was a far more extensive FM broadcasting [industry]."[102]

Receiver production numbers (appendix Table B.5) help summarize FM's declining status. In all of 1946, less than 200,000 FM sets were made, compared to more than 15 million AM receivers. The next year showed a sixfold increase, but that still meant only 1.2 million FM receivers compared to nearly 19 million for AM. Several firms also brought out inexpensive converters, allowing tuning of FM signals on an AM radio. And 1948 began the same way: manufacturers promised large production runs, but just over 1.5 million FM sets were made, compared to ten times that number of AM receivers. By 1948 even television-receiver manufacture was approaching half that of FM and would explode to become far greater the next year and thereafter. Put another way, FM receivers made up only 2 percent of all radio sets made in 1946, 7 percent in 1947, and 11 percent in 1948. This was clearly no way to build a mass audience.[103] Making all this more frustrating was the constant pledge of manufacturers to do better "next year."[104]

Station managers complained persistently that the sets would sell if they were only available. But after a final spurt of growth in 1950, FM-receiver sales sank into a slough that continued for much of the next decade. Faced with these facts, FM stations were forced to continue touting the high socioeconomic status of their small but loyal audiences. In many major markets, FM operators cooperated with both manufacturers and radio shops to develop public-awareness campaigns of just what FM offered.[105] Zenith was especially zealous in this effort, with widespread advertising, point-of-sale booklets, and the like. GE and Westinghouse joined in—the latter offering to provide a complete FM sales campaign for stations that purchased its transmitters.[106] There was even a brief attempt (prompted by a Massachusetts station) to show FM channel numbers on radio dials—just like television—rather than the more complex frequency numbers, but it never took hold.[107]

In one small way, television-set sales helped boost FM radio. Some television receivers included the FM frequencies that fell between television's VHF channels six and seven. For a time in the late 1940s, these made up a large portion (a third in 1949) of FM sets made. After 1950, however, such combination receivers became another small and then disappearing part of the market.

One important factor existed that was hard to quantify: the hi-fi craze noted earlier. High-end, individual-component home entertainment systems included separate tuners, amplifiers, record players, speakers, and related devices. They were pricy and usually messy, with connecting cables running everywhere.[108] A substantial number were imported from Britain or Germany (as it appeared American set makers were not interested in such a small market). Many of the earliest models did not review well in the consumer-buying literature (they were hard to tune or had poor frequency response, the critics reported).[109] But the very existence of listeners willing to spend serious money for quality sound suggested a continuing niche market for struggling FM operators. Indeed, even trade periodicals noted the rising importance of such sales as their quality improved.[110]

Aside from their receiver purchases, however, markedly little was actually known about FM listeners and their tune-in habits. For many years only the overall size of the audience was known, based on receiver sales. The Pulse, Inc., began to survey the New York City FM audience in the late 1940s, showing that by January 1950, FM sets were in 18 percent of the city's homes—about a half million households.[111] By mid-decade, FM sets were found in more than half the homes in the city, while about 40 percent of Washington, D.C., and Chicago households owned FM sets. For the first time, Pulse 1957 data showed that FM listening was higher than AM in some Los Angeles households—a very early indicator of the turnaround to come.[112] On the other hand, Nielsen did not report any FM information in its annual reviews of radio.[113]

EDUCATORS CLIMB ON BOARD

The medium's small audience did not concern some FM licensees. Responding to very different needs, the number of noncommercial FM stations slowly but steadily climbed through this period. After years of talking about radio's educational potential and the wartime-enforced pause in FM development, colleges and universities could now put into practice what they had long sought to do. Indeed, as the commercial FM business suffered in the mid-1950s, educational stations grew to make up about a fifth of all FM outlets on the air. Unlike their commercial counterparts, the number of educational stations never declined. While educational institutions often required a long time to raise funds needed to build and operate a station, they kept at it, encouraged by the FCC's reservation of twenty channels in the 88–92 MHz band.

Several FCC decisions helped promote noncommercial station development. In mid-June 1948, acting on petitions from several educational institutions, the commission proposed rules allowing tiny low-power (10-watt) FM transmitters, but only if they were licensed to educational users. While such ministations could cover a radius of only two to five miles, they were also far less expensive than the smallest (250-watt) commercial stations allowed. The first college 10-watt station was WAER of Syracuse University; the station aired in 1948, though later it became a 50 kw, full-time station still licensed to the university.[114] The first high school FM station (or at least the oldest) was WNAS of New Albany, Indiana, which signed on May 18, 1949.[115] Final rules for the tiny transmitters were established in September.

In mid-1950 a new "Third Class" operator permit required a station employee to know the basics of station operation but did not require in-depth electronic knowledge. Further, the FCC allowed the 10-watt educational outlets to be operated using remote control, a further cost saving, and did not require a minimum number of hours per week on the air, as was the case with commercial stations. By mid-1951 more than 40 percent of the nearly 100 educational stations operated on low power.[116] Five years later, the proportion of low-power stations was the same; but in the meantime, many of the original low-power outlets had increased their transmitter power to regular levels.

Some thirty state governments announced plans for statewide educational FM networks in the late 1940s and early 1950s, though few actually followed through. The Wisconsin legislature in 1945 ordered planning for statewide service, which led to construction of an eight-station FM network to join the two AM stations already operating. The first four FM outlets were on the air by mid-1948 and all were completed by 1952, so that together they reached every county with a full weekday schedule plus a half day on Sunday. More hours were soon added to make the network a seven-day-a-week operation.[117] Programs for the network largely originated in Madison, home of the central campus of the University of Wisconsin, and stations were linked by direct off-the-air pickups, thus avoiding expensive line charges. This state network (see Map 3.3) was the first in the nation.[118]

Development of the Wisconsin network was chiefly the brainchild of Harold "H. B." McCarty, Harold Engel, and other officials of the university's WHA-AM in Madison. Limited to daytime hours by the terms of its license, WHA had placed a colocated FM outlet on the air in March 1947 to allow a full schedule of broadcasts. Transmitting its programs to the state network, the boundaries of the campus were, in a sense, extended to the boundaries of the state—and they were often advertised just that way. Programs carried on the network included several popular university lecture series, the "Wisconsin School of the Air" directed at elementary and high school students, jazz and classical music programs for general listeners, and agricultural and news programs. While the "voice" of the

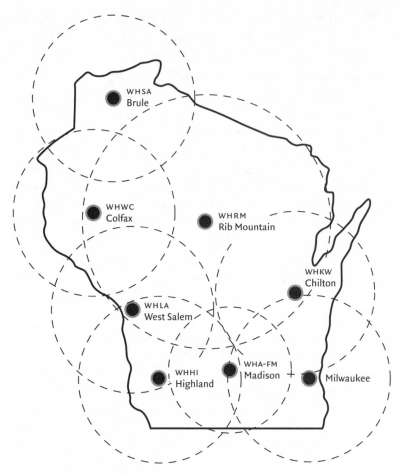

MAP 3.3. Wisconsin FM Network, 1952

network was that of announcers in Radio Hall (a former campus heating plant) in Madison, the individual FM transmitter operators accrued quite a state following for their idiosyncratic weather forecasts (and comments about other local developments or their pet animals) carried several times a day.[119]

Out in leafy Berkeley, California, Lewis Hill formed the Pacifica Foundation as what he later termed a "voluntary listener sponsorship experiment."[120] An English-major dropout at Stanford University, Hill had been a conscientious objector during World War II, doing various kinds of service jobs until serious arthritis sidelined him. He worked for a time with the American Civil Liberties Union, then as a radio newsman in Washington,

D.C. Hill, an antiwar radical, and others formed Pacifica in 1946, and three years later (it took that long to raise sufficient money to buy the 2,500-watt transmitter) they placed KPFA (FM) on the air. Perhaps 100,000 people then owned FM receivers within the station's coverage.[121] KPFA was designed from the start to rely on listener support and present often striking alternative programming to the city's commercial radio outlets. With support from the Fund for Adult Education, an arm of the Ford Foundation, station transmitter power was increased in 1952 to 10 kW, achieving an accordingly larger coverage range over the whole Bay Area. A second Berkeley transmitter began service two years later. Programs on both stations ranged over an eclectic mixture of music, poetry readings, drama, and talk, all drawing on the vibrant cultural life of the city. Audiences were small but loyal: more than 6,000 were regular financial contributors by the late 1950s.[122]

The Pacifica and Wisconsin stations offered an alternative to the second-most-serious issue faced by all educational outlets (the first problem was, and remains, money): the lack of a network for program sharing meant that every station had to rely on what it could produce locally or could find in recorded form. There was some program exchange among "Big 10" (Midwest) state university stations, as well as between the Wisconsin and Pacifica outlets, but most noncommercial schedules were limited by how much any station could either create or purchase.

In yet another parallel to their commercial cousins, educational broadcasters also fell under the spell of television. Books, articles, and authorities argued that television would be an ideal teacher on almost any level or condition. After the FCC approved expansion of television channels into the UHF and set aside several hundred television allotments for noncommercial use in 1952, the focus of noncommercial broadcasters progressively swung over to television, just as had happened with commercial operators. The University of Wisconsin, for example, placed WHA-TV on the air in 1954 as only the third such outlet in the country (KUHT, owned by the University of Houston was first, airing earlier that same year). Several states, including Alabama, Pennsylvania, and later Maryland, developed statewide educational television networks of several interconnected stations. But as with commercial outlets, the greater expense of television absorbed substantial management focus and funding, leaving educational radio as something of a backwater.

By 1956–57 the future of commercial FM appeared in serious doubt. Endless surveys, studies, and journalistic ink and paper went into trying to determine how to "fix" the supposedly superior radio service. A number of newspaper radio-TV editors spoke warmly of FM, trying to get their readers to give it a try, arguing the medium had a great future.[123] The FCC modified many of its rules and created multiplex SCAs to help create revenue. But none of this seemed to make much difference; clearly great sound was not going to be enough to keep FM viable. Spectrum jackals were circling to grab underused FM frequencies. FM was becoming the invisible, and thus vulnerable medium.

Trying to nail down exactly *why* FM all but failed is complicated by the fact that there are so many interrelated causes underlying the medium's setbacks. The war delayed FM, and military research helped promote the frequency shift in 1945, forcing the medium start over. In the short term (for the first decade), that shift proved a disaster, though over the longer term (as we shall see) the expanded FM band formed a vital part of FM's eventual success. The policy and management confusion that followed the shift also contributed to FM losing its initial momentum. The lack of receivers (for which there were many causes) led to small audiences, which turned off most advertiser interest. So did the fact that most FM stations simply duplicated AM programs. Such duplication removed any real reason for consumers to invest in receivers. The classical-music programming that resulted on independent stations was hugely appealing to only a tiny minority of listeners, loyal though they were. The lack of FM networks contributed to the medium's lack of presence. Finally, the competitive growth of AM and television took up the industry's time, personnel, and investment, leaving little or nothing for dwindling FM. The result was a depressing picture with many causes and seemingly few solutions.

Yet if one knew where to look, small signs of a possible FM turnaround were vaguely evident. In 1957 the number of FM stations on the air held steady rather than declined. The number of authorized stations, as well as pending applications, rose. While some operators were still closing up shop, they were counterbalanced for the first time by FM newcomers. A trade paper's survey of the business in April 1957 found a good deal to be optimistic about, ticking off numerous examples of positive developments.[124] Among them was SCA's revenue potential that might keep the broadcast service going. More listeners were being bitten by the hi-fi bug every year, and only FM could provide quality broadcasts for their systems. Looking farther afield, while AM and television continued to expand, both were slowing down as the best spectrum assignments were taken up. Still-available FM frequencies provided the only way to add more service to many markets. Just possibly, some perceived, FM might still develop into a viable business.

 MHz

Turnaround (1958–1965))))))

> The future of FM broadcasting
> looks more encouraging than
> it has for a decade. . . . Main
> encouragement [comes] from
> these potentials: new sources of
> income[;] . . . new audience appeal,
> particularly stereo and hi-fi; a
> budding nationwide promotional
> project that promises to make a
> strong impact on the advertising
> market; important technological
> developments from control room
> to living room; new stations taking
> to the air; [and] signs of growing
> interest in the constantly growing
> FM audience.[1]

This trade-magazine story described a growing excitement in radio circles. Something appeared to be happening to FM after years of decline. Industry people were talking positively about the medium for the first time in what seemed like eons. A number of article titles suggested that FM's fortunes had suddenly improved: "FM Future Brightest in a Decade";[2] "FM: Hot Trend in 1958?";[3] "FM: A New Boom of Interest";[4] " 'Have Audience, Can Sell' — FM";[5] and "A New Head of Steam for FM."[6] After years of depressing news, things very clearly were looking up.

Already in some cities, and for the first time in nearly a decade, the FCC was receiving more license applications than frequencies to place them on. New York had sixteen FM stations on the air (four noncommercial, seven owned by AM outlets, and five independents, with five further applicants for the two remaining channels across the Hudson River in New Jersey); Los Angeles had twenty-two, with another station about to go on the air; and Chicago had sixteen FM outlets, with two more coming (and no remaining frequencies).[7] Many FM managers were especially focused on Chicago, where CBS station WBBM-FM in July began to program separately from its AM sister outlet. A staff of sixteen (three announcers, five engineers, three disc jockeys, four administrative and sales people, and a record librarian) supported the fifteen-hours-per-day schedule.[8] Within a year, Chicago's ABC- and NBC-owned FM stations had followed suit.[9]

To fully appreciate the context of FM's developing turnaround, it is important to understand that television's dominance, and the subsequent decline of the AM-based radio networks, was still churning up the radio business. AM was slowly emerging from the transition forced by the national craze for entertainment television. As advertisers deserted the radio networks, programs dwindled — some shifting to television, but many leaving the air. Drama gave way to cheaper music, variety, and talk. By 1960 the last radio evening drama and daytime serial had left the air.[10] The radio networks offered news and little else,[11] and affiliates long reliant on network programs to fill their schedules became dependent on their own resources. Top 40 radio developed after 1955 to become radio's dominant format, as competition for advertising dollars grew fierce. That competition was made fiercer by the continuing addition of new stations: by 1960 nearly 3,500 AM outlets were operating, and 500 more had appeared by 1965.

TURNING THE CORNER

Amidst this upheaval in radio, and despite the fact that FM generally still looked pretty miserable, early glimmers of change were appearing in the nation's largest cities. The turn may have begun back in 1955. Though little noted at the time, the FCC's decision that year to authorize SCAs opened a vital revenue source for hard-pressed FM outlets. By providing "functional-music" or "storecasting" subcarrier services, an FM station could develop a wholly new market. As SCAs were not available on AM or television, FM was handed a unique opportunity.

Other trends were shifting as well. Chief among them was evidence that the country's urban radio markets had grown overcrowded. In the decade up to 1958, the number of AM stations had doubled, with about 150 new outlets airing each year. In many areas the only remaining AM channels were for daytime-only stations, which were of limited use for some of radio's vital "drive-time" listening hours. By 1958, 40 percent of AM outlets were restricted to daytime-only (or very low nighttime-power) operation. Nearly a third had to use directional antennas to avoid interference, further restricting their coverage and audience reach. FM offered the only way to expand radio service in many cities, and it suffered none of these AM drawbacks.

At the same time, television's dramatic rate of growth had leveled off, with about 450 stations on the air by 1958. This slowing in TV's pace of expansion served to free up time, money, and personnel, which could now be redirected. While most households remained glued to their tube, there were also increasing signs of a growing cultural revolution in the country, inspired by such factors as Cold War tensions, growing racial unrest, and youth rebellion. Theodore Roszak argues these were the result of "machine tooling [of young people] to the needs of our various baroque bureaucracies: corporate, governmental, military, trade union, educational."[12] In a landmark study of the 1960s, he argued that "the young stand forth so prominently because they act against a background of nearly pathological passivity on the part of the adult generation. . . . The fact is, it is the young who have in their amateurishness, even grotesque way, gotten dissent off the adult drawing board."[13] This very youthful dissent would eventually awaken FM to the potential economic and ratings benefits of serving an under-thirty demographic, though it would take nearly another decade.

Technology also helped. The introduction of commercial stereo recordings in 1958 sharply increased interest in high-fidelity sound systems. Catering to this interest were FM outlets providing classical music or jazz formats rarely found on AM. To tune these broadcasts, listeners obviously needed FM receivers, and that market was also showing signs of revival. In 1958, for the first time in five years, FM-set sales exceeded 280,000 units (compared to millions of AM and television receivers). Given the dearth of American output, a slowly increasing proportion were imported from Germany or Japan. Growing sales would lead by the end of the decade to a greater variety of receivers (including AM-FM dual-band portable sets) and lower prices. FM-set sales would exceed 1 million by 1959 and 2.5 million just three years later.

These signs of FM life began to attract advertiser and agency interest. Audience research suggested that FM listeners' high socioeconomic status would attract ads for high-end products and services. As FM air time cost less than half of AM-station rates, slowly and cautiously a few advertisers began to supplement their existing AM advertising with FM spots. Questions and concerns remained, but the ripple of commercial interest was encouraging.

Three studies issued in 1958–59 further publicized FM's prospects, as did the fact that more newspaper radio-television editors were writing positively about FM. A detailed analysis in *Broadcasting* early in 1958 offered considerable evidence of FM "buzz" in several large markets, including stations with new program ideas that broke the light-classics sound that defined the medium. Yet the survey also noted continuing reticence by most advertisers to purchase FM time until more was known about listening patterns.[14]

A 1959 assessment, conducted for Brown University's graduate school by independent Boston-based researcher Lyman Allen, reported results of a national survey to which 281 commercial and educational FM outlets responded. Widely discussed among broadcast managers, Allen's study also reported on stations experimenting with programming independent from their AM owners—and the resultant growing listener and advertiser interest.[15] He concluded that the "most solid indication of steadiness in the FM industry is the trend toward a higher proportion of FM-only operations among new FM-station applications."[16] Yet of his respondents, most still cited classical or semiclassical music as their program focus, reinforcing the traditional image of the medium.[17]

Finally, an internal NBC corporate-planning report issued in March 1959 suggested how that network might best exploit FM by developing more stations and experimenting with separate programming on the five outlets they already owned.[18] But at the same time, it noted that "perhaps the most outstanding characteristic of FM broadcasting is the utter paucity of statistically valid audience research data"—the "numbers" so desired by the advertising community.[19] Still, using FCC statistics, the report noted that more independent FM stations were making a profit each year.[20] It also reiterated that duplicating AM programming was cheaper than independently programmed FM outlets. Summing up, it recommended that NBC independently program one or more of its stations to test the waters and then perhaps purchase more.[21] Just a few months later, however, NBC station managers concluded separate programming "would be financially unsuccessful."[22]

Another statistic also indicated that FM was turning around. The number of licensed FM stations going *off* the air was declining—from twenty in 1957 to seventeen a year later, half that in 1959, and only four by 1960. Struggling FM outlets were now hanging on, encouraged by all the signs of growing interest in their medium by other broadcasters, listeners, and some advertisers. Most were owned by AM operators, as were most new FM stations. For the first time in a decade, radio operators again saw an FM license as protection should AM eventually be superseded. The newspapers' proportion of FM ownership declined as more stations came on the air—from more than 20 percent in the late 1950s to about 12 percent by 1965.[23]

Indeed, there were signs of an incipient bandwagon effect as talk about and interest in FM stations increased. In its *Annual Report* for 1959, the FCC summed up the growing enthusiasm by citing some current statistics: "Increased interest in commercial FM broadcast was manifest during the year. It was evinced by a net gain of 135 such authorizations, 74 more stations on the air, 8 fewer deletions, more competition for facilities (24 applications being designated for hearing), and by higher prices in station sales. [Yet] except for portions of the northeastern part of the country and some of the larger cities (Chicago, Los Angeles, San Francisco, and possibly others), FM channels are still available."[24] Still another indicator of interest was a renewed effort to form an FM trade association. Several FM operators interested in the potential of high-fidelity radio gathered at Chicago's Palmer House Hotel in January 1959 to consider a full-fledged FM broadcasting promotional group. They agreed to form the National Association of FM Broadcasters (NAFMB), which over the next several years would meet prior to the opening ceremony of the annual NAB convention.[25] In 1960 the NAB convention also started to feature its own "FM Day" and began a monthly newsletter about FM activities.[26] The NAFMB soon grew large enough to hold its own convention.

ALLOTTING MORE STATIONS

All this evidence of revived growth, plus projections for a busy future, raised concern among broadcasters and the FCC. While the FM turnaround soon ended attempts to reallocate FM's spectrum to other users,[27] the growing number of station applications suggested some new problems.

Needed first was a more flexible approach to getting stations on the air more quickly. In mid-1958 the FCC abandoned its allotment scheme, adopted as a "temporary" expedient thirteen years earlier.[28] Individual applications could be dealt with faster without constant rule makings for changes in the old table of allotments. For the next five years, FM would lack a formal allotment scheme while the commission pondered how best to plan for what was an increasingly vibrant FM service. In mid-1961 the commission began to create a framework for FM's future. As it explained in its *Annual Report*:

> The need for a revision of the FM rules is due to many technical and other developments since this service was started 20 years ago. The demand for FM facilities is now such as to pose many of the problems which beset AM broadcasting. Therefore . . . the Commission started an inquiry looking toward revamping the FM rules. The considerations relate to two general questions: (1) whether the present system of FM station assignments is the best one for optimum development of this important service; and (2) how the development and expansion of FM can be achieved without the administrative burdens and delays inherent in [the] present AM station assignment process. . . .
>
> Three classes of commercial FM stations are proposed—one with a nominal protected service range of 25 miles, another of 50 miles, and the third of 100 miles. In addition, educational stations will be divided into two classes—one of low power (10 watts) and the other with powers and ranges equal to the commercial stations.[29]

The FCC created some shivers of apprehension among some broadcasters when it added that it would also "consider whether duplication of AM programs on FM stations should be curtailed."

The FCC sought to create an organized scheme for FM allotments to avoid the many assignment problems cropping up commonly on the crowded AM band.[30] The commission was considering eventual approval of "a vast number of local outlets, removing the need for, and it is to be hoped actually replacing marginal AM operations."[31] For the first time in a dozen years, the FCC was again suggesting that FM might partially replace AM.

Comments filed in the proceeding over the next few months raised concern about the limited number of FM stations allowed in major cities. The commission proposal called for fairly rigid spacing between adjacent channels, thus limiting the number of outlets in any one area. Indeed, many pending applications faced rejection for not meeting the proposed

TABLE 4.1. New FM-Station Classification, 1962–1963

Station Type	Power Range	Antenna Height Allowed (in Feet)	Service Radius (in Miles)	Co-Channel Spacing (in Miles)
A	100 watts–3kw	300	15	65
B	5–50 kw	500	40	150
C	25–100 kw	2,000	65	180

Source: "FCC Rules Revision Overhauls FM Band," *Broadcasting*, July 30, 1962, p. 32.

channel-separation distances. In late 1961 the FCC imposed a partial freeze on processing new FM grants, excepting only those in rural areas.[32]

On July 26, 1962, the FCC adopted a modified version of its proposed rule revisions. The three station classes would now cover smaller areas than had first been projected. Complicating things further, the FCC announced that only smaller FM outlets (Classes A and B in Table 4.1) would be allowed in the crowded northeast quadrant of the country and in Southern California.[33] Existing stations would be "grandfathered" with their existing power and coverage assignments.[34] In the final release of the commission plan, some 2,730 specific allotments were made, 1,200 of them already occupied by authorized or operating stations. Generally, the three classes would not be intermixed in the same market, thus largely avoiding the problem faced in television (where powerful VHF and weaker UHF allotments had been intermixed in most markets, creating an impossible competitive situation for the UHF outlets). Indeed, the FCC's FM plan followed the same criteria that had been used a decade earlier to end the freeze on television application processing. The commission's priorities sought "(1) accommodation of existing stations on their channels[;] . . . (2) a first FM service to as much of the U.S. as possible—particular that portion without a local [AM] nighttime service; (3) at least one FM station in each community; (4) a choice of at least to FM services wherever possible; [and] (5) substitutes for AM stations which are marginal from a technical standpoint."[35] Many disagreed with this approach because, combined with rigid channel spacing, the new rules precluded as many as 4,000–5,000 possible additional allotments. Many communities received only a single FM allotment. The final mid-1963 FCC decision modified things only slightly, however, while lifting the eighteen-month-old applications-processing freeze. Only thirteen existing stations had to shift channels, and most did so voluntarily.[36] Nearly 3,000 FM channels had been allotted to some 1,900 communities.

Despite its three-year rule-making process, however, the FCC still faced a host of petitions for modification of the new scheme over the next several years. Most sought to provide the first FM service to a community, and thus most were granted. At the same time, the commission sought to slow the growth of AM; in 1964 it ended a two-year freeze on new AM applications by formulating stiffer technical barriers to new stations that might cause interference.[37] One purpose of the AM rules change was to further shift radio expansion to FM rather than allowing more crowding of AM.

MULTIPLEX SCAS AND STEREO

Feeding pressure on the FCC allocation scheme was the growing revenue potential of FM SCAS. More than eighty FM stations had received SCAS by 1958. Using multiplex transmission (see appendix A), these allowed stations to transmit a regular broadcast channel as well as a subcarrier signal that could be tuned by special receivers. As their financial potential became more obvious, the number of stations applying for the authorizations rose. By 1960 nearly a third of all FM stations on the air had received SCAS (including eight outlets in New York, most of which leased background music services), though not all were in use, in part because of continued equipment technical-standards confusion. As the number of FM stations grew, the proportion holding SCAS stayed about the same into the mid-1960s. By 1964 some 400 SCAS had been issued.

Multiplexed transmission offered even greater potential. In July 1958 the FCC initiated a wide-ranging proceeding to develop more multiplex applications. This unleashed a host of ideas (including network relay, doctor paging, foreign-language services, even traffic-light control). An operating Florida weather-alert network and the ten-station (eight of them FM) Wisconsin state radio network providing weather and stock reports demonstrated what could be accomplished.

> Such a method of instantaneous, statewide communication, using an FM network for relaying, removes three big problems that broadcasters face during a state-wide or local emergency: (1) the scarcity of land [telephone] lines created by the heavily increased demand for these facilities during almost any kind of emergency; (2) the freedom of FM transmission from interference such as is caused to AM transmission by bad

weather or of disruption of land line communications caused by some weather conditions; [and] (3) the sizable expense of using common carrier relay of communications during emergencies of long duration.[38]

In the early 1960s, Alabama and Texas followed suit with somewhat similar state linkups of independently owned FM outlets. But most attention focused on the more exciting notion of broadcasting in stereo.

The stereo-broadcasting concept dated to AM-based experiments in the 1920s.[39] In 1950 the Multiplex Development Corporation demonstrated the first stereo transmission using an experimental transmitter. Working with Crosby Laboratories, the firm continued improving their system over the next several years and sold some equipment for people to tune the test broadcasts. AM and FM outlets owned by Iowa State University offered experimental two-station stereo service in 1948, followed in 1952 by the *New York Times* AM-FM stations sharing live classical concerts.[40] By the late 1950s, Boston's WCRB was offering up to forty hours a week of such broadcasts using stereo tapes after having begun with just four hours in 1954. Typically, FM provided the left channel, and AM the right—not for any technical reason, but just to standardize procedures. While providing a more dimensional sound experience, the process had two drawbacks: it tied up two stations for one broadcast (as, of course, did any simulcasting by AM-FM stations) and the AM audio channel could not match the sound quality of FM.[41]

Interest increased in mid-1958, as both NBC and CBS experimented with stereo broadcasts utilizing pairs of AM and FM stations. So did some forty other station pairs in various cities. In September the first commercial stereo disc recordings went on sale (stereo tapes had existed for some time, but few consumers had tape machines). The availability of stereo discs led to serious consideration of full-time stereo broadcasts. ABC tried TV (with its FM sound channel) two-station stereo that also featured video of the schmaltzy musical *Lawrence Welk Show*, and NBC followed suit with a stereo show starring comedian George Gobel. In addition to adding video, such broadcasts could also be received in more homes than could the AM-FM pairs (since 85 percent of households had a television set by then, while only a quarter owned an FM radio).[42] Boston's educational licensee WGBH used three stations in April 1958—AM, FM, and television—to reach the largest possible audience with a stereo broadcast.[43]

While Howard Armstrong had devised the basics of a multiplex stereo system before his death in early 1954, his scheme was incompatible with existing monophonic receivers. Thus, while two-station experimentation continued, researchers sought a one-station system that could also be tuned (though naturally without the right-left channel separation) by existing receivers.[44] By early 1959 at least seventeen different single-station systems had been suggested, many experimentally used by one or more stations. Some firms even proposed AM stereo systems, further adding to the confusion. Faced with all of this activity and interest, in March 1959 the commission opened its Docket 12517 to expand its exploration of FM stereophonic transmission.[45]

Following past practice in broadcast-standards matters, the Electronic Industries Association formed a National Stereophonic Radio Committee (NSRC) to test the competing systems and recommend a final choice to the FCC. It was directed by W. R. G. Baker, who had headed the wartime FM panel of experts advising the FCC on the FM-frequency allocation issue (see chapter 2). While his group faced a prodigious task wading through the welter of competing systems,[46] by early 1960 they had whittled the pile down to seven. Comparative field testing of those began in July. Whichever manufacturer won final approval stood to make millions of dollars in patent royalties. But some systems could not accommodate SCA and stereo transmission at the same time, which would force a difficult financial decision on stations. The NSRC submitted its recommendations to the commission in October.[47]

On April 19, 1961, the FCC largely approved the industry's recommended hybrid, which melded elements of systems developed by GE and Zenith (both pioneer FM-receiver makers two decades earlier). The chosen standard allowed stations to simultaneously broadcast both stereo and an SCA service and ended consideration of AM stereo in favor of boosting FM.[48] Several squabbles over patents for the chosen system dragged on through the decade but had little impact on stereo implementation.

The development of stereo faced the same "chicken-and-egg" problem of whether new receivers would sell before stations had begun to transmit stereo signals. Neither manufacturers nor broadcasters wanted to make the first move until the "other" side had provided a reason for investment.[49] By June 1961 manufacturers had sorted themselves into three camps: those (such as Zenith) that would develop stereo receivers, others (including RCA) that would build stereo adapters for existing FM sets, and finally companies that would market adapters first and later turn to full receivers.[50]

The FCC chose June 1, 1961, as the day that FM stereo would begin, and three stations managed to obtain FCC approval of their transmission equipment to provide a few hours of stereo broadcasts that day. GE's WGFM in Schenectady was first (by an hour and simply because of time-zone differences), followed by Zenith's WEFM in Chicago and KMLA in Los Angeles.[51] KHGM in Houston was the first FM station to undertake a twenty-four-hour schedule, some of it in stereo.[52] WTFM in New York followed suit and was operating in the black within a year. Making use of a library of some 90,000 recordings plus its own news service, WTFM worked closely with radio dealers to encourage sales of stereo receivers.[53] Nearly forty stations were providing stereo by the end of the year, nearly 200 a year later (about 17 percent of all FMs on the air), and 322 (25 percent) by the end of 1964.[54] Virtually every new FM station went on the air with stereo capability. But full-time stereo broadcasting took several years to develop due to a lack of sufficient recorded stereo music.

Stereo attracted few advertisers at first, a serious drawback in a medium that was strapped for funds and required each station to invest up to $100,000 to add stereo. One station in Boston and another in Chicago considered giving up stereo due to paltry advertiser support.[55] Coverage patterns of stations were often dramatically reduced with stereo, and many stations provided leaflets about special antennas that fringe-area listeners could install. By the middle of the decade, however, most of these start-up wrinkles had been resolved, though advertisers remained wary.

Stereo had an almost immediate impact, however, among high-fidelity listeners. FM now offered not only better frequency response than AM but also stereo—and this coming only shortly after the first stereo recordings had been marketed. Stereo's rollout influenced receiver design as component systems became more popular. Soon it seemed everybody was buying big speakers and high-wattage receivers/amplifiers to tune FM stereo stations as well as to spin growing collections of stereo LPs. The Electronic Industries Association began a big push for console high-fidelity home entertainment centers featuring FM stereo. For those with less space or cash, compact systems combined detachable speakers with a record player and receiver. Even table radios soon featured stereo, though their speakers provided little sense of channel separation.

Stereo breathed new life into FM's "beautiful-music" and classical formats as stations advertised a whole new listening experience. Station manager Lynn Christian remembers "that much of our early FM stereo audience on KODA-FM and WPIX-FM in Houston and New York came over [from AM] for stereo music . . . in Houston for classics and light classics, and in New York for popular artists and orchestras. It was a driving force."[56] The arrival of stereo, just as more independent FM programming was becoming available, combined to create considerable new excitement about the revitalized medium.

REGIONAL NETWORKING

Interest in networking revived as FM turned around, though most of the resulting efforts were more program-sharing cooperatives rather than true interconnected networks on the AM or television model.[57] One reason for this was the substantial cost savings that resulted when "networks" did not have to lease connecting lines from AT&T.[58] Indeed, operating an exchange of tape recordings might cost only 10 percent as much.

Two such tape "networks" soon served northeastern states, which enjoyed the widest ownership of FM receivers. The first was developed by and around New York Times station WQXR in late 1958.[59] Five FM upstate stations joined, at the same time announcing plans to separate programs from their AM owners. By early 1961 nineteen stations were interconnected by relay and another twenty or so had joined by means of shared tape recordings. The network (but not the New York station) changed hands in 1962 as plans were made to expand operations to 100 stations. That fall, WQXR's network could be heard in most of the thirty-five largest markets and was carrying many commercially sponsored programs, some of them in stereo. Early in 1964 the operation changed hands again, becoming the Market 1 Network, which was by then relying totally on tape sharing rather than relay interconnection. After WQXR left the network it had founded, emphasis changed from program sharing to time sales to advertisers.[60]

The other linkup began in early 1958 as the Concert Network in New England. The four-station operation, with relay transmitters in Providence, Hartford, New York, and Boston, was wholly owned by FM-receiver pioneer and broadcaster T. Mitchell Hastings.[61] Of the Concert Network stations, only the New York outlet operated twenty-four hours a day, while the others offered an 11:00 A.M. to 1:00 A.M. schedule. Plans were made to add more stations reaching as far south as Washington, D.C., but the promising operation withered when the New York station was sold in 1963 to meet accumulated debt.[62]

Several other "networks" were really program syndication operations. Heritage Stations, for example, began by providing stations in twenty-five markets with a completely automated FM-program service of eighteen hours a day. By mid-1963 the operation programmed forty-five stations (thirty of them FM and fifteen AM) with its "Heritage" stereo classical music, "Premier," "good music" (easy listening), or the "Sovereign" middle-of-the-road transcription service, continuing into the late 1960s.[63] Quality Music Stations began in 1960 as a sales representative for classical music stations in twenty-six markets. And the FM Broadcasting Service was operated by the Keystone Network. But none of these offered a common identity or brand to subscribing stations and thus did not "sound" like cohesive networks.

Though Mutual and NBC both considered expanding into FM, the first true national FM network would only appear in the late 1960s. ABC began by separating the programming of its owned-and-operated stations, starting with New York. By 1963 WABC-FM was a full-time stereo classical-music operation with no duplicated hours. Within two years, the music morphed into popular tunes. NBC Corporate Planning examined how that network should program its stations and suggested a similar gradual separation of its AM and FM outlets.

PROGRAMMING MUSIC

As the turnaround began, FM service was still characterized by only two programming approaches: classical or background music on most independently owned outlets (about a fifth of all the FM outlets on the air) and duplicated AM programming on the majority of co-owned FM stations. Independent outlets often supplemented their music with cultural programming (not unlike public radio stations decades later). Few made a profit, save perhaps from their SCA subcarrier operations.

The music format that would become the basis of initial FM financial success ironically debuted on an AM station in 1959. Radio legend Gordon McLendon conceived the idea of a full-time good-music format featuring old and popular standards on his KABL (as in "cable" car) in San Francisco. The impetus behind McLendon's initiative was to provide an alternative to the youth-oriented Top 40 music and chatter that had come to dominate the AM band (and that McLendon had helped to pioneer). He set out to create a programming sound especially tailored to appeal to adults—a mature and usually neglected listening demographic. His concept quickly succeeded, and by the mid-1960s dozens of stations around the country were airing the lush orchestrated format.

This good music (later dubbed "beautiful music") found rapid acceptance in the FM community because it fit into the medium's prevailing self-image as the more cultivated and less boisterous audio service. Aside from its relaxing sounds, good music appealed to audiences because of the long-uninterrupted music sweeps that the format encouraged. Clustering of advertising messages (eventually called "spot sets") in quarter-hour breaks created the (usually correct) impression of fewer commercials, which compounded FM's appeal. Wall-to-wall music (derided as radio "Muzak" by its detractors) on AM-FM station pairs pulled some listeners away from AM, much to the surprise of station operators who had implemented the low-cost format on FM as a stopgap approach, primarily to keep expenses down. Beautiful-music programming gradually moved to the better-sounding FM, pioneering a trend that would appear time and again with other music formats and leaving AM managers seeking something else to program.

A growing means of raising revenue for FM stations in larger markets was publishing a monthly program guide supported by both subscription fees and advertising. Most sold for low subscription rates of a few dollars a year and could also be purchased on newsstands.[64] Some were elegant and colorful, others were examples of stark simplicity. A number of stations made use of the bimonthly Hi-Fi Music at Home, which provided individual-station program-schedule inserts in the front of each issue. In February 1959, Cue magazine in New York added an eight-page section of FM program schedules.[65] The fine-arts image was often conveyed on program-guide covers, as when famed conductor Leopold Stokowski posed for Houston's KHGM guide promoting the station as the "Home of Good Music." The maestro was shown sitting in front of an FM receiver and holding the guide as he might a music score. While dignified, the overall snob appeal was both blatant and powerful.[66]

Only such large-market FM stations as classical music–programming WFMT in Chicago were able to successfully sell much advertising time. WFMT had been started by Bernard Jacobs, who had served in the Army Signal Corps and then as a broadcast-station engineer. He took over the equipment and debt of a failed FM outlet (WOAK) in late 1951. Though he had to go on the air twice in 1952 to plead for funds to remain operating (he got $11,000, which was enough), soon the situation turned around and the station, operating in the black by 1953, began to carve out a consistent niche in the crowded radio market. By 1958 WFMT became the country's first FM station to garner sufficient listeners to appear in a local market-audience ratings report.[67] By 1961 the station was ranked ninth (and first among FM outlets) in the city's fifty or so radio stations. The staff worked hard to maintain their position: "A good bit of . . . programming [is] classified as at least unusual if not off-beat. The station carries 150 complete operas and 100 full-length plays a year, plus tapes of nearly 100 world music festivals. WFMT is the only Chicago outlet to carry all Presidential press conferences and, last year [1960], rebroadcast—in full—Fidel Castro's four-hour United Nations address. The result has been a flock of national and international awards."[68] Studs Terkel added iconoclastic commentary and documentary. By the early 1960s, WFMT claimed to have the largest FM audience in the country. None of this came cheaply: Jacobs by 1961 had invested close to $50,000 on the station's impressive record library alone. Having published a program guide for nine years, in 1961 WFMT began to issue its monthly *Perspective* magazine filled with culture, art-event schedules, and plenty of advertising to support it and the station.

An offbeat approach that played to a technically sophisticated audience was found at a Los Angeles FM station: "Stereo recording sessions are being broadcast by KMLA under sponsorship of IFA Electronics. Entitled 'U-Tape-It' and aired four times a week, the series was described as 'fresh, new and exciting' by the *Los Angeles Times*. As a result of its considerate format, IFA has listeners in a hundred thousand homes or more, many of them presently without a tape recorder who nevertheless tune in just for the rare pleasure of so much fine music without interruptions."[69] Washington, D.C., station WWDC offered the same service, though only for a half hour each evening, giving a nod to intellectual property concerns with an announcement that any tapes made should not be sold. The exact timing of selections often was announced, and some stations even suggested the speed and type of tape to use. Whether or not they offered specific programs of music, most outlets provided lighter music during the day, switching to "heavier" classics in the evening.

Amidst all of this FM activity, some stations that had earlier given up the struggle returned to the air. The change at the *Milwaukee Journal* stations came after the retirement of Walter Damm, who had been an FM pioneer before and during World War II. Feeling he had been burned by the FM downturn in the late 1940s (he took WTMJ-FM off the air in 1950), Damm adamantly refused to consider reopening the station despite evidence that FM was gaining listeners in Wisconsin. Damm's retirement, combined with the rapid disappearance of FM channels in the market, made station officials aware that if they did not move quickly, they would be shut out of the reviving medium. They applied for a construction permit in mid-1958, and the following year WTMJ-FM returned to the air—but only as a mere shadow of its prewar self. Using only 5 kw (10 percent of its former power), the station operated as a fully automated music service lacking any live shows. The cautious Journal Company was not going to invest heavily until and unless the FM boom continued—and advertisers showed interest.[70]

Most FM stations owned by AM outlets still shied away from initiating independent programming due to the increased costs (chiefly personnel) of such an action. After the CBS Chicago station WBBM-FM broke ranks and split programming from its AM owner in 1959, for example, CBS officials in New York considered doing the same with WCBS-FM but found that different union rules made such a move prohibitive.[71]

EDUCATION AND CULTURE

Out in California, the noncommercial Pacifica Foundation continued expanding its FM operations. Though founder Lew Hill died in 1957, others steered the nonprofit to add a Los Angeles station, KPFK (FM), two years later. In 1960 a wealthy philanthropist offered his WBAI (FM) in New York City, and Pacifica's reach was exponentially increased. But the growing audience and impact of the foundation also brought unwanted government curiosity.

Complaints about allegedly obscene programming on the Los Angeles station led to the outlet being placed on a short-term license by the FCC. As other Pacifica stations came up for renewal, they too were held up for further consideration, including questions about how the parent foundation was funded—and by whom. Then the story became very complex; a U.S. Senate subcommittee in January 1963 investigated possible security violations in some of the more radical broadcasts.[72] An executive-committee session (the transcript was released for publication about a month later) focused on possible communist influence on or control of Pacifica, an investigation prompted by some of the programs carried by the foundation's three stations. For some 270 pages of transcript, senators and committee staff sought to find out why Pacifica officials would allow communists (among many others) to speak on the air.

This unwanted attention focused on the radical nature of some Pacifica programming, which was a stark contrast to most mainstream AM or FM stations. Most of the three stations' programs were cultural and educational rather than political, and after further consideration, the FCC closed its Pacifica investigation in January 1964 and renewed the licenses. The commission concluded there was no communist influence in the foundation, that overall program trends were more important than specific programs, and that political programming had been balanced, with input from communists but also from the conservative John Birch Society.[73]

Meanwhile, early rumblings of what would become the women's liberation movement were evident on occasional discussion programs and features on WBAI and at a handful of college stations around the country. Pacifica also led the way when homosexuality was first seriously discussed on the air. A live performance of the poem "Howl" by Beat poet Allen Ginsberg on KPFA-FM in 1956 is considered a landmark event in the history of lesbian, gay, bisexual, and transgender radio. Writing in the *San Francisco Bay Reporter*, David Lamble observed: "Memories are foggy and the tapes may no longer exist, but let's just say that the first truly gay radio broadcast occurred whenever Allen Ginsberg first 'Howled' on Pacifica radio's KPFA in Berkeley, California, the nation's first successful non-commercial radio station. The language, rhythms, meaning, and in-your-face intensity of Ginsberg's beat manifesto were quite unlike any message American radio had ever transmitted."[74]

One of the earliest regularly scheduled series devoted to gay issues debuted on WGTB-FM in Washington, D.C., in 1960. *Friends* became the longest-running gay-oriented radio program in the country. Curiously, the station's licensee, Georgetown University, was a Catholic institution emphatically opposed to the homosexual lifestyle. One wonders if the university's administration ever tuned the groundbreaking program, whose message and content were quite audacious for the era, even for stations licensed to secular organizations. According to a local newspaper report, "*Friends* offered information about venereal disease and community support groups, and it challenged mainstream values."[75]

A few years later, another WGTB series would provide an opportunity for lesbians to convey their concerns to the listening public. *Sophie's Parlor* remained on the air for several years but was cancelled (along with *Friends*) in 1976 by the university's administration, apparently under pressure from the Catholic Church. Both programs were continued over Pacifica's Washington, D.C., station.

In 1962 Pacifica's WBAI in New York broadcast "The Homosexual in America," a one-hour program centered on the opinions of a panel of psychiatrists, after which vocal protests by New York Mattachine Society organizer Randolfe Wicker demanded equal time from WBAI management—and got it.[76] Other complaints came in concerning anti-Semitic speakers. This kind of accommodation and openness would have been inconceivable on an AM station at the time and equally unlikely on any commercial FM outlet until the arrival of the underground format a half decade later.

While noncommercial FM outlets broke the mold by featuring programs and personalities hitherto viewed as inappropriate or even unseemly for mainstream radio broadcasts, an increasing number of commercial AM stations (including WDIA in Memphis, WVON in Chicago, and WERD in Atlanta), particularly in the South and in northern industrial cities, began to dedicate programming to African American audiences. Black DJs like Roy Wood, Jack Gibson, and E. Rodney Jones dialogued with listeners about the incipient civil rights movement and focused on news related to racial issues. These same DJs also aired black artists who frequently became crossover hits on white Top 40 stations. Another decade would pass before such black radio would make inroads into FM.

MANDATING INDEPENDENCE

Continuing throughout this turnaround period was the argument over whether FM stations should duplicate (simulcast) programs of co-owned AM outlets. Pushed by independent FM operations and many critics of commercial radio, the argument resurfaced from time to time, especially when a portion of the FCC's 1961 notice announcing plans for an FM reallocation (discussed above) stated the following:

> In an effort to speed the development of the FM service by permitting economical FM operation, the commission has up to now permitted FM stations to duplicate, without limitation, the programming of AM stations, usually AM stations under common ownership. Many, perhaps a substantial majority, of FM stations operate on this basis today.
>
> Probably this has contributed to the growth of the medium for the reasons intended, and also it permits AM stations to reach an additional

FM audience with a service often of higher quality technically; but at the same time a question exists as to whether duplication, or at least unlimited and total duplication, is an appropriate use of FM facilities or amounts to [a] waste of a valuable frequency band.

Comments are invited as to whether complete or partial duplication should be permitted for any FM station, and, if only partial duplication should be permitted, what maximum percentage of program time should be permitted for this type of operation.[77]

Comments flooded in on both sides, most restating old positions. The NAFMB trade association (representing primarily the independent FM outlets) naturally argued for a total ban on duplication, which would be put into place over time. The NAB decided not to touch the issue, as any position would offend some segment of its membership.[78] NBC and CBS modified their longtime support of duplication and favored letting individual stations make the choice. Some commentators held that fully automated stations (even if independent from an AM) were not in the public interest. Others felt the type of program being duplicated (or not) should be the deciding factor. Many concluded that any across-the-board requirement would probably harm FM more than help it.[79]

Not surprisingly, it took the commission a while to sort through all of this. In May 1963, nearly two years later, it issued a tentative decision, concluding again that "the ultimate role of FM broadcasting is to supplement the aural service provided by AM stations."

[W]ith the demand for FM facilities increasing rapidly, we believe it is appropriate to consider a gradual change in our policy regarding duplicated AM-FM programming. . . . We have considerable doubt that AM-FM duplicators are a substantial force acting to put FM sets in the home or automobile. . . . [We have reached] the tentative conclusion that total AM-FM duplication is no longer a force acting to promote FM but is, to the contrary, a practice which, in many areas, will retard the growth of an efficient and viable service. Our ultimate goal, of course, is to achieve a system in which all, or nearly all, of the programming broadcast by AM and FM stations in the same community is separate.[80]

One approach to this end was suggested in the notice: at license renewal (which then occurred every three years), applicants promising less or no duplication could score a major bargaining point over potential competitors. The stunned reaction of many in the radio business was summed up in a *Broadcasting* editorial, which concluded: "And then the rulebook hit the fan."[81] After years of seeming to acquiesce to the majority view that duplication was actually *good* for FM, and thus in the public interest, the commission seemed to draw a new line in the regulatory sand. FM broadcasters were only disappointed in the commission's expressed feeling that FM was still "supplementary" to AM, concluding that would be true "only if [FM] is relegated to that role by restrictive regulation."[82]

What the FCC proposed was gradualism at its best or worst, depending on where one stood on the issue. The commission suggested that in markets with more than 100,000 people and no remaining unused FM channels, AM and FM stations should duplicate no more than half of their total program schedule. But this was perceived as only the first step in a progression of rules that would eventually eliminate all duplication. Not surprisingly, very limited broadcaster support existed for what the FCC proposed. While the usual First Amendment issues were raised, the chief arguments were based on the past: duplication *had* helped FM to this point and thus would likely continue to do so. Banning or even limiting duplication was very risky just as FM was turning around. In any case, as those filing comments argued, this was a question for individual broadcasters to decide, not a government agency.

On July 1, 1964, the FCC issued its final report, approved by a 5-to-2 vote and relying substantially on the minority arguments of the independent FM stations, adopting the rule it had proposed a year earlier. Indeed, the rule was made even stronger in that it now included all markets of 100,000 or more (there were 125 of them, serving about 80 percent of the country's population), not merely those lacking unused FM channels.[83] Yet, worried about the short-term impact of their decision, the commission provided several exemptions for news, sports, and public-affairs programs that would not count against the 50 percent barrier. AM daytime-only stations would be little effected, the FCC concluded, since they were not on the air for much of the time their colocated FM could broadcast, automatically resolving the 50 percent issue. Finally, as a further cushioning of the rule's impact, the commission allowed stations to petition to delay any change during their current license period or for three years, whichever came first.[84] The new rules were scheduled to take effect August 1, 1965. As it turned out, of course, things would not be that simple.

The rules barely had been issued when multiple petitions for waivers began to arrive. Despite the huge debate the rules had created, remarkably few stations were directly impacted by the required change. As the FCC noted in dealing with several petitions for reconsideration, in the 125 affected markets "there are some 551 authorized FM stations in the commercial FM band. 214 of these are not affiliated with AM stations in the same city or nearby, and therefore are not covered by the rule. Of the remaining 337, more than 137 presently are programmed separately, entirely or 50 percent or more of the time, leaving fewer than 200 which would have to change their mode of operation in greater or lesser degree. A number of these are associated with daytime-only AM stations, and numerous others now program separate to a considerable extent."[85]

Not clear from such a summary was that New York was the market most affected by the change. Eight FM stations were involved, though two (WABC and WNYC) already operated with some separate program hours.[86] Petitions for changes in or exemptions to the rules continued to flood into the FCC, which had delayed the rules' effective date to October 15, 1965. Some broadcasters, including the networks and several multiple-station owners, argued that there was already plenty of independent programming in their markets or that their program format was unique, or nearly so. By mid-June nearly 60 percent of the 200 or so most-affected stations had applied to the FCC for waivers or extensions.[87] Virtually all of the stations duplicating more than half their programming in New York, Los Angeles, Chicago, and Washington were among them. The seeming industry revolt was, of course, centered on money—specifically, the added cost of programming (in most cases, a matter of additional personnel) in an FM business still largely losing money due to limited advertiser interest. Some licensees "threatened" to use automation as the only way to meet the FCC requirement while keeping costs reasonable. Others planned to play the same programs on FM as they did on AM but on different days by means of recordings. Still others took on different formats entirely—even all-talk, heretofore restricted to AM. As the FCC rule said nothing about program substance, any of these approaches were considered responsive to the commission's new requirements. Some observers noted that one result of all this would be to make FM sound more like AM with a variety of formats— and with more commercials as advertisers took notice of growing FM audiences.[88]

Another fear lay behind some of the broadcaster responses: a concern that the FCC's separate programming initiative might eventually lead to a forced separation of AM- and FM-station ownership in the same market. That idea had been raised before. New York FM-station manager Lynn Christian suggested that broadcasters consider selling the weaker station of any pair they controlled (such as an AM daytimer) and with the proceeds purchase a station (he suggested an FM before prices rose further) in a different market.[89] He gave the term "separation" a new angle, suggesting that ownership of stations in separate markets could spread a group owner's influence while resolving program duplication issues.

The result of all this give-and-take was the further delay of the rules for those stations that had petitioned for change or waivers to various dates in 1966 (or, as it turned out for a few AM-daytime owners of FM stations, to the end of 1967). But at no time did the FCC retreat from its basic finding that program duplication was to be phased out in stages. Still, a rule making begun in 1961, formally proposed in 1963, and adopted in 1964 (to be effective the next year) was finally in effect only at the start of 1968. After the dragged-out legal battle (blissfully condensed here!), the impact of the rule would only become apparent by the late 1960s and early 1970s. It is sufficient to note that the FCC's forced creation of a separate FM program "voice" would prove to be the vital factor in FM's eventual dominance over AM.

EXPANDING APPEAL

The chief result of the FCC's stereo and program-nonduplication rule makings was a growing audience interest in FM. Whereas just over 200,000 FM receivers had been sold in 1957, eight years later annual sales of FM sets approached nearly 8.5 million units.[90] Along with the growing number of stations, these receiver statistics define the scope and pace of the FM turnaround. Yet despite this progress, advertiser interest was (again) slow to follow suit. Several things served to retard placement of ads on FM stations, any one of which would have been sufficient to cause problems for broadcasters.

Chief among these was the continued dearth of audience information — the research "numbers" beloved by all ad agencies and their customers. Simply touting a "quality" audience, as FM operators had done through the 1950s, did not suffice. Outside of New York and a few stations in other large cities, there was precious little solid information on which to base advertising decisions. While stations pleaded a lack of income to fund the needed surveys, agencies refused to invest in FM without the needed numbers. Making this confrontation more difficult to resolve was a lack of standardization in providing what information *was* available, whether about listeners or station rates. Overriding all of these concerns was the continued giving away of FM advertising time to AM time buyers. That the FM audience could be reached at no cost made the job of independent FM stations seeking to sell time almost impossible without a proven separate audience. Finally, while FM rates seemed very low, their actual cost per thousand listeners (the standard advertiser pricing measure) was high given the relatively small audiences involved.

Early in 1961 the Radio Advertising Bureau, heretofore devoted to AM radio, issued *Advertisers Are Asking Questions About* FM, a fifteen-page booklet of pie charts and text that provided some estimates and firm figures for most aspects of FM. Each page hammered home its purpose with a section called "Meaning for YOU," which made the advertiser impact of FM's changes clear. A Kenyon & Eckhardt executive told FM broadcasters at a 1963 meeting that what potential advertisers needed was "the size, the sex, the education, and the location of your audience. Not only in total, but at specific times of day, and how it varies seasonally."[91] But few FM stations then possessed that data, nor could they afford to gather it, contributing to a vicious cycle of no data and thus little advertising.

Advertisers might be reticent, but the public was seemingly not so. In 1958 the Electronic Industries Association reinstated FM information in their tracking of receiver manufacture and sales—yet another indicator of rising industry interest. More sets costing under $50 were on the market, and by the early 1960s receivers costing less than $30 were becoming more common. The year 1959 saw the first million-set FM sales year since 1951, and the retail numbers kept rising. While only 8 percent of all radios sold in 1960 included FM, by 1965 the proportion had nearly doubled to 15 percent.[92] It seemed clear that the FM-receiver market would continue to grow.

Several trends pushed these increasing FM-receiver sales. As transistor radios became more widely available, cheaper, and of higher quality in the early 1960s, an ability to tune FM stations became a feature of a growing proportion of them. Zenith advertised what they called "America's first all-transistor portable FM/AM radio" in mid-1960.[93] At the other end of the market, expanding interest in high-fidelity listening, prompted by availability of commercial stereo records in 1958 and FM stereo broadcasts in 1961, prompted a growing market for high-end FM tuners. Stereo was promoted even in small portable FM receivers, where the stereo effect was almost impossible to discern because the speakers were but inches apart. By the mid-1960s the growing likelihood of separate FM programming promised a further impetus to potential FM-set buyers.

Availability of FM radios in cars, however, lagged well behind the home market, rising to only about 6 percent of all cars sold in 1965. Given the importance of commuter drive-time radio listening in most major cities, this was a vital market sector for FM to penetrate. The problems were technical (the need to shield the radio from engine interference) and market-driven (the "catch-22" cycle of high cost due to limited sales). At first, American set makers largely ignored the market: "Most of the FM sets going into Chicago area cars come from Europe, mainly from West Germany. Only a few auto FM sets are turned out in the United States. Lack of volume in demand, up to now, has kept the big American radio companies from venturing into the field."[94] As with many products (including digital-satellite radio tuners four decades later), the market began with high-end models. The Lincoln luxury line of automobiles may have been the first to offer an FM option (adding about $100) on its 1959 models. The next year, several third-party manufacturers offered FM sets for cars, including Motorola (the pioneer in making AM car radios decades earlier).[95] Three years later, Ford was offering the FM option on all of its cars, and a third of Cadillac buyers took FM receivers as well. Something on the order of 75,000 FM car radios were sold in 1962, a number that rose to 300,000 the next year and doubled again by 1964 (see appendix B.6). This rising trend was due in part to growing on-air FM advertising that such receivers were available.

Trying to determine who was actually listening to all these FM receivers was a question explored in different ways. Early studies focused on receiver availability (or penetration) in selected urban markets. Here the data was scattered but hopeful: the proportions were generally rising and at a faster pace by the mid-1960s (see appendix B.7). But audience information was somewhat dependent on both the total number of FM stations and the number providing programs separate from AM outlets. Penetration in most rural areas and smaller towns was little more than 10 percent before 1960—but nobody really knew for sure. And many stations had no idea how many FM sets were in the hands of potential listeners.

A more traditional indicator was whether and how FM stations showed up in audience ratings surveys. For years the answer was simple: no FM outlet registered at all (with simulcasting listeners rarely knowing whether they were hearing AM or FM). In 1959, for the first time ever, two FM outlets were included in Chicago ratings, with classical station WFMT coming in eighth of thirty-six stations and WFMF coming in eleventh. By mid-1960 *U.S. Radio* reported that thirty-five FM stations were appearing in Hooper ratings in twenty-one different markets (thirty-two of them were independent and thus featured their own programming).[96] By 1962 FM outlets were showing up in market ratings in forty-four cities.[97] A listing meant reaching at least 1 percent of the audience, and typical FM stations were achieving 5 or 6 percent. By the middle of the decade, Pulse, ARB, and other ratings companies announced plans to separately list FM stations in local radio market reports—a real sign of progress.

HOPE RENEWED

FM proponents found the late 1950s and especially the early 1960s to be an exciting period—the first time since the late 1940s when FM appeared to be on the path to eventual success. In a sense, FM survivors picked up where things had left off in 1949–50. Hardly a month now passed without some new study or article extolling the medium's growing commercial potential. In late 1960 U.S. FM appeared as a new (if thin) monthly magazine aimed at FM broadcasters and advertisers, though it lasted less than a year.[98]

Many other indicators demonstrated FM's changing status. Prices paid for stations were rising, as were license applications for new outlets. Long recalcitrant advertisers finally seemed to be taking notice, as was evidenced by rising FM revenue in many markets. Though stereo service began slowly, it provided a continuing boost to FM's turnaround, offering something unavailable on AM or television. And while many AM-owned FMs argued hard against program nonduplication, that FCC rule change would underpin an explosion of creativity that within fifteen years would finally push FM ahead of the older AM service.

FM 95.5 MHz

A Sound Alternative

(1966–1980)))))

The cloistered little world of FM radio has been invaded—by rock and roll, big bands, hockey game play-by-plays, and sexy girl announcers making slightly off-color remarks. You can hardly hear the string quartets for the din. By the end of this year, there will be some 800 independently programmed, commercial FM stations, quadruple the number of a few years ago. Most of them bear no resemblance to the intellectual and exclusive image—classical music, field-recorded folk songs, and trios playing 14th century instruments—that has characterized FM radio to its tiny but intensely loyal listening audience.[1]

So reported *Business Week* in September 1966 as FM's impressive turnaround continued, leading to considerable turmoil both in the business and on the air. FM had become the fastest-growing part of American broadcasting, and station purchase prices were rising. To emphasize their stations' growing program independence and audience appeal, some managers suggested that FM stations should create new call letters separate from their AM owners.[2]

Radio's big question in 1966 was just how far and fast the FCC would push FM to separate programming from the AM outlets that controlled most FM stations. Though the first decision had been made in 1964, industry legal maneuvers delayed full implementation into late 1967. Seen in retrospect, what is ironic about this fight is that most broadcasters were on the wrong side of their own interest. As would soon be demonstrated by rising ratings of independently programmed FM stations, cutting down on duplication was the best thing that had happened to FM since World War II. But an AM-dominated business, concerned about added program costs—and the division of their own audience—resisted strongly. By 1969, however, the NAB found that 70 percent of FM stations owned by AM operators were programming separately, many of them for more hours than FCC rules required.[3]

Armed with growing evidence of the benefits of its original order, the FCC in 1974 proposed to expand the nonduplication requirement to stations in smaller markets (those with fewer than 100,000 people). Broadcaster resistance was almost as strong as to the original order a decade earlier, though some citizen groups said the FCC had not gone far enough.[4] As before, station requests for exemption for certain programs (often classical music) abounded. Yet this time, broadcasters were divided, for based on their early experience with program independence, more FM-station owners agreed with the FCC proposals. Some commentators were changing their focus and growing concerned about the future viability of AM radio. Urging caution, they still perceived FM as a supplement to, not a competitor of, AM.[5] A few critics saw the whole matter as more fundamentally an issue of cross-ownership than programming, arguing that no owner should operate AM and FM stations in the same market.[6]

The FCC maintained its course, and in 1975 it proposed rules to limit duplication to no more than 25 percent (rather than half, as the existing rule called for) of programming in markets with at least 100,000 people and 50 percent in smaller markets down to 25,000 (which had not been covered in the original rules). Some FCC staff argued that the 25 percent limit should apply to all markets, perhaps even those as small as 10,000 people. After all, they noted, the point was to make efficient use of spectrum by providing diversified programs. The commission finally decided on a two-step approach to reach a 25 percent limit in markets of 25,000 or greater, to be phased in by 1979.[7] Complaining all the way, FM was dragged into greater competition—and eventual success.

Yet the spread of independent programming was just one factor driving further change in FM. Another was growing listener dissatisfaction with what AM radio had become. Many showed growing disdain for the formulaic pop on AM, made even more so by Top 40 consultant Bill Drake, who narrowed music playlists and curtailed deejay chatter. Stations under the influence of Drake's rigid programming baton were said to have been "Draked." Younger listeners still tuned to such AM fare, but many of those over twenty-five were looking elsewhere as AM stuck to its formula. FM's blossoming variety—including better versions of old AM program standbys—began to siphon off AM's listeners.

So did the era's social upheaval, which *Life* magazine described as "violent, nostalgic, preposterous, maddening, amusing, sometimes immensely evocative and moving."[8] Political assassinations (Martin Luther King Jr. in March 1968 and Robert Kennedy in June), racial upheaval (seemingly annual summer riots in major cities), the expanding yet increasingly unpopular war in Vietnam, and the growing use of mind-altering drugs all contributed to a blossoming counterculture, which in turn inspired a dramatically different "underground" sound on FM.[9] The rebellious, antiestablishment messages of musical groups such as Jefferson Airplane, Mothers of Invention, Jimi Hendrix Experience, and Country Joe and the Fish (few of them played on AM) resonated with college-based and other counterculture fans. FM reflected sharper divisions in American society, incorporating alternative and counterculture content as well as increasingly mainstream music and talk.

GOING UNDERGROUND

To begin with, many FM stations provided fertile ground for experimenting. Few commercial stations were yet profitable, which provided flexibility for innovation. Any idea that might lead to larger audiences and thus revenue was welcome. Experimentation with previously unusual or taboo programming became common. This ultimately gave rise to a short-lived "underground" sound, starting with nominally commercial stations in New York and then San Francisco (home to a thriving hippie culture). College-campus outlets also sought student audiences with music and ideas they wanted to hear.

These early underground stations fancied themselves as a voice for the disenchanted, and through their contrarian approach to programming they ingratiated themselves with thousands of (generally) young people who could no longer abide the status quo in commercial radio, let alone the society it reflected. Exemplifying the diversity of the era are the many names used to label and describe the format: progressive, alternative, free-form, psychedelic, and even the "anti-format format."

Indeed, it was on such programs that rock music for the first time established an FM beachhead. In contrast to AM, however, FM underground stations aired long album cuts by groups such as Canned Heat, Vanilla Fudge, Mothers of Invention, and Traffic. The underground outlets featured DJs (a moniker often rejected by iconoclastic underground practitioners) who personified the hippie manner and comportment: laid back and seemingly stoned (which may have been contrived to better relate to the counterculture audience). This approach thrived until 1971, when the FCC came down hard on stations airing music with drug-related messages no matter how subtle or imagined they might be. What little advertising was aired was downplayed due to the often anticapitalist sentiments of the on-air staff. Waterbeds, leather goods, and head shops were among the most frequent sponsors in the early days of underground radio.

New York City station WOR-FM introduced an alternative format that would soon be emulated by hundreds of stations across the country. One of the driving forces behind its underground sound was Bill "Rosko" Mercer, a onetime performer at New York's fabled Apollo Theater. Rosko came from urban black radio, where he specialized in airing soul and rhythm-and-blues music. In 1966 he helped pioneer progressive or freeform FM rock by shifting WOR-FM's attention to album-rock music. With the demise of that format just a year later, Rosko migrated to WNEW-FM, where he continued to concentrate on the album-rock sound. There, "he invited his listeners to 'take a mind excursion, a little diversion, the hippest of all-trips—the return to reality.'"[10]

Another free-form radio hero was Scott "Scottso" Muni, also heard on WNEW-FM. Raised in New Orleans, he had arrived in New York in the late 1950s after a radio career that began with the Marine Corps. After trying free-form on WOR-FM, he, too, moved to WNEW, soon to become program director as well as an on-air DJ. The atmosphere could be zany:

Musicians were constant guests at the station. During one interview, Jimmy Page of Led Zeppelin collapsed in mid-sentence; . . . Muni played an album, revived the guitarist and finished the interview with . . . Page lying on the floor. In another interview, . . . Muni played cards on the air with members of the Grateful Dead. In the early 1970s, a . . . robber named Cat Olsen, who was holding hostages at a bank, demanded to speak to . . . Muni and hear some Grateful Dead. [Muni] helped defuse the situation.[11]

Often dubbed "the professor" for his knowledge of music and musicians, Muni stayed on WNEW-FM for a quarter century, his calm and authoritative voice serving New Yorkers even as formats came and went.

Noncommercial outlets played their part in this underground movement. New York–area FM outlets WBAI (the Pacifica station noted earlier) and WFMU were among a relative handful around the country airing eclectic and nontraditional programs to small but loyal audiences. At WBAI, young DJ Bob Fass worked the overnight slot, airing *Radio Unnameable*: "Taking the concept of freeform (or birthing it himself), he began with music. He set out to show that all music [be it] rock, classical, folk, classical . . . relates to each other and that none of it has to be categorized. . . . The show was completely free, and there you had freeform."[12] These noncommercial stations were a reaction against most everything radio had to offer. Many college stations were outspoken against the Vietnam War and considered it their mission to take an opposing path.

To many on the West Coast, the underground approach to music selection and presentation was epitomized by Larry Miller. In late 1966 he began hosting an all-night show on KMPX-FM in San Francisco, an eclectic city that featured the thriving if radical community of Haight-Ashbury near a university. Underground DJ Dave Dixon, among others, cited Miller as one of the architects of this breakthrough sound: "Miller was there in front of everyone. He was doing the show that inspired the format."[13] Fellow underground pioneer Dave Pierce concurs: "Larry Miller really introduced the programming concept that would be more fully developed by Tom Donahue. I think Miller's was the first seed in the underground radio movement."[14] Former Top 40 impresario Tom Donahue (known affectionately as "Big Daddy" because of his enormous girth) would bring the format to full fruition at KMPX within months of tuning Miller's idiosyncratic program. Hired as program director, Donahue expanded and embellished Miller's approach to create the West Coast's first full-time commercial underground station. Onetime underground personality and *Rolling Stone* editor Ben Fong-Torres later reflected on the genre as he painted a portrait of another San Francisco station: "Back in the early '70s, KSAN ('Jive 95') was the hippest of all stations and, among young listeners, the only spot on the dial worth tuning in. It was freeform, free-for-all radio; intensely personal and political; outrageous and unpredictable, much like the '60s scene that inspired its birth."[15]

In a move somewhat prescient of the low-power FM movement that arose decades later, in 1970 another San Francisco group filed for a new station. They planned to raise $6,000 to build a 10-watt station that would rely for some of its operational funding on the panhandling abilities of a fifteen-year-old! The aptly named Poor People's Radio, Inc., group (made up of two attorneys, a real-estate man, an engineer, and the head of a local broadcasting school, none of whom would seem to qualify for the "poor" title) planned a "controversial" service suggesting alternatives to resolve social problems. Among other things, they projected talking books for the blind on the station's SCA (just as such services were first becoming available). Though the FCC issued a construction permit for a noncommercial channel in November, KFPR (for Free People's Radio)[16] proved to be short-lived.

Ironically, while these underground stations often touted themselves as radio's "human rights alternative" based on their support of antiwar protesters, black activists, drug advocates, and other groups, some women's rights groups and would-be underground female DJs claimed the stations were actually sexist. Historian Donna Halper recalls an incident in 1970 at Boston's WBCN-FM that made the local newspapers:

> The gist of the story was that the station ran an ad for office help which ended with the tag line that the company had openings for "chicks who can type." Debbie Ullman, an account executive there (who longed to be on the air), was insulted and so were 35 protesters from Bread and Roses, a local feminist group. The group picketed WBCN for its attitudes toward women. The *Boston Globe*, not getting the point, referred to the protesters as "a radical female liberation" group. The protesters and Ms. Ullman simply wanted to know why it was assumed that only women could type and were patronizingly called "chicks." To make their point, the group gave the station's management some baby chickens. . . . It was hoped the guys on the staff could make the distinction between baby chicks and human females, but evidently that was a distinction that many men in the format could not make.[17]

Yet despite the growing women's liberation movement, not all aspiring female underground disc jockeys were as put off by the apparent sexism at these stations. "I was just glad to be in on the new FM groove," notes early underground radio pioneer Dusty Street.

How did it happen that I became the so-called First Lady of commercial underground radio? Well, let me tell you. I was a student of San Francisco State, and I took acid one day and decided that being a student wasn't what I wanted to do. . . . I saw this guy on the street, [and] he said they just started a radio station called KMPX, and they were looking for female engineers. All the engineers [there] were women—young girls, actually. I was Dusty "Super Chic" Street, and the others were Susie Cream Cheese and Katy "The Easter Pig" Johnson. . . . [Eventually] we decided that the ladies should be able to get on the air because we really kept the place operating. They gave us a show that I think was called "The Chicks on Sunday" or something weird like that. Anyway, it was Raechel Donahue (Raechel Hamilton then), Buzzy Donahue (Tom Donahue's daughter), and the three female engineers, and we pretty much did our own thing. . . . I really got a lot of support from the guys. I find that there is a lot more suppression of women today than there was in the late 1960s and early 1970s.[18]

PERSONALITIES ON THE AIR

While AM had always been home to radio's personalities, FM had the opposite reputation until it embraced a broader, more mainstream approach to programming. FM's primary focus for years was on both the quality and quantity of the music. "More music/less talk" was its quintessential programming strategy and selling point. On most FM outlets, on-air personnel were "announcers" rather than "DJs"—the latter designation suggesting a more personal, informal, and engaging presence. Certainly FM offered some familiar voices behind the microphone (often highly regarded program "hosts"), but AM was where radio's real luminaries—the "super jocks"—resided.

The FM band was synonymous with uninterrupted sweeps of Mozart or Mantovani until rock music invaded its hallowed ether in the late 1960s courtesy of the FCC's nonduplication rules and also antiestablishment programmers. The next two decades witnessed a seismic change in the role of FM's on-air personnel. Pure music programming gave way to a greater presence of voices inspired by a raft of newly implemented formats. AM stars such as Bruce Morrow, Robert W. Morgan, Murray the K, Larry Lujack, and Dan Ingram were challenged by a new generation of radio personalities on FM, especially in morning drive time. In addition to the FM notables cited earlier (Muni, Donahue, Rosko, Fass), names like Scott Shannon (WHTZ-FM), Jay Thomas (WKTU-FM), Peter Fornatale (WNEW-FM), Shadow Stevens (KROQ-FM and later in syndication), Rick Dees (KIIS-FM and later in syndication), and Casey Kasem ("American Top 40") were among many that soon rivaled the recognition levels of their AM hit-music predecessors. Other FM DJs were gaining impressive reputations with particular programming genres. For example, in album-rock radio, Charles Laquidara (WBCN-FM), Vin Scelsa (WNEW-FM), J. J. Jackson (KLOS-FM), Jonathan Schwartz (WNEW-FM), and Dr. DeMento (KMET-FM and syndicated) were among the dozens of successful personalities drawing young male adults to tune in FM. On noncommercial radio, Bob Edwards (hosting *Morning Edition* on National Public Radio [NPR]), Robert J. Lurtsema (WGBH-FM's *Morning Pro Musica*), Noah Adams (NPR's *All Things Considered*), and Lowell Ponte (KPFK-FM's *Rapline*) soon became household names. In every large market, FM enjoyed growing recognition for the voices it aired.

And more women achieved renown on FM. NPR provided an exceptional venue for women to showcase their journalistic skills. By the late 1970s, Susan Stamberg, Linda Wertheimer, and Nina Totenberg had acquired enviable reputations as reporters, while at commercial FM outlets, Alison Steele (see chapter 6), Yvonne Daniels (WGCI-FM), and Carolyn Fox (WHJY-FM) were just three examples of women attracting large and loyal followings. Indeed, if AM had been the "old boys" radio band, FM was the new equal opportunity employer.

DIFFERENT DRUMS

FM radio provided alternative programming in other ways as well. Beginning in the 1960s, for example, Pacifica Foundation stations began to offer programs aimed at gay and lesbian listeners. Queer radio mainstay IMRU (initially called *The Great Gay Radio Conspiracy*) began its many years on the air in 1971. The show was locally produced, and one of its founders, Greg Gordan, would help to develop similar programs elsewhere over the next two decades.[19] An increasing number of noncommercial FM outlets, particularly those in the community-radio sector, took up the cause as well. Six months before the introduction of IMRU, Philadelphia's WXPN-FM launched what would be one of gay radio's most noteworthy and enduring programs, *Gaydreams*: "As legend stands, [it] was the first weekly gay radio program on the East Coast and, possibly, in the nation. . . . The founder of *Gaydreams*, John Zeh, also created another *Gaydreams* on WAIF-FM in Cincinnati in the late 1970s."[20]

Another of FM's significant cultural accomplishments came with the rise of Native American radio. In the waning days of the counterculture movement, Native Americans began to see radio as an affordable way to better address the many pressing issues confronting their tribes. The catalyst that brought radio to the forefront of their thinking was the 1969 takeover of Alcatraz by Native American people from various tribes who sought to point out the misdeeds perpetrated against them by the federal government and Anglo society. American Indian interest in radio as a tool for combating discrimination and cultural hegemony was launched when Pacifica station KPFA-FM in Berkeley lent the island's occupiers a transmitter to broadcast their myriad concerns, which they did between November 1969 and June 1971. The fact that Native American radio would become a public- and community-FM enterprise is made understandable given the low likelihood of any commercial station finding success on the barren reservations where half of the country's 2 million Native Americans reside.

Native Americans perceived radio as one means of empowerment. Inspired by the 1960s' civil rights movement that ultimately led to the occupation of Alcatraz, indigenous leaders adopted FM to help inspire solidarity within their impoverished tribes. Fearing loss of their ancient traditions and languages through overassimilation of Anglo culture, Indians began to apply for radio licenses to serve their far-flung reservations. KTDB-FM in Pine Hill, New Mexico, became the first licensed indigenous station in 1972. More would soon follow.

From their inception, Native American radio stations were perceived as a crucial element in the preservation of Indian life because they are "free to express the values of their own unique cultures in both their Native language and in English. They are free to provide a forum for the expression of their needs and desires. They are free to provide public service announcements and other information important to their listeners. In short, they can be a liberating and creative force in their mission to get the 'word' out to their communities."[21] Further, there were plenty of FM channels lying fallow in the great open spaces of the American West. Noncommercial station applicants could obtain start-up money from government or foundation entities. The National Telecommunications and Information Administration, for example, helped many Native American broadcast projects through its Public Telecommunications Facilities Program, while the Corporation for Public Broadcasting made funds available through several minority-broadcasting initiatives.[22]

AUTOMATING THE MAINSTREAM

As some underground and alternative lifestyle FM stations began to make money, their potential to earn more prompted greater interest from companies holding their licenses. At the onset station owners had only modest financial expectations and hoped at best to break even or make a small return, but as ratings climbed for underground stations, the idea that they could be transformed into major profit centers took hold. Even networks noted the trend. ABC FM Special Projects launched "LOVE" in 1969 under the direction of program innovator Allen Shaw. He produced twenty-five hours of weekly programming that was duplicated on high-speed tape recorders for airing by the seven ABC-owned FM outlets. Looking back three decades later, Shaw noted that though audiences doubled in six months, "the underground press . . . panned us as 'overly slick,' 'corporate rock,' and 'the network giant ripping off the counterculture.' "[23] Lamented Fong-Torres on the encroaching co-option of the format in 1970: "It appears 'underground radio,' under the repressive nursing of network and/or corporate owners, is becoming just another spin-off of commercial, format radio. Top 40, middle-of-the-road, classical, country, R&B, and, now, 'underground.' In short, underground radio is safe stuff nowadays, no more 'progressive' in terms of hard politics, experimentation with music, or communication with the so-called 'alternative' culture than the everyday AM station."[24]

Thus commercial FM's brief free-form endeavor was soon supplanted by the more mainstream and populist version album-oriented rock (AOR), the brainchild of programmer Lee Abrams (later the chief programmer for XM Satellite Radio). Although inspired by the bottom line, AOR did constitute a listening option, albeit in its own watered-down way. Despite the morphing of underground to the more mainstream AOR sound, FM stations continued to attract young adult listeners. "Soft-rock" (sometimes dubbed "mello-rock") FM stations also began to appear in larger markets in the early 1970s. That format would evolve into adult contemporary, which would become FM's most popular music program format by decade's end.

As FM's music offerings changed, so did the technology behind them. A year before FCC implementation of its nonduplication rules, the first radio automation systems appeared that would allow a station to operate almost free of on-site employees. For a modest initial investment, outlets could put their facilities on a kind of autopilot, and many did so with alacrity, as was described in *Business Week* in September 1966: "So-called station automation [is] a set of [audio] tapes, featuring bland, middle-of-the-road popular music, coded for automatic switching and broadcast. The object, of course, is to economize on live engineering and announcing staff. A single staff announcer . . . can easily operate a station all day."[25] These systems used carefully timed tapes and "silent tones" (below the level of human hearing) that triggered electronic switching devices. Often one tape would contain music from a syndication firm and another the announcements, with tape cartridges providing commercials.[26] All of this was interleaved using the timed switching device. By mid-1969 some 2,000 stations, most of them FM, were automated, served by a half-dozen national-program syndicators.[27] These early systems were *not* foolproof, however, and stories arose of embarrassing moments when the mechanisms ran amok before a human could intervene.

Because of the beautiful-music format's limited use of talk, it was ideally suited for automation. Oversized tape reels containing lush instrumentals and low-key ballads could run for hours and free programmers to focus more resources on their profitable AM stations. This was not exactly what the FCC had in mind, but if combo operations were not providing FM listeners with something wholly fresh and innovative, they were at least fulfilling their obligation to offer separate programming, albeit as economically as possible. While critics of automation argued it would do little to bolster FM's appeal and potential, despite their concerns, this would prove to be another important landmark in FM's improving fortunes.

By the late 1960s, the beautiful-music format had become FM's most profitable mainstream offering. WPIX-FM in New York, for example, had in just two years created a solid audience with its evening "PIX Penthouse," a mixture of "popular hits and sweet, swinging standards." The station also promoted "the Sound of the Good Life" as it daily presented "the best part of AM, news, weather, traffic, stock market reports, sports, and the one thing that FM does so much better: High quality stereo music minus the annoying interruptions."[28] In Hartford, Connecticut, WRCH-FM appealed to adults over forty with its "Rich" music format, as did WYOR-FM in Miami, which promoted itself as the city's "soothing" alternative. Among other pioneering beautiful-music stations were KIXL in Dallas, KABL in San Francisco, and WPAT in Paterson, New Jersey—each representative of the "more music/less talk" ethos. FM radio had its first bona fide ratings winner.

Indeed, not long afterwards, virtually any music (including formats once heard only on AM) could be found on FM. Disco music, for example, began to surface on some urban FM stations in the late 1970s. Stations in Boston, Chicago, New York, San Francisco, and several other major markets began to draw listeners away from AM Top 40 and urban black outlets by mixing disco songs into their playlists. In 1978 WKTU-FM in New York became the first all-disco station in the country. By the next year, just as FM's national audience first surpassed that for AM, many other FM stations, such as Boston's WXKS (branding itself as "KISS 108"), employed the format and enjoyed ratings success. WXKS was the launching ground for top black/urban performer Sonny Joe White, whose hip monologues and flamboyant personality made him a major attraction of the station for years as it evolved into the urban-contemporary format in the 1980s.

This (to some, surprising) popularity of disco made clear that FM was becoming the preferred place for almost any music, as the popular formats led quickly to improving stations' bottom line. The price for this success, however, was that as FM approached audience equity with AM, it began to lose its listening cachet as a classy alternative.

FM's growing voracious demand for content revived the syndicated-music industry, which provided stations fully produced and prepackaged programming. It was the "widespread use of automation equipment commencing in the 1960s [that] sparked significant growth in the field of programming syndication. Initially, the installation of automation systems motivated station management to seek out syndicator services."[29] Beautiful-music stations, for example, no longer had to cobble together their own music and could reduce staff. Furthermore, this preassembled programming was professionally produced, adding to the format's overall appeal. Syndicators took the next step.

True modernization of the format began in 1968, at the hands of Jim Schulke and his staff. Schulke, who had a background in television, started working in radio to capitalize on the FM boom he anticipated. In 1968 he founded Stereo Radio Productions, to provide tapes and advice to Beautiful Music stations. By 1970 he had made two stations number one in their markets—the first FM stations of any type to be rated number one—with WOOD, Grand Rapids, Michigan, and WEAT, West Palm Beach, Florida. Schulke's SRP set the standard of excellence for this type of automated programming services.[30]

Other key players in the development of the beautiful-music format included Lee Seagall, who applied the concept of "match flow" (arranging program elements so they followed one another smoothly), and Marlin Taylor, who refined the sound to appeal to a broader audience and extend their listening time. Taylor began assembling his own music tapes for WRFM, the beautiful-music station he was running in the late 1960s. He began sending the produced reels to other Bonneville-owned outlets, and this led to the creation of Bonneville Program Services in 1971. Marlin became president of the new division, which soon was providing programming to stations around the country. Another pioneer was Darrell Peters, with his "FM 100 Plan" in Chicago. He was the first to utilize both the Chicago and London Symphony Orchestras to produce beautiful-music "cover" versions of 1960s and 1970s hit tunes, providing them to his major-market affiliates. Schulke later purchased and expanded this operation.[31] Such music syndication was just a step short of true networking.

NETWORKING

Recognizing FM's growing impact, all four national radio networks (ABC, CBS, Mutual, and NBC) continued their close monitoring of FM opportunities. Internal reports continually reassessed the roles each might play with their owned-and-operated (O&O) FM stations and possible network service. Only in 1968, however, did the first national network plan come to fruition.

CBS was the first to experiment with independent programs for one of its O&O FM outlets when Chicago's WBBM-FM separated content from its AM counterpart in July 1958.[32] Seven years later, CBS began to brand all of their FM stations with the theme "The Young Sound," recorded music aimed at a young adult demographic. Initial success with both audience and advertisers suggested similar action to other networks.[33] NBC developed a taped, semiclassical, stereo-music service for use by its O&O stations.[34] For years the weakest radio network, ABC reviewed these examples and, combined with the impetus provided by the FCC's nonduplication rule making, began to actively plan several separate networks, one of which would constitute the first nationwide FM linkup.

The 1967 planning effort resulted in three format-driven AM networks and a more generic FM service (perhaps inadvertently underlining the fact that many still saw FM as a distinct medium). ABC gave its affiliates first crack at joining the new American FM Network, which began operating at the beginning of 1968 with ninety-two stations in the top 200 markets. Affiliations had grown to 136 by mid-March and reached 162 by July.[35] By mid-November the FM web reached 176 stations in the top 213 markets—not quite up to predictions of a station in each of the largest markets, but close enough.[36] The FM network provided hourly newscasts, long a weakness in FM programming. As ABC was sharing a single AT&T network interconnection to transmit its four networks to keep costs down, the FM newscast (emphasizing more business news than its other networks) was broadcast at fifteen minutes past the hour (from 11:15 A.M. to 11:15 P.M. EST) when few other stations would be offering news.[37] Brief (usually five minutes) weekly features on travel, books, theater and recordings were provided, as was a fifteen-minute "Vietnam Update" on the status of the ongoing war in Southeast Asia. Few stations took these programs, despite the fact that all advertising slots were for local sale.[38] Unlike traditional networks, no compensation was involved either way—the affiliates simply sold the available advertising slots locally.

In retrospect, ABC's FM service was more a network in name than in reality, though it helped provide the medium with more identity. The network helped its affiliates with an extensive marketing program. Over the next few years, it grew only slowly (it had nearly 200 affiliates by 1978 and the same five years later),[39] with stations making use of affiliation to appear more "plugged in." Its cumulative weekly audience peaked at 17.2 million listeners in 1978 in a period of continually expanding FM listening, but then it stagnated, suggesting that many FM stations were affiliating with format-related networks or bypassing networks altogether.[40]

Paced by the new network, but even more by their separate program efforts, ABC's O&O FM outlets did increasingly well. By 1975 its Los Angeles and Detroit stations were reported to be making more money than their AM counterparts, though all stations were earning higher revenues.[41] A year later the entire ABC group of O&O FM outlets moved into the black financially for the first time,[42] paralleling the improving financial outlook for all of FM.

SNIFFING SUCCESS

More evidence of FM's growing viability was evident in the prices that buyers were willing to pay for existing stations. By mid-1967, *Broadcasting* noted that while most FM stations were still losing money, sale prices had moved higher in two years: "A few years ago the owners of an FM station in the East Coast were considering selling their outlet for $250,000. A few months ago they turned down $500,000 for the station. One station broker pointed out that two years ago he couldn't get $75,000 for a[n] FM in Detroit but last year sold [it] for $310,000. Two months ago, the owners of [a station in] Philadelphia turned down $600,000."[43] Sales in early 1970 suggested a continuing trend. A Los Angeles FM outlet sold for nearly $1.6 million,[44] several other sales approached the million-dollar price level,[45] and a similarly valued Chicago station was donated to an educational group to avoid continuing legal problems.[46] A prime reason for rising station valuations was FM's growing listener appeal. In at least six major markets, FM stations rated highly (sometimes first) among eighteen- to forty-nine-year-olds, the listeners most sought by advertisers.[47] Despite all this, it surely did not hurt sales that FM-station prices were still "about 500 percent cheaper than for an AM outlet."[48]

FM-station sale prices continued to climb. By mid-1972 the record FM-station price moved up to $3.6 million (for GE's takeover of a Boston station), and another buyer had put down $2.75 million for a Chicago outlet.[49] Five years later, a Kansas City station moved for $5.1 million, pushing the valuation of big-market FMs even higher.[50] And by late 1978, a Denver station changed hands for nearly $7 million (a $4 million deal had nearly been consummated just a year earlier). As one station broker put it, FM had fairly quickly become "ocean front property—there's only so much available."[51] (Despite these indicators of growing success, however, a few long-time FM broadcasters were still checking out. Westinghouse Broadcasting, in a rare lapse of judgment, decided to sell its two FM outlets in Boston and

Pittsburgh, despite the medium's growing vitality. In the 1980s they would spend a huge amount to buy back into what was by then far more expensive FM-station ownership.)[52]

Demonstrating their growing value and independence, FM stations owned by AM operators began to use separate call letters to emphasize that they were no longer merely duplicating the AM signal. With the new designators, stations could also drop the "-FM" suffix that some felt restricted them to a second-class role or image.[53] Providing new on-air identity had another valuable result: listeners polled in audience surveys were no longer confused about which station they were hearing (shared call letters often confused audiences, whether they were tuning AM or FM). Reported FM ratings improved accordingly.[54]

Still another indicator of FM's growing importance was the ever-larger annual meeting of the NAFMB—up from 175 attendees in 1965 to 345 just two years later and more each year thereafter.[55] These were usually held just before the annual NAB conventions (until 1974, when the FM group began to program its own conferences at different times and cities), which, along with the NAFMB, held increasingly well-attended "FM Day" sessions covering programming, advertising, and engineering matters.

Speakers at these industry gatherings continued to bemoan the medium's one intractable problem: poor advertising sales belied FM's growing success as measured by other means. The lag was again blamed on a lack of sufficient audience "numbers" to please advertisers and agencies, but it was really more a matter of how FM was perceived. Decades of relying on classical or background music and touting small but "high-class" audiences were hard to overcome for sales people now trying to persuade mass advertisers to buy airtime. Few station representative firms actively sold FM, and more traditional "reps" and agencies still paid FM no heed. The medium continued to be known on Madison Avenue as a tough sell that had not yet "been colored green." A few agencies did take notice of emerging advertiser curiosity about FM's rapid development—a curiosity that only grew as FM stations crept higher in market ratings reports.[56]

Perhaps predictably, innovative Top-40 radio pioneer Gordon McLendon took the "next step" with his KADS (FM) experiment in Los Angeles, which briefly broadcast nothing but advertising. Announced (after approval by the FCC) in mid-1966, the station planned a schedule filled with classified advertising as an aural competitor to local newspaper pages. The commission agreed to the experiment given that thirty-two other stations (twenty of them FM) already broadcast in the city.[57] Licensed only for one year (instead of the then-normal three) and required to submit a series of progress reports to the commission, KADS was scheduled to broadcast from 6:00 A.M. to 10:00 P.M. daily. The ad format first aired in early November, with plans to expand to twenty-four-hour operation. Said McLendon, "I am sure that when our experiment has proved successful, every major market in the United States will have an all want-ad radio station."[58] Sadly for his investment, however, the usually insightful McLendon soon had to throw in the towel when it proved hard to collect the payments for air time from hundreds of small advertisers. After a loss of more than $100,000, he converted KADS to KOST (perhaps a play on what he had expended), which, more traditionally, devoted 75 percent of its time to music.[59]

Early in 1971 the Ted Bates agency released an extensive study of the expanding FM marketplace and concluded that FM could increasingly serve advertisers' needs. Focused on the twenty largest market areas (serving about a third of the country's population), researchers assessed FM's service to the "housewife" part of daytime schedules. Summing up their 1968–70 data, Bates found that for some audiences and times of the day, FM listening approached half of all radio listening—a startling figure to many in both radio and advertising.[60]

A year later the N. W. Ayer agency noted that radio's teenage audience was growing away from its once total reliance on AM and that daytime FM listening was up (the medium had long been known for its evening appeal). Ayer was one of the first to conclude that FM should now be marketed simply as "radio" rather than something separate or special.[61] That finding contributed to a fundamental change in thinking among many industry leaders, who agreed that FM should no longer be seen as different from AM. As the head of ABC radio put it in startling fashion at one industry conference, "FM radio is dead."[62] Others more positively began claiming that "FM is radio," often with emphasis on the last word.

One barrier to greater FM popularity was overcome in 1973, when Top-40 music first appeared on some FM stations.[63] The small shift became an avalanche by fall of the next year, when fully a quarter of the ten largest markets' FM stations programmed Top 40 music, compared to only 16 percent of their AM counterparts.[64] Noting this and other changes, many broadcasters questioned further need for a separate FM trade organization, though they readily acknowledged just how central NAFMB had been to the medium's turnaround over the past decade. In seeming response, NAFMB became the National Radio Broadcasters Association in 1975 and admitted AM stations as members.[65] Underlining the point was the last of what had been an almost annual series of special reports on FM in *Broadcasting* in the fall of 1974. Though one brief reprise ran five years later, these were now replaced with surveys of the current state of *all* radio, both AM and FM. At the same time, however, one textbook on radio-station management included only four FM outlets among fourteen stations profiled.[66] Some patterns of traditional thinking were hard to break.

DEVELOPING "PUBLIC" DISCOURSE

Paralleling expansion—and growing success—on the commercial side of FM, noncommercial broadcasters continued developing what they perceived as a band of opportunity. FM's educational stations, many of them based on colleges or in small communities, contributed to the variety that kept FM from becoming a static-free echo of AM. Most educational stations combined broadcasts to schools with programming aimed at an adult audience. By the 1960s many shared programs with National Educational Radio (NER), a tape-exchange "network." NER made available thousands of hours of recorded music and talk programs to help share production costs. In 1967 the National Association of Educational Broadcasters issued a report on educational radio, titling it *The Hidden Medium* to sum up what most stations lacked: sufficient funding and audience recognition.[67]

Coming to their rescue was one of the last Johnson administration "Great Society" domestic policy bills to pass Congress. Based on the Carnegie Commission, a private foundation-supported effort that created a series of path-breaking policy recommendations early in 1967,[68] the Public Broadcasting Act in October created a Corporation for Public Broadcasting (CPB) to fund and administer a new *public* (rather than educational or noncommercial) system. Congress declared that the public interest should encourage the growth and development of public radio and television broadcasting, "including the use of such media for instructional, educational, and cultural purposes." Such stations should focus upon "development of programming that involves creative risks and that addresses the needs of unserved and underserved audiences, particularly children and minorities."[69]

Inclusion of a public radio network, though added only late in the legislative process, seemed to promise federal support for both existing and future noncommercial FM stations. With the financial assistance of CPB (which received most of its revenue from annual congressional appropriations), the population of the redubbed public FM stations increased threefold, from nearly 300 outlets in 1967 to almost 1,000 by 1979. The law's provision banning CPB from interconnecting stations itself inspired its March 1970 formation of National Public Radio, soon to become "a dominant intellectual force in American life and a primary source of news for millions."[70]

Glowing promise met grim reality when disagreement over goals and means plagued NPR from the beginning, especially over the degree of system centralization. For decades, educational FM stations had funded their own operations from limited but often loyal sources, and longtime managers were loath to let young Washington-based upstarts tell them what to do. At the same time, the CPB system, designed to separate public funding from programming decisions, would prove only partially successful. The presidential administration of Richard Nixon (1969–74) proved increasingly hostile to a public radio and television system that seemed, in turn, too liberal and thus hostile to its initiatives.

Against these developing tensions, NPR filled its senior posts with people sharing noncommercial radio experience. William (Bill) Siemering, for example, was named the network's first program chief and largely drafted NPR's original mission statement. He had for several years run a noncommercial station in Buffalo, melding elements of Canadian radio into his mixture of talk and music on the air. He saw NPR's role as "listening to the country" and was an out-of-the-box thinker who bubbled with program ideas. He tended to hire people in their twenties, some with little broadcast experience, for the new ideas they might bring to the air.[71]

Siemering encouraged creativity among his young charges as they worked up to the premier of the magazine-style *All Things Considered* in early May 1971. The late afternoon program went out to about eighty NPR member (affiliate) stations and was uneven to put it mildly, initially offending the ears of longtime professionals at the affiliate stations. Material for the program sometimes arrived late, making a hash of scheduling. At the same time, however, NPR also offered live coverage of events in Washington, D.C., and other places that were heretofore unavailable to the stations. Behind the scenes, the clash of cultures between the older, more traditional managers and the younger and idealistic, though at times disorganized, program staff finally boiled over, and Siemering was let go as a "poor manager" late in 1972—to his shock and that of many in the public radio world.[72]

In truth, NPR faced a daunting task: creating a viable national public service in the face of an established commercial radio business that defined "radio" to American listeners. As if this were not enough, there was widespread disagreement on how best to accomplish the task. Local noncommercial FM outlets, some with decades of hard-won experience at what worked and what did not, chaffed at the new national service that sought to take the limelight. Some stations stayed out of the new network, sometimes because of a desire to stay independent and locally oriented in nature.

For most, however, the problem was an inability to meet the CPB's fairly stringent requirements for membership.[73] Faced with the need to develop a viable national public radio system, CPB realized it dared not spread its limited radio funds across too many overlapping public stations. Dribs and drabs of money given to all the outlets would not accomplish much. Instead, the corporation adopted a policy to provide grants to the limited number of stations that already demonstrated their local viability, as measured by existing financial support, at least a minimal level of paid staff, and operating hours on the air, among other criteria. Thus developed a new division among the few hundred "CPB-qualified" stations that became a part of NPR and the far greater number of small community stations that did not. Public radio presented a far more varied face to listeners than did public television, where the smaller number of operating stations allowed virtually all to receive CPB support.

For college radio stations programmed largely by and for students, programming continued to center upon music often not found elsewhere. By dividing programming into discreet segments or blocks that featured an array of music genres (jazz, rock, folk, blues, and so on), many college radio stations served up some of FM's most eclectic on-air schedules. Block programming insured that most tastes would be served—if for only an hour or two a week. Assuming the role of radio's only exclusively free-form alternative music source following the demise of the commercial underground format, college broadcasters developed a loyal though not vast audience. College stations also served as a springboard for many rock artists whose music became standard fare on commercial stations once they generated impressive-enough record sales.

The number of college stations grew rapidly through the 1960s and 1970s, in part because of the FCC's low-powered Class D licenses. The cost of putting these 10-watt, entry-level stations on the air was modest, which appealed to the college administrations funding them. But expanding public broadcasting changed perceptions of the tiny radio stations, though hundreds broadcast on the low end of the FM band. In 1972 CPB, seeking to develop a stronger national noncommercial radio system, petitioned the FCC to eliminate the tiny school stations as not being an efficient use of spectrum. The commission gave Class D stations until 1978 to either increase their minimum power to 100 watts or face secondary operating status on a commercial channel. Most Class D stations sought and received the power increases, somewhat thwarting CPB's intention to obtain more full-service public radio stations on those frequencies.

In the meantime, another small FM transmitter option appeared when, in 1970, the FCC authorized FM-translator transmitters to help fill in coverage holes (by rebroadcasting with up to 250 watts on a different channel) of full-power stations. As the Class D stations were being phased out, translators—heretofore largely ignored—came into their own. Translators could use any FM channel and were inexpensive to establish and maintain. A variation, the booster transmitter, rebroadcasts a full power station on the same channel to fill in unserved pockets. Boosters must be owned by the primary station; translators need not be, though there is no limit on how many of each may be owned.[74]

Community stations (those not qualified to receive CPB grants) developed somewhat like their college radio cousins, as both sought to provide content—alternative music and highly specific local features—not typically found on commercial stations. Community broadcasters are principally funded by corporate, civic, and listener contributions, concentrating their efforts on the political, cultural, and social issues and concerns of their listening area. While alternative-music programming has been and remains a significant ingredient of many community-station schedules, interview and talk features focusing on a broad range of timely and sometimes controversial topics are abundant and serve to define and distinguish this type of radio from the rest of the pack. These usually small community outlets have often been viewed as a medium of and for "the people."

Radio critic and gadfly Lorenzo Milam spearheaded the community-based FM initiative through the 1960s and into the 1970s. More than anyone, he showed small nonprofit groups and organizations how to get a station on the air. His efforts were a precursor to the low-power FM (LPFM) movement nearly three decades later. Meanwhile, as the ranks of community broadcasters swelled in the 1970s, a "group of 25 visionaries and counter culture mavens gathered in Madison, Wisconsin, to ponder the future of community radio."[75] Out of this came formation of the National Federation of Community Broadcasters (NFCB), whose initial mission "was to develop training manuals for stations, help stations obtain their FCC licenses, and set up the Program Exchange to facilitate sharing of programming [material] among stations."[76] During the ensuing years, the organization was instrumental in providing independent producers with program distribution assistance (exchanging tapes, which became known as a "bicycle network").

Under the early direction of Tom Thomas and Terry Clifford, the organization extended its activities and influence to reflect the era's heightened concern for the civil rights of minorities. In addition, the NFCB "proved instrumental in bringing people of color into public radio. The organization staged the first-ever Minority Producers' Conference . . . and played a key role in the development of national policies to enhance community stations—for example, NFCB helped make it possible to non-NPR stations to receive grants from the Corporation for Public Broadcasting."[77]

Another type of public service or educational station that began to multiply in this period focused on religion. Religious radio dated to radio's earliest days, but modern religious outlets, nearly all of them FM operations, are a relatively recent phenomenon. So-called mainline or traditional Catholic, Protestant, and Jewish religious programming had been an established and self-sustaining (not advertiser-supported) part of many AM stations for decades. By the 1970s, however, more conservative Protestant church groups began to spread their gospel message by acquiring noncommercial FM educational licenses. Their efforts to do so were initially rejected by the FCC on the grounds that they did not qualify as "non-profit *educational* organizations" as required by the Communications Act. FCC industry analyst Allen Myers recalls, "We did tell them that they could form a separate not-for-profit educational organization to be a licensee, but faced with the loss of control that would have involved, most churches opted to be licensed as commercial stations."[78]

Alarmed by a growing trend to do just that, in December 1974 Jeremy Lansman and Lorenzo Milam petitioned the FCC to inquire into the operating practices of noncommercial stations licensed to religious educational organizations. Their request, intended to drive religious broadcasters from the air, was denied in August 1975: "The Commission explained then that it is required by the First Amendment 'to observe a stance of neutrality toward religion, acting neither to promote or inhibit religion.' It also explained that it must treat religious and secular organizations alike in determining their eligibility for broadcasting channels."[79] Wrongful rumors (spread from pulpits and letter campaigns) that the FCC was planning to eliminate all religious broadcasting resulted in 12 million letters being sent to it in the six years following the rejection of the petition. And the angry response did not stop; letters, calls, petitions, and, by the late 1990s, e-mails continued to flood into FCC offices protesting an action the FCC had never seriously considered taking. The so-called petition against God took on a life that lasted for more than a quarter century.

TWO CHANNELS, OR FOUR?

The advent of stereo transmission in 1961 had provided a huge boost to FM's reviving appeal. By the end of the decade, 668 FM stations were broadcasting in stereo. Stereo by then had become an accepted part of the FM marketplace: virtually all commercial and most public stations signing on, regardless of format, included the capability to broadcast two-channel sound. More stereo recordings became available. Earlier stations continued their conversion to the standard. Indeed, while the public could purchase receivers with a stereo indicator light, those soon disappeared as virtually every FM-station broadcast in stereo, making such a feature pointless.

Even as more FM stations provided stereo, however, engineers were developing what appeared to be "the next thing" for radio: four-channel sound. As early as 1970, one firm was selling four-channel audiotape equipment, and several experiments using two FM outlets had taken place in Boston (WGBH and WCRB), New York (WNYC and WKCR, both non-commercial outlets), and San Francisco (KSAN and KPFA).[80] The paired stations were linked with high-quality telephone lines, and listeners had to have two FM receivers—and four speakers—to pick up the quadraphonic signals. Listening to either station alone provided but a part of the overall signal—exactly the problem that had afflicted earlier AM-FM stereo broadcasts.

Two problems cropped up right away: there were a variety of different and competing quad systems (some developed by those who had been active with stereo a decade earlier), and it seemed likely that any quad system would occupy spectrum used by stations for their revenue-producing subcarrier transmissions. And obviously a single-station technical standard was needed for the most efficient operation and use of spectrum. Record manufacturers were ready for the change, as most had been taping four-channel versions of their music for several years.

By 1972 activity picked up in the attempt to develop viable four-channel recording and broadcast systems. CBS, for example, was backing a "matrix" system that encoded four signals down to two for transmission, then decoded back up to four at the receiver. RCA announced plans for midyear release of the first "discrete" quad recordings, which retained four channels from recording to playback but were compatible with stereo players for two-channel performance. Other companies offered variations.[81]

In April 1972 the National Quadraphonic Radio Committee (NQRC) was formed by radio-equipment manufacturers to compare the various systems and recommend one to the FCC (this approach was following the pattern used many times before).[82] After extensive review and testing of five competing systems (all using the discrete method), the NQRC sent its two volumes of recommendations to the FCC late in 1975. The group determined that such a system was practical and could be made compatible with existing receivers.[83] After further testing, the FCC subsequently agreed.[84] In June 1977 the commission inquired whether there was sufficient interest to adopt a technical standard. Some 2,000 comments were received, most in favor of the idea.[85]

Yet after all this development, testing, and promotional effort, remarkably little happened. There was a flurry of interest,[86] and some quad tape recordings were issued, but little further action took place; broadcasters decided quad was not worth the investment in equipment, and manufacturers decided to stick with promoting already-successful stereo. Discussion of quad had all but disappeared by the end of the decade, though it was a precursor of Dolby's surround-sound system.

A GROWING AUDIENCE

Until the late 1960s, FM's audience had remained small and demographically narrow, restricted largely to that 10 to 15 percent of the radio audience that was both socially and economically well-off. Their limited number belied their loyalty and impact. For those advertisers seeking an older, upper-income market, FM stations offered genuine appeal. And thus

FM outlets continued to sell their "class-not-mass" audience. But a substantial change was already evident.

First, the receiver market was expanding and changing in character. By the late 1960s, FM (and all radio) sets were increasingly imported from the Far East. While imports made up only a fifth of the market in 1966, they had grown to two-thirds just two years later.[87] By the 1970s, there was virtually no domestic manufacture of radio receivers, AM or FM.

Second—and for FM proponents the more important point—was the growing proportion of all radios that included FM reception (see appendix Table B.8). From just a quarter in 1966 to half in the early 1970s and two-thirds by late in the decade, these receiver figures underlined the growing importance of FM listening. As early as 1967, half of the country's homes had at least one FM radio.

The remaining trouble spot, and the one factor contributing most to FM's continuing listening lag behind AM, was the lack of FM car radios.[88] Only by 1976 did even half the new cars come equipped with FM receivers. FM might be portable, but until it was readily accessible on the road, AM retained an important edge to listeners and advertisers alike. Despite the appeal of FM stereo, automobile stereo systems took even longer to achieve parity, as the added wiring and speakers were a cost factor automakers resisted.

The steady buildup of the FM-receiver market, delayed though it seemed to many longtime FM proponents, ironically killed off several attempts to get Congress to legislate that all radio receivers had to include the capability of tuning both the AM and FM bands. In 1964 legislation to require reception of UHF stations by all television receivers had become effective. FM proponents hoped to follow that precedent, though FM radio was in far better shape than UHF television had been. The first radio "all-channel receiver" bills appeared in both the House and Senate in the late 1960s,[89] but other than airing the issues, they did not go anywhere. More were introduced regularly, with (predictably) FM proponents arguing for passage and the consumer-electronics manufacturers resisting legal action, saying that FM was achieving its goal in the marketplace. In the early 1970s, congressional committees passed bills that later died in the legislative process. Hearings in the Senate in 1974,[90] and the House in 1977,[91] again considered bills to promote manufacture of home and automobile FM radios. By that point, however, the effort seemed unnecessary given FM's gains, for by then the service was available in virtually all households and a rising proportion of automobiles.

Paced by the increasing availability of both inexpensive and high-end receivers, the attraction of stereo, and increasingly independent programming, FM's share of radio's listening audience continued to grow. The rise toward parity with AM was evident first in major cities (as shown in appendix Table B.8), which offered multiple stations and increasing program variety. FM-receiver ownership soared by the early 1970s. Across the top ten markets, the overall trend in FM's share of radio listening grew from 15 percent in 1967 to 35 percent by 1976. National listening levels lagged, however, due to the slower growth of FM audiences in poorly served rural regions.

FM stations first began to appear in major-market ratings reports in the late 1960s, and their stature only grew as the 1970s progressed. Yet even informed estimates could miss just how quickly the FM audience was growing. A Cox Broadcasting 1976 report on the state of the medium suggested FM would control 40 percent of radio audience by 1980 (just four years hence), when FM's actual share by then would be closer to 55 percent.[92]

Most indicative of FM's growth and potential, however, was the changing nature of FM audience research. Pushed by advertisers demanding "the numbers" before committing to purchase of air time, those studying FM began to move away from a focus on receiver availability (so-called penetration studies) toward findings more in line with what had long been provided for AM radio and television: *who* was listening and *when*. In part this was driven by the FCC's program nonduplication rule, which raised FM broadcast-operation expenditure and thus added pressure for more revenue.[93]

By mid-1967 the monthly trade paper *Media/Scope* was speaking of FM as a "mature medium" and noting that its audience was concentrated among listeners eighteen to forty-nine, who especially appealed to advertisers. Most FM listeners were still in major markets.[94] CBS radio began to survey FM listeners that same year and by 1972 found a 106 percent increase in FM's listening share in the top eight markets. Young people were listening more (83 percent of those under thirty, but only half of those sixty or older), and the medium continued to appeal most to those with more education (85 percent of those with at least some college, versus 58 percent of those who did not complete high school). Given the location of most stations, listening was far higher in major metro areas than rural regions.[95] But the operative word was growth on all fronts.

ON THE MOVE

The logjam of historical barriers to FM development was clearly giving way by the 1970s. Building on the momentum already achieved, FM's audience grew by leaps and bounds. Such success had numerous sources, although that was difficult to determine from the industry trade press. *Broadcasting* praised "stubborn [FM] believers and later . . . owners of powerful AM stations" for making the difference,[96] totally ignoring the FCC's force-feeding of separate programming—against which those same broadcast leaders had fought tooth and nail but which turned out to be the single most important factor in FM's arrival as the dominant radio service. The commission's earlier decisions approving FM stereo standards (1961) and SCAS (1955) contributed to lifting FM out of decline. By finally resolving the decades-old controversy over program duplication, the FCC provided a crucial impetus for FM's arrival as a commercial equal to AM service.

And how quickly the radio worm turned. Even at the start of the period covered in this chapter, established FM radio operators in major markets were already casting a jaundiced eye on the flood of newcomers that sought to further divide FM's audience and still-limited revenue.[97] Predictions that FM would surpass AM were widely heard once again.

Behind the scenes, however, a more subtle change was evident in this period—though it is understood more in retrospect than it was at the time. During the 1960s, FM was an exciting place to be, for while almost nobody made any money, neither were corporate bean counters breathing down programmers' necks to toe a given company line or image. Experimentation was often encouraged or at least tolerated. FM's "alternative" role to AM (and sometimes everything else) peaked in the 1960s and early 1970s. Then, as the financial signs for the medium improved, the flexibility and experimentation began to disappear in equal proportion. Once the medium was seen to have the potential to make money (by rising in market ratings and thus attracting more potential advertisers), it could no longer be treated as a programming sandbox. FM had to play radio's game just as AM long had, pushing a few set-music formats (from soft rock in 1971 to disco in 1979, the latter viewed as the coup de grace by many old-line FM disciples) to grab the most desired audience groups. And it worked:

FM became a great success by late in the 1970s, but at the cost (to many of its adherents) of losing its programming soul to the bean counters. As a California music magazine put it in mid-1978:

> Corporate broadcasters are products of paranoia. The pressure on major market stations for those coveted ratings is incredible. Unfortunately, no matter what the ratings indicate, they will never speak for the entire mass market. They are an indicator, a barometer of base popularity. Not the final word, and hardly the gospel truth. And the ratings also make everyone forget that the people who listen to radio are not demographic numerical equivalents, marketing specifications, or jerks. They're real flesh and blood souls who boogie to different drummers.[98]

The one bright development that tempered this mainstreaming trend to blandness was the rise in importance of noncommercial stations, thanks especially to the creation of National Public Radio. NPR experienced its own exciting (and also brief) flirtation with different approaches to and styles of programming, until it, too, had to toe a more institutional line, albeit varied from the commercial variety. NPR gave the first national prominence to the noncommercial service that had been ignored for years. After a somewhat shaky start, the network's expanding number of stations provided mainstay news and cultural programs across the country. During the decade that saw the nation abandon its costly misstep in Vietnam and begin a swing to the political right, public and community radio stations addressed a myriad of social and cultural issues largely ignored by commercial outlets. Through distinctive, evocative, and often courageous programming that focused on a wide range of timely topics pertaining to race, gender, religion, ecology, politics, and economics, these public, college, and community outlets prevented FM from sinking into the morass of corporate-driven programming long prevalent on AM. For its willingness to address controversial issues, public stations often inspired the ire of conservatives and even an occasional liberal or moderate. That dissent was exactly what many of FM's pioneers had sought: to provide a breath of fresh air.

FM   96.5 MHz

Dominance : *FM Is Radio*

(1980–1995))))))

FM audiences led AM for first time in RADAR radio usage report for spring 1979. Overall Monday–Sunday figures show 24-hour FM share at 50.5 percent, 42 percent for 6 A.M. to 10 A.M. and 58 percent for 7 P.M. to midnight. Teen-agers and young adults (18–24) devote 59 percent and 65 percent of their listing to FM, respectively, while the figure for persons above 50 is 37 percent.[1]

This startling news appeared in a brief paragraph, buried among four others about different topics on a back page of the trade weekly. But the reported facts heralded a radio revolution: FM was finally beginning to outpace AM. A quarter-century after Edwin Howard Armstrong's untimely death, the medium he pioneered was finally coming into its own. The much-predicted dominance of the newer FM over AM seemed to be at hand, though getting there had taken far longer than FM's pioneers had predicted—about four decades. FM began 1980 with a bare majority of the radio audience, but within a dozen years it accounted for fully three-quarters of all listening. Indeed, articles with titles such as "Can AM Radio Be Saved?" were becoming common,[2] suggesting just how much had changed.

Most measurements of FM's role reflected its growth through these years. One prime example was continuously climbing station sales prices, demonstrating growing demand for a limited number of outlets and that FM was rapidly approaching parity with AM. And for just that reason, trying to isolate FM's specific story becomes more difficult as it increasingly merges with—and ultimately supercedes—the story of AM. This shift occurred on several levels, most obviously in programming, where AM and FM differences were quickly disappearing. Long gone were FM's lonely days of classics and background music. The medium's long-separate identity (and so much that flowed from that separateness) largely disappeared by the mid-1980s.

GROWTH AND WALL STREET

Larger audiences and positive financial news by 1980 built the platform for continued FM expansion throughout the decade, as is evident in appendix Table A. Demand for new licenses brought more than 2,000 new commercial and 700 new educational outlets by 1995. Compared to FM's expansion, AM nearly stood still.

Despite high interest rates in the early 1980s, FM-station sale prices rose steadily. In 1980 six FM stations sold for $5 million or more, the record being $12 million for one Los Angeles outlet.[3] Within five years that figure seemed like a bargain: another Los Angeles station sold for $44 million, demonstrating the value that investors placed on strong FM outlets in major markets.[4] Even more indicative was that FM stations were sometimes selling for twenty to thirty times their cash flow in a business where ten times had been a more usual price predictor.[5] The FM-station sales record rose yet again in 1989, when a Washington, D.C., outlet changed hands for nearly $50 million.[6]

Helping to stoke interest in FM (as well as in AM and television) were a series of ownership rule changes made by the FCC making it easier to own more stations. For three decades, no entity could own more than seven FM stations in the country and never more than one in a given market. Taking into account the huge growth in the overall number of radio stations in the country, the FCC, starting in 1982, progressively loosened radio ownership restrictions, first to twelve, then to eighteen, and finally to twenty AM or FM stations nationwide. Under some circumstances, one owner could even control more than a single station in a market. Given that more FM outlets were going on the air all the time, these changes made sense to most observers, and they paralleled similar changes in AM and more-limited modifications of television ownership.

As the number of FM stations on the air continued to climb, however, the commission was faced with how to accommodate them all. The original mid-1940s' allotment scheme had projected as many as 2,000 FM stations. Its early 1960s' replacement boosted that to about 3,500 outlets. But two decades later, it was increasingly evident that channels had to be found to accommodate the continued flow of new applicants.

Technology lent a hand: as transmitter and antenna designs improved and use of digital equipment became standard, engineers could more precisely project station coverage patterns. This helped avoid most interference, even with more stations on the air. FCC changes in FM allotments, however, narrowed spacing between stations, thus increasing the likelihood of interference. The NAB cited interference concerns as they lobbied against placing more stations on the air, though many concluded the organization's negative stance was protectionist thinking in favor of stations already on the air. The weak link was increasingly the cheap radio receiver, featuring circuit designs that had changed little over the years and were weak at rejecting interference. As imports struggled for market share, manufacturers were investing less in receiver improvements even as FM drew more listeners.

Early in 1980, the commission began a proceeding to squeeze more stations on the air within FM's existing spectrum allocation. Docket 80–90 was initiated because many applications for new FM stations did not fit within the FCC's existing allotment plan. Further, the National Telecommunications and Information Administration (NTIA) sought to make available more opportunities in FM radio. The commission offered several options for comment.[7] The gist of most was to "drop in" additional FM allotments within the existing scheme, though this quickly raised the usual concerns about the interference that such drop-ins might create. As often happens in FCC proceedings, many research studies were filed to support differing viewpoints. Most widely cited was an ABC-sponsored engineering study that predicted substantial regions of interference as the newly dropped-in allotments were occupied by operating stations. Only NPR— then seeking more affiliates—was in general agreement with the commission's proposal.[8] To minimize interference, NTIA urged that FM stations make use of directional antennas. Long used by AM outlets, these can be designed to propagate signals in specific patterns to lessen interference.[9] The commission eventually approved the directional-antenna option.[10]

After considerable wrangling, in May 1983 the FCC adopted the drop-in scheme, arguing it could allow up to a thousand additional stations (though internal disagreements showed when the chairman's office said the number might be more like 600).[11] Essentially, the FCC created new subclasses of FM stations to supplement those established in 1963. Under specified conditions, FM stations of one class could utilize channels originally reserved for another. Expecting what could become thousands of applications for the new allotments once they were finally approved, the commission said it was considering a lottery system to more speedily process potential competitors. Critics (including dissenting commissioner James Quello, a former Detroit radio/television manager) complained that technical studies supporting the decision had neither been made public nor subjected to outside review.[12]

Nearly a year later, the FCC listed some 700 projected new FM allotments for public comment.[13] Most were for the least-powerful Class A stations and located in southeastern states. Several commentators argued that operators of daytime-only AM stations should receive priority in applying for the new FM outlets so they could broadcast full time.[14] While that suggestion raised ghosts of FM as being "ancillary" to AM, it also made clear that the nation's radio service used two types of transmission and getting the most out of each was a primary goal. The FCC adopted the suggested daytime AM-station preference.[15] The final list of FM allotments was released at the end of 1984.[16] Depending on the application processing approaches used, the commission estimated it would take three years to review and assign new licensees.[17]

Going a step further, the commission decided that processing priority would be given to applications controlled by women (who had been granted a preference back in 1978 for FM stations) and minorities, two groups that generally owned few radio stations.[18] These preferences would be determined by means of a lottery to select applications for processing. Just a few months later, however, a federal appeals court struck down the intended preference for women on the grounds that it was "based on the offensive presumption . . . that women as a group have a distinctly female point of view."[19] The case concerned a Georgia station awarded to a woman with little experience over a man with two decades of experience running stations, though other than their gender, there was little else to distinguish the two. As one of the judges concluded in criticizing the FCC's approach,

"A mandate to serve the public interest is not a license to conduct experiments in social engineering conceived seemingly by whim."[20]

As more FM stations crowded onto the air, each had a more difficult time being heard—sometimes literally. In 1986 several industry groups proposed doubling the maximum power that a small Class A FM station could use (to 6 kw) so their coverage area could increase up to 40 percent. Though it took three more years, the FCC agreed, affecting about a thousand stations (none of which were operating in the crowded Northeast.[21]

The commission also loosened rules restricting SCAs in a 1982–83 proceeding, thus allowing commercial and noncommercial stations the freedom to use subcarriers for any service, not just one that was broadcast related.[22] Furthermore, the SCA could now be used twenty-four hours a day rather than restricted to the hours of broadcast operation. Most important was a change allowing public stations to lease their SCA for commercial gain.[23] Within a couple of years, nearly 1,000 FM stations had leased their subcarrier.[24] One group, however, expressed concern about this trend: reading services for blind listeners. There were many of these across the country, nearly all using an SCA channel belonging to a local noncommercial FM outlet.[25] They feared the siren call of more income, for the parent licensee might force them off the air with no place to go. Indeed, the Mutual network, among others, announced plans for specialized voice and data network services utilizing SCAs leased from FM stations nationwide.[26] But FM suffered some weaknesses—limited range, reception problems amidst tall buildings, and a slow rate of data transmission (about 9.6 kilobytes per second), which made many commercial applications impracticable.[27] As a result, most reading services for the blind continued their valuable services.

MICRO-RADIO RUMBLES

A more radical proposal simmered on an FCC back burner. Based on an application from the Moody Bible Institute in Chicago in mid-1981, the FCC's media-bureau staff considered creating a class of LPFM stations— essentially a revival of the 10-watt educational operations that had been on the air for three decades (1949–79), although now they would be allowed for either commercial or noncommercial use.[28] Under strong broadcaster pressure against the notion, the commission appeared to close the door on such stations nearly a decade later.[29] One concern was whether small FM translator stations (used to provide signals in ill-served areas) might be allowed to originate programs—and thus become independent FM operations in their own right. Not surprisingly, broadcasters lobbied against this idea by again citing interference, but certainly they were also concerned about adding more competing voices.

Interesting, if not prophetic, was a proposal in 1970 by a St. Louis group called "Challenge for the 70s" for the creation of what it termed "mini" stations designed to serve low-income neighborhoods. From the perspective of the chief of the FCC's educational broadcasting branch at the time, Dr. Robert L. Hilliard, the plan had the potential to serve society in a variety of ways, in particular in the area of education. "These [low-power outlets] will stimulate self-identity and pride," observed Hilliard, "particularly among inner-city residents. The idea for mini stations, operated by and for residents in these [poor] areas, has great potential for motivating them to go on to successful learning in the formal, schoolroom setting. . . . [The stations] can be used to reach out into so-called white suburbia to inform those residents about problems faced in the city and to motivate them to take action to alleviate the problems."[30] According to St. Louis radio historian Frank Absher, at least one such station actually got on the air:

> It was KBDY in the Montgomery-Hyde Park neighborhood of North St. Louis. The CP was granted in the summer of 1972. . . . It was at 89.9 MHZ and operated with 20 watts effective radiated power. The station promoted itself as "the first non-commercial radio station in the country to be owned and operated by a neighborhood organization." Unfortunately, it ran into several problems in the ensuing years due to mismanagement and was eventually shut down after having exceeded power restrictions so frequently that another non-com[mercial outlet] (WLCA at Lewis & Clark Community College in Godfrey, Illinois) challenged them at the FCC and won . . . in April 1988. There was a [special temporary authority] order allowing KBDY back on the air at 6 watts, but the station basically died off.[31]

Aside from these, there was a more troubling precedent: many low-power transmitters operated as "pirates" (the term used by licensed broadcasters and the FCC) without a license. Operated by radio enthusiasts with up to 50 watts of power, these tiny outlets ranged up to five miles and often took on more of a political bearing during the social and cultural turmoil of the 1960s (unless discovered and closed down by the FCC as violating the Communications Act). During the 1980s and 1990s, some of these illegal "micro-radio" FM outlets railed against big media's bottom-line fixation at the expense of local- and public-interest programming. While it is impossible to nail down numbers due to their illegal nature, there were often several micro stations operating at any one time.

Peace activists in Yonkers, New York, led by Allen Weiner, placed micro station WKOV-AM on the air in 1969 and a year later jumped to the FM broadcast band, changing the station's call letters to WXMN (in honor of Howard Armstrong's pioneering experimental station, W2XMN). Its surprisingly effective 50-watt signal drew listeners from several surrounding communities and helped launch the micro-radio movement in earnest. Several other low-power stations (WSEX and WBRX in New York, among them) were soon operating. Weiner's illegal enterprise resulted in his arrest in August 1971, but other pirate stations continued to appear. Within a decade there may have been "at least 20" pirate operations in the New York area alone.[32]

In California, African American activist Walter Dunn put micro station "Zoom Black Magic Radio" on the air in Fresno in 1985. For many low-power aficionados, his operation, with targeted neighborhood programs that included "grassroots music, militant talk, and ads for black businesses,"[33] symbolized what micro could be. Some felt this was where the "modern microbroadcasting movement [began]."[34] Dunn's operation became a model for other micro stations in urban ghettos and housing projects, most notably WTRA in Springfield, Illinois, led by DeWayne Readus (also known as M'banna Kantako), who "begat hundreds more"[35] low-power outlets. Kantako's station focused on the police brutality he claimed plagued his impoverished community, and as such it served as a beacon "for Springfield's dispossessed."[36] Broadcasting their message to the "street," ghetto-based micro stations ("Human Rights Radio," as Kantako came to call his operation) offered programming on a wide range of highly charged topics, including the AIDS epidemic, drug use, and police abuse, as well as rap music rarely aired by mainstream FM stations.

The ghetto pirate's "for-the-people" orientation fueled something of a broader "free-radio" movement, which emerged during the Reagan administration (1981–89) and came to full fruition the next decade. Inspired by the FCC's seeming affinity for commercial broadcasting and what they saw as the subsequent decline of local public-interest programs and diversity, pirate micro broadcasters accelerated their crusade against corporate radio's monopoly of the licensed airwaves.

The number of clashes between the FCC and the illegal micros increased during the 1990s as the NAB and public radio (especially NPR) launched campaigns to remove unlicensed stations from the air.[37] Arguing that micros interfered with their signals, both the NAB and NPR (odd bedfellows, given they disagree on most other issues) urged the FCC to aggressively eliminate rogue stations, despite the latter's claim to a freedom-of-speech right to be heard.

Perhaps the best-known micro station activist and censorship foe was Stephen Dunifer, who put Free Radio Berkeley on the air in April 1992. An admirer of M'banna Kantako, Dunifer did battle with the FCC for several years, during which time his case became a cause célèbre with the American press, which portrayed the conflict in David-versus-Goliath terms. Declared Dunifer, "[Free] radio has been an intimate friend of many struggles for self-determination and liberation from oppression."[38] Dunifer closed down his Free Radio Berkeley in 1998, but by then the micro-radio movement had garnered many influential supporters—among them members of Congress, as is discussed in the next chapter.

MAKING MUSIC

Several FM programming patterns became increasingly apparent throughout the 1980s. First, while stations continued to emphasize music and their low-fidelity AM brothers concentrated more on various talk (and sometimes news) formats, this division was not always observed. Music remained on many AMs, while talk increasingly appeared on FM. Second, though music formats continued to splinter, reflecting changing musical tastes, more than a few critics argued that stations were beginning to sound increasingly alike. Third, and more seriously, it seemed to close observers that FM's growing audience appeal—and thus financial success—was creating growing caution and less innovation. Increasingly, stations took the safe approach of imitating successful formats rather than developing new directions. And thus this era can be seen as one of increasingly minor format shuffles rather than substantial change. Some critics claimed FM was declining to the bland and prosaic—albeit with growing profits—just as had AM before it.

A causal relationship seemed apparent between the loss of the cultural ferment characterizing the two previous decades and the decline of innovation in FM programming. The medium in the 1980s and 1990s seemed rudderless and uninspired, save when it came to seeking greater profits. Passions that typified earlier social and political protest movements had been supplanted by ennui and self-absorption, with more emphasis on "me" rather than "we." With the exception of the anti-industry micro-radio crusaders and the altruistic sensibilities of many noncommercial program schedules, FM was drifting onto the shoals of stagnation. Observed underground-radio pioneer Larry Miller, "The hopefulness for something extraordinary and far-reaching had faded. You might say the 'spirit' had been abandoned by the medium as the consequence of its acute corporatization. FM became a business model rather than a model of invention and freshness like it once was—at least for a few shining moments back in those years that 'if you can remember them, then you weren't there, as the quote goes."[39]

Music was, as always, at the center of both FM's appeal and debate. Formats continued to meld with changing musical tastes as well as new performers. Music became less a selling point for AM as a broader variety of formats appeared on FM. The difference in presentation between the two services could be seen in how they arranged program elements. Whereas AM outlets held to the old "song–commercial spot–DJ talk–song" formula, FM stations vigorously promoted their playing of two to four songs in a row, followed by sets of perhaps three to five commercials and minimal DJ chatter. The difference was least apparent during morning drive time, when both AM and FM offered more "wake-up" personality chatter and commercial interruptions.

FM beautiful-music format was updated to counter declining and aging audiences by mixing in more adult contemporary and soft rock. It was billed as "easy listening" by the 1980s, with less emphasis on dreamy background sounds to create a more energetic beat. More airtime was given to contemporary artists such as Dan Fogelberg, the Beatles, Ann Murray, Bread, and Barry Manilow.[40] Most stations offering this "background" or "subliminal" sound relied on syndicators. Century 21, Peters Productions, and Drake-Chenault were among the largest suppliers of prepackaged, customized sound hours designed for automation systems that slowly were replaced by computerized satellite feeds. In the late 1980s, "an NAB survey concluded that over three-quarters of the nation's stations receive[d] some form of satellite programming."[41] Most were outlets featuring the syndicated easy listening sound. Local origination was rare, which would soon be the case with other formats, raising concerns about the decline in FM's parochial character and grassroots orientation.

Top 40, once the sole province of AM and long the epitome of what would never be found on FM, began to shift toward FM's better fidelity, redesigned as "contemporary hit radio" (CHR). The sound became more streamlined with less talk, paralleling Bill Drake's changes in AM's Top 40 outlets two decades earlier. Music playlists were narrowed to typically thirty songs and less variety to create a more cohesive sound. Programmer Mike Joseph (often cited as the father of radio consulting) devised the approach to include fast rotations (more airplay for songs/artists whose records were hot, less for music whose sales were declining), up-tempo songs, and surrounding production elements that included promotional announcements, station or advertiser contests and jingles, commercials, and occasional public service announcements. By the mid-1990s, CHR outlets weighted their playlists with more rock music while still avoiding heavy rock and oldies.

Adult-contemporary (AC) music increasingly dominated FM in the 1990s, relying on current or recent pop favorites while steering clear of hard rock. AC mutated into two distinct varieties: so-called hot and soft AC. While their music and announcers sometimes reflected a Top 40 sensibility, hot-AC stations avoided anything too raucous — no hard-edged rock beats or grating guitar riffs, for example. The soft-AC stations assumed a quasi–easy listening persona through presentation of such artists as Lionel Richie, the Carpenters, Stevie Wonder, and Olivia Newton-John, along with more laid-back DJs. A melded AC variation, fittingly dubbed "mix," was characterized with an emphasis on popular soft rock, dance, and ballads from the previous two decades. These related program approaches would become enormously successful by mid-decade, ranked among FM's top-rated and most profitable stations.

The AOR of the 1980s was slowly supplanted by classic-rock (CR) and classic-hits (CH) formats in the 1990s. While CR relied on album-rock favorites from the 1960s and 1970s — such as "Light My Fire" (the Doors), "Stairway to Heaven" (Led Zeppelin), and "Jumpin' Jack Flash" (the Rolling Stones) — CH aired pop tunes that had topped music charts during the same period, including "Horse with No Name" (America), "I Shot the Sheriff" (Eric Clapton), or "Dreams" (Fleetwood Mac). CR typically served its music in two- and three-song sweeps like its predecessor AOR, whereas

CH stations frequently emulated the faster pacing of the bygone Top 40 sound. The 1990s also saw the emergence of a modern-rock format, which distinguished itself from CR and CH by focusing on new rock artists and groups (such as INXS, Depeche Mode, or the Cure) that were often drawn from small import record labels and college stations. Modern-rock stations were sometimes described as alternative or progressive because they emphasized more obscure music.

The disco craze of the late 1970s, conversely, proved short-lived; by the mid-1980s, it had morphed into "urban contemporary" (UC), with a dance-oriented sound that included compatible rock tunes. UC stations, most in larger markets, were faster paced, though longer dance selections were featured. This proved trendy and was closely keyed to what was hot in pop culture. By the early 1990s, many UC stations added hip-hop hits to their mix. The UC emphasis was found on many black stations and AC–soft rock operations seeking a youthful audience, including blacks, Hispanics, and whites—the "melting pot" format, as it was also called.

DJs of UC stations were among FM's most popular and diverse. The dean of the format was Frankie Crocker, who the *New York Times* reported "catapulted WBLS-FM, the black-music format radio station, to the No. 1 spot among listeners ages 18–34 in New York City twice in the last three decades."[42] The paper credited Crocker (who called himself the Chief Rocker) with conceiving the term "urban contemporary" in the 1970s. As was the case with Bill "Rosko" Mercer (chapter 5), Crocker had performed hosting duties at New York's Apollo Theater before concentrating on his radio career. Another early UC personality, Matty Siegel, started holding court on Boston's UC108 in 1981. He made good use of humor with a distinct local flavor and frequent celebrity guests and continued to dominate Boston morning radio into 2008. Tom Joyner was perhaps best known among UC DJs. He was dubbed the "hardest-working man in radio" as he jetted between daily shows in Dallas (on KKDA) and Chicago (over WGCI). In the 1990s, Joyner passed up further frequent-flyer miles for a syndicated show that attracted large audiences.[43] Alison Steele joined New York's WNEW as one of four females (selected from 800 who tried out) for an all-women experiment in 1966. When that ended just eighteen months later, Steele stayed on as the "Nightbird," working an early-morning shift with her sultry tones. She interspersed music with telephone calls—upwards of twenty-five or thirty each night—from her insomniac listeners, while her poodle chewed on a bone nearby. For a brief time she affected miniature cigars. She was later named to the Rock and Roll Hall of Fame and became the first woman to win *Billboard* magazine's "FM Personality of the Year" award.[44]

Country music also became more popular on commercial FM in the mid-1980s. By then it was the nation's most widely programmed format, dominating more than 2,300 AM and FM stations. Of all AM formats, country seemed the least likely to make the FM transition. Earlier, FM broadcasters had balked at playing "hillbilly" music on their more culturally conscious stations, but several FM outlets achieved success by wrapping it in a more urbane package. By featuring crossover hits and artists (such as Glen Campbell, Johnny Cash, Marshall Tucker, and the Allman Brothers) from other formats, in particular AC and Top 40, FM stations marketed themselves as "urban" country, "countrypolitan," "modern" country, or "hit" country. Such terms were presumed to give the music greater appeal to a hipper audience. Countrypolitan, for example, denoted a sophisticated, nonrural approach. Modern country rejected the traditional "hee-haw" sound. "Hot" country suggested a zingy Top 40 or "now" sound. Each variation helped expand the base of traditional country and enjoyed growing ratings.

Whatever their musical emphasis, FM stations mixed in more talk during the 7:00–9:00 A.M. morning drive time. In major markets this focused on news and information and wake-up banter. A fairly short-lived variation was the phenomenon dubbed "Morning Zoo." The idea was to engage listeners through zany and irreverent antics of an on-air team fronted by a main personality. Comedy was central, as was audience involvement via call ins. Testifying to its success was the fact that nearly every station with a Morning Zoo invariably captured high ratings. Scott Shannon and Cleveland Wheeler were among the first practitioners when they introduced it in Tampa. The format was brought to wider attention by Shannon over New York City's WHTZ-FM. By the early 1990s, however, the Morning Zoo's "hellzapoppin" ambiance had worn thin, and its goofiness and outrageous stunts and contests had been toned down in favor of a more moderate style.

While a number of AM stations concentrated on oldies (pop hits from the 1950s through the 1970s) and even earlier nostalgia (popular songs from the big-band era of the 1930s and 1940s), both formats were aimed at older adults who liked songs from their own past. As just one example, Al Hamm's "Music of Your Life," focusing on the big-band era, was widely syndicated on AM stations and eventually migrated to FM. These vintage variations trickled over to FM in the late 1980s and enjoyed modest success. Indeed, two Philadelphia FM outlets switched from other formats to play oldies within twelve hours of each other.[45]

FM's oldest commercial offering—classical music—found itself in a battle to share listeners with public radio's increasingly popular use of the format. In many markets, NPR affiliates filled the hours between *Morning Edition* and *All Things Considered*, as well as evening hours, with chamber and orchestral music. While the noncommercial stations could offer long sweeps of uninterrupted music, commercial outlets had to break for ads, putting them at a disadvantage. To mitigate this handicap, commercial classical stations reduced their spot loads and skewed their format to the shorter and more familiar works often neglected by public radio. Classical-music purists derided this trend by comparing it with hit-music stations. Nevertheless, the few markets with commercial classical FM stations (among them San Francisco, Chicago, New York, Washington, and Boston) retained a loyal though modest following.

Other format permutations were rolled out with varying degrees of success in the 1980s and early 1990s, reflecting the continuing fragmentation ("niching" or "narrowcasting" in radio parlance) of music radio's demographics if not an increased awareness of the nation's growing diversity. Among the added formats heard on FM were arena rock (live rock concerts), male adult contemporary (geared to men thirty-nine and older with a low tolerance for dance rhythms), eclectic-oriented rock (a diverse blend of lesser-known songs and artists), digital hits (exploiting the growing CD Walkman market), ARROW (an acronym for "All Rock-and-Roll Oldies," targeting classic hits from the 1970s and 1980s), Gen-X (featuring new-wave and dance hits), Triple-A (adult album alternative, airing songs from the margins of pop and rock), and boomer rock (the various AC versions with a harder edge). Although FM appeared to be offering greater diversity, skeptics rightly claimed that the new concoctions merely varied long-standing formats and thus lacked inventiveness. Rather than invest in new directions, FM appeared content to rework existing formats to maintain its bottom-line stability.

Perhaps ultimate recognition of the seemingly thriving program variety on FM came with the FCC's 1986 decision to eliminate its program non-duplication rules established two decades earlier. While deregulatory ideology drove the action, the underlying concern focused on AM radio's fortunes, a complete reversal of the earlier situation. Now successful FM formats, many copied from AM, could be shared over weaker AM outlets to keep the latter on the air.[46]

FM TALK: SHOCK AND SERVICE

Talk programming on commercial FM generally trailed similar formats on AM. This proved especially so as the number of AM talk shows increased in the wake of the FCC's 1987 elimination of its Fairness Doctrine.[47] Broadcasters no longer had to provide time to individuals or groups with differing views from those aired by a station. Very quickly, uninhibited and usually conservative talk programming became the financial salvation of AM. But the political and issues-oriented call-in shows remained scarce on FM into the early years of the new millennium, when FM programmers began to see the benefit of implementing all-talk in light of increasing listener migration to other audio music sources.

Radio news also declined on both AM and FM. As late as 1984, 85 percent of independent FM stations reported having a newsroom (91 percent of AM-FM combinations did), though news was already filling less airtime. The trend began with stations in crowded urban markets that offered audiences multiple news choices. Outlets offering news began to drop in 1990.[48]

Arguably taking the place of news was a new and different kind of talk. Radio "shock jocks" drew large audiences made up of mostly adolescent males. The most infamous of this breed was Howard Stern, who first aired in 1982 with increasingly scatological on-air antics that prompted numerous FCC fines for indecency rule infractions. Though based in New York, his program by the mid-1990s was syndicated to more than forty markets, including some FM outlets. His greater reach increased his fines. Of course there was another side to this: "Howard Stern is the most-fined personality in radio and actually encourages the fines and touts these FCC fines as if they were medals of honor."[49] A slew of later syndicated Stern wannabes, such as Mancow (Chicago), the Greaseman (Washington, D.C.), and Opie and Anthony (Boston, then New York), went out of their way to provide listeners with the same brand of locker-room humor and puerile skits— insipid, perhaps, but hugely popular to a highly desired audience demographic: young males and a surprising number of females. Most of these shock jocks held court during morning drive time and had a profoundly positive impact on station profits, if not on the listening public's moral sensibilities.

Progress in gay radio would slow in the 1980s, partially as the result of a growing antigay mindset with the spread of AIDS. The so-called gay plague was discussed and demythologized on programs such as *Lambda Weekly*, which aired on several community stations starting in 1983. Pacifica's WBAI New York outlet and other stations broadcast gay and lesbian interview and talk features on a fairly frequent basis, beginning about the same time. The many right-wing, often-rabid talk shows that appeared on AM following elimination of the Fairness Doctrine inspired additional efforts to get more gay programming out to the public. Once again, FM noncommercial stations provided an alternative. By the mid-1990s, more than 250 radio programs targeted the gay audience, all but a few broadcast by public, community, and college FM stations. On the other hand, discourse on gay issues was scant on commercial outlets and was usually of a derogatory nature as FM's own growing number of shock jocks showcased over-the-top stereotypes for cheap laughs.

Community stations also gave voice to the Native American community. A telling 1987 report outlined the many cultural contributions of Indian radio.

The stations are able to break down barriers which exist between the reservations and the off-reservation community. They are a strong vehicle for educating non-Indians about the history, culture, conditions, and activities of reservation population. They are able to share cultural values, experiences, and events, making them accessible to listeners. By broadcasting in Native languages and focusing on local customs and practices, they reinforce the value of tribal cultures and the identity of Indian people. At the same time, by broadcasting positive images, they can counter many of the negative racist stereotypes held by non-Indians. The stations also broadcast news, information, and other programming relating directly to the needs and concerns of reservation populations. This gives legitimacy to these concerns and strengthens their importance, especially when they are not addressed by other media. They have a unique identity. The reservation-based public radio stations are special in the public radio arena, because they represent a particularly unique and little understood segment of ethnic culture.[50]

By the 1990s more than twenty Native stations were broadcasting in the continental United States, all but two on FM. There were five in Arizona, a handful scattered in New Mexico and the Dakotas, and one each in New York, Montana, Colorado, Washington, Oregon, California, and Wisconsin. Seven indigenous stations broadcast in Alaska, though Hawaii had none. These stations offered diverse programming but almost always focused on Indian cultural heritage. Tribal language, indigenous music, and traditional storytelling programs were widely scheduled: "Tribally owned radio stations are offering a new sound on the radio dial—drum beats, powwow music, and Native American news stories of their own choosing. Several Native stations receive programming from public radio distributors and a specialized satellite service, American Indian Radio on Satellite (AIROS), was launched in the mid-1990s with federal funding and assistance from [Native American Public Broadcasting Consortium]."[51] Most programs, however, were produced in-house. Native broadcasters also partnered with the National Federation of Community Broadcasters to further enhance local programming.

PUBLIC RADIO

National Public Radio continued to expand during the 1980s thanks to its innovative news and cultural programs. Audiences for *Morning Edition* (which first aired with a news and features format in 1981) and *All Things Considered* continued to grow. Together these morning and early-evening live programs, which combined hard news with in-depth audio features, became the best known of NPR's growing menu of programs. *Car Talk* began in 1977 over Boston station WBUR-FM and was carried nationally on NPR a decade later. It quickly established an impressive following; listeners loved the two Magliozzi brothers' (nicknamed "Click" and "Clack") brand of irreverent car humor combined with serious repair advice.[52] *Fresh Air* ran for a decade on Philadelphia's WHYY and then expanded to the NPR national service in 1985. Host Terry Gross's interviews and features on the arts and public issues held a loyal audience.[53] Indeed, the overall size of NPR's audience more than tripled in the 1980s, climbing from just under 2 million at the start of the decade to nearly 7 million in 1989.[54] But NPR also made mistakes, two of which had long-term impact.

The first mistake concerned a program. When offered Garrison Keillor's idiosyncratic *A Prairie Home Companion* variety review based in the mythical

Lake Wobegon, Minnesota, NPR programmers turned it down as being too regional in appeal. Its popularity in Minneapolis (where it began in 1974) encouraged Minnesota Public Radio to develop a structure for its syndication. Soon American Public Radio (APR, later Public Radio International) was providing *Prairie* to appreciative audiences nationwide. Indeed, many stations rebroadcast the Saturday night program the next day.[55] Soon APR was distributing other public radio staples, such as the Los Angeles–based *Marketplace*, a business-news half-hour show airing on weeknights. NPR's original rejection gave birth to an increasingly potent competitor for public-station airtime.

The second mistake involved money. Seeking to broaden its sources of financial support, NPR nearly disappeared during the mid-1980s when an overly ambitious program of diversification forced the network to seek a financial bailout from CPB. Paying back the $9 million loan, equivalent to a third of NPR's annual budget at the time, led to a period of stringent cost cutting, staff layoffs, and a delay in the introduction of much of the network's cultural programming.[56] Indeed, a longer-range impact was NPR's refocus on news and public affairs to the detriment of cultural and other program options.

At the same time, the public radio spectrum was growing more crowded. With the end of the FCC Fairness Doctrine and softening of a policy preventing religious groups from directly holding noncommercial licenses,[57] more religious stations took to the air. As the FCC's Allen Myers put it, "The change really began when organizations such as American Family Association decided to construct new stations, convert its [FM] translators to full-service stations, and to [re]license its existing commercial stations as [noncommercial educational outlets]."[58] Other religious organizations likewise began to relicense their stations, and the practice quickly burgeoned. This increased religious interest in noncommercial FM outlets stemmed from a growing scarcity of commercial frequencies as well as the high building or purchase prices and FCC fees levied on commercial stations. Myers notes that noncommercial "stations were and still are exempt from those fees. Religious organizations tried to save money by filing for (or renewing licenses for) existing stations as [noncommercial educational outlets]."[59] Most succeeded, and at some, conservative Protestant and evangelical strains of Christianity blossomed on FM's airwaves. The number of religious AM outlets also grew as more stations became available at significantly lower prices because of FM's burgeoning listener popularity.

LISTENING ON THE GO

The story of FM's growing popularity after 1980 is completely different from the dismal tale of earlier decades. Rather than begging for receivers and listeners, FM stations enjoyed a steadily growing lead over AM stations in audience numbers—from about half the national total in 1980 to about three-quarters of all listeners a decade later. With success, FM audience research began to more closely resemble the patterns long found in AM, thus better matching advertiser needs.

FM broadcasters no longer bewailed a lack of receivers. That complaint that had defined discussions of FM for three decades had finally faded in the face of growing demand and receiver availability. Virtually all radios, from the smallest portables to extensive home-stereo systems, now featured FM, sometimes to the exclusion of AM tuning capability. The one specific market where FM lagged behind AM was also finally catching up. FM automobile-radio penetration reached 78 percent in 1980 and 88 percent just five years later.[60] Though "drive-time" listening was still dominated by AM news and talk stations in most major markets, FM outlets were gaining there as well. FM was now every bit as portable as its AM forebear. Distance from a wall plug no longer meant a declining FM audience.

Even at the beginning of the 1980s, FM stations were among the top-three ratings leaders in all but one of the ten largest markets.[61] Slowly but steadily, the proportion of top-rated FM stations climbed, as did overall radio-listening levels.[62] Some variance was evident, even in the largest cities. By late 1981, FM's share of total radio listening ranged from more than 69 percent in the Dallas metro area to only 49 percent in the more hotly contested New York market.[63] FM listening still lagged in rural areas of the South and West. But every year saw these differences diminish.

As FM's audience swelled, research attention turned from a focus on set penetration to the more usual analysis of who was tuning to what and when. A survey conducted for CBS in mid-1982, for example, showed listening patterns and interests to be much alike for both AM and FM, adding to the growing perception that longtime distinctions between the two had finally all but disappeared.[64] What distinctions did exist were defined along gender or social lines, not by the type of radio service.

Despite its growing audience, however, one aspect of FM still had not changed much by the early 1980s. Though FM was now the most popular radio medium, that fact was hardly reflected in its advertising income. Advertisers continued to shy away from the longtime "second service," not yet persuaded by increasing evidence of growing audience and listener loyalty. On the positive side, the long-standing image of FM as having an older, smaller, and deeply loyal audience was giving way in the face of the ratings success of a growing number of FM stations. With this trend came more ad buying, especially at rock stations with their much-sought-after teenage and young adult audiences. The ad agencies still shying away from FM were generally those buying time for cars, food products, national retail chains, and soap and drug firms.

Despite the poor showing, however, this time there were no national campaigns to encourage FM advertising as had occurred in earlier years. This was partially due to the lack of a focused FM trade organization but more a consequence of the changing role of the medium itself. The subject of how best to utilize FM continued to be discussed at radio and advertising conferences. Sessions compared best practices and case studies of what had worked and how it might work for others. Local advertising, however, was something else, though stations worked hard to convince agencies and advertisers of their growing audience. This new station promotion more often included the specific audience numbers so beloved by agency staff.

By the mid-1980s, FM was being sold differently than before. Major-station representative firms were now aggressively pursuing owners of successful FM outlets in major markets and then applying pressure on their sales personnel to deliver results. Many sales people were in the same age bracket as the audiences targeted by the stations. There were growing signs that many AM sales managers were growing jealous, concerned about the time spent upon FM advertising. The Radio Advertising Bureau largely sidestepped the issue by promoting better training and research services for all of radio.

These trends became clearer as new sales alliances began to form throughout the country. Large radio rep firms, including Crystal, Eastman, Katz, and McGavrenGuild, began joining ostensibly competitive local stations together (something always avoided in the past) and selling their time to national accounts. One of the early examples took place in

San Francisco, when Crystal's Bob Duffy enticed two pairs of differently programmed stations to work together. KABL (both AM and FM) played easy-listening music, while KMEL (FM) broadcast AOR music. Working together under Duffy's guidance, the three stations doubled their national business in two years.[65]

Contributing to FM's growing financial success was its own developing professionalism, improved greatly during the 1980s thanks to better training, improved compensation plans to attract other media sales people to radio, and more timely audience and demographic research. This was the typical process of development: as more success bred more income, that money could help improve the product and further increase listening. By the early 1990s, FM revenue finally began to match the medium's audience clout.

LAYING DIGITAL TRACKS

Amidst the growing success of the medium, technology issues continued to evolve, sometimes providing options that remained unexplored. Early in 1980, the FCC sought input on the likely usefulness of a possible technical standard for quadraphonic (four-channel) FM transmission.[66] The resulting flow of comments expressed worry about harming revenue-producing SCA services. The Muzak Corporation, heavily dependent on leased SCAs in markets across the nation, strongly underlined this concern. So did others representing services for the handicapped that often used noncommercial-station SCA channels.[67] The situation was confused by parallel consideration of a competing system of stereo radio.

Increasingly concerned about the economic status of AM stations, the FCC had begun to consider allowing stereo broadcasts by the older service. A 1980 decision to select a system developed by Magnavox was withdrawn under a storm of engineering scorn. Two years later, the FCC approved the *idea* of AM stereo, but not a specific system, claiming "the marketplace" should decide among the five or six systems then competing for approval. Only a decade later, under specific orders from Congress, did the FCC retrace its steps and select a specific system (this time one created by Motorola), but by then it was too late, and AM stereo had failed to take hold.[68] FM would remain the only stereo broadcaster.

Interest in FM quadraphonic faded (in great part due to the expense of four separate speaker systems required of consumers), though the notion of "surround sound" arrived with the introduction of Dolby Surround technology. Designed to reproduce the motion-picture theater's Dolby Stereo surround soundtracks in a home environment, it consisted of three channels: left, right, and a single "surround" channel, which was melded with the front two channels (this single surround channel was frequently sent to two rear speakers, resulting in a four-speaker system as shown in appendix A). This Dolby system was upgraded in 1987 with the Dolby Pro Logic system, a four-channel version of the earlier three-channel technology, with a separate center channel, used mainly for dialogue.[69] But it was not widely adopted, again due to cost for both broadcasters and consumers.

Also widely discussed was FMX, a noise-reduction system invented by Tom Keller and Emil Torick, engineers with the NAB and CBS, respectively. FMX was said to expand FM stereo-signal coverage by two to three times, thus proving useful in fringe listening areas. FMX was also said to improve the listener's sense of stereo separation. Costs of adding the system were low—a few thousand dollars for stations and only a few dollars each for manufacturers of FM stereo receivers. About a third of independently programmed FM outlets reported plans to adopt the FMX technology in the late 1980s.[70]

Most radio stations, AM or FM, were making extensive use of satellite program delivery by the mid-1980s. After six decades, the radio broadcast networks terminated their contracts with AT&T for network interconnection, replacing wire with cheaper and more flexible satellite links. Nearly sixty program services (syndication networks for all practical purposes) were soon available to stations, including ten digital, forty analog, and another seven using both. Storecasting was another service rapidly converting to direct satellite reception, thus bypassing use of FM-station SCAs, though luckily that revenue was no longer central to the stations' survival. Some 3,000 customers had made the switch by 1986, and experts projected a tenfold increase in business by the early 1990s. Combining all of these services, 90 percent of AM and FM stations were making use of satellite delivery, a practice most evident in smaller markets with fewer program options. The vast majority were used for network feeds.[71]

Digital technology soon provided a broader application. On their consumer introduction in 1984, compact discs (CDs) were welcomed as being far easier to handle and offering sharper digital sound while being virtually indestructible (though the latter later proved not to be the case). Only with their widespread sale did the picture change—first as the traditional LP record disappeared and then as the portable tape-cassette player was replaced by the CD-based Sony "Walkman" device that had originally appeared as a portable cassette five years earlier. The superiority of digital-sound reproduction over analog provided the impetus for the transition (just as FM had over AM four decades earlier), which proved to be swift and decisive. Digital equipment soon replaced broadcast cartridges, vinyl records, and cassettes as the primary source for radio's presentation of music in the early 1990s. Beyond the on-air studio or control room, the production studio also saw a shift to digital. Likewise gone were cart and tape players/recorders (cassette and reel-to-reel), replaced by minidisk machines and computerized mixing. Real-time audio production was made obsolete with the introduction of the minicomputer, which allowed for the manipulation of mixing elements or data (voice tracks, beds, sound effects, and the like) without the traditional constraints of the clock or old-line razor editing. Digital audio put the studio in a box, and with the touch of a finger against a computer monitor, producers and DJs could perform tasks that were once labor and time intensive. A metamorphosis in audio had taken place.[72]

(((By the mid-1990s, the FM business had grown comfortable on top of radio's competitive hill. Success had taken a lot longer than many had expected in the exciting days when FM was brand new and showed potential. The medium had persevered and finally succeeded. FM stations enjoyed the audience and (belated) advertiser acceptance that ruling the ratings provides. But here and there were signs of future problems.

While AM was by 1995 described as a "band on the run,"[73] FM had taken on some of the less savory aspects of the older service. Though continuing to benefit from its better sound and stereo transmissions, many FM stations carried high commercial loads and lots of DJ chatter and provided a narrowing choice among a few highly popular genres—just the factors that had combined to drive listeners away from AM. Those seeking specialized formats, such as classical or jazz, among others, rarely found them on commercial FM anymore. Nor did they find much peace amidst the barrage of advertising. The fight to gain and retain high ratings and ad dollars was driving FM just as it long had driven AM. Amidst FM's success in redefining the radio business, however, something had been lost. And that loss would help pave the way for development of alternative listening technologies that would emerge with the approaching millennium.

FM 97.5 MHz

Clouds in the Air (Since 1995)))))

FM radio was beginning to be plagued with the same vulnerabilities that faced AM in the late 1960s —over commercialization, dated technology that didn't meet the audio standard of the day, limited format choices, extremely profitable to the point of denial about its inherent weaknesses, an old play book that was fast becoming out of date and style, and failure to engage the emerging music styles. Coupled with an overly scientific approach that was geared more for Wall Street than Main Street and the promise of a new medium like satellite the decision [to leave FM] was not difficult and not unlike taking the plunge into FM 35 years ago.[1]

This critique from Lee Abrams—a longtime FM programmer, a pioneer in AOR-radio formats, and later the program chief of XM Satellite Radio—suggested a growing "perfect storm" of problems for FM. Granting his bias in promoting his newer venture, the comment is insightful coming from someone central to commercial-FM, music-format decisions over three decades. Despite, or because of, its success, FM seemed to be breeding stagnation and thus conditions for change.

As will become evident, FM's development since the mid-1990s is largely the story of the radio business generally as AM and FM become harder to separate. It is also a story of rising digital competition that will soon replace analog broadcasting. Given FM's increasing dominance of the business, comments made about "radio" mean FM, as most AM stations have been slowly reduced to a secondary role.

By 2006 broadcasters began to heavily promote HD (high-definition, or digital) radio service. Though only a minority of stations broadcast in HD as opposed to traditional AM and FM analog transmission, there was expansive talk about a coming radio revolution. The excitement, even some of the terms and words used, gave one a sense of déjà vu, for they repeat much of what was said about then-new FM seven decades ago. The same talk of a technology-based radio revolution filled trade reports and a good deal of consumer writing as well. Whether HD will mark a real change, however, remains to be seen.

As these words are written, complaints about the bland sameness of radio are being widely heard. One important factor behind this situation is a landmark but ill-considered piece of legislation.

WATERSHED: THE 1996 ACT

Though the Communications Act of 1934 has been amended many times, its basic thrust and role have remained largely intact. Early in 1996, however, came a fundamental change that would soon change the face of radio. After years of effort, the Telecommunications Act of 1996 was passed by Congress at the beginning of February and signed by President Bill Clinton a week later.[2] Taken as a whole, the 100 or so printed pages of amendments were the most substantial package of revisions of the 1934 law ever enacted.[3] Almost lost amidst a forest of provisions designed to reshape the telephone industry, radio broadcasting was a brief afterthought. The few sentences devoted to radio, however, would to create a revolution in station ownership. As a start, radio licenses became valid for eight years (they had run for three-year periods until 1981, when they were extended to seven years). That was only the beginning.

Less noticed at first were more important changes in how station licenses would henceforth be renewed. Though all stations must regularly renew their FCC license, the vast majority remain on the air for decades, even with changes in ownership. Generally speaking, it is the rare licensee that leaves the air voluntarily.[4] Even rarer are stations taken off the air by

FCC action because of some transgression of commission rules. Recognizing this continuity, and under strong lobbying pressure from the NAB, Congress changed the law to essentially mandate license renewal unless a station had seriously broken the rules. The FCC was directed to change its regulations to renew radio and television licenses if each of the following three statements held true: the station has (1) served the public interest, convenience, and necessity (the same words that have guided FCC operations for seven decades); (2) been found guilty of no "serious violation" of either the act itself or FCC rules; and (3) committed "no other violations" of the act or FCC rules "which taken together, would constitute a pattern of abuse."[5] As required elsewhere in the amendments, the FCC was no longer allowed to even consider any competing applicant until and unless it denied an existing station its renewal—a considerable change from past practice. While other 1996 provisions left some discretion to the FCC, this one was very specific and clear. Further, it was made retroactive a year and a half (to May 1, 1995), unlike any of the other changes.[6] The change was a lobbying triumph for the broadcast industry.

And there was more. The act's changes in broadcast ownership limits prompted a radical restructuring of the radio business. While Congress directed the FCC to study television-station ownership, it was far more specific concerning radio. The commission was instructed to eliminate its existing limits (caps) on how many radio stations could be owned nationwide (they stood then at twenty for AM and twenty for FM), opening the option of one entity buying up dozens or even hundreds of stations. As we describe later, that is exactly what happened, and the change came very quickly.

Somewhat more complex was the situation regarding how many stations one entity could control in any single market. For decades, the FCC allowed ownership of only one AM, one FM, and one television station per owner per market (and in some cases, even less). As shown in Table 7.1, Congress now decided that market size would dictate how many stations could be controlled. In the largest markets, one owner could now have up to eight stations (no more than five of either AM or FM)—more than the FCC rules before 1982 had allowed any owner across the whole country. This change, again pushed by the broadcasting lobby, portended dramatic shifts in radio-station operation with the greater efficiencies that centralized ownership allowed.

In many ways, this market-level rule was more important as, excluding

TABLE 7.1. Single-Market Station Ownership as Allowed under the 1996 Act

Market Size	Number of Commercial Radio Stations a Single Entity May Control
45 or more radio stations	Up to 8 stations, though no more than 5 in the same service (AM or FM)
30–44 stations	Up to 7, no more than 4 in the same service
15–29 stations	Up to 6, no more than 4 in the same service
14 or fewer stations	Up to 5, no more than 3 in the same service

In no case may a single owner control more than half of the stations in any market unless it can be demonstrated that such an action will "result in an increase in the number of radio broadcast stations in operation."

listening over the Internet, listeners can only tune local stations. By allowing a single owner to control up to a third or more of those stations, the law threatened to transform a business that had long centered on ownership diversity.

PROFITS VERSUS DIVERSITY

Within weeks, the new ownership provisions were having an impact. Ostensibly, the law's radio provisions were designed to help what lobbyists had described as an ailing industry. Excessive competition from too many stations and explosive growth in their numbers over the last two decades had caused profits to slump dramatically in the late 1980s and early 1990s. Many AM stations had left the air, and others seemed likely to do so. The act's virtual elimination of national radio-station ownership limits, however, inspired a frenzy of buying never before seen. The change also allowed the rapid consolidation of newly acquired facilities into clusters of multiple station (or "malls") in most American cities. The result was a sharp rise in profits and station valuations, as described by the *Atlantic Monthly* in April 2005: "Throughout most of the decade, the industry's revenues increased by more than 10 percent a year. The average cash-flow margin for major radio companies is 40 percent, compared with more like 15 percent for large TV networks; and the mean price for a radio station has gone from eight to more than thirteen times cash flow. . . . The emergence of huge, dominant radio conglomerates like Clear Channel and Infinity is a direct consequence of the '96 Act."[7] Money fueled this corporate strategy, of course, both to make the purchases and to maximize bottom-line potential. And profits did rise. Housing several stations under one roof with

TABLE 7.2. Largest Group Owners of Commercial Radio Stations, 1996–2007

Company (Listed in 2002 Order)	1996 No.	1997 No.	1997 Rank	2000 No.	2000 Rank	2002 No.	2002 Rank	2007 No.	2007 Rank
Clear Channel	62	172	4	959	1	1,207	1	1,162	1
Cumulus	N/A	48	9	303	2	268	2	303	2
Citadel	25	87	6	176	3	218	3	225	3
Infinity/CBS	47	N/A	N/A	161	4	184	4	164	4
Entercom	12	28	17	91	5	105	6	104	5
Salem	N/A	N/A	N/A	N/A	N/A	91	7	97	6
Regent	15	30	14	N/A	N/A	76	8	68	12
Cox	18	49	8	71	—	76	9	79	8
ABC	22	27	19	43	—	74	10	70	10

Sources: Data for 1996 from FCC, *Review of the Radio Industry, 1998*, appendix C, "Top 50 Owners," <http://www.fcc.gov/mb/policy/radio.html> (accessed July 2007). (Data accurate as of March 1996, but ranks were not provided.) Data for 1997 from FCC, *Review of the Radio Industry, 1998*, appendix B, "Ownership of 20 or More Stations," <http://www.fcc.gov/mb/policy/radio.html> (accessed July 2007). (Data accurate as of November 1997.) Data for 2000 from *Who Owns What*, January 10, 2000, pp. 1–2. Data for 2002 from "The State of the News Media, 2004," <http://www.stateofthenewsmedia.org/narrative_radio_ownership.asp?cat=5&media=8> (accessed January 2005). Data for 2007 from *Who Owns What*, March 26, 2007, p. 2.

shared staff was a very effective way to reduce expenses while generating capital. *Business Week* reported that "just adding a second station can cut 25 percent in costs the first year. . . . Owners also are eager to buy stations because it lets them offer advertisers a bigger share of listeners—at a higher price" by offering different formats and thus audience segments.[8]

When the act was approved, there were 5,133 different radio-station owners.[9] In just the first two years following its passage, that number declined by 14 percent.[10] According to one industry publication, 2,045 stations were sold during the first year alone.[11] Observed *USA Today* two years later: "The pace of consolidation—highlighted by the loss of 700 individual owners since March 1996—transformed radio practically overnight."[12] Radio consultant Ed Shane noted that "the mergers of radio companies and acquisitions of new properties was so intense, the daily publication *Inside Radio* added a weekly edition called *Who Owns What* as a scorecard for consolidation. That weekly tabulation of groups, numbers of stations, rankings, and revenues became a metaphor for the state of the industry."[13] Some of that information is summarized in Table 7.2.

This table is somewhat misleading because it only shows the number of stations owned, regardless of their market or audience (or revenue). After 2000, for example, only Clear Channel held the same position (first) in number of stations, total audience reach, and total annual revenue. Most of Clear Channel's stations were FM outlets. The other group owners differed sharply; while Infinity was fourth in stations in 2004, for example, it ranked second in audience and revenues because its fewer stations were located in larger markets. ABC, ranked tenth or eleventh in number of stations (depending on the year), was number three in audience reach and annual revenue for the same reason. Note how comparatively little the list has changed in the early 2000s; the fast growth came in the first four years after the 1996 act. This listing includes only commercial stations. There are also some group owners of public stations (where there had not been any limits even before 1996), notably Salem Communications Corporation, holding more than 100 outlets. A growing number of the public outlets focus on religion.

Clear Channel Communications became the obvious poster child of what can happen under a changing regulatory climate. Long heading Clear Channel was L. Lowry Mays, who founded the corporation in 1972. Born in Texas in 1935, Mays earned an MBA at Harvard and became a successful investment banker before creating the San Antonio Broadcasting Company and purchasing his first radio station in San Antonio (it remained the firm's headquarters) in 1972. From the start, he focused on radio as a more flexible medium for local advertisers than either print or television. After slow but steady growth, Clear Channel became a public company in 1984. The 1996 easing of radio ownership limits marked the beginning of a quick corporate climb to the top as the world's largest owner of radio-station licenses and the employer of 60,000 people. As a member and then chairman of the National Association of Broadcasters board of directors in the late 1980s and early 1990s, Mays played a key role in lobbying the FCC and Congress for radio-ownership deregulation.

Through purchase or merger, Clear Channel had accumulated more than 550 stations by October 1999, when it bought—for $25 billion—the 443 stations of AMFM, Inc., in what at the time was the second-biggest media merger ever.[14] Writing two years later, reporter Eric Boehlert expressed the widely held views concerning the voracious consumption of radio stations by Clear Channel: "Radio stations that once were proudly local are now being programmed from hundreds of miles away. Increasingly, the very

DJs are in a different city as well."[15] At its peak, Clear Channel had roughly 1,200 stations, 70 percent of which were FM.[16]

Chagrin with Clear Channel's buying spree began to reach a vitriolic crescendo early in the new century. Despite publishing in the same state, *Texas Monthly* summed up the story: "Unleashed by government deregulation in 1996, founder Lowry Mays shelled out billions for properties like Jacor Communications and Tom Hick's AMFM, formerly the biggest radio conglomerate in the country. For several years, one of every ten commercial radio stations in the United States belonged to Clear Channel, . . . a total of more than 1,200 domestic channels in some 250 markets.[17] Naturally, being the largest radio owner attracted negative reactions. Reviewing radio's growing problems, critics argued that consolidation is one cause: "They claim Clear Channel and other big groups have ruined the airwaves by homogenizing song lists, politicizing the dial with conservative talk and sucking out local flavor with voice-tracking technology. . . . Clear Channel contends that its cost-cutting measures have saved hundreds of stations from bankruptcy."[18]

Late in 2006, just over a decade after the law that allowed it to grow so large, Clear Channel changed course and announced plans to sell more than 400 stations in smaller markets, as well as its more than forty television stations.[19] Over the next several months, groups of stations (160 outlets) were spun off to new owners and Clear Channel considered a takeover by a private equity firm. This took place in September 2007 as shareholders approved a $19.5 billion buyout. The decisions may have been motivated by Clear Channel's inability to offer advertising time across the country or by region as it had hoped to do, as well as by stagnant radio revenues.[20]

Table 7.3 illustrates the rapidly declining number of separate owners of radio stations in most of the nation's ten largest markets. In many smaller markets, the number of different owners declined by half. In almost every case, the actual number of stations varied little in the five-year period covered. The changes are largely due to the 1996 law.

More specifically, it appeared that minority ownership of stations was significantly affected by consolidation and downsizing. As USA *Today* reported in July 1998:

Minorities are losing ground. From 1995 to 1997, minority-owned AM and FM stations dropped 9 percent — to 284 from 312 — according to a USA *Today* analysis of Commerce Department ownership data. In FM

TABLE 7.3. Decline in Number of Radio-Station Owners
in the Top Ten U.S. Markets, 1996–2007

Market	March 1996	November 1998	March 2001	March 2007
1. New York	33	27	23	21
2. Los Angeles	39	33	25	27
3. Chicago	55	43	41	31
4. San Francisco	22	19	19	15
5. Philadelphia	32	28	24	22
6. Dallas/Ft. Worth	30	24	23	25
7. Detroit	24	19	17	15
8. Boston	36	38	35	35
9. Washington, D.C.	31	25	21	23
10. Houston	28	26	26	23

Source: George Williams, FCC, *Review of the Radio Industry, 2007*, appendix F, <http://hraunfoss.fcc.gov/edocs_public/attachmatch/DA-07-3470A11.pdf> (accessed July 2007).

radio, where stations have clearer, more desirable signals, the numbers are even more striking. Black-owned stations fell 26 percent, to 64 [percent] in 1997. Hispanic-owned stations dipped 9 percent to 31 [percent]. The Commerce Department listed just two Asian-owned FM stations and three owned by Native Americans.[21]

Yet the official data suggested that the impact may not have been quite that strong (see Table 7.4).

The law's impact spread to other areas, too. Station staffs also decreased dramatically. For example, a company owning seven stations in one city did not need the services of seven different traffic managers or news directors. In a "cluster" operation, one or two of these people could get the job done, and the money saved by eliminating the other salaries could go into group coffers for other purposes. Amidst the consolidation, thousands of radio employees—perhaps as many as a third of the total—were laid off to seek other jobs in or away from the broadcast field.[22]

Concerns as to the impact such downsizing would have on station programming were quick to surface as well. At issue was the potential loss of content diversity and "the degradation of commercial radio as a creative, independent medium."[23] Industry observers predicted that an increase in cookie-cutter formats would be the result of the corporate takeover of the medium. Less than two years after passage of the act, Andrew Schwarzt-

TABLE 7.4. The Number of Radio Stations Owned by Ethnic Minorities,
1990–2000 and 2007

Minority	1990	1994	1998	2000	2007
Black	175	191	168	211	346
Asian	5	4	5	23	90
Hispanic	88	111	130	187	289
Native American	4	5	2	5	30
Total Minority Stations	272	311	305	426	755

Sources: Data for the years 1990 to 2000 as reported by National Telecommunications and Information Administration in its occasional reports on minority station ownership. See <www.ntia.doc.gov>; or for the 2000 report specifically, see <http://search.ntia.doc.gov/pdf/mtdpreportv2.pdf> (accessed February 2005). Data for 2007 from S. Derek Turner, *Off the Dial: Female and Minority Radio Station Ownership in the United States* (New York: Free Press, June 2007), table entitled "Full Power Commercial Radio Ownership by Gender and Race/Ethnicity," p. 15, <http://www.stopbigmedia.com/files/off_the_dial.pdf> (accessed July 2007). Turner cautions that data for 2007 should not be directly compared with earlier years since NTIA and FCC methods of determining ownership have varied and suffered a lack of consistency while excluding many minority-owned outlets (see Turner, *Off the Dial*, p. 10).

man, longtime head of the Media Access Project and a consistent critic, observed, "Radio mergers have highlighted longstanding listener complaints about repetitious music programming."[24]

Concerns about consolidation's effects gave rise to growing opposition by new citizen groups and vocal critics. Foremost among them was Americans for Radio Diversity, which in 1997 reported that "over 4,000 of the nation's 11,000 radio stations have been sold, [and] in the 50 largest markets, three firms controlled over 50 percent of the ad revenue."[25] Another protesting group was the Future of Music Coalition (FOMC), born of a desire to combat what it perceived as the negative, if not ruinous, impact of consolidation on radio programming. It decried the "corporatization" of the airwaves and the downgrading of radio content and music playlists. Reporting on one FOMC survey, the *New York Times* surmised that "radio listeners want local disc jockeys to have more control over programming, and they oppose federal laws that encourage more consolidation among radio conglomerates."[26] Observed media critic Robert McChesney, "That the 1996 Telecommunications Act's most immediate effect was to sanctify this concentrated corporate control is not surprising; its true mission never had anything to do with increasing competition or empowering consumers.[27]

Opponents of consolidation were not without important allies. In the early 2000s, FCC commissioner Michael Copps (later joined by Commissioner Jonathan Adelstein) took growing umbrage at what he regarded as the "undemocratization" of the airwaves. His denunciation of radio conglomerates and their effects on the industry was manna to anticonsolidation and big-media opposition groups and helped inspire the emergence of more of them. A decade after the act's passage, Copps continued to voice alarm over its effects as he encouraged an audience of program executives to oppose greater consolidation, adding that "fewer companies own and control media companies. Big companies already control radio. . . . They own the production of programming. They own its distribution. Increasingly, they control creativity itself."[28]

Senator John McCain (R-Ariz.) grew critical of his own party's staunch support of big media and its monopoly of radio and ultimately supported the expansion of LPFM. In particular, McCain feared the loss of free speech stemming from consolidation. When the popular country group Dixie Chicks spoke out against President George W. Bush during their 2003 tour, several large radio owners (most notably Cumulus, along with many Clear Channel stations) barred them from the air. "While McCain was offended by the statement from the Dixie Chicks, he said 'to restrain their trade because they exercised their right to free speech to me is remarkable . . . and it's a strong argument about what media concentration has the ability to do.'"[29]

Not surprisingly, the new giant radio group owners responded that station consolidation was not comprising programming diversity and free speech but actually increasing both. Lowry Mays, the chairman/CEO of Clear Channel Communications, held that "consolidation has, on the contrary, provided for more diversity and programming. . . . There is absolutely no question whatsoever that there is a significant amount of diversity that did not exist prior to consolidation. . . . All you have to do is go and look at the markets and look at the formats [then] and look at the formats today."[30] In 1998 Jacor Corporation CEO Randy Michaels also defended the consolidation movement, arguing that it had spurred development of more formats: "What we have for the very first time is the opportunity to think about our business the way any other retailer would think about their business, and that's regionally."[31] Jacor was soon acquired by Clear Channel and Michaels was shown the door, despite having been a staunch proconsolidation spokesman.

The common view in both the general and trade press was that radio ownership consolidation was having—or soon would have—a pejorative impact on its program diversity and localism. Decline of the former had become a boon to satellite-distributed national channels, which, in turn, fostered concern about the state of the latter. Editorials and op-ed pieces derided the gobbling up of radio stations by media conglomerates and saw a dark future for homegrown, indigenous broadcasts. For example, columnist Marc Fisher wrote in the *Washington Post* that "what's already clear is that the listener is the loser. . . . Not only is the number of people who turn on their radios in decline, but in city after city, listeners are fighting the loss of creative programming."[32] Research in academic journals confirmed these sentiments, one study concluding, "When it was found that more than 50 percent of all U.S. listeners who tune to a specific music format were reached by four radio station groups, a nationwide format oligopoly was documented."[33] Yet another examination of the effects of consolidation on program diversity confirmed

> the assumption that there have been negative effects of ownership concentration. . . . The findings in this study showed the relationship between the loss of competition within a radio market and the loss of audience choice in terms of the number of different formats, and in some cases, the number of different types of songs played within that market. The results confirmed that markets with more competition played a wider variety of radio formats and provided a larger selection of gold unique titles than markets operating in more concentrated markets.[34]

As the number of FM stations grew by 20 percent between 1996 and 2004, the splintering of their music formats continued apace. For example CHR morphed into several variants, including CHR pop (focusing on current chart toppers), CHR '80s (playing hits of that decade), and CHR dance (airing more urban rhythms). Ratings company Arbitron was by now monitoring the machinations and permutations of nearly fifty recognized formats on both AM and FM stations. Adult contemporary and its multiple subgenres led audience ratings through this decade—though home listening declined 4 percent between 1998 and 2002,[35] and the number of young adults (age eighteen to twenty-four) tuning in dropped 8 percent between 1996 and 2004.[36]

The variation in FM's music formats continued after 1996 and came to include AC (and its manifold variations of hot, lite, adult, smooth, alternative, urban, mix, and spectrum—all slightly adjusting their music, and avoiding harder rock, to appeal to listeners aged twenty-four to thirty-nine); CR (album-rock hits of the 1970s and 1980s); country (in all its incarnations, such as "hot," with faster pop country hits; "lite," the easy-listening version; and "traditional" country, with its down-home sound of bluegrass and other forms of American rural music); Latin (both traditional and the faster contemporary vein); smooth jazz (featuring artists like Winton Marsalis, Kenny D, Harry Connick Jr., and George Shearing); alternative (with such variations as Triple-A, which embraced a hybrid of rock, folk, and jazz appealing to adults); Christian (again, with several variations, including contemporary/modern Christian—featuring current pop melodies with a life-affirming message—and "adult" Christian, offering its own version of mainstream adult contemporary, though with the same affirming message); and modern rock (emphasizing edgier, harder sounds from contemporary-music charts).

Trends in many other urban markets showed FM shifting from rock, country, and other once mainline music to Hispanic and black-appeal formats, whose listeners spent far more time with broadcast radio than did white audiences. In 2005 longtime Washington, D.C., rock station WHFS converted to WLZL (El Zol) and Hispanic music—and saw its audience double. A year later, Los Angeles's only remaining country station, KZLA-FM, dropped its format in favor of rhythmic pop featuring popular dance and rhythm-and-blues sounds. Many saw this as a sign of the continuing bottom-line orientation of corporate radio as well as the changing demographics of the nation's second-largest city. New York City lacked a single country station. These missing formats in the country's two largest markets helped feed a competing service: more than a dozen rock or country channels were started on each of the country's two satellite-radio networks (which we describe in more detail later).[37]

Some new (if only in name) FM music formats did emerge in the mid-2000s. Some had peculiar- and eclectic-sounding monikers that inspired both curiosity and a cynical smile. Among them were "Bob" (a rock-pop music hybrid), "chill" (soft and soothing electronica), "red" (both new and older adult standards), and "Jack," a kind of AC/AOR hybrid:

Jack mixes up a lot of '80s music—some classic rock, a slew of one-hit wonders, a few oldies, a touch of Top 40 and a tiny bit of rap. It has surgically removed everything that is annoying about radio. In most markets Jack is just music—no weather, no traffic, no song IDs—and is completely automated, so there aren't even any wrongheaded DJs to endure. At 1,200 songs, the playlists are three times bigger than average, so it doesn't grate with repetitiveness and the commercial breaks are noticeably shorter.[38]

Jack first appeared in Vancouver in 2002 then moved to several other Canadian stations before spreading to American outlets, sometimes dubbed as "variety hits." Some critics argued this kind of "less-old" oldies format was the biggest thing since Morning Zoo formats of the early 1980s. The format was created for Internet use by Bob Perry, a former DJ and station manager.[39] One sign of changing times was the conversion of an oldies format mainstay, WCBS-FM in New York, to the iPod-inspired Jack format. A casualty of this change was legendary DJ Bruce "Cousin Brucie" Murrow, who was out after decades of spinning the "moldy-oldies." Observed Peter Fox in the *New York Times*, "Slowly but surely all the great radio behemoths who have strode the landscape have been felled. [Morrow] is from an era in which you created a character and played that character on the air."[40]

One longtime FM program staple—classical music—continued to fade. By 2007 there were perhaps two dozen surviving commercial classical stations, half of those on the air a decade earlier. The format was dwindling on public radio as well, as news and public-affairs talk programs were increased. Boston's WCRB (Classical Radio Boston), for example, had to abandon its long-held frequency (102.5) when it was purchased by a company intent on offering country. Ultimately, it moved to a lower channel (99.5) with a somewhat diminished signal. The passing of each of these long-lived FM outlets made noise in the press and led to outcries from their small but very loyal audiences.[41]

Sports and other talk formats on FM radio grew more important. One trade magazine proclaimed that "talk on FM is the most profitable format in radio"[42] and that its increase was "being sparked by the need to respond to the questionable future of music programming in the face of satellite radio and several other technological advances that give the music consumer additional clout and less dependency on the tastes and timidity of playlists controlled by bean counters and consultants."[43] There were increasing signs that some FMs were dropping music in the face of growing competition from digital services. Noted one observer: "The next logical step for spoken word radio is over to the FM band. . . . According to industry spokesman Jack Swanson, talk and sports are going to FM. Music is going to iPod, PDAs, websites, and WiFi, and religious and foreign [formats] are going to AM."[44] By the mid-2000s, there were already many successful FM talk stations in various markets around the country, including Boston, Chicago, Seattle, Nashville, and Dallas. After Howard Stern departed his New York station at the end of 2005 for satellite radio, the station converted to an all-talk format.[45]

The future of liberal talk radio, if there is one, may be on FM. That such talk was on the move was evidenced by the rollout of Air America in 2004, which, although off to a very shaky start, gained momentum a year later as its number of mostly AM affiliates rose. By early 2005 the liberal radio network had arrived in Washington, D.C., and expanded its reach to forty-five markets.[46] In 2006, however, Air America was forced to declare bankruptcy. Reorganization was soon underway, and in May 2007 the troubled network was relaunched under new ownership.

Further specialization attracted more FM listeners in the 2000s. New talk formats "including financial, health, home improvement, relationships, computer, travel, ethnic, religious and others . . . have made significant strides."[47] Despite the exodus of some talk-radio figures to satellite radio, media experts believe that the information format remains terrestrial radio's best bet. Radio consultant Holland Cooke argues that "news/talk/ sports is radio's last bastion. . . . The traffic tangle up ahead, the quickly changing weather forecast, the Red Sox game, and other content too perishable to store, will continue to compel users to exit new-tech for AM/FM radio."[48]

While talk increased, traditional radio news continued the retreat begun in the early 1990s. Many stations dropped news entirely, noting that one or more other outlets in the same market already provided newscasts. Trying a different approach, Clear Channel stations in Madison and Milwaukee, Wisconsin, both sold "naming rights" for their news departments to commercial sponsors. News over WIBA (AM and FM) in Madison, for example, as of early 2006 was being touted as coming from the "Amcore Bank News Center." The potential ethical issues this raised (at the very least suggesting to listeners than the bank in question might have some say in which news was broadcast) were widely debated as news of the naming spread.

Talk was a growing trend on public radio as well. Indeed, a handful of public radio stations showed impressive large-market ratings with their news and talk formats. For example, KQED in San Francisco achieved a 5.7 share in mid-2005, while WUNC reached 7.1 in Raleigh, North Carolina.[49] Audiences for NPR's news and talk features continued to grow. As radio reporter Tom Taylor noted, "Radio's most-listened-to morning show isn't Howard Stern—but *Morning Edition*. In fact, NPR's *Morning Edition* is second only to Rush Limbaugh among all radio shows."[50] In some cases, however, such shifts to talk did not bode well for public stations. Washington's WETA-FM lost listeners and donations in the first nine months after a 2004 shift from primarily classical music to all news and talk.[51] Classics lovers were angry and made their views known. In 2007, as part of a complex deal involving two other stations in the market, WETA-FM returned to full-time classical music. National audience research shows that news and talk stations usually do better in fund-raising than the classical-music outlets—perhaps because people have to pay attention to talk and can use music as a background to other activities.

The number of commercial FM stations programming in a foreign language, either part- or full-time, also increased in the early 2000s, reflecting increased immigration in major markets. Spanish-language stations led in this category and, in fact, were rated number one in several cities. Indeed, as the nation's Hispanic population grew into the largest minority early in the new century, so did the number of stations programming Hispanic music and talk. The first Hispanic station to achieve a number-one ranking among the largest markets was KLVE in Los Angeles, which reached that point in 1995 and grew even bigger in the months to follow.[52] Among the most popular radio stations in New York City by the early 2000s were no less than four FM outlets programming exclusively to a Hispanic audience. No other FM format, with the exception of sports talk, showed as much growth potential as did Hispanic music and talk.

INDIGNANT OVER INDECENCY

Though complaints and a few high FCC fines had arisen earlier, several radio talk-show hosts raised questions about whether their use of indecent words should be controlled or punished. Most attention focused on television, reaching a peak when a soon-notorious halftime program during the Super Bowl football game of February 1, 2004, featured an apparently unintended split second of partial female nudity.[53] The resulting political firestorm focused attention on both radio and television as legislators seeking reelection raced to make clear that such programming was not proper for American homes. By 2006 Congress had raised the FCC limit on fines for licensee transgressions to $325,000 for each proven violation. Fines at that level threatened the very viability of smaller stations.

Radio's perpetual bad boy in this regard was, of course, New York–based Howard Stern. Hugely popular with both young male and female listeners and thus attracting millions in advertising revenue, Stern had been pushing the envelope of acceptable program content for more than twenty years. Stern's show cost Infinity Broadcasting the highest fines ever imposed by the FCC for indecency ($2.5 million) but also garnered the largest audiences for programs cited by the FCC as indecent. Of added concern to many was that his program aired in morning hours, when children might be listening. Finally exasperated by the constraints of broadcasting and seemingly beleaguered by persistent claims of indecency against his program (though he also reveled in the attention), Stern shifted his program to satellite radio early in 2006, extolling his greater freedom of expression.[54] Over the next few months, research showed that he took about 1.5 million, or 12 percent, of his terrestrial listeners with him as new satellite subscribers.[55]

Stern left in his wake a gaggle of others who had been emulating his on-air antics for years. They inspired 280 formal complaints to the FCC in 2001, which rose the next year to forty per month.[56] New York's outrageous duo known as Opie (Gregg Hughes) & Anthony (Cumia), also programmed by Infinity, were dropped from WNEW's afternoon-drive program and the nearly twenty other stations that syndicated their program after what they said was a live broadcast of a couple having sex in St. Patrick's Cathedral in August 2002.[57] However, the "schlock" pair (as Stern, no fan of his competitors, derisively referred to them) would soon develop a well-paying channel on XM Satellite Radio. They were suspended from that in 2007 for making egregious sexual comments regarding Secretary of State Condoleezza Rice. Ironically, Opie & Anthony were allowed to continue with the terrestrial version of their show because their inflammatory comments had been made on satellite radio—a medium quick to promote its ability to accord performers full freedom of speech. Shortly before that, Don Imus had been fired for a racial/sexist slur on his widely heard New York morning show, seemingly ending his more than three decades on radio. (Just nine months later, however, another New York outlet put him back on the air.) No less infamous for his off-color behavior on the many FM outlets that carried his broadcasts was Todd Alan Clem, star of the syndicated *Bubba the*

Love Sponge program. It was ousted in Florida for airing a skit in which "cartoon characters discuss sexual activities . . . meant to pander to listeners." The FCC proposed a fine of $755,000.[58]

The indecency crusade, heavily pushed by conservative religious and family-values groups, seemed likely to continue and strengthen. Several members of Congress stoked the fire with bills to limit indecent programming on cable and other pay services—including satellite radio—despite dubious legal grounds.[59] Congress and the FCC may fulminate and issue laws and mandate agency rules, but federal courts (and probably the Supreme Court) will have the final word. More insulated from daily political pressures, high-court decisions are often more mainstream than overheated cultural debates in the political sphere.

STILL MORE STATIONS

Despite growing complaints that stations sounded too much alike and competition from other options (which we will discuss later), new FM stations continued to go on the air. By early 2007 more than 6,266 commercial and 2,817 educational FM outlets were broadcasting (not counting more than 770 low-power FM outlets). Combined, FM stations outnumbered AM stations by nearly two to one.[60] Indeed, facing an ever-tighter competitive market, the number of AM stations continued to slowly decline.[61]

Under pressure from would-be FM applicants, not to mention congressional interest in developing additional revenue to offset regulatory expenditures, the FCC initiated its first open auction of available FM channels.[62] Over three weeks (and sixty-two bidding rounds) in November 2004, 110 bidders eventually won nearly 260 FM-station construction permits with bids totaling $147.4 million. Winning bidders were given three years to complete construction but had to pay their bid in full before receiving the construction permit. Virtually all the new stations were located in small markets.[63] Noncommercial FM applicants, held up by an FCC freeze imposed in 2000 (and including some applications dating back to the early 1990s), continued to accumulate until the commission developed a comparative point system (rather than an auction, as for commercial stations) to choose the best applicants and began to issue construction permits in 2007.[64] Based on this clear and continuing demand for FM outlets, the commission projected holding more commercial auctions and noncommercial point-system comparisons to come. But one FM marketplace faced a very different future.

Pressured by micro-radio advocates (as we described in chapter 6) and facing three 1998 petitions proposing the creation of small FM stations, the FCC on January 28, 1999, announced its intent to create three new categories of LPFM outlets. These could broadcast with up to 1,000 watts, depending on local conditions (the more typical 100 watts of power would provide a usual range of about 3.5 miles). The commission hoped to parallel the model established two decades earlier for low-power television outlets, more than 2,200 of which were licensed by 2007. Left up in the air at first was whether or not these proposed LPFM stations could be commercial or were required to be noncommercial. The FCC cited 13,000 inquiries it had received from individuals and groups interested in operating such stations.[65] Among these was the city of Atlanta, which wanted to broadcast traffic and weather reports as well as city council meetings; several Native American groups that otherwise lacked local programming; a group of independent musicians; and more than a few religious groups.[66]

But in another example of the industry creating strange bedfellows, commercial *and* public radio groups quickly agreed to argue against the FCC proposal, expressing concern about an increasingly congested FM band and thus rising interference. There was more than an element of "I've got mine, Jack," involved here, with established stations, commercial and noncommercial alike, seeking to quash new entrants with research showing how much interference would result under the FCC plan. What they were actually most concerned about, of course, was more radio signals competing for and thus dividing up their audiences. Reaching new heights of hyperbole, the NAB called the LPFM threat "the most serious issue to face the radio industry in thirty years."[67] Citing its own engineering research, which had found little or no interference from experimental low-power transmitters, a year later the commission adopted its plan and authorized operation of noncommercial micro stations.[68] The decision included a limited amnesty for those who had already been engaging in unlicensed (pirate) operation.[69]

Though the FCC decision seemed final, the battle was only warming up. The commission received opposition from would-be LPFM licensees who felt the decision favored such establishment organizations as churches, social-service agencies, schools, civic groups, and labor unions. Far more damaging to the prospects for LPFM, however, was continued strong opposition to the whole idea by existing FM broadcasters, who now took their case to Congress.[70] After President Clinton threatened to veto a free-standing bill severely limiting LPFM by creating extensive protections for existing station coverage areas (and rather provocatively called the "Broadcasting Preservation Act of 2000"), Congress added the provisions as a rider to an omnibus budget authorization for 2000, which the president did sign. This had the effect of tightly limiting LPFM before it could even begin; the law even went a step further and rescinded the amnesty for unlicensed operators. The radio establishment had succeeded in shutting off most LPFM competition in cities and towns, leaving only some rural and suburban options.

Suggesting the great interest in even the severely restricted service allowed, however, by late 2002 nearly 2,000 LPFM applications had been filed (many by religious organizations), though few stations had been authorized. The FCC conducted additional interference research, demonstrating conclusively (as it said in a report to Congress) that the congressionally imposed restrictions on LPFM (actually prepared by the broadcast lobby) were unnecessary.[71] Pending a congressional change of mind about restricting LPFM, however, the FCC made clear the very limited opportunities: "LPFM stations are available to noncommercial educational entities and public safety and transportation organizations, *but are not available to individuals* or for commercial operations. Current broadcast licensees with interests in other media . . . are not eligible to obtain LPFM stations."[72] Further, no licensee could control more than one LPFM station.

Perhaps to avoid continuing criticism, the commission for some time did not publicize on its website the number of LPFM authorizations that had been allowed despite these restrictions. By May 2004, however, more than 600 construction permits had been issued and some 275 LPFMs were on the air.[73] Those numbers doubled in the next year,[74] reaching 770 on air by early 2007. Most were issued to religious outlets, with community groups coming in second and educational or municipal stations trailing behind.[75]

What long-term impact LPFMs would have on the future of FM generally remained uncertain. One activist suggested, "By granting LPFM licenses to local nonprofit community groups the FCC has assured communities that radio will maintain a local presence [but] . . . funding for LPFM is limited by its nonprofit status."[76] On the other hand, the NAB restated its concern about LPFMs interfering with long-established primary-service

FM radio.[77] Given the policy standoff, LPFM increasingly appeared to be a small-potatoes issue for broadcasters facing substantially more important competition elsewhere.

Facing the policy deadlock in Washington, some tiny operations took things into their own hands, as they had earlier. "Radio Free Allston" made waves as the pirate Boston station appealed for listeners and support. It first appeared as a 20-watt, unlicensed station on 106.1 MHZ in February 1997, operating from 5:00 P.M. to 1:00 A.M. on weekdays until it was closed down by the FCC in November after another station complained about interference. Its programs were eclectic to say the least, ranging from coverage of the local city council to music, political discussions of all kinds, and even programs in foreign languages.[78] The operation reappeared as a tiny (less than a single watt, and thus not subject to FCC oversight or concern) AM-based "Allston-Brighton Free Radio" three years later, with much the same community-based program idea.[79] While it also created an Internet presence, both had died by the early 2000s for lack of funding support.[80]

DIGITAL DEMISE?

While radio listeners have long had multiple "sound casting" options from which to choose, by the 1980s technological developments suggested they would soon have more. A growing variety of digital technologies promised an expanding menu of options to entice listeners. Providing vastly improved sound and better listener control, these systems will eventually replace analog AM and FM broadcasting (although those traditional designations may survive for some time). It is only a matter of time. As *Business Week* put it while assessing radio's status: "The digital revolution took its time getting to radio. Now it's exploding. . . . As radio shows are turned into digital bits, they're being delivered many different ways, from Web to satellite to cell phones. Listeners no longer have to tune in at a certain time, and within range of a signal, to catch a show or a game. As the business goes digital, the barriers to entry—including precious airwaves—count for less and less."[81] Put another way, radio now has to compete in a world where listeners control when (and to what) they listen. This situation has been coming for some time.

Early signs of FM audience erosion became apparent in the mid-1990s, when new digital audio options began to attract music fans, especially younger ones. Several studies made clear that listeners were making less use of broadcast radio; Arbitron ratings data suggested a 14 percent drop in radio audiences in the decade after 1994.[82] Arbitron also reported a 2.5-hour-per-week decline in the overall time spent listening to radio between 1997 and 2004, again most noticeable among the twelve-to-twenty-four age bracket.[83] While many factors contributed to the decline, more listening options was chief among them, though some were more than two decades old.

Power to the People

With the late 1990s' appearance of multi-CD players and then CD-jukeboxes that could hold 200 to 300 discs, the compact disc began to impact radio audience numbers. People could play what they wanted and when merely by pushing a few buttons—and they did not have to listen to advertisements. Availability of portable CD players greatly increased the CD threat to radio. Demonstrating the continuing morphing that so characterizes digital technology, in early 2005 Sony announced a combination Walkman–cell phone that would allow users to download selections from their home CD collections onto their mobile telephone.[84] Clearly, sound quality was not a major issue! Indeed, "the convergence of wireless technology, content and size make the cell phone the perfect host for taking your favorite sounds to the beach, a doctor's waiting room, or a park near your home. Many higher-end cell phones have already incorporated the ability to receive FM signals. This ability will continue to increase as new generations of low-end phones offer more options."[85]

Among consumer audio choices, the emergence of music downloading around the turn of the century represented the biggest competitive threat to radio (and record stores). The exodus of radio-music listeners, especially the under-thirty audience, was predicted to continue. While digital MP3 players already were on the market, Apple Computer's introduction of its iPod device in late 2001 really pushed the technology. This tiny, lightweight digital-music storage device redefined portability and ease of operation. Nearly 4 million were sold in 2004 alone—and 6.2 million more were sold in the second quarter of 2005.[86] In 2006, when satellite carriers introduced iPod-like devices that allowed downloading off the air, the threat to terrestrial radio became stronger.

Orbital Signals

As with digital recording, digital satellites developed over many years. It has long been known that the higher the transmitting antenna, the greater the signal area that any station can cover. And of course, transmitting from hundreds of miles above the earth is better than transmitting from a tower, no matter how tall it may be. A transmitter orbiting the earth had tremendous potential, as was demonstrated with the scratchy analog signals sent back to earth from the first artificial satellites in the late 1950s. International radio broadcasters during the Cold War dreamed of (or feared) propaganda signals beamed down from space. Development of geostationary orbit satellites (the GSO is some 22,300 miles above the earth and beams uninterrupted signals, unlike satellites in lower orbits whose transmissions are blocked when they are on the opposite side of earth) increased the stakes by allowing one satellite to cover a third of the world.

The origin of modern (direct-to-home) satellite-radio broadcasting dates to 1990 when, in response to a petition, the FCC initiated a proceeding to develop a policy for a GSO-based digital-radio service. In 1992 an allocation in the 2.3-GHz range was defined for what was dubbed the satellite digital audio radio service (DARS). An industry advisory committee began to develop DARS technical standards.[87] In 1997 the commission approved the new service and established basic rules. While the FCC did examine the possible impact of this new service on existing AM and FM stations, it decided that the subscription basis of any national DARS service, plus the need for special listening equipment, would provide only limited competition.[88]

A 1997 FCC auction led to the awarding of licenses to Satellite CD Radio (which would soon become Sirius) and American Mobile Radio Corporation (later renamed XM). XM's two Hughes-designed satellites (dubbed "Rock" and "Roll") were launched into the GSO in 2000. Sirius ordered three satellites and launched them into lower orbits so that two were always in position to broadcast across the nation. XM built more than eighty studios in its Washington, D.C., headquarters—a renovated nineteenth-century printing plant—to house its initial offering of more than 100 channels (seventy music and thirty talk). It aired first in the Dallas and San Diego markets, though it unwittingly selected an inauspicious day to launch— September 12, 2001, the day after the 9/11 terror attacks on New York and Washington. XM delayed its rollout by two weeks, and full national service came by November. After numerous delays, Sirius finally launched its competitive service early in 2002.

Throughout this whole process, broadcasters continued to file strong objections with the FCC, trying to stop, or at least hamstring, the potential new competitors. They filed petitions to delay DARS, but they faced the precedent of existing television direct broadcast satellite (DBS) service, on which the FCC had based its DARS decisions. Broadcasters then focused on the many terrestrial repeater antennas that both DARS services would require to produce clear signals in urban areas, claiming this was terrestrial, not satellite broadcasting, and thus a violation of at least the principle of DARS. During this legal skirmishing with terrestrial broadcasters, both satellite services conducted a constant quest for cash to continue operating while growing their subscribing audiences.

Somewhat ironically, XM's program chief was Lee Abrams, who had pioneered the AOR format on FM in the early 1970s and consulted for hundreds of broadcast stations. In doing so, he "designed numerous other highly successful radio formats, including the first Classic Rock format at San Francisco's KFOG, the first Urban/Dance format at New York's WKTU, and the first New Age/Jazz format."[89] These initiatives helped do in commercial FM underground radio and transform it to mainstream album rock. He was also a key contributor to the "overly scientific approach" to the radio-programming process, which helped foster the bland FM sound that critics decried.

XM and Sirius, each programming well over 150 channels (music services were commercial free), provided much of the variety terrestrial radio lacked.[90] Adding significantly to satellite radio's appeal was their showcasing of high-profile music celebrities such as Sting, Quincy Jones, and Ted Nugent, who were given their own channels. Migration of some of terrestrial radio's foremost personalities, among them former NPR *Morning Edition* host Bob Edwards and the controversial DJ duo Opie & Anthony (both to XM), added to that appeal. The well-publicized 2006 jump to Sirius by Howard Stern helped raise public awareness about (and controversy over) the satellite services since Stern promised to bring his millions of FM listeners with him. Television talk-show host Oprah Winfrey signed to develop a talk channel for XM.

Countless articles explored the threat that satellite services posed to terrestrial radio, whose stock and station prices were already in decline. Yet the satellite services faced their own problems. By 2006 *Radio Ink*, a daily trade newsletter, was suggesting that satellite services had been overly touted. Evidence suggested that their rate of growth was slowing down (and might impinge radio less than 5 percent) and that profits were farther away than had been expected.[91] Given their financial state, rumors were rife of a possible merger between the two satellite-radio companies. Sirius chief Mel Karmazin turned rumors into fact with an offer to merge with xm in 2007. Chances for the required regulatory approval appeared dim in mid-2007 but improved later thanks to widespread endorsements.

To enhance their appeal, xm and Sirius offered receivers for use beyond the car and home. Available to subscribers by 2005 were the first tiny (about the size of an iPod) portable satellite radios—xm's "Myfi" and Sirius's "Plug & Play." More car manufacturers offered built-in satellite radio (adding another concern for broadcasters, whose biggest audiences are in drive time). By mid-2007 xm and Sirius shared some 15 million subscribers, and perhaps overly optimistic projections suggested satellite-radio subscriptions might reach 20 million by 2010. Although even that figure would be only a small percentage of the estimated 250 million terrestrial-radio listeners, satellite-service competition continued to concern traditional broadcasters.

On the Web

Yet another option—this one serving both existing stations and their competition—appeared in cyberspace. The creation of the "Real Audio Player" software by Progressive Networks in 1995 allowed computer users with Internet access to upload and play audio clips. Soon, other firms announced their own Web audio programs, though many faded with the dot-com crash of 2000–2003. Web-based radio services were one result, allowing listener access from anywhere in the world.[92] Web audio operations are of two types: those that "stream" existing am and fm broadcast signals, and those that provide original content, dubbed "Web-only" stations or "webcasters." The first full-time Web-only station appeared in February 1995 when Radio hk began broadcasting recordings of independent bands. It was created by an advertising agency in Marina del Rey, California.[93] klif in Dallas became the first station to stream its signal. Broadcasters had mixed feelings about these Web operations, considering them at once a form of competition and yet also a means for expanding their own audiences while promoting their stations. The competition arose because Web stations (either Web-only or from distant stations) eroded local audiences as they increased the number of listening options.

By early 2000 some 4 million people (about the size of the Philadelphia radio market) were tuning into Web stations over a given week.[94] Nearly 3,000 broadcast stations were streaming their audio signal, 100 more were adding Web service every month, and nearly 250 Web-only operations were available to Internet users. A few broadcasters were adding things not heard on the air. And listeners gained options to listen to radio services from other nations as well. Some 8,000 U.S. stations used the Web merely for online promotion rather than programming.[95] Such information typically included details about upcoming station events, biographies of on-air personalities, and how to reach the station with requests (though few made it possible to easily comment on the music played). Surveys showed that listeners were seeking program streaming rather than mere promotion.[96]

The bright future of Web-radio expansion began to darken, however, when owners and performers of music sought compensation for the use of their music by various digital media. ASCAP, BMI, and SESAC argued that additional revenue was due their writer and composer members to supplement what they already earned from traditional radio and other sources.[97] Working with the Recording Industry Association of America (RIAA), they successfully promoted a series of laws that extended copyright payments to various digital means of providing or storing music.

The Digital Performance Right in Sound Recordings Act of 1995 began the process,[98] and among its provisions was the creation of a new compulsory license for particular types of noninteractive, digital-subscription transmissions. Three years later, the Digital Millennium Copyright Act (DMCA) of 1998 became, to many webcasters at least, the killer.[99] Though little noticed at the time, the DMCA called for a study of how webcasting broadcasters should pay for the rights to use music. After the various parties could not agree on the issues, the librarian of Congress, James H. Billington, established a panel in 2001 to sort out the complexities, and it reported its recommendations in February 2002. Four months later, Billington turned down their projected fees and established rates about half as high (though even these were, as the law required, retroactive to the October 28, 1998, date of the DMCA's passage), which the Copyright Office then included in its regulations in July 2002.[100]

Predictably, representatives of the music business said the new fees were too low, while webcasters called them distressingly high. Many nonprofit webcasters faced the end of their service or potential financial ruin. Critics claimed the whole copyright mess was going to terminate the diversity that webcasting had only begun to provide. As a result, and at the request of many smaller webcasters, Congress stepped in with the Small Webcaster

Settlement Act of 2002,[101] which delayed initial payments for small private and noncommercial operations that many felt had not been properly included in all the previous negotiations. These annual payments of music royalties for webcasters were scheduled to be adjusted for 2006–10.

As the regulatory dust settled, fears that webcasting would all but disappear because of onerous payments proved overwrought, and most signals remained available. The smallest Web-only services paid as little as $500 a year for their music, while larger commercial webcasters paid according to a complex formula of the number of songs used per hour and the number of listeners served. By the end of 2004, "Arbitron led the way back to Internet streaming by announcing that it would again measure audiences for radio websites."[102] By that point, some 19 million were tuning online radio at least once a week—up from just 7 million four years earlier.[103] Reported the *Boston Globe* in early 2005, "The Internet radio audience is growing, and likely to get bigger as more Americans get high-speed Internet connections. . . . The immense variety of offerings is [the] main benefit of Internet radio . . . and it can only get better as more of America's 200 million Internet users tune in."[104]

In 2007, however, the boom dropped yet again when the Copyright Royalty Board recommended that Web stations pay a fee *each time each listener* heard a song. The implications were massive, for by mid-2007, some 14,000 webcasters (as many as traditional radio stations) served some 34 million listeners.[105] The implications of this were seen by many as cataclysmic. "The decision . . . could raise royalty rates paid by some online radio stations more than tenfold—enough to put many smaller stations out of business."[106] Opposition against the ruling caused a firestorm among webcasters and broadcasters alike, many of whom streamed audio on their own station websites. But the board stood its ground, and Congress seemed unlikely to act. On June 26, 2007, many webcasters went silent for a day to try and demonstrate the likely result of the Copyright Royalty Board decision. The action stirred many news stories but no change in the outlook. Starting in mid-July 2007, when the decision took force, thousands of webcasters began to close down, unable to pay the required fees due to their very limited revenues. How this will play out in the longer term remained to be seen. Meanwhile, in late 2007 the RIAA launched a crusade to require traditional broadcasters to pay a performance fee for music they play. As expected, opposition from radio operators was substantial, a bill was introduced in Congress to ban the charge, and as this book went press, the issue appeared far from resolved.

A good example of the sort of additional service that Web radio made possible—and that was closed down by the copyright decision—was "Radioparadise," originating, perhaps not surprisingly, from central California. The brainchild of Bill Goldsmith and based in part on his three decades of FM radio experience, Radioparadise offered a free Web-only radio service featuring an idiosyncratic mixture of music (Beatles to Nora Jones to the Strokes). While only 5,000 people tuned in, they contributed some $120,000 to keep the service (and the Goldsmiths) afloat, save for the new copyright fee payments.[107] Despite all the upheaval, the *New York Times* reported in September 2007, "About 55 million Americans listen to Internet radio every week (compared with the 279 million who listen to terrestrial radio), a jump of 26 percent in the past year, according to Bridge Ratings, a survey firm in Glendale, California."[108]

Wireless broadband technology allows every kind of audio extant on the Internet and other public data networks. Indeed, by the mid-2000s it was showing potential to be one of the most disruptive forces in communication. Wireless broadband is a high-speed way to access the Internet and other data services. It makes it possible for end users (listeners) to upload a veritable cornucopia of audio options—Web streams, cable systems, satellite signals—and what are called "podcasts."

Podcasting simply refers to independently produced online radio. It allows iPod or other MP3 users to download prerecorded radio shows from the Internet. This new audio technology promises everyone a chance to operate their own radio station, a prospect that does not exactly warm the hearts of traditional over-the-air broadcasters. Indeed, adoption of the new idea seemed impressive by 2005, and broadcasters were right to fear how far it might expand. Because anybody can create a podcast with a computer, receiving software (aggregator), and an MP3 player, the medium was dubbed "homemade radio," and it steadily gained a following around the globe. Indeed, no Web-based audio innovation has caught on as quickly as podcasting. An Internet search for the term returned fewer than 100 results in September 2004, but within a few months the number had grown to more than a million. Quick to exploit the newest digital device, conventional radio jumped aboard the podcasting bandwagon. Clear Channel and CBS Radio began featuring podcasts on their member stations in 2005.

While it is too early to predict the eventual impact podcasting might have on conventional radio, many saw it as yet another sharp thorn in the medium's side. Some observers compared podcasts and radio to blogs and print journalism. In both cases, the huge reduction in the costs of communicating placed the ability to operate in the hands of anyone interested. By 2006 hundreds (probably thousands) of podcasters were making a wide range of programs available, and some suggested that existing broadcast programs like *All Things Considered* and *Rush Limbaugh* might become available before long.

One good indication of podcasting's potential viability as a popular audio medium was ASCAP's decision in late 2004 to establish podcast music license agreements at $250 a year. (Whether this will change in light of the later and larger copyright decision described above was not clear in mid-2007.) The posting of prerecorded podcasts (essentially programs) on the Internet for worldwide access creates yet another challenge for FM broadcasters in competing for listeners. A strong indication of podcasting's place in the current audio landscape is its swift acceptance by the public.

TERRESTRIAL RADIO FIGHTS BACK

Facing these challenges, radio responded by substantially revising its approach. Quoting an industry newsletter, the *Washington Post* viewed the rollout of various changes as a result of increasing audio competition: "Radio, losing a generation of listeners to music downloading and facing threats from satellite and internet radio, is finally starting to fight back. The nation's biggest radio companies are responding to a grousing and mercurial audience by cutting the number of commercials per hour, expanding the range of music played on the air and experimenting with new formats."[109] Making clear that much of the problem was radio's "lost youth," critic Andrew Keen bemoaned the impact of the Web: "Radio is in the midst of its own identity crisis. Teenagers, historically radio's biggest and most devoted audience, simply aren't listening to radio anymore. Over the last ten years, the listening hours of eighteen- to twenty-four-year olds have dropped 21 percent."[110] Added *Radio and Records* editor Roger Nadel, "We have to adapt. . . . The radio business may be undergoing it biggest shakeup ever. So many new technologies are beckoning to its traditional listeners and it's hard to know what radio is anymore."[111] Worried by the growing popularity of their competitors, one of the publicity campaign slogans used by broadcasters to discourage listeners from tuning to satellite radio has been "The Best Radio is Free." (Satellite-radio users must buy special receivers and pay a monthly subscriber's fee of about $13 monthly for each service, with discounts for multiyear contracts.) Broadcasters cautioned that just as cable-TV fees have jumped dramatically over the years, so will charges for satellite radio.

Doing more than merely complaining about its new competitors or taking legal action, radio began to adopt some of the same digital technology. HD radio service is one part of the industry's future—as demonstrated by the planned digital conversion of 95 percent of Clear Channel's hundreds of stations by 2010. A company official praised its CD-quality sound and ability to deliver complementary data and audio services.[112] HD operators must consider the FM lesson of the 1940s and 1950s, however. Without new and different program content, better sound alone will not appeal to consumers. As one observer noted late in 2006, "Alas, HD radio—at least as it exists today—is largely the same vast wasteland as conventional radio, with stations offering short playlists of music in a few repetitive formats."[113] Further, whether radio digitization will help rebuild radio's popularity remains to be seen, for other digital options continue to erode radio listening.

HD—or digital audio broadcasting (DAB), as it was long known—had been discussed for some time when the FCC, prompted by the broadcast and manufacturing industries, initiated in 1990 an inquiry into its potential implementation. At the same time the Eureka-147 digital-radio system, developed, manufactured, and adopted in Europe, was demonstrated in Canada. This system employed the L-band (390 MHz to 1.55 GHz) but was not adopted in the United States because of the many other services already using those frequencies. While much of the world appears convinced that L-band offers the best DAB or HD spectrum, the FCC is not because of the difficulty in shifting those existing users.[114]

In 2002 the FCC adopted the industry's proposed "in-band, on-channel" (IBOC) system for offering digital HD radio on existing AM and FM broadcast channels. IBOC was developed primarily by engineer Glynn Walden at iBiquity Digital Corporation in the early 1990s. The commission declared IBOC best for enhanced sound fidelity, improved reception, and provision of possible new data services (such as station, song, and artist identification or stock and news information).[115] The technology allows broadcasters to use their existing channels to transmit AM and FM analog signals simultaneously with new higher quality digital signals, while preventing mutual interference.

By mid-2007, more than 1,300 radio stations offered HD radio. HD receivers were becoming more available and affordable, and most large radio groups were actively converting their outlets to HD operation.[116] The Corporation for Public Broadcasting announced a continuing series of grants (approaching 500 by 2007) to help public radio stations convert to HD as well. A significant potential of HD radio, one that might persuade broadcasters of its potential to provide parity with satellite and Internet radio (see below), is its capacity to carry multiple programs per channel. Once stations have turned off their analog signals (there was as yet no deadline set at the time this book went to press), they will have several additional paths with which to transmit digital audio. A market with fifteen terrestrial-radio outlets could end up with as many as sixty channels of diverse programming to attract and retain listener frequency. NPR, for example, was planning to split its HD broadcasts into as many as six channels per station, allowing multichannel competition in an increasingly multichannel world.[117] Several public stations already offered a second (HD) stream when WUSN in Chicago became the first commercial outlet to do the same in May 2005.[118]

While improved sound fidelity will be HD radio's foremost selling point, digital receivers will offer users additional appeals, including a visual component. "Smart" receivers add sight to radio with a small LCD screen to provide a myriad of options, such as geographical location information and station data accessed by a search engine designed to locate preselected programming. Smart receivers also promise interaction between the listener and station. Audience members are expected to be able to participate in two-way communication in such things as song selection, music testing, product giveaways, and promotions and contests.

TRANSITIONS

Multiplying audio options are redefining the very essence of the term "radio," as increasing competition crowds radio broadcasters. The problem facing those broadcasters is easy to state but harder to accomplish: how best to incorporate digital technologies to present more diverse or specialized programming and thus retain listeners?

By the middle of the first decade of twenty-first century, FM had just about peaked in terms of the number of stations on the air, and thus, for the first time in decades, the future held little potential for further expansion. Predictions about radio's future were sounding more bleak, even from some of the medium's most devout supporters. Clear Channel Radio's one-time head, Randy Michaels, held out little hope that things would improve for terrestrial radio: "There is no question that today's radio model is a leaky bucket. . . . The way people get their entertainment and information is changing, and radio had better adapt to the changing ways and look at what's happening."[119] He shifted his own focus to television. Underlining his concern, a study in 2005 showed that potential listeners age eighteen to twenty-four felt that radio lacked "buzz." The medium was seen as a mere utility, lacking any ability to raise audience passion. The survey suggested that "usage tends to be narrowing to the car."[120] Given FM's long fight to get receivers into cars, this is ironic, indeed.

Although apprehensive about the swiftly changing listening landscape, broadcast radio began a promotional campaign in 2006 intended to help retain existing fans and possibly attract new ones. A *Pittsburgh Post-Gazette* writer astutely observed, "Stations are cutting ads per hour, jumping back into [Internet] streaming and emphasizing live local shows to restore the 'companionship' factor in commercial radio."[121] Others agreed that "radio is taking steps to stop the bleeding."[122] One major step was the continuing rollout of HD-radio service.

And others also struck an optimistic tone. One of the digital age's fore-most publications, *Wired* magazine, argued early in 2005 that "New Tech will not kill, but 'resurrect,' broadcast radio." Suggesting that the new audio options have forced radio to reinvent itself just as happened when television appeared, the publication concluded: "Rather than being on life support, radio in fact is on the verge of its boldest technological change since the introduction of FM stereo in the 1960s. Not only that, it may be on the threshold of another golden age, one which could have almost as powerful an impact as the first."[123] As just one example, in 2005 some radio stations began to offer download options for their listeners—a direct reaction to the iPod revolution. There are risks in such an approach, of course—enabling such downloading encourages music listening through technologies other than radio—and stations make but pennies on each song sold.[124] Whether this belated entry into the download world makes a real difference remains to be seen.

FM radio's slowly declining audience in the early 2000s is reminiscent of events four decades earlier. Listeners originally shifted to FM in the 1960s because they were tired of AM's bland programming, excessive commercials, inane chatter, and inferior (static-filled and single-channel) sound. They sought something better—high-quality content that makes effective use of its improved technology. Decades later, many listeners (and some practitioners) seem to be abandoning FM for many of the same reasons, defecting to satellite radio or Web-based downloading and mobility.

In the end, of course, the question of who or what survives all this competition is less a matter of technology than of content (though ease of consumer use is a huge factor). Providing the same content with newer technology rarely goes anywhere, as evidenced by the first two decades of FM's own history in duplicating AM programs. Provide something wholly new, or a wider and better choice, on the other hand, and customers beat a path to your door. The future is all about controlling that door.

Defining the Context of FM

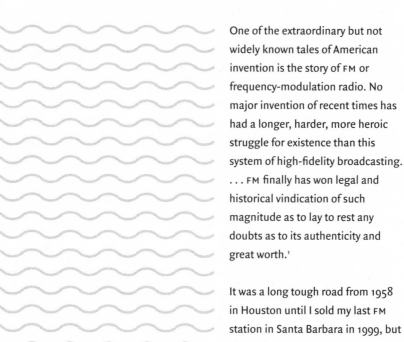

One of the extraordinary but not widely known tales of American invention is the story of FM or frequency-modulation radio. No major invention of recent times has had a longer, harder, more heroic struggle for existence than this system of high-fidelity broadcasting. . . . FM finally has won legal and historical vindication of such magnitude as to lay to rest any doubts as to its authenticity and great worth.[1]

It was a long tough road from 1958 in Houston until I sold my last FM station in Santa Barbara in 1999, but along the way I always believed in the FM radio medium, because as I said repeatedly over forty years of FM management and ownership, in this country, sooner or later the quality product always wins out with the American consumer . . . and with FM we had the best. I only hope it stays that way with digital FM/HD in the twenty-first century.[2]

These statements express the remarkable nature of FM radio's rise to dominance, as well as the passion and determination of the people who dedicated their lives to the medium's growth. To this point, we have described how FM developed and eventually succeeded. On our remaining pages, we take a very different approach to the FM story. Here, in an attempt to better understand the patterns in that story, we apply several theoretical approaches. Our purpose is both to summarize FM's development and reconceptualize its history from different points of view. Each approach sheds light on how and why the medium developed as it did.

One can begin with key people such as FM system inventor Howard Armstrong or the technology itself. Another option is to trace the development and operation of individual stations through the years. Changing policy offers a different subject of focused study. FM program patterns shed light on public taste as well as social issues over seven decades. Noncommercial FM stations provide very different stories. One can also explore FM's audience to better understand why it grew so slowly for so long. No single topic, however, fully tells the tale.

Arriving two decades after the inception of AM broadcasting, FM became the first test of whether an improved technology could successfully compete with a well-established legacy service. FM provides different answers to this question over the years, as much of its history demonstrates just how steep a cliff any new service must climb. Clearly, any "better mousetrap" will succeed to the degree that it offers users good reason to seek it out—and too often, FM did not.

FM'S INVENTION AND INNOVATION

We begin with the inventive process itself. The most insightful study of radio's innovation appeared while FM radio was still a nascent service.[3] W. R. Maclaurin's *Invention and Innovation in the Radio Industry* (1949) devotes only seven pages to the rise of FM, which then seemed to be taking hold. He concludes that it was Armstrong's combined strengths as both an inventor and an innovator that proved essential to the new medium's survival. Maclaurin argues that RCA was mistaken to bypass FM, suggesting FM's innovation is a good example of "competitive sources of new ideas" that can help a business grow.[4]

Nearly a decade later, *The Sources of Invention* (1958) offered a broad investigation into patterns of invention and innovation in both Britain and the United States.[5] The authors described the twentieth-century development of corporate research as evidenced in the declining number of patents granted to individuals. While corporations received 18 percent of all patents at the century's start, that proportion rose to 58 percent by 1936, when FM was emerging from the laboratory; the percentage grew even higher later in the century.[6] FM is only briefly noted in *The Sources of Invention*,[7] as the book appeared when the second radio service seemed to have faded. The authors agree with Maclaurin that Armstrong's active role was essential in the face of widespread disinterest in FM. Yet they make clear that the era of the lone inventor was fast disappearing. Increasingly well-funded corporate research teams with sufficient facilities, money, and long-term support (such as those of RCA, GE, and AT&T's Bell Labs, to name three) would soon dominate technological progress. Corporations contributed little to FM's core technologies, however, though GE and later Zenith helped to both improve and promote them.

STAGES IN FM'S DEVELOPMENT

Reviewing FM's development can be considerably clarified with tools originally designed for very different purposes. For example, W. W. Rostow's *The Stages of Economic Growth: A Non-Communist Manifesto* (1961; rev. ed., 1991)[8] sought to redefine the development process as former colonies became independent nations. Using his terminology, we can perceive the rise of FM broadcasting in a very different way.

Rostow posits five "stages" in a country's development. His first, the predevelopment, or "traditional," society, can be said to describe radio broadcasting during its formative decades through about 1945. For two decades, American AM radio grew and thrived, while important decisions about its infrastructure (including station and network operations, program types and patterns, support by advertising, regulatory policies, and means of audience research) were developed. Much of that was achieved by 1930, and the Depression years that followed restricted the new business's ability to modify its established model. What had been new in 1920 became a self-satisfied legacy by 1940. But behind the sheen of commercial success lay problems.

Rostow's second, or "preconditions-for-takeoff," stage sets the groundwork for change. In our case, this parallels the innovation of FM and television before and during World War II—essentially, the decade from 1935 through 1945. One primary precondition was growing public dissatisfaction with AM's plague of static noise. Some demanded more cultural and educational programming, which broadcasters had largely abandoned. Critics sought to open up the closed, club-like atmosphere of the small AM network-based business. Within this decade Armstrong and others laid the technical and business groundwork for establishing his new radio service. These pioneers touted FM's improved sound, suppression of static, and potential for new stations and program ideas. To ease FM's introduction, its backers adopted traditional features of AM, including local stations, many notions of programming, and advertising for financial support. FM allowed a revival of educational radio—which was then a small service characterized by more studies than operating stations—thanks to its additional and reserved channels encouraging cultural alternatives. While FM offered technical improvements, it had to appear sufficiently familiar to encourage its adoption by potential listeners.

Rostow's "takeoff" stage, where the pace of development quickens, took place not once but twice in commercial FM radio. The first occasion came with the "false-start" period of 1946–49, when FM enthusiasm outpaced underlying reality. But the excitement quickly faltered and died, and commercial FM faded for another decade. Only after 1957 did FM's takeoff stage reappear, when conditions for its success improved. Television and AM radio expansion had slowed, and only FM offered open channels in major markets. Audience interest in high fidelity was increasing, and FM subsidiary services offered new revenue options. This time, growth continued. Educational FM experienced a different arc, growing more slowly but also steadily and never experiencing the 1950s dip of the commercial business.

Rostow's "drive to maturity" exploits technology to speed development. This FM period runs to 1979, when the newer medium eclipses AM in total national audience. Educational FM reached this point even earlier with the achievement of federal support in 1967 and the appearance soon afterwards of National Public Radio. The rapid increase in the number of commercial and public FM stations, and their growing popularity, expanded the medium's importance to broadcasters, advertisers, and audiences. Two FCC policy decisions were hugely important: the approval of stereo-broadcast technical standards early in 1961 and the later and more vital mandating of AM-FM program separation. Both proved central to FM's growing appeal.

Finally, Rostow's "era of self-sustained growth," or "high mass consumption," characterizes a nation with fulsome trade and established industries. This can apply to both commercial and public FM over the past quarter century as the medium increasingly dominated radio. This final success had taken decades longer than its proponents had once presumed and hoped it would. From half of the nation's radio listening audience in 1980, FM expanded by the mid-1990s to three-quarters or more, retaining that level into the new century. Growth in station numbers if not program variety, receivers of all types and price ranges, and advertisers combined to make FM a huge success.

Already, however, we can discern a further period, one not found in Rostow's analysis. We know that analog radio will soon phase out, to be replaced by already-growing digital services. As FM faces this technology-driven change (which is ironic given its own origin as a dramatic improvement over AM), the medium has become increasingly troubled over the past decade. FM took on many characteristics of AM. Wall Street–driven industry consolidation has helped promote a numbing sameness in FM programming, substantially increased commercialization, and is resulting in a slowly declining audience. FM is also under pressure from newer digital technologies (iPods and satellite radio chief among them), suggesting there is an additional and final stage: decline.

A more complex approach to the process of invention and innovation, written around changing communications technology, does not focus on radio or even use it as an example. Brian Winston's study, originally titled *Misunderstanding Media*, first appeared decades after those noted above.[9] He posits a circular scheme of development that makes clear that there are often external reasons why one option develops and another does not. He includes factors that can delay or hinder development of an otherwise successful technology. And the stages in his model can more realistically overlap in time.

Winston begins with the "existing competence and scientific knowledge" with which any new technology must build. In FM's case, this would include the scattered engineering theory and research done prior to 1930, much of it concluding that FM transmission created more problems than panaceas for radio broadcasting. FM was only one of many technical alternatives examined as radio broadcasting flourished, based on what was then known about electronics, radio transmission, and spectrum—the existing knowledge of that era.

Armstrong enters the picture at Winston's critical step of "ideation": by about 1930, Armstrong realized that a wide-channel system of frequency modulation might overcome many perceived FM drawbacks to create something not only useful but also better. The defining of Armstrong's core "idea" behind FM continued through the granting of his four basic FM patents in late 1933. Some researchers call this step "invention," the base on which all further development proceeds.

The "prototypes" stage of Winston's model takes in all of Armstrong's experimental work of the 1930s, as well as the first broadcast tests and early receivers through 1939. Within this short period of time, most of FM's technical bugs were worked out, and a viable alternative radio system was tested and improved with the vital help of people like the Yankee Network officials. Winston's model allows for realistic overlap in its steps; thus we see another FM prototype stage with the early 1960s' introduction of stereo, just as the early 2000s witnessed yet another such stage with the spread of digital technologies.

At this point, Winston introduces the first of two crucial external inputs—what he terms the "law of supervening social necessity," which helps to propel a successful technology further. FM developed because it resolved AM's vital drawback of static interference. Finding a way to reduce or eliminate static was the vital "supervening" necessity that drove the creative juices behind FM. More broadly, though not fully appreciated at the time, FM served several other "social necessities" as well. The new service required station equipment and receivers, and it thus contributed to the manufacturing sector just as the country passed through the "little" or second Depression in the late 1930s. FM also serviced the later desire for a higher fidelity system of broadcasting. And FM offered the potential addition of many new broadcasters into what was then a relatively small business club. Indeed, the new broadcast system offered a chance to revisit, if not overcome, several limitations in existing broadcasting.

What Winston confusingly calls "invention" comes next, though he really means what most would term "innovation," or the successful marketing of a new device or service. With FM, this process took a long time; indeed, we argue that it stretched from 1940 well into the 1970s. This was a job of persuasion—first of engineers, broadcasters, and regulators, then of listeners, and finally of advertisers—that FM could fulfill their respective needs. This long period was made more difficult by a deep split in broadcast-industry thinking about FM's potential, either as a mere supplement to existing AM or as an audio medium in its own right. The critical debate over program duplication played out in the context of this split.

Winston's most fascinating external input comes next, which he dubs the "law of the suppression of radical potential." What he means is the sometimes Luddite reaction of older businesses or technologies seeking to retard expansion of something newer that might prove fatally competitive. Sometimes dubbed the "not-invented-here" syndrome, this is a natural impulse to constrain developments in which your own organization has no role or little to gain. This occurred to FM on numerous occasions, perhaps most successfully when AM broadcasters argued that FM stations should duplicate or "simulcast" their programs. While this seemed helpful on the surface (FM could use AM's popular programs to attract listeners), in reality duplication eliminated any separate identity for most FM stations. Listeners or advertisers cared little for a service that offered nothing new. FM's decline through most of the 1950s was largely a matter of such indirect "suppression," though many participated in the process, not seeing it as such.

Noncommercial radio illustrates an application of Winston's suppression idea. As NPR was forming around 1970 and a new generation was building the Washington-based structure of what would become public radio, many of educational radio's old guard resisted change. This was partially generationally driven: longtime survivors in local stations did not speak the same language as the younger programmers with national audiences in mind. There was a classic power conflict, as the old guard was steadily pushed aside to make way for younger people touting a wider spectrum of ideas of what public FM radio could be. But there was also an element of political fear—worry that greater involvement in the Washington political arena would drag stations into increasing controversy, possibly threatening their newly gained financial support. Those fears were well grounded, as funding problems did appear later. Finally, part of the tussle was rural versus urban, as local educational stations in smaller towns resisted being told what to do by Washington-based public radio zealots.

Winston's final stage, "production," indicates that the technology or service is made widely available on a continuing basis. There are few fundamental changes or innovations. There can be "spinoffs" (variations such as stereo) or "redundancies" (duplications or failures, such as quadraphonic sound) at this ultimate stage. But these are variations, not fundamental shifts in the core service. They may contribute to ultimate success, or they may not. In dominating AM, FM radio has occupied this stage since the 1980s.

Winston's model is useful in assessing segments in FM's development. It is especially valuable for adding factors lacking in most thinking about the diffusion of newer technologies—the social needs that push for change, for example, and the counter push to slow innovative potential. As with Rostow's earlier scheme, however, Winston ignores the eventual decline and replacement of a service or technology, something FM analog radio is now facing with digital innovations.

The seminal work surveying the innovation literature remains the late Everett Roger's *Diffusion of Innovation*.[10] Rogers's book demonstrates the growing complexity of the innovation process, as researchers shift away from the linear models that had long dominated study of the process. Rogers speaks of the "rate" or "pace" of innovation and the many factors than affect it—such things as perceived advantage (for example, FM sounded better, especially with stereo); compatibility (the new radio service did require new transmission and reception equipment, a delaying drawback in its innovation); the type of decision (many different players had to make choices, another factor delaying FM); and the extent of proponents' promotion efforts (which varied by period).[11] And Rogers reviews the importance of the "critical mass," or what some have termed the "tipping point," when an innovation finally achieves self-sustaining growth and widespread adoption.[12] This is similar in concept to Rostow's ultimate period of self-sustaining growth. We know that FM reached that stage by the late 1960s, propelled by the FCC's controversial program nonduplication decision. There were no further major policy decisions or business changes to affect the medium from that point; building on its recent momentum, it simply continued to expand to reach a dominating role by 1980.

THE KEYS TO FM'S HISTORY

There are several further ways to consider the FM story. Each of these—and there are surely others as well—helps to fill in holes or shortcomings of the analyses developed thus far.

Lone Innovator?

FM has most often been described as the innovative product of a lone inventor working without corporate support. Indeed, just as Armstrong was receiving his four basic FM patents, American corporations were for the first time applying for more patents than were individual inventors.[13] This version of the tale focuses on Armstrong and makes for often emotional reading, as his constructive and friendly relationship with RCA's David Sarnoff turned negative and then bitterly adversarial. One book about Armstrong all but posits that Sarnoff's company was guilty for the despairing inventor's 1954 suicide.[14] Many articles do the same. Armstrong's chief biographer, Lawrence Lessing, shies away from such absolutes but makes clear where his emotional loyalties lie.[15] Most writers of history in this vein focus on the personalities and thus shed less light on other important factors informing the complex FM story. They see early FM in stark black-and-white tones, almost as a morality tale. One example was Tom Lewis in his gripping *Empire of the Air* (1991), which became an equally compelling PBS television documentary in the hands of producer Ken Burns.

Yet, as noted in Maclaurin's study discussed above and as seen in our first and second chapters, FM was also an innovation pioneered by risk-taking broadcasters. Though few in number, these respected members of the broadcasting community (especially Shepard of the New England–based Yankee Network) played a vital role by helping convince their fellow station managers to invest in FM. These broadcasting pioneers also tipped the scales at the 1940 FCC proceeding in favor of getting the service on the air as a regular commercial offering.

In many ways, FM's story is perhaps most usefully seen as the first of a continuing flow of "new" technologies that would develop to challenge older-legacy broadcasting services. The next of these—and one to which FM was often compared at the time—was UHF television, which, while technically similar to VHF, was located in the higher spectrum and thus suffered severely in coverage compared to the legacy VHF stations. The parallels between the two are instructive. Both FM and UHF (as the industry "have-nots") served and suffered for years as secondary services to AM and VHF (the "haves"). In both cases there was a concerted push to require "all-channel" receivers in order to more rapidly build audiences. A law finally required UHF reception in television receivers, but no parallel legislation ever resulted (nor, as events turned out, was needed) for radio. Continuity was in the interest of the haves—continuing the existence of the have-nots, but not to the degree that they might become fully competitive. And through the 1960s, neither FM nor UHF posed any threat. FM eventually succeeded on its own merits in the 1970s, while UHF finally overcame its drawbacks thanks only to the spread of cable television, which equalized both types of broadcast television.

"Second" Service

Some of FM's troubles until the mid-1960s were caused by a crucial split among FM managers concerning what role their medium should play. The few independent stations, those not owned by colocated AM outlets, sought to develop FM with a clearly separate identity and appeal. The majority of AM-owned FM outlets, on the other hand, sought audiences by cooperating with the more powerful AM business and simply simulcasting AM programs and advertising. They thus provided the same program service on both frequency bands, and (wittingly or not) suppressed the identity of FM as a separate service.

During this long-running program duplication battle, FM lacked much appeal for potential listeners. This was due not only to program duplication and the background/concert music carried by most independent FM stations, but also to the relative scarcity and thus expense of FM receivers. And here we come upon another of the numerous "chicken-and-egg" quandaries that characterize FM's history: the receivers were expensive because so few of them were sold (fewer than 200,000 a year in the mid-1950s); yet making an FM receiver of any quality and low cost clearly was not worth the manufacturer's effort given the small market.

Another result of this long-lasting pattern of program duplication was FM's inability to evoke interest among the advertising community, an essential step in achieving financial viability. For years, commercial time on most FM stations was given away as a bonus for purchase of time on their AM owners. Many in and out of the business argued this did not really matter, since FM's audience was too tiny anyway. FM stations seeking advertisers (most did not bother) took to selling the class and taste of their admittedly small audiences—much as public radio and television would do decades later. Highbrow products took notice and advertised, but few others did. But even here, FM was captured in a "catch-22" when it later tried to break away from the class image to reflect its growing mass audience. It took years to shift advertiser perceptions.

Educational radio was used to being "secondary," so this was not so much of an issue for those operations. After all, barely two dozen educational radio stations still survived on the AM band when FM was first approved. Once noncommercial channels were set aside for FM in 1941 and again in 1945 on the new higher band, the educational FM market grew—slowly at first, but steadily. After World War II, several hundred colleges—even a few high schools—placed low-power FM stations on the air to provide both community service and on-air training for students. Many remain on the air today. Further, another category of noncommercial outlets—small community stations—began to develop in the 1960s and has now expanded to nearly 1,000 outlets across the country. More recently, a host of religious outlets have added their generally conservative Protestant voice to those noncommercial channels. In their own markets, these public, college, community, and religious stations (all classed as "noncommercial" by FCC regulators) have achieved credible and loyal, if often small, audiences. And those listeners are often society's movers and shakers, far more than their mere numbers might suggest.

Policy Boost

FM radio's development is studded with regulatory decisions that dramatically affected its course. For the most part, these actions by the FCC were intended to be helpful; the reservation of channels for noncommercial stations in 1940 and 1945, the larger though higher spectrum allocation of 1945, the creation of subsidiary communication authorizations in 1955, the approval of stereo standards in 1961, and the inception of program nonduplication in the 1960s all come to mind. Each provided a vital boost to FM's eventual success, none more than the expanding application of nonduplication rules in the late 1960s, forcing FM to become a separate service. This, in turn, led to a growing audience and more advertiser interest and support—Rostow's "takeoff" to sustained growth. Two very different examples illustrate the importance of these policy decisions.

FM development was hugely affected by the FCC's frequency shift in 1945. This had terrible short-term effects but positive, and more important, long-term effects, as we described earlier. Unlike AM radio or television, FM was the only operating commercial service that began life on one frequency band (42–50 MHz in 1941) and ended up on another (88–108 MHz). While we explored the reasons behind the shift, the important point is that FM had to start anew just as money and personnel were being directed to postwar AM expansion (and would soon be diverted to the rising medium of television). For a dozen years, FM had little chance to grow in such circumstances and was limited to playing but a secondary role behind both AM and television. The frequency shift was not the only cause of this stagnation, but it was a prime contributor. Yet, in the long run—as early as the 1960s in some large markets—the larger spectrum allocation made possible the eventual vast growth of the FM business. Indeed, FM's thousands of stations would not dominate the business today had not their allocation been enlarged in the closing days of World War II.

At least as important in achieving FM's ultimate status was the later shift in thinking about duplicated AM-FM programming. Long subject to debate—usually expressed in terms of what was best for the public interest when in fact the arguments were nearly all about money—simulcasting was finally restricted by the FCC in the mid-1960s. The decision was fought hard by radio owners, including some FM-station operators who should have known better. Within less than a decade, positive results of the policy shift were evident, as major-market FM-station audiences climbed well into the ratings books. More than any other factor, the substantial elimination of duplicated programming paved the way for FM's eventual supremacy over AM radio.

Disruption

There is yet another way to look at the FM radio story, one that is more in agreement with RCA boss David Sarnoff's initial shocked reaction when he got an advance peek at Armstrong's innovation in late 1933. FM radio was no mere improvement on an existing technology; it was clearly a "disruption"—and the first one of importance to occur in broadcast radio. Disruptors in recent technological innovation theory are new products or approaches that almost never come from existing companies or dominant players.[16] They differ from "sustaining" innovations that are usually improvements in the existing base and that most often derive from an industry's dominant player(s). To describe disruptions using slang phrases, they sometimes appear from "left field" and are "Pans" ("pretty awesome new stuff") compared to the "pots" that already exist. Disruptions rarely originate within the established or dominant industry, for there is little financial or market incentive for them to do so. The World Wide Web application of the Internet is an excellent recent example of such a disruption that began to greatly change existing patterns of electronic communication after becoming commercially available in 1995.

A disruption works or is successfully innovated because it offers something that the existing mainstream does not (in FM's case, better sound quality and no static), or it appears to be simpler to use (not as applicable in this case). Winston's "law of the suppression of radical potential" can also be seen in this context as the understandably defensive reaction of a legacy player (such as RCA, a dominant AM radio manufacturer and broadcaster) to the perceived new disruptive threat—Armstrong's proposed FM system.

Yet, as with the complex multistage development and diffusion models, even disruption can best be seen as part of a continuing process. Just as FM was a disruption for dominant AM radio, its own disruption is already discernable. FM now largely defines the mainstream of commercial radio broadcasting and has done so in the United States for a quarter century. It is on track to be disrupted, in turn, by a variety of digital options. Indeed, the process has already begun, as witnessed by the growing audiences for digital-recording devices and subscription satellite audio services.[17]

What If?

There are many places in FM's story where a different decision could have dramatically changed FM's development. Dubbed "counterfactual history" by some practitioners, the idea of changing key decisions from those actually taken can shed further light on the real story. We offer just two examples here, one from FM's formative years and one occurring two decades later. Both were turning points.

As noted, FM's spectrum shift in 1945 had a disastrous short-term effect on the medium. To a substantial extent, FM had to start over again after the war while competing with resurgent AM and the fascination of television. But what if FM had *not* been shifted and instead had retained or perhaps expanded its original spectrum allocation? Would this have made a difference in the medium's development? Clearly it would, in both the short and long term. FM would have had one less thing to fight in the late 1940s and might have gained a stronger competitive toehold to continue its growth despite AM and television popularity. Receiver manufacturers were already tooled up for the 42–50 MHz spectrum, and they could have turned out FM sets right away and in large numbers. But this original spectrum (even slightly expanded, which is all that would have been possible even in 1945) would have severely constricted FM's later growth. The original seventy channels would never have been able to contain the dramatic post-1965 expansion in FM-station numbers, and the medium would have been strangled just as it was achieving success.

And, two decades later, what might have been the effect had the FCC not decided to force AM-FM program separation? Here the evidence is even stronger. Continued simulcasting would have restrained FM into continuing its supplemental role to AM. FM's expansion during the 1970s and dominance after 1980 would never have taken place, for there would be precious little reason for listeners or advertisers to migrate from AM radio or for broadcasters to develop more stations. Fought tooth and nail by most elements of the radio business at the time, the FCC stuck to its guns and slowly separated AM programmers from their dominance of FM stations. Had the commission not stayed its course, FM could never have blossomed in the way it did over the next three decades. It can indeed be argued that the program-nonduplication decision was the single most important FCC contribution to FM's development after the commission's basic role of allocating spectrum. The earlier stereo decision surely helped, as did FCC support of independent FM-station operators, but the program-nonduplication struggle was of paramount importance.

Imitation and Decline

We can, finally, perceive FM in yet another way: as an imitator of much that AM radio had already pioneered. Given that broadcast industry infrastructure was largely created in the first dozen years or so of AM operation, this is perhaps not surprising. Certainly for the first three decades of its own operation, FM sought desperately to closely parallel AM's structure and success. Station operators tried to establish their own FM networks (the first attempt dated to the war years), sought to provide many of the same program types (this led to the ultimate imitation of program duplication), and tried to appeal to the same advertisers.

Only with the forced inception of program variety in the mid-1960s did the trend to AM imitation decline—or did it? While a period of creative underground and other alternative programming was tried at many FM stations in the late 1960s, most were short-lived, as few made sufficient revenue to continue. And thus today's FM stations look and operate much like their AM brethren, albeit usually with more music and less talk. Virtually all sell time to advertisers as their prime means of support. FM managers watch ratings closely and adjust their program choices accordingly, just as radio has done for decades.

(((Looking ahead, the ultimate demise of analog FM broadcasting is already visible. While we cannot venture exactly when this will take place since there is no mandated deadline, our best guess is sometime during the second decade of the twenty-first century. FM will ultimately imitate AM again in this final stage of disappearing from the scene. Both are based on analog technology and are thus outflanked by the vastly sharper sound of digital transmission. The FCC will eventually close both analog services in favor of the more efficient digital operations. Millions of Americans enjoy satellite digital service as this is written, with more subscribing all the time. Terrestrial digital or HD radio service is not far behind. Just as FM radio was a marked improvement over AM, so these digital services mark a huge advance over FM.

After a seven-decade history, FM—which has dominated radio for nearly thirty years—will soon give way to something newer and better. Howard Armstrong would be the first to understand.

AM, FM, and HD Radio Technology

Howard Armstrong's innovative breakthroughs, which are central to FM broadcasting, involved (a) changing the means of modulating a transmitted radio signal
from amplitude modulation, which had been the long-accepted standard method;
and (b) utilizing wider channels—200 kHz rather than AM's 10 kHz. Out of those
two changes—easy to summarize, yet difficult to conceive initially—came much of
the listening difference between the two services. This appendix provides a brief
comparison between AM and FM radio. Important in the comparison is the combination of political and regulatory decisions—such as which spectrum band will be
used for a given service—and technical "givens," or the laws of physics that define
what can be done with specific services. Overseas, for example, many AM stations
use 9 kHz channels, while FM is often called VHF radio; the assigned frequencies
may vary; and digital broadcast standards differ. Otherwise, the comparisons below
are largely similar.

1. SPECTRUM BAND

Amplitude Modulation (AM). U.S. AM stations operate in the medium waves (MW),
or so-called standard band—that is, from 535 to 1705 kHz. Each station operates
on a channel 10 kHz wide (half above and half below the center frequency). The
107 AM channels are each assigned to many stations in different areas to reduce
interference.

Frequency Modulation (FM). Since the 1945 band shift, FM has been allocated the
88–108 MHz frequencies in the VHF spectrum band. Each FM station is assigned
a channel of 200 kHz. FM channels are also assigned to many stations in different
regions.

2. STATION CLASSIFICATIONS

AM channels are classified into three types: clear (60), regional (51), or local (6). The
FCC further modified the system to define AM-station classes by Roman numerals
and more recently by letters. Only Class C stations are assigned to local channels,
while Classes A, B, and D may use clear channels and Classes B and D can use regional channels. There is no allotment scheme for AM radio. More than half of AM
stations leave the air at local sunset. Most stations also utilize directional antennas
to reduce interference. But the range of any AM station can vary between day and
night and by season because of MW propagation variance.

TABLE A.1. AM-Station Classifications

Station Class	Transmitting Power	Percent of AM Stations
Class A	10,000–50,000 watts	1
Class B	250–50,000 watts	35
Class C	250–1,000 watts	21
Class D	250–50,000 watts	42
(daytime-only operation)		

FM channels. The FCC has issued several different classification systems for FM, beginning in 1945. The present system is outlined in the table below. FM channels are allotted (prelocated) across the country. Class A and B are used in the more crowded Northeast and Southern California. Class C stations are only allotted outside those regions, along with Class A and B. Unlike AM, FM channels are not separately classified.

TABLE A.2. FM-Station Classifications

Station Class	Transmitting Power	Approximate Range
Class A	100–6,000 watts	15 miles
Class B	6,000–15,000 watts	30 miles
Class C	12,000–100,000 watts	60 miles

3. CHANNELS

AM: The narrow AM channel (10 kHz) is one factor behind that service's narrower frequency response ("tinnier" sound—see number 9). Inadequate spectrum space made development of AM stereo more challenging and prevented SCAs (see number 11) from being authorized for AM.

FM: The wider FM channel (200 kHz) can accommodate a "high-fidelity" (audio bandwidth of 15 kHz), two-channel stereo audio signal, as well as ancillary signals called FM subcarriers, which are used for services such as low-speed data transmissions and radio reading services.

4. SIGNAL PROPAGATION

AM: This variable depends on the radio frequencies used by AM, not on the modulation system. In the medium-wave band (see number 1), coverage is affected by many things: power, antenna height, time of day, ground conductivity, and the frequency. Medium-wave signals propagate by both sky and ground waves (see Diagram A.1), and any station's coverage varies by time of day (since skywaves propagate only at night) and season.

FM: FM radio's VHF channels utilize direct or line-of-sight waves (see number 1). The result is more limited coverage than powerful AM outlets, but FM coverage patterns do not change with the time of day because there are no skywaves in the VHF

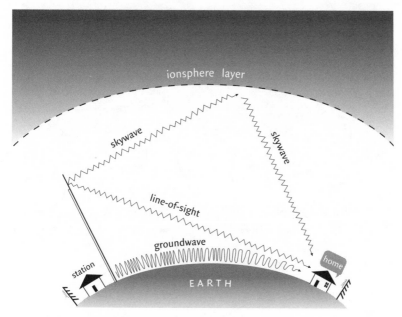

DIAGRAM A.1. Skywaves, Groundwaves, and Direct Waves

spectrum. The primary variables to improve station coverage are a higher antenna and increased transmitter power.

5. NIGHTTIME OPERATION

AM stations, because of nighttime skywave signal propagation (see number 4), generally use less power at night or, by terms of their license, must go off the air entirely at night; this is to reduce interference as much as possible.

FM stations may operate all day, every day and are not in any way restricted in their evening operation because VHF waves do not use the interference-causing skywaves. An FM station's coverage is thus the same day or night.

6. WAVE FORM

AM: The carrier wave (the basic signal used to carry the desired program information) is amplitude modulated; that is, the power output (amplitude) of the transmitter is adjusted (modulated) proportional to the modulating signal, which in the case of AM radio is an audio signal that is typically band limited to 10 kHz. Seen in a diagram as a line (Diagram A.2), each wave changes in height.

FM: The carrier wave is frequency modulated; the amplitude remains the same at all times, but the carrier-wave frequency changes in relation to the program material (Diagram A.3). Seen in a diagram as a line, waves change in width (frequency), not height.

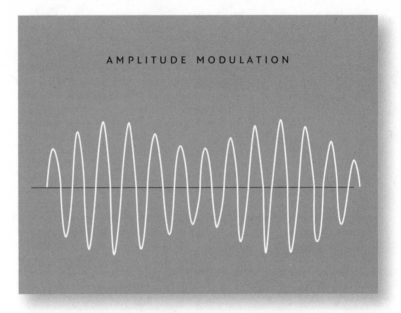

DIAGRAM A.2. AM Wave

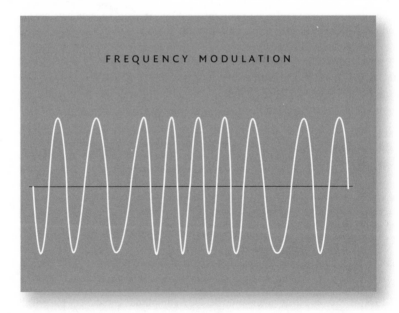

DIAGRAM A.3. FM Wave

7. STATIC AND INTERFERENCE

AM: Being naturally amplitude modulated, static attaches itself to the intended program material and cannot be electronically separated or eliminated. An AM signal must be twenty times more powerful than an interfering AM transmitter, or noise may result.

FM: Static may flow with, but cannot meld with, FM waves. It is normally separated and eliminated at the FM receiver. An FM signal need be only twice as strong as another station on the same channel to avoid interference. FM signals are, however, susceptible to a phenomenon known as "multipath fading," which is a characteristic of line-of-sight VHF signals. This occurs when the FM signal reflects off of trees, buildings, and other objects, resulting in multiple signals arriving at the receiver from different directions.

8. RECEIVER

AM: Detects and amplifies the AM waves just as received, discarding the carrier wave to leave only the program signal. But AM sets cannot distinguish between intentional signals and noise or interference, much of which is amplitude modulated.

FM: Detects the FM wave, eliminates any AM static or stray electronic noise, and amplifies and converts the FM signal to audible sound. If multipath fading is present, then the received signal may be subject to rapidly fading in and out.

9. FREQUENCY RESPONSE

AM: An AM radio channel is capable of passing an audio signal that is 10 kHz wide; however, the vast majority of AM receivers are band limited to 5 kHz or less, thus cutting out much of the base and some of the treble tones audible to the human ear.

FM: With their wider channels, FM stations can transmit audio signals with bandwidth up to 15 kHz, and the majority of FM receivers have this bandwidth as well. This allows broadcast of most tones audible to the human ear (which is capable of hearing up to 20 kHz; see Diagram A.4).

10. STEREO

AM: First allowed by the FCC in 1982 (although no specific standard was adopted), AM stereo never became an important factor, despite belated selection of a standard a decade later. Before approval of FM stereo in 1961, several AM outlets had stations teamed with FM outlets to provide stereo with one channel on AM and the other on FM, though this was wasteful of spectrum (see Diagram A.5).

FM: Approved early in 1961, FM stereo allowed one station to broadcast both right and left channels, thus saving spectrum space. Beginning in mid-1961, a growing number of FM stations adopted the FCC-approved technical standard for FM stereo transmission (see Diagram A.6). The service is nearly universal today.

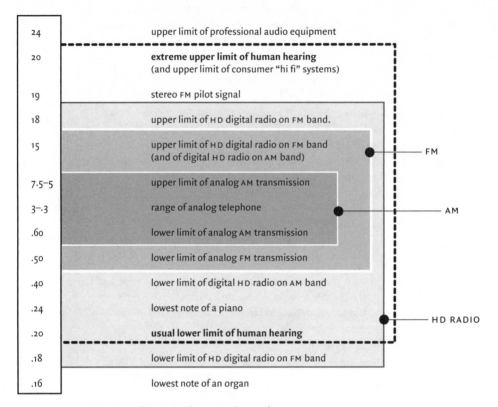

kHz	SOUND ELEMENT	
24	upper limit of professional audio equipment	
20	**extreme upper limit of human hearing** (and upper limit of consumer "hi fi" systems)	
19	stereo FM pilot signal	
18	upper limit of H D digital radio on FM band.	
15	upper limit of H D digital radio on FM band (and of digital H D radio on AM band)	FM
7.5–5	upper limit of analog AM transmission	
3–.3	range of analog telephone	AM
.60	lower limit of analog AM transmission	
.50	lower limit of analog FM transmission	
.40	lower limit of digital H D radio on AM band	
.24	lowest note of a piano	
.20	**usual lower limit of human hearing**	HD RADIO
.18	lower limit of H D digital radio on FM band	
.16	lowest note of an organ	

DIAGRAM A.4. Frequency-Response Comparison

II. SUPPLEMENTAL SERVICES

AM stations, with their narrower channels, were not as easily utilized for supplemental transmission of nonbroadcast signals. In the 1980s, however, the FCC approved their limited use for various kinds of electronic monitoring service, such as for utilities.

FM stations. Based on work by Armstrong and others, the FCC in 1955 approved FM SCAs, a multiplexed use of the FM transmitter that allowed more than one signal to be broadcast. SCAs were intended to create a revenue stream for hard-pressed FM outlets, and most were used to transmit music into stores and offices. The SCAs are also referred to as FM subcarriers and are frequency modulated onto the carrier wave along with the main-channel audio program (see also numbers 3 and 12).

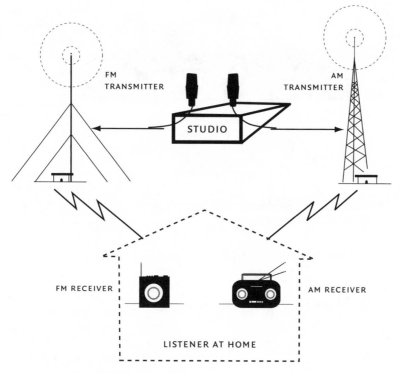

DIAGRAM A.5. Two-Station Stereo

12. DIGITAL RADIO

Early in the twenty-first century, the FCC authorized U.S. analog radio broadcast-ers—both AM and FM—to transmit in-band, on-channel (IBOC) digital services, which is based on technology developed by iBiquity Digital Corporation (their brand for this technology is HD radio). Since other countries are planning to im-plement digital radio using other technologies, it is likely that digital radio sys-tems will be incompatible across national borders, while current analog systems are readily transportable. IBOC digital radio broadcasting provides CD-quality sound for FM and roughly FM quality for AM stations (see number 9). Both the AM- and FM-band IBOC systems provide other data-carrying options, includ-ing the display of the station's call letters, program or song titles, artist or guest names, or even news and weather on a receiver. Because of their wider channels, IBOC stations in the FM band can carry Supplemental Program Services; this is called "multicasting." One FM station can typically have one or two multicast channels in addition to their main (audio) channel. Finally, since the IBOC digi-tal radio signal contains the traditional analog signal along with the newer digi-

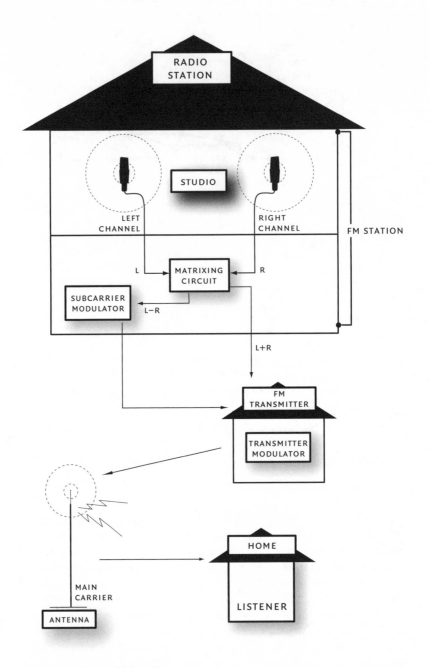

DIAGRAM A.6. FM Multiplexed Stereo

tal signal, it is compatible with existing analog receivers, so that much existing equipment and consumer receivers (of which there are some 700 million in use in the United States, or more than two for each person) can be used during the transition to fully digital operation. (However, existing receivers cannot pick up the multicast channels.)

FM Historical Statistics, 1945–2005

INTRODUCTION

Prior to about 1980, historical data on FM tends to be scattered, variable, and rarely comparable. On the other hand, some information has become less visible since 1980 (FM-receiver sales, for example) or is now made available only on an expensive commercial basis (free trade-association data is a thing of the past, and the government collects less than it did). With those caveats in mind, we have gathered here the best of what is available to provide more precise indicators of the medium's development. Tables provide information for the greatest number of years where comparable data is available. Tables with similar titles but different years appear separately if their data is not comparable.

Station information is all derived from official FCC records, although for various dates each year, depending on the changing federal fiscal year. In recent years, monthly station totals can be retrieved from the FCC's extensive website, <www.fcc.gov>.

Program information is the most variable and least trustworthy information in this appendix. For one thing, program definitions keep changing, and one person's ideas of where to place a given genre or format varies from another's. Additionally, data has never been kept by any government agency and only rarely by ratings firms. We are thus left with different counts done by different entities for varied purposes — hardly the neat comparable information we would like to have.

Receivers and audience information is a bit better, especially receiver sales data. Though no longer reported by the Electronic Industries Alliance, set sales data does exist from 1945 into the 1980s and is summarized here. From that information, other sources over the years have estimated the availability or penetration of FM receivers among consumers, both in selected cities and nationally. This penetration information is, it must be emphasized, only estimated and must therefore be used carefully. Audience-share information derives from Arbitron ratings surveys and is comparable for the years shown.

For more context for this information, as well as discussions on the reliability and validity of the data sources more generally, see Christopher H. Sterling, *Electronic Media: A Guide to Trends in Broadcasting and Newer Technologies, 1920–1983* (New York: Praeger, 1984).

TABLE B.I. Postwar FM Stations, 1945–1957

Year	Commercial FM Stations			Educational Stations on Air
	Authorized	On Air	Pending	
1945	N/A	46	N/A	6
1946	456	55	250	8
1947	918	238	431	8
1948	1,020	587	90	22
1949	856	737	65	34
1950	732	691	17	62
1951	659	649	10	83
1952	648	629	9	92
1953	601	580	8	106
1954	569	553	5	117
1955	552	540	6	124
1956	546	530	10	126
1957	560	530	24	135

Source: FCC data shown as of June 30 each year.
For ease in discerning development, the high point in each column is shown in italics.

TABLE B.2. FM-Station Expansion, 1945–2005

Factor	1945	1950	1955	1960	1965
Total FM stations on the air	54	781	674	850	1,525
Commercial FM stations on the air	46	733	552	688	1,270
As a percentage of all commercial stations	5%	26%	17%	17%	24%
Noncommercial FM stations on the air	8	48	122	162	255
As a percentage of all FM stations	15%	6%	18%	19%	17%

Source: FCC.

TABLE B.3. FM Program Format Trends, 1966–1978 (All Figures Percentages)

Year and No. of Stations	Middle of the Road	Top 40/ Contemp.	Beautiful/ Background	Country	Talk/ Other
1966					
Top 50 mkts. (244)	49	15	30	—	6
Other mkts. (564)	64	4	23	5	4
1971					
Top 100 mkts. (643)	18	25	39	10	8
1975					
Top 40 mkts. (475)	13	21	24	9	33*
1978					
All mkts. (1,174)	6	41	26	11	16*

Source: Christopher H. Sterling, *Electronic Media: A Guide to Trends in Broadcasting and Newer Technologies, 1920–1983* (New York: Praeger, 1984), table 570-A, pp. 180–81 (drawing from a variety of sources that are detailed there).
* In 1975 just 6 percent of reporting FM stations were providing classical-music formats. By 1978 that proportion was cut in half.

1970	1975	1980	1985	1990	1995	2000	2005
2,597	3,353	4,193	4,888	5,792	6,842	7,832	8,751
2,184	2,636	3,155	3,716	4,357	5,109	5,766	6,218
34%	37%	41%	44%	47%	51%	55%	57%
413	717	1,038	1,172	1,435	1,733	2,066	2,533
16%	21%	25%	24%	25%	25%	26%	29%

TABLE B.4. FM Program Format Trends, 1990–2004 (All Figures Percentages)

Format	1990 Public (1,636 stations)	1995 All (7,128 stations)	1995 Public (1,943 stations)	1999 All (8,052 stations)	1999 Public (2,342 stations)	2004 All (9,026 stations)	2004 Public (2,734 stations)
Country	—	22.7	—	19.4	—	16.2	—
News/talk	1.9	4.3	14.0	7.2	22.8	7.4	22.0
Adult Contemp.	—	10.5	—	7.9	—	6.7	—
Oldies	—	6.2	—	6.0	—	5.8	—
Top 40 Contemp.	4.3	5.0	2.6	5.3	1.6	5.8	1.2
Christian	—	3.0	6.3	5.7	15.4	5.8	15.5
Religion	20.3	6.1	18.3	4.4	14.5	5.6	18.6
Classic Rock	14.8	4.2	14.8	3.8	11.6	4.9	—
Hot AC		3.4		3.9		4.6	—
Variety	23.2	5.3	19.6	4.8	16.9	4.3	14.3
Spanish	2.0	2.5	1.9	3.1	2.7	3.7	2.8
Classics	19.6	3.7	11.8	1.8	4.6	1.7	4.7
Jazz	4.6	2.0	4.1	1.6	2.8	1.7	2.7

Source: *The M Street Radio Directory* (<www.MStreet.net>) for years cited. Data for noncommercial/public stations and "all" stations refers to their "primary format," except for the year 2004, where "all" FM outlets data are simply a "format count." Dash indicates less than 1 percent.

TABLE B.5. Postwar FM-Receiver Sales, 1946–1957

Year	No. of Sets Sold (in Thousands)	Year	No. of Sets Sold (in Thousands)
1946	181	1952	670
1947	1,140	1953	659
1948	1,529	1954	233
1949	800	1955	277
1950	2,228	1956	229
1951	1,267	1957	204

Source: Electronic Industries Alliance data.

TABLE B.6. FM-Receiver Sales and Penetration, 1950–1980

Factor	1950	1955	1960	1965	1970	1975	1980
No. of FM sets sold (in thousands)	2,228	277	1,994	6,337	21,332	22,420	39,822
As a percentage of all radios sold	17%	2%	8%	15%	48%	65%	78%
No. of FM automobile sets sold (in thousands)	N/A	N/A	75*	636	1,427	3,482	8,892
As a percentage of all car radios sold	N/A	N/A	1%*	6%	14%	38%	78%

Sources: Electronic Industry Association data as reported in Christopher H. Sterling, *Electronic Media: A Guide to Trends in Broadcasting and Newer Technologies, 1920–1983* (New York: Praeger, 1984), pp. 225–26 (for 1960–80 data); and Christopher H. Sterling, "Second Service: A History of Commercial FM Broadcasting to 1969" (Ph.D. diss., University of Wisconsin–Madison, August 1969), p. 788 (for 1950 and 1955 data).

* 1962 data, which is the first year for which the information is available.

TABLE B.7. FM-Receiver Availability in Selected Markets, 1958–1965
(Showing Estimated Percentage of Households Owning FM Radios)

Market	1958	1959	1960	1961	1962	1963	1965
Boston	51	50	—	51	—	—	—
Chicago	42	42	—	—	44	45	—
Cleveland	34	36	—	—	—	40	63
Houston	30	30	31	32	34	—	—
Los Angeles	48	49	—	—	—	49	—
Milwaukee	22	30	—	35	37	41	52
New York	57	—	57	—	53	—	—
Philadelphia	36	—	—	40	—	—	—
San Francisco	47	—	—	—	48	—	—
Washington, D.C.	—	40	41	42	—	—	—
U.S. Average	—	—	—	10	—	—	23

Sources: Table data is drawn from several sources, primarily data reported by and to the Radio Advertising Bureau and the National Association of FM Broadcasters. Milwaukee information is from Journal Company annual analyses. See Christopher Sterling, "Second Service: A History of Commercial FM Broadcasting to 1969" (Ph.D. diss., University of Wisconsin–Madison, August 1969), table 26, p. 595.

TABLE B.8. FM-Receiver Availability in Selected Markets, 1966–1975
(Showing Estimated Percentage of Households Owning FM Radios)

Market	1966	1968	1970	1975
Atlanta	54	58	76	96
Boston	50	62	67	95
Chicago	63	73	85	95
Denver	58	50	62	92
Houston	56	N/A	76	97
Los Angeles	67	69	83	95
Miami	52	60	65	92
New York	51	64	71	99
Philadelphia	67	76	88	99
San Francisco	60	62	78	94
Seattle	56	55	73	93
Washington, D.C.	62	77	86	98

Sources: The Pulse, Inc., press releases.

TABLE B.9. FM-Audience Listening Share in Selected Markets, 1967–2002
(All Figures Percentages)

Market	1967	1969	1970	1972	1974	1976	1978	1980
Top 10 Markets								
New York	17	22	23	28	33	40	48	53
Los Angeles	16	21	21	28	28	39	46	52
Chicago	10	16	13	23	28	35	50	55
Philadelphia	18	21	20	35	35	41	54	60
San Francisco	24	28	21	25	30	35	42	51
Detroit	13	22	21	32	38	44	54	62
Boston	22	29	19	25	32	39	46	48
Washington, D.C.	8	19	28	37	39	46	64	68
Dallas–Ft. Worth	10	20	21	28	38	49	61	68
Pittsburgh	13	22	15	20	30	34	44	48
Other Markets								
Atlanta						40	51	63
Denver						40	46	50
Kansas City						49	49	52
Madison						43	57	58
Miami						44	49	53
Seattle						31	42	52

Sources: Statistics for the years 1967 to 1976 are from Arbitron Radio Survey, "Reporting Metro Persons 12 and Older Tuning in Monday–Sunday, 6:00 A.M. to Midnight," as reported in *Broadcasting*, September 22, 1975, p. 30, and October 10, 1977, p. 70. Data for 1967–69 are from *Cox Looks at FM Radio Past, Present, Future* (Cox Broadcasting), p. 35. Data for 1978–2002 are from the Arbitron Radio Survey, summarized in James H. Duncan Jr., *An American Radio Trilogy: 1975 to 2004*, vol. 1, *The Markets* (Tesuque, N.Mex.: Duncan's American Radio, 2004).

TABLE B.10. Share of Total National Radio Audience, 1980–2005

Year	FM Share	AM Share
1980	54	46
1985	68	32
1990	79	21
1995	81	19
2000*	83	17
2005	85	15

Source: 1980–2000 data from *State of the Radio Industry, 2000* (Chantilly, Va.: BIA Research, Inc., 2000).
* Actually 1999 data

1982	1984	1986	1988	1990	1992	1994	1996	1998	2000	2002
55	59	63	65	67	71	70	73	75	77	77
57	61	66	65	68	68	72	74	77	79	81
57	64	67	70	70	68	69	70	73	73	76
65	70	73	75	77	76	77	78	79	79	77
53	57	60	64	62	66	65	66	68	71	70
67	68	69	69	73	73	75	77	76	79	78
58	61	62	66	71	71	69	69	73	74	77
74	76	78	80	81	82	81	82	85	84	81
71	72	78	77	78	76	79	77	79	82	83
53	61	62	64	69	70	68	70	77	74	74
65	68	80	82	82	81	83	83	84	82	81
59	59	66	73	75	76	75	74	76	77	76
55	65	66	63	67	69	70	74	76	75	76
59	62	62	67	78	76	79	77	77	82	82
58	62	65	69	71	70	72	74	75	74	76
53	59	62	65	69	72	72	71	72	74	75

In 1976, the only date that overlaps between the two sources, Duncan shows higher audience shares than shown here, though the baseline data is the same in each case. Thus the jump shown for most markets between 1976 and 1978 may be some kind of statistical anomaly. The "other" markets were added to provide a bit of regional balance; and Madison, Wisconsin (about the 100th market), was added because the senior author grew up there.

Changing FM National Coverage, 1949–2005

These maps provide a visual record of FM broadcasting's expanding coverage of the United States over more than half a century. Based on an amalgamation of individual station coverage information, each of these maps provides something of a snapshot of FM's status at different times. As FM coverage is the same day or night (unlike AM), such maps show those areas able to tune at least one FM station. But as each map derives from different sources and utilizes different methods of compilation, they must be seen only as approximations rather than as a detailed record.

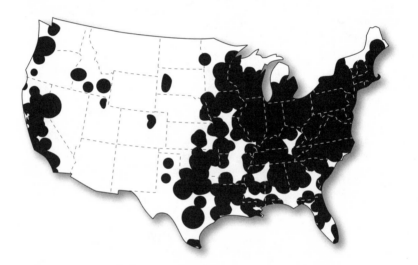

MAP C.1. FM Coverage, 1949 (Source: WASH-FM, Washington, D.C.)

The pattern evident here makes clear that FM, with some 725 stations on the air, was largely available in the East and Midwest in this period, with a number of states — Montana, Wyoming, Arizona, and New Mexico among them — unable to receive any FM stations. Indeed, coverage of the country west of the Mississippi was very spotty and mostly restricted to major cities. Several states were largely not served (as to land area, if not population), including Washington, Oregon, Idaho, Nevada, Utah, Colorado, the Dakotas, Nebraska, and Kansas.

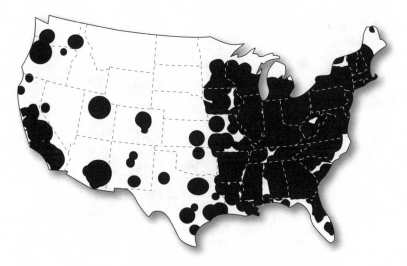

MAP C.2. FM Coverage, 1957 (Source: National Association of Broadcasters, Engineering Department)

We see little progress here—indeed some backsliding, as there are fewer stations (about 650) on the air and coverage at the bottom of FM's 1950s decline has shrunk from levels of eight years before. Note that Idaho and the Dakotas lack any FM coverage, while they had some in 1949. Likewise, coverage in Texas and Oklahoma is far more spotty. More of the South and much of Maine have lost FM service.

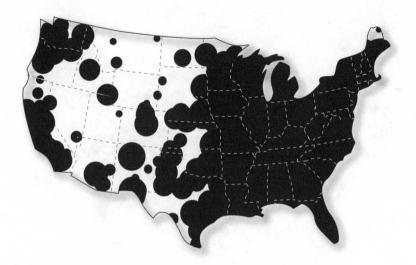

MAP C.3. FM Coverage, 1966 (Source: National Association of Broadcasters, Engineering Department)

After nearly a decade of FM renewed growth, and with some 1,700 FM outlets on the air, the picture has substantially improved; indeed, there is no state lacking FM service. East of the Mississippi, the country is totally covered save for parts of northern Maine. Washington and California are now largely covered, as is far more of Idaho and Montana.

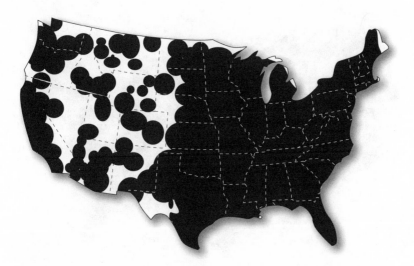

MAP C.4. FM Coverage, 1975 (Source: Office of Telecommunications, U.S. Department of Commerce, FM Broadcast Coverage of the Coterminous United States [Washington, D.C.: Government Printing Office, 1976])

The pattern evident a decade earlier continues here: more filling out of formerly underserved areas, as well as—though not evident on the map—more service in major cities. Making use of automatic data processing (for the first time) and a detailed data base, this map shows that the more than 4,000 FM stations in service are covering most of the population and more of the country's land area. While many parts of the West lack service, these are regions with little population density.

MAP C.5. FM Coverage, 2005 (Source: Chip Morgan of Chip Morgan Broadcast Engineering, Vermont)

This map, assembled especially for this book, shows that, after three more decades of FM expansion, the "white areas" lacking FM coverage have diminished to regions supporting few people. More evident in the West are FM stations in communities along interstate highways (as in Montana, for instance, along I-90). There are no communities of any size lacking at least one FM station, given the nearly 9,000 transmitters on the air. Making use of computer-based mapping software, this map is an amalgamation of thousands of individual-station coverage maps.

NOTES

INTRODUCTION

1 Europeans called AM frequencies medium-wave for their location in the spectrum rather than following the American custom of identifying a radio service by its type.

2 George Santayana, *The Life of Reason*, vol. 1. (London: Constable, 1905; repr. Dover Books, 1980).

3 In his *History of the French Revolution* (London: Chapman & Hall, 1837).

4 Susan J. Brinson, "From Marconi to Cop Rock," in *Transmitting the Past: Historical and Cultural Perspectives on Broadcasting*, ed. W. Emmett Winn and Susan J. Brinson (Tuscaloosa: University of Alabama Press, 2005), p. 4. The editors are on the Auburn University faculty.

5 Economists, at least the purists among them, discourage us from talking about a broadcast "industry" since there is no physical product manufactured.

6 Numerous English professors have "discovered" cinema studies as a way out of the narrow strictures of scholarly work in their own literary fields. So have area studies scholars and many others. Scholars revel in the mass of past and present films suitable (or not) for all kinds of social and cultural analysis. Broadcasting has yet to develop a similar appeal.

7 Frederick H. Lumley, *Measurement in Radio* (Columbus: Ohio State University Press, 1934; repr. in "History of Broadcasting: Radio to Television" [New York: Arno Press, 1971]).

8 Hadley Cantril and Gordon W. Allport, *The Psychology of Radio* (New York: Harper, 1935; repr. in "History of Broadcasting: Radio to Television").

9 Hadley Cantril, *The Invasion from Mars: A Study in the Psychology of Panic* (Princeton, N.J.: Princeton University Press, 1939).

10 Hugh Malcolm Beville Jr., *Social Stratification of the Radio Audience* (Princeton, N.J.: Princeton Office of Radio Research, 1939).

11 Paul F. Lazarsfeld, *Radio and the Printed Page: An Introduction to the Study of Radio and Its Role in the Communication of Ideas* (New York: Duell, Sloan, and Pearce, 1940; repr. in "History of Broadcasting: Radio to Television").

12 *Radio* (London: Faber, 1936; repr. in "History of Broadcasting: Radio to Television").

13 For two broad surveys of broadcasting's cultural and historical literature, see Michael C. Keith, "A Survey of Cultural Studies in Radio," chapter 8 of *Methods of Historical Analysis in Electronic Media*, ed. Donald G. Godfrey (Mahwah, N.J.: Lawrence Erlbaum Associates, 2006), pp. 187–205; and Christopher H. Sterling, "Assessing the Record: A Century of Historical Research," chapter 15 of

the same volume, pp. 349–74. The present discussion draws from these essays, with some necessary updating.

14 The *Journal of Radio Studies* first appeared as an annual in 1992. It is now published twice a year by Routledge and edited through the Broadcast Education Association. More recently, the *Radio Journal* has begun appearing thrice-yearly in Britain, publishing work from both sides of the Atlantic.

15 Susan J. Douglas, *Inventing American Broadcasting, 1899–1922* (Baltimore: Johns Hopkins University Press, 1987). Douglas then taught at Hampshire College but later transferred to the University of Michigan.

16 We are not ignoring the vitally important research by Hugh G. J. Aitken with this statement. But Aitken's *The Continuous Wave: Technology and American Radio, 1900–1932* (Princeton, N.J.: Princeton University Press, 1985), and its predecessor *Syntony and Spark: The Origins of Radio* (New York: Wiley, 1976), focus entirely on the technology story, while Douglas interweaves that with the business and nascent policy side of the growing radio business as well as the public perceptions of early radio.

17 The Canadian-born Smythe (1907–92) pioneered the application of political economics to the study of media power structures, first within government—he served at the Federal Communications Commission (subsequently cited as FCC) as an economist in the 1940s—and then as an academic in the United States and finally back in Canada. See Bill Melody's brief appreciation of Smythe and some of his published work, as published in the *Canadian Journal of Communication* 17, no. 4 (1992), <http://info.wlu.ca/~wwwpress/jrls/cjc/BackIssues/17.4/melody.html> (accessed June 2006).

18 Schiller (1919–2000) wrote widely and is perhaps best known for his *Mass Communication and American Empire* (New York: Augustus M. Kelley, 1969), which many feel helped launch the modern American critical studies' interest in media analysis. His own writing reflected his increasing alarm at the corporate takeover of media. See Richard Maxwell, *Herbert Schiller* (Lanham, Md.: Rowman & Littlefield, 2003). In a relatively rare example of familial pursuits, Schiller's son Dan now tills some of the same research vineyards from his post at the University of Illinois.

19 For an early and relevant example of his work, see Vincent Mosco, *Broadcasting in the United States: Innovative Challenge and Organizational Control* (Norwood, N.J.: Ablex, 1979), in which he argues that established interests dominate the policy process.

20 Much of Wasko's work has focused on Hollywood and its funding, more specifically on the Disney organization. She teaches at the University of Oregon.

21 See especially his *Understanding Media: The Extensions of Man* (New York: McGraw-Hill, 1964) for a convoluted but still insightful historically based survey of changing media impact.

22 Innis (1894–1952) has never been an easy academic to read or understand; he fills every sentence with sometimes dense information. Among his more relevant work are *Empire and Communications* (Toronto: University of Toronto Press,

1950) and *The Bias of Communication* (Toronto: University of Toronto Press, 1951).

23 Carolyn Marvin, *When Old Technologies Were New: Thinking about Communications in the Late Nineteenth Century* (New York: Oxford University Press, 1988).

24 Daniel J. Czitrom, *Media and the American Mind from Morse to McLuhan* (Chapel Hill: University of North Carolina Press, 1982). Czitrom then taught history at Mount Holyoke.

25 Michael Brian Schiffer, *The Portable Radio in American Life* (Tucson: University of Arizona Press, 1991).

26 Jonathan Sterne, *The Audible Past: Cultural Origins of Sound Reproduction* (Durham, N.C.: Duke University Press, 2003).

27 David Holbrook Culbert, *News for Everyman: Radio and Foreign Affairs in Thirties America* (Westport, Conn.: Greenwood Press, 1976).

28 Douglas B. Craig, *Fireside Politics: Radio and Political Culture in the United States, 1920–1940* (Baltimore: Johns Hopkins University Press, 2000).

29 Edward D. Miller, *Emergency Broadcasting and 1930s American Radio* (Philadelphia: Temple University Press, 2003).

30 These can be useful even if they are not scholarly in their apparatus of source notes and the like. See, for example, the many radio genre books by Jim Cox (most published by McFarland) or John Dunning's invaluable directory of radio programs, *On the Air: The Encyclopedia of Old-Time Radio* (New York: Oxford University Press, 1998). All of these provide useful grist for the researchers' mill.

31 Ray Barfield, *Listening to Radio, 1920–1950* (Westport, Conn.: Praeger, 1996). Barfield is a Clemson professor of English.

32 Michele Hilmes, *Radio Voices: American Broadcasting, 1922–1952* (Minneapolis: University of Minnesota Press, 1997). Hilmes has done more than most to help overcome radio's research-image problem in recent years with her own writing, conference papers, and a useful radio Listserv. She is on the communication arts faculty at the University of Wisconsin, Madison.

33 Jason Loviglio, *Radio's Intimate Public: Network Broadcasting and Mass-Mediated Democracy* (Minneapolis: University of Minnesota Press, 2005). Loviglio teaches American studies at the University of Maryland, Baltimore County.

34 Michael C. Keith, *Signals in the Air: Native Broadcasting in America* (Westport, Conn.: Praeger, 1995). Keith teaches at Boston College.

35 Michael C. Keith, *Voices in the Purple Haze: Underground Radio and the Sixties* (Westport, Conn.: Praeger, 1997).

36 Michael C. Keith, *Talking Radio: An Oral History of American Radio in the Television Age* (Armonk, N.Y.: M. E. Sharpe, 2000). In a sense, Keith's volume carries on the approach begun by Barfield, who in his earlier book provided an oral history of the period before television.

37 Michael C. Keith, *Sounds in the Dark: All-Night Radio in American Life* (Ames: Iowa State University Press, 2001).

38 Phylis A. Johnson and Michael C. Keith, *Queer Airwaves: The Story of Gay and Lesbian Broadcasting* (Armonk, N.Y.: M. E. Sharpe, 2001).

39 Robert L. Hilliard and Michael C. Keith, *Dirty Discourse: Sex and Indecency in American Radio* (Ames: Iowa State Press/Blackwell, 2003).

40 Robert L. Hilliard and Michael C. Keith, *The Quieted Voice: The Rise and Demise of Localism in American Radio* (Carbondale: Southern Illinois University Press, 2005). Hilliard teaches at Emerson College.

41 Michele Hilmes and Jason Loviglio, eds., *Radio Reader: Essays in the Cultural History of Radio* (New York: Longman, 2002).

42 Susan Merrill Squier, ed., *Communities of the Air: Radio Century, Radio Culture* (Durham, N.C.: Duke University Press, 2003).

43 W. Emmett Winn and Susan J. Brinson, eds., *Transmitting the Past: Historical and Cultural Perspectives on Broadcasting* (Tuscaloosa: University of Alabama Press, 2005).

44 Robert W. McChensey, *Telecommunications, Mass Media, and Democracy: The Battle for Control of U.S. Broadcasting, 1928–1935* (New York: Oxford University Press, 1993). This is a good example of the main title telling little about a book and the subtitle being all-important.

45 Louise M. Benjamin, *Freedom of the Air and the Public Interest: First Amendment Rights in Broadcasting to 1935* (Carbondale: Southern Illinois University Press, 2001).

46 Susan Smulyan, *Selling Radio: The Commercialization of American Broadcasting, 1920–1934* (Washington, D.C.: Smithsonian Institution Press, 1994).

47 Kathy M. Newman, *Radio Active: Advertising and Consumer Activism, 1935–1947* (Berkeley: University of California Press, 2004).

48 Thomas Streeter, *Selling the Air: A Critique of the Policy of Commercial Broadcasting in the United States* (Chicago: University of Chicago Press, 1996).

49 James C. Foust, *Big Voices on the Air: The Battle over Clear Channel Radio* (Ames: Iowa State University Press, 2000).

50 Hugh R. Slotten, *Radio and Television Regulation: Broadcast Technology in the United States, 1920–1960* (Baltimore: Johns Hopkins University Press, 2000).

51 See, for example, two books published the same year: Richard Neer, *FM: The Rise and Fall of Rock Radio* (New York: Villard, 2001); and Jesse Walker, *Rebels on the Air: An Alternative History of Radio in America* (New York: New York University Press, 2001).

CHAPTER I

1 "Staticless Radio," *Scientific American*, May 1939, p. 291.

2 See C. H. Sterling and J. M. Kittross, *Stay Tuned: A History of American Broadcasting*, 3rd ed. (Mahwah, N.J.: Lawrence Erlbaum Associates, 2002), appendix C, table 6-A, p. 862.

3 Bureau of the Census, *Historical Statistics of the United States, Colonial Times to 1970*, pt. 2 (Washington, D.C.: Government Printing Office, 1976), p. 783.

4 See, for example, Alfred M. Goldsmith and others, eds., *Radio Facsimile: An Assemblage of Papers from Engineers of the RCA Laboratories Relating to the Radio Transmission and Recorded Reception of Permanent Images* (New York: RCA Institutes Techni-

cal Press, 1938), especially "Part 1: Historical Development of Facsimile," pp. I–III.

5 Fan magazines were becoming common in the 1930s. One early book in the same genre was Joseph Gurman and Myron Slager, *Radio Round-Ups: Intimate Glimpses of the Radio Stars* (Boston: Lothrop, Lee & Shepard, 1932).

6 There is a substantial and growing literature on the so-called golden age of radio, but nothing surpasses the first two volumes of Erik Barnouw, *A History of Broadcasting in the United States*, 3 vols. (New York: Oxford University Press, 1966–70). Volume 1, *A Tower in Babel* (1966), takes the story to 1933, and vol. 2, *Golden Web* (1968), covers 1933 to 1953.

7 For more on this use of radio, see Douglas B. Craig, *Fireside Politics: Radio and Political Culture in the United States, 1920–1940* (Baltimore: Johns Hopkins University Press, 2000).

8 Sterling and Kittross, *Stay Tuned*, appendix C, table 3-A, p. 838.

9 See two network reports to advertisers: *Radio Takes to the Road* (New York: NBC, 1936) and *An Analysis of Radio-Listening in Autos* (New York: CBS, 1936). See also Donald W. Matteson, *The Auto Radio: A Romantic Genealogy* (Jackson, Mich.: Thornridge Publishing, 1987).

10 See, for example, Hadley Cantril and Gordon W. Allport, *The Psychology of Radio* (New York: Harper, 1935; repr. in "History of Broadcasting: Radio to Television" [New York: Arno Press, 1971]); or Azriel L. Eisenberg, *Children and Radio Programs* (New York: Columbia University Press, 1936).

11 Lawrence Lessing, *Man of High Fidelity: Edwin Howard Armstrong* (Philadelphia: J. B. Lippincott, 1956), p. 218. Reprinted by Bantam Books in 1969, both versions are long out of print and now difficult—and expensive—to find. Though suffering a number of limitations (including a lack of documentation), this journalistic account remains the only full biography of the inventor. For a wonderful online annotated collection of photos and documents from throughout Armstrong's life, see the extensive website at <http://users.erols.com/oldradio/index.htm> (accessed October 2004).

12 The FCC has always referred to AM broadcast stations as "standard" radio, a terminology that for many years rankled struggling FM operators because it seemed to further isolate the newer service. The commission adopted the term in the late 1930s to differentiate the existing basic system from various additional technologies, including FM.

13 For a technical description of this device, see C. F. Elwell, *The Poulson Arc Generator* (New York: Van Nostrand, 1923).

14 Cornelius D. Ehret, "Art of Transmitting Intelligence" (patent 785,803) and "System of Transmitting Intelligence" (patent 785,804) in *Specifications and Drawings of Patents*, pt. 2, by the U.S. Patent Office (March 1905) pp. 3661–72. Ehret had applied for both of these three years earlier.

15 As discussed in Edwin H. Armstrong, "Mathematical Theory vs. Physical Concept," *FM and Television*, August 1944, p. 11.

16 Alfred N. Goldsmith, *Radio Telephony* (New York: The Wireless Press, 1918), p. 11.

17 John R. Carson, "Notes on the Theory of Modulation," *Proceedings of the Institute of Radio Engineers* 10, no. 2 (February 1922): 57–64.

18 *The History of Broadcasting and KDKA Radio* (Pittsburgh: Westinghouse Broadcasting, n.d.), p. 29.

19 Orrin E. Dunlap, *Dunlap's Radio and Television Almanac* (New York: Harper, 1951), p. 94. The relatively low frequencies used in these tests no doubt contributed to the great distances covered.

20 See Lessing, *Man of High Fidelity*, pp. 26–28.

21 For his own version of the innovation, see Edwin H. Armstrong, "Some Recent Developments in the Audion Receiver," *Proceedings of the Institute of Radio Engineers* 3 (September 1915): 215–47; repr. in *Proceedings of the IEEE* 1 (August 1963): 1083–97.

22 For a summary of this patent fight, see W. Rupert Maclaurin, *Invention and Innovation in the Radio Industry* (New York: Macmillan, 1949), pp. 119–23.

23 Pupin was renowned for his work on long-distance telephone transmission and circuits, which allowed multiple messages to be sent at one time.

24 See Edwin H. Armstrong, "The Story of the Super-Heterodyne," *Radio Broadcast* 5 (July 1924): 198–207; and his more technical "The Super-Heterodyne: Its Origin, Development, and Some Recent Improvements," *Proceedings of the Institute of Radio Engineers* 12, no. 5 (October 1924): 1–14.

25 The military title also became part of an annual programming award given in the years after his death.

26 Mary Ellen Hogan, "The Innovation of FM Radio: Armstrong vs. the Radio Corporation of America" (master's thesis, Temple University, April 1972), p. 62. Hogan cites a 1920 agreement as reported in Federal Trade Commission, *The Radio Industry* (Washington, D.C.: Government Printing Office, 1924), p. 168.

27 RCA had a fair bit of space toward the top of the building, which some had dubbed the "Empty" State Building given the poor office-rental market in the depths of the Depression.

28 The term came from the then-typical kitchen breadboard, as radio components were mounted directly on wooden boards to facilitate shifting them about as experiments warranted.

29 Hogan, "The Innovation of FM Radio," p. 63. See also the useful narrative in Thomas J. Buzalski, "Field Test of the Armstrong Wide-Band Frequency Modulation System from the Empire State Building, 1934 and 1935," *Antique Wireless Association Review* 1 (1986): 108–16. Buzalski was one of the NBC engineers who worked with Armstrong at the time.

30 Hogan, "The Innovation of FM Radio," pp. 64–68, outlines the arguments as RCA saw them.

31 The published version of his New York presentation is Edwin H. Armstrong, "A Method of Reducing Disturbances in Radio Signaling by a System of Frequency Modulation," *Proceedings of the Institute of Radio Engineers* 24 (May 1936): 689–740.

This is the fundamental paper announcing and describing the principles of Armstrong's FM system.

32 Lessing, *Man of High Fidelity*, pp. 209–10.

33 The scene is described in ibid., pp. 208–11.

34 "A Method of Reducing Disturbances in Radio Signaling by a System of Frequency Modulation," *Proceedings of the Institute of Radio Engineers* 24 (May 1936): 689–740. This was the first detailed public description.

35 The tower still stood in 2007 as this was written; it could clearly be seen, for example, from the Tappan Zee Bridge to the north. For good pictures of the structure on its completion, see "Revolution in Radio," *Fortune*, October 1939, pp. 86–88, 116B, 119, 121.

36 A transcription, sometimes called an electrical transcription (ET), was a special high-quality recording made for broadcast use. ETs used 12- or 16-inch discs in this era before tape recording technology had appeared.

37 See the excellent "Edwin H. Armstrong" website, <http://users.erols.com/oldradio/index.htm> (accessed October 2007). The site includes facsimiles of important documents and photographs from the inventor's life.

38 For details on and photos of these pioneering REL sets, see the Armstrong website, <http://users.erols.com/oldradio/eha68.htm> (accessed October 2007).

39 Leland Bickford in collaboration with Walter Fogg, *News While It Is News: The Real Story of Radio News* (Boston: G. C. Manthorne, 1935).

40 Much of this background information on Shepard is drawn from Donna Halper, "John Shepard—Boston's Showman," <http://www.oldradio.com/archives/people/shepard.htm> (accessed October 2004). Though he sold the Yankee Network (to General Tire & Rubber) in late 1942, Shepard completed a five-year contract as board chairman. Amidst substantial change in the radio business, the Yankee Network offered its final broadcast in 1967.

41 "Half Million Will Be Spent for Tests," *Broadcasting*, January 15, 1938, p. 15.

42 See "Earliest FM Stations," <http://members.aol.com/jeff560/fmfirst.html> (accessed October 2004), for further details. With the inception of commercial FM operations in January 1941, W1XOJ's power was boosted to 50,000 watts, and in April the call letters became W43B. The first commercials that aired exclusively on FM were broadcast in May (they advertised Socony Oil [later Mobil]).

43 Donna Halper, "John Shepard's FM Stations—America's First FM Network," <http://www.bostonradio.org/radio/shepard-fm.html> (accessed October 2004).

44 See "Yankee Frequency Modulation about Ready," *Broadcasting*, June 1, 1939, p. 53; and Lessing, *Man of High Fidelity*, p. 238.

45 For further background on this operation, which was purchased by the *New York Times* in 1944, see Elliott M. Sanger, *Rebel in Radio: The Story of WQXR* (New York: Hastings House, 1973).

46 See C. H. Sterling, "Second Service: A History of Commercial FM Broadcasting

to 1969" (Ph.D. diss., University of Wisconsin, Madison, 1969), table 1, "Pioneer FM Stations, 1934–1940," pp. 31–32.

47 Ibid., pp. 35–37.

48 "How to Promote FM," *Radio and Television Retailing*, November 1940, p. 26. The story includes a photo of the Macy's display.

49 Dunlap, *Dunlap's Radio and Television Almanac*, p. 126.

50 Christopher H. Sterling, "WTMJ-FM: A Case Study in the Development of FM Broadcasting," *Journal of Broadcasting* 12 (Fall 1968): 341–52." This drew on the author's unpublished master's thesis of the same title at the University of Wisconsin, Madison, a year earlier.

51 "Zenith Tests FM," *Broadcasting*, January 15, 1940, p. 31.

52 See Paul deMars, "Frequency Modulation: History and Progress," in 1940 *Broadcasting Yearbook* (Washington: Broadcasting Publications, 1940), p. 372.

53 FCC, *Fourth Annual Report for the Fiscal Year Ended June 30, 1938* (Washington, D.C.: Government Printing Office, 1938), p. 66.

54 FCC, *Fifth Annual Report for the Fiscal Year Ended June 30, 1939* (Washington, D.C.: Government Printing Office, 1939), pp. 48–49.

55 *Broadcasting*, February 1, 1940, p. 80.

56 [Dick Dorrance], *Broadcasting's Better Mousetrap* (New York: FM Broadcasters, Inc., n.d. [1940?]), pp. 9–10.

57 "F-M Is Exhibited to Capitol Group," *Broadcasting*, February 1, 1940, p. 48. There was considerable variation in how the new service was labeled in these early years; it ranged among "FM," "F.M.," and, as here, "F-M."

58 See, for example, "Staticless Radio."

59 "Revolution in Radio," *Fortune*, October 1939, pp. 86–88, 116B, 119, 121.

60 The following description of these FCC hearings is taken from the 25,000-word story filed after the hearings in the industry's main trade biweekly. See Sol Taishoff and Lewis V. Gilpin, "Birth of Commercial FM This Year Seen," *Broadcasting*, April 1, 1940, pp. 18–21, 80–93.

61 Samuel Lubell, "Comes the Radio Revolution," *Saturday Evening Post*, July 6, 1940, p. 32.

62 Even this early in broadcasting's development, a frequency shift for a station or a full reallocation almost always meant moving higher in the electromagnetic spectrum. Lower frequencies (such as those medium frequencies utilized by AM service), having been allocated first, were filled with a variety of telecommunications services. Only the VHF and higher ranges remained largely unused in 1940.

63 "FCC Delays Decision on FM as Television Holds Spotlight," *Broadcasting*, April 15, 1940, p. 28.

64 FCC, *Sixth Annual Report for the Fiscal Year Ended June 30, 1940* (Washington, D.C.: Government Printing Office, 1940), pp. 66–69.

65 As quoted in Andrew Inglis, *Behind the Tube: A History of Broadcasting Technology and Business* (Stoneham, Mass.: Focal Press, 1990), p. 128.

66 "One Thousand New FM Stations Foreseen," *Broadcasting*, June 1, 1940, p. 18.

67 FCC, *Sixth Annual Report*, p. 67.

68 These last were somewhat analogous to the "clear-channel" AM stations that had been established in 1928 by the Federal Radio Commission. AM clear-channel outlets (so named because there had originally been only one transmitter operating on their frequency during nighttime hours) used 50,000 watts of power and, depending on conditions, could often reach out several hundred miles, thus providing radio service to rural areas that might otherwise not be served.

69 This was because, with FM's location in the VHF spectrum, it did not suffer from skywave propagation, which often caused interference. See appendix A for further discussion of this point.

70 FCC, *Sixth Annual Report*, p. 68.

71 "FM Challenge," *Broadcasting*, June 1, 1940, p. 58.

72 Lubell, "Comes the Radio Revolution," p. 33.

73 Advertisement in *Broadcasting*, June 1, 1940, p. 77. Emphasis in the original.

74 See *Broadcasting*, June 15, 1940, p. 20.

75 Inglis, *Behind the Tube*, p. 128.

CHAPTER 2

1 "Final Decision on FM Frequencies: We Don't Want a Successful Operation and a Dead Patient on Our Hands," *FM and Television*, March 1945, p. 19.

2 "FM: What 'Green-Lighted' Stations Are Doing to Get Started," *Radio and Television Retailing*, December 1940, pp. 26, 59.

3 "Application of the Journal Company for a High Frequency Broadcast Station Construction Permit," July 17, 1940, exhibit 31, FCC station files, National Archives, Washington, D.C.

4 "New FM Grants Bring Total to 29," *Broadcasting*, January 20, 1941, p. 55; and *Broadcasting*, March 3, 1941, p. 40.

5 "Call Letter Plan Is Proposed for FM," *Broadcasting*, November 15, 1940, p. 17.

6 "Gee, Whiz Dept.," *FM Bulletin of the FMBI*, July 28, 1942, p. 3. This mimeographed newsletter is often cited in this chapter. Its title varied, as did the means of numbering issues and the city of publication (New York and then Washington). For simplicity we cite a common title and specific dates.

7 A full listing is in *Broadcasting*, November 15, 1940, p. 17.

8 By mid-1942, Sleeper's monthly had broadened to add "Radio-Electronic Engineering and Design" as a subtitle, and by 1944 it was called *FM and Television*. Given the holding pattern of civilian broadcasting (no new stations or receivers for the duration), content increasingly focused on wartime radio applications.

9 See, for example, "More Attention for FM," *FM Bulletin of the FMBI*, January 17, 1942, p. 2, which details several of these in Detroit, Boston, and Worcester, Massachusetts.

10 "The G-E Frequency Modulation Primer" (GE Radio and Television Dept. Publication 13-197, Bridgeport, Conn., n.d.); and "Facts about FM" (Stromberg-Carlson Publication No. 1060, Rochester, N.Y., n.d.), p. 15.

11 "General Electric Presents Listen—It's FM!" (company four-page illustrated promotional brochure 13-171-A, n.d.).

12 "News from FM Centers," FM Bulletin of the FMBI, June 30, 1942, p. 5, for example, makes mention of such a use in the Philadelphia schools.

13 "System of Calls for FM Devised," Broadcasting, December 15, 1940, p. 50.

14 "We Just Don't Like Them," FM Bulletin of the FMBI, July 11, 1943, p. 2.

15 "Something Special to Report," FM Bulletin of the FMBI, August 31, 1943, pp. 1–2. A list of the stations on the air with both their old and new call letters appeared in issue 33 of this publication (October 19, 1943, pp. 1–2).

16 Broadcasting, March 10, 1941, p. 46.

17 Broadcasting, December 1, 1941, p. 48.

18 "FM Saturation?," Broadcasting, February 17, 1941, p. 30.

19 Harvey J. Levin, Broadcast Regulation and Joint Ownership of Media (New York: New York University Press, 1960), p. 54. Emphasis in the original.

20 The FCC's Report on Chain Broadcasting appeared in May 1941 and would eventually lead to NBC's sale of the Blue Network (1943), which by 1945 had become ABC.

21 FCC, Order No. 79 (Washington, D.C.: FCC mimeo 48496, March 20, 1941).

22 "FCC Starts Newspaper Ownership Drive," Broadcasting, March 24, 1941, p. 8.

23 "Gordon Gray's Grant Only FM Station Excepted from FCC's Newspaper Ruling," Broadcasting, April 14, 1941, p. 42.

24 At this point only a handful of Washington, D.C., buildings were air-conditioned. The FCC, then housed in one of the Federal Triangle government buildings, was not in one of them.

25 "FCC vs. Press," Business Week, July 26, 1941, p. 33.

26 Broadcasting, August 4, 1941, pp. 50–51.

27 Murray Edelman, The Licensing of Radio Services in the United States, 1927 to 1947 (Urbana: University of Illinois Press, 1950), p. 108. One factor in dropping the proceeding may have been Fly's departure as FCC chairman.

28 FCC, Eighth Annual Report for the Fiscal Year Ended June 30, 1942 (Washington, D.C.: FCC mimeo edition, 1942), p. 33. FCC annual reports for 1942 to 1944 were never formally published but rather appeared only in a very limited number of copies. They were included in the reprint of FCC reports from 1934 through 1955 ("History of Broadcasting: Radio to Television" [New York: Arno Press, 1971]).

29 "A Smattering of News," FM Bulletin of the FMBI, January 24, 1942, p. 2.

30 "FMBI Has a Meeting," FM Bulletin of the FMBI, March 7, 1942, pp. 1–2.

31 "And That's That," FM Bulletin of the FMBI, April 18, 1942, p. 1.

32 Broadcasting, July 22, 1942, p. 18.

33 "FCC Announces Lenient FM Policy, Battling Wartime Material Shortage," Broadcasting, August 10, 1942, p. 55.

34 "Meet the Boys," *FM Bulletin of the FMBI*, August 11, 1942, p. 3.

35 "FM Station List Shows 37 Outlets Now in Operation," *Broadcasting*, November 9, 1942, p. 28.

36 "Snow in the South," *FM Bulletin of the FMBI*, March 21, 1942, p. 3.

37 "In Response to Request," *FM Bulletin of the FMBI*, September 30, 1943, pp. 1–2.

38 "Forecast for FM," *FM Bulletin of the FMBI*, May 27, 1942, p. 2.

39 "FM No Mystery to This Young Lady," *FM Bulletin of the FMBI*, May 9, 1942, p. 3.

40 "Nothing, It Seems, Is Sacred," *FM Bulletin of the FMBI*, September 22, 1942, p. 5.

41 "Those Indomitable Women," *FM Bulletin of the FMBI*, November 30, 1942, p. 4.

42 "Word from Fort Wayne," *FM Bulletin of the FMBI*, December 14, 1942, p. 4.

43 "That the Day Should Ever Have Come," *FM Bulletin of the FMBI*, February 15, 1943, p. 5.

44 "All-Girl Staff Mans W1XTG," *FM Bulletin of the FMBI*, May 15, 1943, p. 4.

45 *Broadcasting*, March 29, 1943, p. 58.

46 "FM Applications Involve $8,300,000 Cost," *Broadcasting*, April 24, 1944, p. 11.

47 "Milestone for Mutual," *FM Bulletin of the FMBI*, November 17, 1943, p. 1.

48 O. B Hanson to John F. Royal, Vice President for New Developments, internal memo, November 26, 1941, box 110, folder 28, NBC collections, State Historical Society of Wisconsin, Madison.

49 Ibid.

50 "Independent-Owned FM Net Covering 40 Markets Planned," *Broadcasting*, July 1, 1940, p. 12; and "Action Is Planned on FM Network," *Broadcasting*, July 15, 1940, p. 74.

51 "FM Market Group to Hold Meeting," *Broadcasting*, February 3, 1941, p. 50.

52 "The Noise-Free Network," *FM Bulletin of the FMBI*, November 29, 1941, pp. 1–2.

53 *Broadcasting*, December 1, 1941, p. 57.

54 "The American Network Again," *FM Bulletin of the FMBI*, January 5, 1944, p. 2.

55 *Broadcasting*, February 14, 1944, p. 43. Emphasis in the original.

56 *Broadcasting*, May 1, 1944, p. 67.

57 William B. Lewis, "The Possibility of a Fifth Network," *FM and Television*, November 1944, pp. 18–19.

58 It should be noted that there is little information on which to base generalizations about early FM programming. Trade periodicals only occasionally made any note of programming, usually for various "firsts." Some newspapers listed local FM-station programs, but not all.

59 As will be seen, the same thing happened again two decades later in the early 1960s with the introduction of stereo broadcasts, when listeners were subjected to broadcasts of tennis matches so they could position their speakers.

60 *Broadcasting*, January 20, 1941, p. 70.

61 Today the *Journal* stations still operate from the considerably expanded facility.

62 "NBC Makes Programs Available to FM," *Broadcasting*, January 17, 1944, p. 12.

63 John Royal to Frank Mullen, internal memo of July 25, 1945, box 110, folder 29, NBC Collections, State Historical Society of Wisconsin, Madison.

64 "CBS, Blue Favor Duplicating on FM," *Broadcasting*, June 16, 1944, p. 14.

65 "FM Rate Card," *Broadcasting*, April 28, 1941, p. 42.

66 "First FM Sponsor," *Broadcasting*, October 15, 1940, p. 50.

67 See "First FM Sponsors," *Broadcasting*, April 14, 1941, p. 42; and *Broadcasting*, January 20, 1941, p. 55.

68 "FM Chain Ready," *Business Week*, June 14, 1941, p. 58.

69 *Broadcasting*, May 18, 1942, p. 72.

70 *Broadcasting*, October 11, 1943, p. 44.

71 "Muzak Projects Nationwide FM Circuits," *Broadcasting*, October 15, 1944, p. 3.

72 "W47NY's Program Booklet," *FM Bulletin of the FMBI*, August 27, 1943, pp. 2–3.

73 David Eshelman, "The Emergence of Educational FM Broadcasting," *NAEB Journal*, March–April 1967, p. 57.

74 Ibid., p. 58.

75 Ibid., pp. 57–58.

76 See, for example, Ray C. Wakefield, "FM and Education," *Quarterly Journal of Speech* 31 (February 1945): 39; and Henry L. Ewbank, "Statewide Plans for Educational FM Broadcasting," *Quarterly Journal of Speech* 31 (October 1945): 333.

77 Donald N. Wood and Donald G. Wylie, *Educational Telecommunications* (Belmont, Calif.: Wadsworth, 1977), p. 31.

78 Robert J. Blakely, *To Serve the Public Interest: Educational Broadcasting in the United States* (Syracuse, N.Y.: Syracuse University Press, 1979), p. 78.

79 U.S. Office of Education, *FM for Education* (Misc. Publication No. 7, Washington, D.C.: Federal Security Agency, 1944).

80 "FM Promotion Activity to Be Extended as Survey Shows 14 Firms Making Sets," *Broadcasting*, September 1, 1940, p. 97.

81 Ibid.; and *Broadcasting*, October 1, 1940, p. 42.

82 "FM Fans Reported Increasing at Rate of 5,000 Every Day," *Chicago Tribune*, September 21, 1941, p. NA1.

83 "120,000 FM Sets in Homes Claimed," *Broadcasting*, November 10, 1941, p. 46; and *Broadcasting*, January 5, 1942, p. 40.

84 "By Way of Introduction," *FM Bulletin of the FMBI*, May 9, 1942, p. 1.

85 "So, What Did We Find?," *FM Bulletin of the FMBI*, June 16, 1942, p. 2.

86 See, for just one example among many, "We Have Our Reasons," *FM Bulletin of the FMBI*, November 3, 1942, p. 3.

87 "Battle over FM," *Business Week*, November 11, 1944, p. 20.

88 See, for example, *FM Broadcasting* (Princeton, N.J.: RCA Laboratories, 1944), which in forty-five pages of technical description and comparison with AM

does not mention Armstrong's name once; *FM: A Statement of NBC's FM Policy by Niles Trammel, President* (New York: NBC, 1944); and *New Approaches to Broadcasting* (Camden, N.J.: RCA Victor Division, 1944).

89 See, for example, *Broadcasting*, April 26, 1943, p. 36.

90 *Broadcasting*, November 22, 1943, p. 12.

91 "FM Broadcasters Pledge Action on Post-War Allocation Plans," *Broadcasting*, August 9, 1943, p. 10.

92 "Effects of Bursts on FM Are Studied by FCC: Satisfactory Solution Seen," *Broadcasting*, June 12, 1944, p. 20.

93 "Discussion of Postwar Broadcasting," *FM and Television*, October 1944, pp. 22–25, 65, is a complete transcript of Howard Armstrong's FCC testimony.

94 This came from an extensive report on the hearings. See "Rapid FM Growth in High Band Indicated," *Broadcasting*, October 15, 1944, supplement, pt. 1. See also Milton B. Sleeper, "Outline of the FCC Hearing on FM," *FM and Television*, October 1944, p. 13.

95 Ibid., p. 2.

96 Ibid., p. 9.

97 Ibid.

98 Ibid., p. 16.

99 *Postwar Shortwave, FM, and Television* (New York: CBS, 1944) is a transcript of Keston's testimony.

100 "Norton Urges FM over 120 mc, Television 500–1,500 mc Band," *Broadcasting*, November 6, 1944, pp. 23–26.

101 FCC, *Report on Docket 6651, FM Broadcast Service* (Washington, D.C.: Government Printing Office, 1945); "Allocations Proposals Announced by FCC," *Broadcasting*, January 16, 1945, p. 13 quotes the entire document.

102 *Broadcasting*, January 22, 1945, p. 17.

103 Panel 5 chairman C. M. Jansky made these points at a New York IRE special meeting assessing the FCC plans. See *Broadcasting*, February 5, 1945, p. 66.

104 "Military to Confide Secret Data to Radio," *Broadcasting*, March 5, 1945, pp. 64, 68.

105 "Shifting of FM Upward in Spectrum Seen," *Broadcasting*, March 19, 1945, p. 18; see also FCC, *Report on Docket 6651, Section 8 — FM Broadcast Services* (Washington, D.C.: FCC mimeo 82387, May 15, 1945), pp. 60–61.

106 "Congress Keeps Hands off FM Allocation," *Broadcasting*, April 9, 1945, p. 18.

107 FCC, *Report on Docket 6651*, p. 84.

108 Using a Midwest test location, it found that at an eighty-mile range signals at 91 MHz were usable only about 30 percent of the time, while at 45.5 MHz, listening was acceptable at 90 percent of the time. This suggested long-range FM listening would not work at the new, higher allocation. See C. W. Carnahan, N. W. Aram, and E. F. Classen, "Report on Propagation of 45.5 and 91.0 Megacycles between Richfield, Wisconsin, and Deerfield, Illinois, July 20, 1945, to September 20, 1945" (submitted to the FCC, October 1, 1945).

109 "FCC Allocates 88–106 mc Band to FM," *Broadcasting*, July 2, 1945, p. 13.

110 Ibid.

111 "Broadcast Leaders See FM Replacing AM," *Broadcasting*, August 6, 1945, p. 16. This paragraph is also informed by the full transcript of the hearing issued by the National Association of Broadcasters: *Special Allocations Hearing Bulletin: FM Hearings, Docket 6768* (Washington, D.C.: NAB, August 24, 1945).

112 FCC, *Rules and Regulations: Subpart B — Rules Governing FM Broadcast Stations* (Washington, D.C.: FCC, September 12, 1945). See also the FCC report on these rules, as reprinted in *Broadcasting*, August 27, 1945; and in "Frequency Modulation," chapter 6 of *Radio and Television Law*, by Harry Warner (Albany: Matthew Bender, 1948).

113 Established by the Federal Radio Commission in 1928, the so-called clear channels — so named because originally no other station was to broadcast on these frequencies (which would be "cleared" for the purpose) — were to be high-power AM outlets operating in major cities but designed to serve large rural regions, especially at night. By this time, there were some small stations operating on a secondary level on some clear channels, but they remained pristine (used only by the assigned large station) in nighttime hours, when AM signals traveled further. See appendix A.

114 By mid-1945, almost half of all AM stations on the air were limited to daytime hours only because of nighttime skywave interference in the medium-wave frequencies they used. See appendix A.

115 Warner, *Radio and Television Law*, p. 604.

116 Things moved faster in those days, it seems. The petition from Zenith was filed on January 4, 1946, and the hearing was held on January 18 and 19. And the latter was a Saturday! The final decision was issued on January 24. Such speed would have been astonishing a half century or more later when, it seemed, everything took longer and was often delayed further by appeals.

117 "FM High Band Controversy," *Broadcasting*, January 6, 1946, p. 15; and "FM Is Open Question as Hearing Begins," *Broadcasting*, January 21, 1946, p. 18.

118 "FCC Report Explains FM Allocation," *Broadcasting*, March 11, 1946, p. 36.

119 U.S. Congress, House of Representatives, *Radio Frequency Modulation: Hearings on H. J. Res. 78*, 80th Cong., 2nd sess., February (part 1) and March–April (part 2) 1948. The two parts are paginated consecutively.

120 U.S. Senate Committee on Interstate and Foreign Commerce, *Progress of FM Radio: Hearings*, 80th Cong., 2nd sess., March–May 1948.

121 Ibid., pp. 102–3. Senator Homer Capehart (R-Ind.) was the complainer.

122 For a detailed though by no means neutral description of the long lawsuit, see Lawrence Lessing, *Man of High Fidelity: Edwin Howard Armstrong* (Philadelphia: J. B. Lippincott, 1956), pp. 279–94.

CHAPTER 3

1 J. Frank Beatty, "FM's Pulse Beat," *Broadcasting-Telecasting*, October 9, 1950, p. 23.

2 Irv Marder, "Armstrong Sues: RCA Target in FM Fight," *Broadcasting*, July 26, 1948, pp. 21, 67.

3 "Armstrong, FM Inventor, Dies in Leap from East Side Suite," *New York Times*, February 2, 1954. The lawsuit against RCA was settled a year later for $1 million. See *Broadcasting-Telecasting*, January 10, 1955, p. 84.

4 For further background and detail on this sometimes confusing but fascinating postwar period, see Christopher H. Sterling and John M. Kittross, *Stay Tuned: A History of American Broadcasting*, 3rd ed. (Mahwah, N.J.: Lawrence Erlbaum Associates, 2002), especially chapter 7.

5 See Christopher H. Sterling, *Electronic Media: A Guide to Trends in Broadcasting and Newer Technologies, 1920–1983* (New York: Praeger, 1984), especially tables 180A and 680A.

6 See Ronald Garay, *Gordon McLendon: The Maverick of Radio* (New York: Greenwood, 1992); there is thus far no published biography of Storz.

7 For an excellent history of how "Top 40" originated and developed, see David T. Macfarland, *The Development of the Top 40 Radio Format*, in "Dissertations in Broadcasting" (New York: Arno Press, 1979).

8 The literature on Presley and his impact is huge and growing, but one interesting recent survey is Will Friedwald, "Elvis Today," *American Heritage* 56, no. 1 (February/March 2005): 22–28.

9 See, for example, *A Discussion of Radio: Past, Present and Future* (New York: Batten, Barton, Durstine & Osborn, Fall 1956).

10 George Rowe (Office of Information, U.S. Department of Agriculture), *FM for You* (Washington, D.C.: Government Printing Office, November 1945). See "Agriculture Dept. Issues FM Primer for Guidance of Farm Organizations," *Broadcasting*, November 19, 1945, p. 77.

11 *Journal of Frequency Modulation* (New York: Telecasting Publications) was the title for the February, March, and April issues; the changed title appeared on the May issue. Martin Codel, cofounder of *Broadcasting*, was president and publisher. The monthly continued until November 1947, when it was absorbed by *Sponsor*.

12 U.S. Congress, Senate Special Committee to Study Problems of American Small Business, *Small Business Opportunities in FM Broadcasting*, 79th Cong., 2nd sess., Senate Committee Print No. 4 (April 10, 1945). Its twenty-one pages explained and promoted the service as a good option for war veterans and offered recommendations for applying for a construction permit.

13 Milton B. Sleeper, ed., *FM Radio Handbook: 1946 Edition* (Great Barrington, Mass: FM Publishing Co., September 1946). This included illustrated information on FM's background, how to apply, studio operations, use of coax lines for FM transmitters, high-fidelity reproduction, antennas, receivers, railroad radio installations, facsimile equipment, and FM standards of good engineering practice. Clearly intended as an annual, it was the only edition to appear.

14 Charles A. Siepmann, *Radio's Second Chance* (Boston: Little, Brown, 1946). A

former BBC official, Siepmann (1899–1985) came to the United States early in the war and became a consultant to the FCC. His book cited countless drawbacks of commercial AM operations and looked to FM as something of a panacea to improve the situation. He entered academe and published *Radio, Television and Society* (New York: Oxford University Press, 1950), a widely used college text.

15 In comments before the FMBI convention on January 26, 1944, as quoted in *Broadcasting*, February 7, 1944, p. 50.

16 Paul A. Porter, "As I See It," *Frequency Modulation Journal*, February 1946, pp. 10–11.

17 Charles R. Denny Jr., "How the FCC Views FM," *FM and Television*, February 1947, pp. 24, 54. These were his remarks before an FMA luncheon meeting the previous month.

18 Quoted in *Broadcasting*, February 2, 1948, p. 84.

19 Milton B. Sleeper, "FM Prepared for Nation-Wide Expansion," *FM and Television*, July 1945, p. 27. Sleeper was an important publisher of FM-related periodicals and guidebooks in this period.

20 *Broadcasting*, January 14, 1946, p. 91 cites these two examples as holding up the New York stations from rapidly converting to their new frequencies.

21 Ibid.

22 "FM Shifts to High Band in Two Weeks," *Broadcasting*, December 17, 1945, p. 20.

23 Ibid., p. 93.

24 The station was KRNT in Des Moines, Iowa, as noted in *Broadcasting*, March 17, 1947, p. 44.

25 "FCC Sets 231 AM cases; Uses CBS FM Plan," *Broadcasting*, November 15, 1945, p. 18.

26 *Broadcasting*, May 12, 1947, p. 87. He spoke in a May 1947 talk at Ohio State University.

27 *Broadcasting*, December 29, 1947, p. 76.

28 "FM Misnomer," *Broadcasting*, December 24, 1945, p. 48.

29 "FCC Announces FM Allocation Proposals," *Broadcasting*, December 24, 1945, p. 17. A word on nomenclature here. For decades, the FCC spoke only of broad allocations and specific station assignments. Only in the late 1970s did it adopt a term already used in Europe: "allotments," meaning a specific channel in a specific location, whether or not an actual station was using it. For clarity we've used allotments here, even though American use of the term was three decades into the future.

30 Ewell K. Jett, "The Community FM Station," *Journal of Frequency Modulation*, March 1946, pp. 10–13, 46–47. Commissioner Jett used coverage maps of stations in Washington, D.C., and Minneapolis–St. Paul, Minnesota, to illustrate his point.

31 "Power of 1kW Proposed for Community FM," *Broadcasting*, June 3, 1946, p. 15. This was craftier than it may have appeared, for the new labeling was opposite

the labeling approach used in AM. For the latter, Class I was a high-powered station, and Class IV was a local, low-powered outlet.

32 See FCC, *Thirteenth Annual Report for Fiscal Year Ended June 30, 1947* (Washington, D.C.: Government Printing Office, 1947), p. 21; and "FCC Issues New FM Allocation Plan," *Broadcasting*, April 14, 1947, p. 15.

33 "Labor Unions Request 16 Stations," *Broadcasting*, November 26, 1945, p. 20. The Chicago Federation of Labor was an AM exception—it had operated Chicago station WCFL for years.

34 "Investment Required for FM Surveyed," *Broadcasting*, December 17, 1945, p. 17.

35 "Plan to Reserve FM Channels Adopted," *Broadcasting*, July 22, 1946, p. 18.

36 "FCC Approves 65 More FM Stations," *Broadcasting*, November 5, 1945, p. 16.

37 It should be remembered, of course, that the population shift to the West and South had barely begun at this point, and thus more of the country's people still lived in the older cities of the Northeast.

38 Another factor limited and slowed station construction—a temporary government policy (lifted in mid-1947) to direct materials to the critical housing market rather than commercial applications such as broadcast stations. A number of stations had to operate with temporary authorizations and facilities for about a year.

39 *Broadcasting*, July 28, 1947, p. 22. While at first FM licenses lasted only one year, in mid-1948 licenses for the then-standard three years were granted to operating FM outlets. See FCC, *Thirteenth Annual Report*, p. 22.

40 FCC, *Fourteenth Annual Report for Fiscal Year Ended June 30, 1948* (Washington, D.C.: Government Printing Office, 1948), p. 33.

41 AT&T had been the provider of network links since the 1926 sale of its station WEAF in New York to RCA. Part of the agreement signed between the then-feuding telephone and radio "groups" into which the industry was divided in the early 1920s held that AT&T would stay out of station operations, but it would be the sole provider of the links necessary for regional or national networking of stations. The same agreement was extended to television, and until the inception of satellite services in the 1980s, AT&T microwave and coaxial cable links provided network connections for television as well. AT&T filed its first intercity connection rates for FM, providing a frequency response three times better than those used for AM—but at nearly double the cost. See "FCC Gets AT&T FM Inter-City Rates," *Broadcasting*, January 26, 1948, pp. 17, 75. At the time very few FM operations could pay such rates (sixteen hours a day of connection between New York and Washington would run just over $2,000 per month, or about $20,000 in 2005 figures).

42 *Broadcasting*, June 4, 1945, p. 80.

43 "Rural FM," *Broadcasting*, March 1, 1948, p. 73; and "New York FM: Rural Radio Network Relays WQXR Music and News," *Broadcasting*, June 19, 1950, p. 43. The latter includes a map of the stations involved.

44 "Dixie FM Network," *Broadcasting*, April 19, 1948, p. 46.

45 Everett Dillard, "The FM Facts of Life" (remarks before the FM Association Sales Clinic, New York, April 1, 1949), p. 1.

46 "Hanna Network: FM Station Feeds AM Outlets," *Broadcasting*, August 29, 1949, p. 35. WBRC-FM transmitted with more than 500kW (purportedly making it the most powerful radio station in the world at the time) and achieved a coverage range of some 200 miles, making the relays possible.

47 "A Nationwide Network for FM," *Frequency Modulation Business*, May 1946, p. 40; and "CBS FM-AM Plan Would Cost 10 Million," *Broadcasting*, May 13, 1946, pp. 17, 98–99. See also the booklet of Frank Stanton's April 1946 FCC testimony, *FM—The Key to Future Radio Allocations* (New York: CBS, 1946), which includes two maps showing the huge AM stations to be located in Denver and northern Kentucky.

48 "ABC's Projected FM Network," *Frequency Modulation Business*, August 1946, p. 34. ABC had emerged in 1945 from the Blue Network, once a part of NBC that had been divested as a result of a 1941 FCC ruling and 1943 Supreme Court decision in *NBC v. United States*.

49 Interview with Everett Dillard, president of Commercial Radio Equipment Co., Washington, D.C., November 19, 1968.

50 Ibid.

51 "Continental Pioneers FM Networking," *Broadcasting*, September 15, 1947, p. 62.

52 *Broadcasting*, April 21, 1947, p. 38.

53 C. M. Jansky, "The Demonstrated Potentialities of Frequency Modulation Broadcasting on Very High Frequencies" (address before the International Telecommunication Conference, Atlantic City, August 6, 1947).

54 *Broadcasting*, June 2, 1947, p. 82.

55 Everette L. Dillard, "Continental Pioneers FM Networking," *Broadcasting*, September 15, 1947, pp. 62, 64.

56 Testimony of Everett Dillard to the House Commerce Committee, *Radio Frequency Modulation: Hearing*, 80th Cong., 2nd sess., 1948, pp. 139–46. Many FM stations owned by AM outlets simply duplicated the latter's programming and were thus not interested in linking with Continental.

57 Interview with Everett Dillard.

58 Ibid.

59 Ibid.

60 Letter from Walter J. Damm, vice president and general manager of Journal Broadcasting, to the FCC, March 23, 1950, as quoted in Christopher H. Sterling, "WTMJ-FM: The Milwaukee Journal FM Station, 1939–1966" (master's thesis, University of Wisconsin–Madison, 1966), p. 92.

61 *Broadcasting*, December 26, 1949, p. 89. WMCA-FM had been costing $25,000 a year to operate—with little countervailing income. It had won its license in a comparative FCC hearing with seventeen applicants for five available channels in New York, a process only completed in the spring of 1948.

62 "FM Meet Almost Passes Toll Issue," *Broadcasting-Telecasting*, May 30, 1955, p. 93.

63 See "FM's Aches, TV's Balm?," *Broadcasting*, June 11, 1951, p. 52; "Spectrum Speculation," *Broadcasting*, July 9, 1951, p. 50; and "Port in the FM Storm," *Broadcasting*, July 23, 1951, p. 48. The magazine's editorial policy was often said to match that of major parts of the broadcast business.

64 E. M. Webster, in remarks before the National Association of Radio and Television Broadcasters District 14 Meeting, Sun Valley, Idaho, September 21, 1953, as reprinted in *Broadcasting-Telecasting*, October 12, 1953, p. 56.

65 "NAM Committee Requests Use of Shared FM Band for Industry," *Broadcasting-Telecasting*, February 7, 1955, p. 78.

66 "Broadcasters Rally to Hold Off Poachers in TV, FM Frequencies," *Broadcasting*, December 2, 1957, p. 50.

67 "FMA First General Session on Friday," *Broadcasting* (January 6, 1947), pp. 17, 72.

68 "FM Gets Formal NAB Recognition," *Broadcasting*, September 1, 1947, p. 16.

69 Edwin S. James, "FMA Group Hits 'Hip-Pocket' Licensees," *Broadcasting*, April 21, 1947, p. 26.

70 "FM Assn. Dissolves: To Merge with NAB," *Broadcasting*, December 12, 1949, p. 28.

71 "Should There Be an IFMB Association?," *FM and Television*, August 1946, pp. 28–29. 37.

72 "FM Group Being Set Up outside NARTB," *Broadcasting-Telecasting*, April 23, 1956, p. 110.

73 Lynn Christian and Christopher H. Sterling, "FM Trade Associations: Promoting Radio's Second Service," in *Encyclopedia of Radio*, ed. Christopher H. Sterling (New York: Fitzroy Dearborn, 2004), pp. 608–9.

74 *Broadcasting*, January 12, 1948, p. 86.

75 Quoted from *Hi-Fi Music at Home* 4, no. 3 (July–August 1957).

76 Advertisement for RCA Victor records, *National Geographic* (November 1936), as cited in Robert Oakes Jordan and James Cunningham, *The Sound of High Fidelity* (Chicago: Windsor Press, 1958), p. 33.

77 Siepmann, *Radio's Second Chance*, p. 253.

78 "Serious Delay to FM Is Seen by Owners in Duplication Ban," *Broadcasting*, October 13, 1947, p. 75.

79 Testimony of Charles Joliffe to the House Commerce Committee, *Radio Frequency Modulation: Hearing*, 80th Cong., 2nd sess., 1948,, p. 246.

80 Petrillo (1892–1984), by his own admission not a particularly good trumpet player, had helped organize Chicago musicians starting in 1919, become head of the AFM local in 1922. From 1940 to 1958 he was national AFM president. He had banned AFM members from recording music during the war in a dispute with record companies for better payments to players. While lauded among his members, he was loathed by the political establishment.

81 "NAB, FMBI Link Forces to Face Petrillo," *Broadcasting*, October 29, 1945, p. 16.

82 "Featherbedding" was by that time the accepted pejorative term to describe union demands (especially in the railway business) for duplicate or otherwise unnecessary employment of union members.

83 "Mr. Petrillo Again," *New York Times*, October 25, 1945, as reprinted in *Broadcasting*, October 29, 1945, p. 16.

84 The Lea Act (after Clarence F. Lea, D-Calif.) added a new section (506) to the Communications Act banning "coercive practices affecting broadcasting." On appeal, a federal court of appeals in Chicago found in favor of Petrillo, finding the Lea Act unconstitutional on several grounds. Further appeal to the Supreme Court upheld the Lea Act in June 1947.

85 This section draws on Richard L. Beard, "The Short Unhappy Life of Transit Radio," *Journal of Broadcasting* 12 (Fall 1968): 328. See also George W. Keith, "Sic Gloria Transit Radio," *Public Utilities Fortnightly*, September 28, 1950, pp. 3–11.

86 William Ensign, "Transit Radio Rolls Along" (remarks before the FM Association sales clinic, New York City, April 1, 1949), pp. 1–2.

87 Advertisement for Transit Radio, Inc., in *Broadcasting*, June 19, 1950.

88 Keith, "Sic Gloria," p. 11.

89 "TR Opposition: Riders Assn. Asks FCC to Ban Transitcasts," *Broadcasting-Telecasting*, February 20, 1950, p. 50.

90 Beard, "The Short, Unhappy Life."

91 *Chicago Skyway Broadcasting v. FCC*, 8 RR 876 (1952).

92 This story is detailed in Lorne Parker, *SCA: A New Medium* (Madison: University of Wisconsin Extension, 1967).

93 See Lawrence Lessing, *Man of High Fidelity: Edwin Howard Armstrong* (Philadelphia: J. B. Lippincott, 1956), pp. 293–94.

94 FCC, *Twenty-Fifth Annual Report for Fiscal Year Ended June 30, 1959* (Washington, D.C.: Government Printing Office, 1959), p. 187. See also Walter B. Emery, *Broadcasting and Government* (East Lansing: Michigan State University Press, 1961), p. 104.

95 Hugh D. Lavery, "How the Time-Buyers View FM," *FM and Television*, February 1947, p. 25.

96 "In FM Poll, 90% Vote for No Commercials," *Broadcasting*, March 24, 1947, p. 75.

97 *Broadcasting-Telecasting*, June 8, 1953, p. 37.

98 Hugh R. Slotten, *Radio and Television Regulation: Broadcast Technology in the United States, 1920–1960* (Baltimore: Johns Hopkins University Press, 2000), pp. 134–35.

99 Frank Mansfield, "$600,000,000 Market," *Frequency Modulation Business*, February 1946, pp. 18–19, 44–45.

100 *Colliers* was then a highly popular general circulation weekly magazine. See "What Does FM Mean to Consumers?," *Frequency Modulation Business*, May 1947, pp. 19, 47.

101 *The Zenith Story* (Chicago: Zenith, 1955), p. 19; and *Broadcasting-Telecasting*, March 5, 1951, p. 37.

102 Transcript of Edwin L. Dunham interview with T. Mitchell Hastings (Boston, November 1, 1966; now in the files of the Library of American Broadcasting, University of Maryland), p. 5. See also "FM Payoff Is Explored," *Broadcasting*, May 4, 1953, p. 32 for a contemporary report on the industry meeting where the Hastings car radio was announced.

103 Receiver sales data is based on records of the Electronic Industries Association (later Alliance). See, for example, "Set Production," *FM and Television*, February 1950, p. 4.

104 For just one example of this, see "Nationwide FM Service Seen by 1948," *Broadcasting*, April 14, 1947, p. 84, which has manufacturers promising 2 million sets in 1947 and 5 million a year later.

105 See, for example, *Broadcasting*, August 12, 1946, p. 15; and Edward R. Taylor, "Cooperation in Building FM Audiences," *FM and Television*, October 1946, pp. 31, 76.

106 See the advertisement in *Broadcasting*, January 26, 1948, pp. 58–59.

107 *Broadcasting*, October 15, 1945, p. 32. The trade weekly editorialized in favor of the idea a week later; see *Broadcasting*, October 22, 1945, p. 32.

108 For one contemporary view, see "Low-Down on Hi-Fi," *Broadcasting-Telecasting*, October 26, 1953, pp. 86–88, 93.

109 See, for example, "AM-FM Tuners for High-Fidelity Use," *Consumers' Research Bulletin*, March 1953, pp. 22–24; and "FM Tuners: Let the Buyer Beware," *Consumer Reports*, October 1957, pp. 454–59, which said set makers claimed far more than their products usually delivered.

110 See, as one example, "Set Production," *FM-TV*, December 1952, p. 39. This feature ran nearly every month and broke out industry receiver sales figures more carefully than summary numbers could.

111 "A Report on FM Listening in New York," *NAB Member Service*, February 20, 1950, pp. 5–11.

112 NBC Corporate Planning Division, "Frequency Modulation" (New York: NBC, 1959).

113 A. C. Nielsen Co. provided radio ratings until 1965, when it left that market. Its annual *Radio* booklets began to appear in 1955 with brief summaries of audience information nationally, but none of them even mentioned FM — mute testimony to the medium's sad state in this period.

114 *M Street Journal*, August 31, 2005, p. 3. The first transmitter was donated by General Electric. Among the tiny station's alumni were sportscaster Bob Costas and newsman Ted Koppel.

115 *M Street Journal*, August 24, 2005, p. 3. The facility, dubbed "The Voice of the Bulldogs," began on 91.5 MHz and is now a Class A station on 88.1 MHz.

116 David Eshelman, "The Emergence of Educational FM Broadcasting," *NAEB Journal*, March–April 1967, pp. 60–61.

117 Sterling worked for this system during his years at the university (1961 through

most of 1969, when he completed his Ph.D.). This paragraph is drawn from that experience.

118 During the 1960s, Sterling worked as a student announcer for the University of Wisconsin's WHA, which fed the state network. This material is drawn from various file documents produced by WHA or the State Radio Council in this period.

119 This paragraph also draws on Sterling's experience at WHA from 1961 to 1969.

120 Lewis Hill, *Voluntary Listener-Sponsorship: A Report to Educational Broadcasters on the Experiment at KPFA, Berkeley, California* (Berkeley: Pacifica Foundation, 1958), offers a first-person account of the formation of this iconic entity.

121 Jeff Land, *Active Radio: Pacifica's Brash Experiment* (Minneapolis: University of Minnesota Press, 1999), p. 42.

122 Matthew Lasar, *Pacific Radio: The Rise of an Alternative Network* (Philadelphia: Temple University Press, 1999).

123 For example, see Boots LeBaron, "Outlook for FM Fans," *Los Angeles Times*, June 16, 1957.

124 J. Frank Beatty, "How Bright a Future for FM? Certainly Brighter Than in the Past, Maybe Brighter Than You Think," *Broadcasting-Telecasting*, April 8, 1957, pp. 116–32. This is a good example of the sort of "taking stock" piece on the FM business that would appear frequently in coming years.

CHAPTER 4

1 "FM Future Brightest in Decade," *Broadcasting*, May 5, 1958, p. 98.

2 Ibid.

3 "FM: Hot Trend in 1958?," *Sponsor*, March 29, 1968, p. 78.

4 "FM: A New Boom of Interest," *Sponsor's Radio Basics*, July 1958, p. 86.

5 "'Have Audience, Can Sell' — FM," *Broadcasting*, February 9, 1959, p. 124.

6 "A New Head of Steam for FM," *Sponsor*, June 13, 1959, p. 34.

7 "FM: A New Boom of Interest," p. 88.

8 "CBS Boosting FM on Chicago Outlet," *Broadcasting*, July 21, 1958, p. 54.

9 Les Brown, "'All of a Sudden It's an Advertising Medium' Sparks FM's Bid in '60," *Fifty-Fourth Variety Anniversary Issue*, January 6, 1960, p. 9.

10 See George A. Willey, "End of an Era: The Daytime Radio Serial," *Journal of Broadcasting* 5 (Spring 1961): 97–115.

11 NBC sought to break this pattern of decline with *Monitor*, a forty-hour weekend offering that began in 1955 with news, interviews, talk, music, and sports. It lasted for years.

12 Theodore Roszak, *The Making of a Counter Culture: Reflections on the Technocratic Society and Its Youthful Opposition* (New York, Doubleday, 1969), p. 23.

13 Ibid., p. 26.

14 "'Have Audience, Can Sell' — FM," pp. 124–35.

15 Lyman Allen, "What Makes FM Succeed" (mimeograph report produced by the

author, South Lincoln, Mass., n.d., but noted as received in February 1959). Copy found at the Radio Advertising Bureau offices in New York City, 1968. See also "'Have Audience, Can Sell'—FM," p. 125.

16 Allen, "What Makes FM Succeed," p. 1.

17 Ibid., p. 10.

18 NBC Corporate Planning Division, "Frequency Modulation" (New York: NBC, 1959); a copy was located at the Radio Advertising Bureau, New York, in 1968.

19 Ibid., section 3, p. 1.

20 Ibid., section 4, p. B-2.

21 Ibid., section 8, p. 3.

22 "NBC Station Manager's Report—Separate FM Programming," July 9, 1959, p. 1. Copy in files of Radio Advertising Bureau, New York, 1968.

23 Based on data computed from *Broadcasting Yearbook* listings, 1958–66, as reported in C. H. Sterling, "Second Service: A History of Commercial FM Broadcasting to 1969" (Ph.D. diss., University of Wisconsin–Madison, August 1969), table 13, p. 431.

24 FCC, *Twenty-Fifth Annual Report for Fiscal Year Ended June 30, 1959* (Washington, D.C.: Government Printing Office, 1959), p. 68.

25 Lynn Christian and Christopher H. Sterling, "FM Trade Associations: Promoting Radio's Second Service," in *Encyclopedia of Radio*, ed. Christopher H. Sterling (New York: Fitzroy Dearborn, 2004), p. 609.

26 "FM Star Grows Even Brighter," *Broadcasting*, April 11, 1960, p. 64.

27 "UHF, FM Want to Stay Put," *Broadcasting*, June 29, 1958, p. 58.

28 "Class B FM Plan Dropped," *Broadcasting*, August 6, 1958, p. 68.

29 FCC, *Twenty-Seventh Annual Report for Fiscal Year Ended June 30, 1961* (Washington, D.C.: Government Printing Office, 1961), p. 55.

30 "Is FCC Making FM Basic Medium?," *Broadcasting*, July 3, 1961, p. 25.

31 Ibid.

32 "Some FCC Applications Put in Cold Storage," *Broadcasting*, December 11, 1961, p. 81.

33 "FCC Rules Revision Overhauls FM Band," *Broadcasting*, July 30, 1962, p. 32. The "Northeast" was defined as east of Madison, Wisconsin, and north of the Ohio River Valley—an expansion of the old 1945 regional divide and indeed an expansion that had been predicted then. The classification of Southern California the same way reflected the dramatic growth of that region in the fifteen years since World War II.

34 "Grandfather Rule to Protect FMs," *Broadcasting*, December 3, 1962, p. 67. The term arose out of late nineteenth-century voting procedures used in southern states to keep blacks from the polls. They would be asked if "their grandfather" had voted (which was usually not the case since he had probably been a slave) and were allowed to vote only if he had. So a term once applied to a discriminatory process came to mean, instead, allowing people or companies to keep doing what they had been doing even if rules changed.

35 "FM Allocations Filings Due Aug. 31," *Broadcasting*, August 6, 1962, p. 53. A word about terminology: while this story and FCC documents of the period refer to "allocation," under modern spectrum management usage this proceeding really concerned *allotments* of channels within the existing FM allocation.

36 "FCC Releases its Design for FM," *Broadcasting*, July 29, 1963, p. 24.

37 "AM Freeze Nears Thawing Stage," *Broadcasting*, June 8, 1964, p. 38.

38 "A New Dimension in Broadcasting," *Broadcasting*, August 10, 1959, p. 56.

39 Franklin Doolittle of station WPAJ in New Haven tested a two-channel AM stereo system in 1925. See John Sunier, *The Story of Stereo: 1881–* (New York: Gernsback Library, 1960), pp. 31–51. See also Burt Hines, "FM Multiplexing: A New Approach to Stereophonic Sound," *Radio & Television News*, November 1955, pp. 55–57ff.

40 Sunier, *The Story of Stereo*, pp. 114, 141.

41 It could be confusing for station staff as well as listeners. Sterling worked a number of such two-station broadcasts as an announcer at the University of Wisconsin's WHA and WHA-FM in 1961–62 and recalls the rather complex announcements broadcast to tell the audience how best to set up their receivers.

42 "Stereo Cues Two-Way Air Media Buys," *Sponsor*, October 4, 1958, p. 35.

43 Sunier, *The Story of Stereo*, pp. 117–18.

44 Ibid., p. 125.

45 FCC, *Report and Order on Docket 12517* (Washington, D.C.: FCC mimeo, April 20, 1961), as reprinted in *Broadcast Engineering*, May 1961, p. 28.

46 See a listing of the many questions facing the engineers in "FCC's FM Probe Gets Stereo Issue," *Broadcasting*, March 16, 1959, p. 97.

47 Ronald Salek, "The Development and Growth of FM Stereophonic Broadcasting: A History" (master's thesis, Michigan State University, 1965), pp. 29–30.

48 FCC, *Report and Order*.

49 "Outlook for FM Stereo," *Broadcasting*, May 15, 1961, p. 80.

50 "Three FM Stereo Roads Converge in Chicago," *Electrical Merchandising Week*, July 24, 1961, pp. 2–3, as noted in Salek, "Development and Growth," p. 45.

51 "Three FMs Meet Date for Multiplex Stereo," *Broadcasting*, June 5, 1961, p. 58.

52 Communication with Lynn Christian, September 15, 2005. The station now operates as KODA-FM in Houston.

53 "Profile of an FM Stereo Station: The Dealer and FM Stereo," *Tape, Record and Radio Retailing*, May 1963, pp. 1–2.

54 The station counts come from the National Association of Broadcasters' monthly newsletter about FM affairs, *FMphasis*, as summarized in Sterling, "Second Service," p. 483.

55 "Stereo: Will It Be FM's Big Break?," *Broadcasting*, April 9, 1962, p. 50.

56 Lynn Christian, in communication with the authors, November 17, 2005.

57 See Martin Williams, "Networks for FM," *Saturday Review of Literature*, January

26, 1963, pp. 55–56, 93, which includes a map of several of the networks described here. Further useful details show up in the letters resulting from this article; see *Saturday Review of Literature*, February 23, 1963, pp. 51, 59; and *Saturday Review of Literature*, March 30, 1963, p. 50.

58 See Ray Stone, "FM Radio and Group Broadcasting" (Maxon, Inc., study undertaken for the FM Association, May 5, 1958), p. 8, which determined that line costs connecting the top-10 national markets alone might total $1.5 million a year. See also "Stone Proposes FM Network," *Broadcasting*, November 3, 1958, p. 86.

59 There had been an earlier attempt to do this with WQXR in 1950, but the decline in FM fortunes led to its closure in 1953.

60 For part of this story, see "QXR to Abandon FM Relay System," *Broadcasting*, August 5, 1963, p. 78; and "Cadillac Dips into FM on 25-Station Network," *Broadcasting*, September 7, 1964, p. 50.

61 A decade later (1968), Hastings would inaugurate progressive rock radio on his flagship classical radio outlet, WBCN in Boston, and in doing so hugely increase FM's popularity.

62 Transcript of interview of T. Mitchell Hastings, conducted by Edwin L. Dunham, Boston, November 1, 1966, in files of the Library of American Broadcasting, University of Maryland, College Park.

63 See "Demand Increases for Syndicated Music," *Broadcasting*, July 31, 1967, p. 94.

64 "Those Fancy FM Program Guides," *Sponsor*, September 19, 1960, p. 37.

65 "Why FM Is Picking Up Speed," *Sponsor*, April 30, 1960, p. 34.

66 Personal correspondence with Lynn Christian. See also "Those Fancy FM Program Guides," pp. 37, 56, which includes that cover among others.

67 "Catering to Highbrows Pays Off," *Business Week*, October 21, 1961, p. 120.

68 Ibid., p. 122.

69 National Association of Broadcasters, *FMphasis*, February 1963, p. 3.

70 Christopher H. Sterling, "WTMJ-FM, The Milwaukee Journal FM Station, 1939–1966" (master's thesis, University of Wisconsin, 1966). See especially chapter 4. See also Christopher H. Sterling, "WTMJ-FM: A Case Study in the Development of FM Broadcasting," *Journal of Broadcasting* 12 (Fall 1968): 341–52.

71 Memo from Alex Smallens Jr. of the CBS Radio Systems and Procedures Department, reporting results of a meeting with Sam Slate, WCBS station manager, October 21, 1958. Provided to authors by Mr. Smallens, later a key figure in FM programming at ABC.

72 Senate Judiciary Committee, Subcommittee to Investigate the Administration of the Internal Security Act and other Internal Security Laws, *Pacifica Foundation: Hearings*, 88th Cong., 1st sess. (January 10–25, 1963), published in three parts.

73 FCC, *In the Matter of Pacifica Foundation* . . . 36 FCC 147, and 1 RR2d 747 (1964).

74 David Lamble, "How We Are Seen; How We See Ourselves: The Lavender Airwaves," *San Francisco Beat Reporter*.

75 Guy Raz, "Radio Free Georgetown," *Washington Free Weekly*, January 29, 1999, p. 15.

76 Edward Atwood, *Straight News: Gays, Lesbians, and the News Media* (New York: Columbia University Press, 1996), p. 51.

77 As reprinted in *Broadcasting*, July 3, 1961, pp. 24–25.

78 Communication with Lynn Christian, September 15, 2005. This kind of conflict would come to increasingly plague the NAB, making its role as an umbrella trade group tenuous at times.

79 "FM—Basic or Supplemental Medium?," *Broadcasting*, November 20, 1961, p. 78.

80 FCC, *Notice of Proposed Rule Making on Docket 15084* (Washington, D.C.: FCC Mimeo 63-468, May 15, 1963), excerpted from paragraph 19.

81 "FM Has Led a Rugged Life," *Broadcasting*, July 29, 1963, p. 62.

82 National Association of FM Broadcasters, "Comments of the NAFMB [on FCC Docket 15084]" (Washington, D.C.: NAFMB, September 16, 1963), p. 4.

83 FCC, *Report and Order on Docket 15084* (Washington, D.C.: FCC mimeo 64-609, July 1, 1964).

84 Ibid., p. 21.

85 FCC, *Memorandum Opinion and Order on Docket 15084* (Washington, D.C.: FCC mimeo 65-195, March 10, 1965), p. 7.

86 Jack Gould, "Radio: Booming FM Ponders Future," *New York Times*, March 22, 1965.

87 "FM's Drag Feet on Program Splits," *Broadcasting*, June 21, 1965, p. 40.

88 Frederick C. Klein, "New Sound for FM? More Stations Attempt 'Popular' Programming to Increase Listeners," *Wall Street Journal*, November 27, 1964, pp. 1, 14.

89 Lynn A. Christian, "What Are You Going to Do with Your New Radio Station?" (remarks before the NAB Management Meeting, New York, November 14, 1966). Christian then managed WPIX-FM in New York City. At the time, one owner was restricted to no more than seven AM and seven FM stations anywhere in the country.

90 Electronic Industries Association data.

91 Stephen Dietz, senior vice president and director of marketing services, Kenyon & Eckhardt, Inc., "Only His Mother . . ." (remarks before the annual convention of the National Association of FM Broadcasters, March 30, 1963), p. 3.

92 Christopher H. Sterling, *Electronic Media: A Guide to Trends in Broadcasting and Newer Technologies, 1920–1983* (New York: Praeger, 1984). See tables 670-A and 670-B, pp. 224–25, drawing data from a variety of original sources, including EIA, the Radio Advertising Bureau, and NBC.

93 Advertisement in *Broadcasting*, May 16, 1960, p. 99.

94 Larry Wolters, "FM Radio Is Coming into Its Own," *Chicago Tribune*, June 21, 1959.

95 See, for example, "FM Auto Radios," *Consumer Reports*, September 1960, pp. 466–68.

96 "FM Reaches for the Honey," *U.S. Radio*, July 1960, p. 33.

97 "Stereo: Will It Be FM's Big Break?," *Broadcasting*, April 9, 1962, p. 51.

98 U.S. FM was a spin-off of the monthly trade publication *U.S. Radio*, and like the parent magazine it offered short news clips and two or three feature pieces each issue.

CHAPTER 5

1 "FM Radio Has to Change Its Tune," *Business Week*, September 24, 1966, p. 173.

2 Claude Hall, "FM Is Challenging AM's Reign, Asserts Christian," *Billboard*, June 18, 1966 (quoting WPIX-FM [New York] station manager Lynn A. Christian).

3 "Separate FM Programming," *FMphasis*, June 1969, p. 1.

4 "No Votes for FCC's Ideas on Simulcasting," *Broadcasting*, August 19, 1974, p. 87.

5 "Broadcasters Sit on Both Sides of Fence on FCC Proposal to Extend Duplication Ban," *Broadcasting*, September 2, 1974, p. 26.

6 "The Third Round on AM-FM Duplication," *Broadcasting*, September 16, 1974, p. 26.

7 "FCC Will Trim Allowable Amount of Duplication," *Broadcasting*, December 22, 1975, p. 22.

8 *Life*, December 26, 1969, p. 72.

9 Michael C. Keith, *Voices in the Purple Haze: Underground Radio and the Sixties* (Westport, Conn.: Praeger, 1997), p. 15.

10 Paul D. Colford, "Bill 'Rosko' Mercer, 73, Unique NY Voice," *Newsweek*, August 3, 2000.

11 John Parales, "Scott Muni, 74, a Radio D.J. of FM Rock Programming," *New York Times*, September 20, 1974.

12 Lynda Crawford, *East Village Other*, March 11, 1971, p. 9.

13 Keith, *Voices in the Purple Haze*, p. 25.

14 Ibid.

15 Ben Fong-Torres, "On Radio," *San Francisco Chronicle*, May 20, 1993.

16 "Shoestring Station Is Set for the Bay," *Broadcasting*, February 15, 1971, pp. 59–60.

17 Donna Halper, in communication with the authors, November 10, 2005, referring to a *Boston Globe* article (February 17, 1970, p. 3).

18 Keith, *Voices in the Purple Haze*, pp. ix–xi.

19 Phylis A. Johnson and Michael C. Keith, *Queer Airwaves: The Story of Gay and Lesbian Broadcasting* (Armonk, N.Y.: M. E. Sharpe, Inc., 2001), p. 33.

20 Ibid., pp. 29–30.

21 Michael C. Keith, *Signals in the Air: Native Broadcasting in America* (Westport, Conn.: Praeger Publishing, 1995), p. 98.

22 Ibid., p. 27.

23 Keith, *Voices in the Purple Haze*, p. 45.

24 Ben Fong-Torres, "FM Underground Radio: Love for Sale," *Rolling Stone*, April 2, 1970, p. 6.

25 "FM Radio Has to Change Its Tune," p. 177.

26 These were loaded into machines dubbed "carousels" after the then-popular consumer slide-projection machines.

27 "Automated Radio: It's Alive and Prospering," *Broadcasting*, June 9, 1969, p. 54. For profiles of three of the automation program providers, see "Here Come (Three of) the Automaters," *Broadcasting*, August 23, 1971, pp. 44–45.

28 "Profile of a Station: WPIX-FM," *FM Guide*, December 1966, p. 10, quoting program manager Charlie Whitaker.

29 Michael C. Keith, *The Radio Station*, 7th ed. (Boston: Focal Press, 2007), p. 348.

30 Peter Fornatale and Joshua E. Mills, *Radio in the Television Age* (Woodstock, N.Y.: The Overlook Press, 1980), p. 79. Schulke had been the first and only full-time paid president of the NAFMB before taking on this new venture. Communication with Lynn Christian, September 15, 2005.

31 Communication with Lynn Christian, September 15, 2005.

32 Les Brown, "'All of a Sudden It's an Advertising Medium' Sparks FM's Bid in '60," *Fifty-Fourth Variety Anniversary Issue*, January 6, 1960.

33 CBS Interoffice Correspondence in the files of Alexander Smallens, who was then (1969) with the American FM Network, New York (he had been employed by CBS before shifting to ABC).

34 "What Networks Are Doing about FM," *Sponsor*, October 3, 1966, p. 38.

35 ABC FM Radio Network affiliate map, March 15, 1968; and "11 More Stations Sign with ABC Networks," *Broadcasting*, January 15, 1968, pp. 53–55.

36 Interview with Alex Smallens, program director, American FM Radio Network, New York, November 19, 1968.

37 Ibid. A 7:15 A.M. newscast was added in December 1968.

38 Ibid.

39 Statistical Research Inc., RADAR reports as summarized in *Broadcasting*. See also Christopher H. Sterling, *Electronic Media: A Guide to Trends in Broadcasting and Newer Technologies, 1920–1983* (New York: Praeger, 1984), p. 233, table 671F.

40 Ibid.

41 "Hot Properties," *Broadcasting*, July 28, 1975, p. 19.

42 "FM in the Black," *Broadcasting*, November 21, 1975, p. 21.

43 "FM Sniffs Sweet Smell of Success," *Broadcasting*, July 31, 1967, p. 55.

44 "Los Angeles FM Sold to Large Toiletry Firm," *Broadcasting*, February 26, 1970, p. 70. Faberge later pulled out of the deal and the station went to two New York investors. See "Faberge Balks at Buying L.A. FM," *Broadcasting*, March 30, 1970, p. 60.

45 "A Sellers' Market Proves a Point," *Broadcasting*, February 23, 1970, p. 47. Listed were details on sixteen station sales, ranging from $250,000 for a station in Houston to several that neared the $1 million dollar mark.

46 "FCC Approves Almost $1-million Gift," *Broadcasting*, February 16, 1970, p. 42. The station involved was fine arts–programmed WFMT, which had been sold to WGN (the *Chicago Tribune*) in 1968 but then was subjected to various citizen protests over media concentration and fear of losing the fine-arts content. When the license was designated for hearing after a court upheld the citizen protests, WGN donated the license to the Chicago Education Television Association.

47 "FM, at Long Last, Is Making Its Move," *Broadcasting*, February 23, 1970, p. 47.

48 Jack Gould, "FM Glows Lustily Despite the Recession," *New York Times*, July 22, 1971.

49 "Price Rise," *Broadcasting*, June 26, 1972, p. 7.

50 "Seller's Market," *Broadcasting*, June 6, 1977, p. 7.

51 "Special Report—FM: The Great Leaps Forward," *Broadcasting*, January 22, 1979, pp. 32, 36.

52 "Severing the Last Link to the Old Group W FMs," *M Street Journal*, March 2, 2005, p. 2.

53 "Why the Trend toward Separate AM-FM calls?," *Broadcasting*, November 27, 1972, p. 44.

54 See the comment in the third column of *Broadcasting*, March 29, 1976, p. 36.

55 Ibid., p. 57.

56 "FM's Need to Explode Some Myths," *Broadcasting*, July 31, 1967, pp. 58, 60.

57 "All-Ad FM Intrigues FCC," *Broadcasting*, July 4, 1966, p. 36.

58 Tony Liftgate and Gil Faggen, "FM . . . Gold in Them Thar Hills?," *Timebuyer*, August 1966, p. 38.

59 "McLendon Gets Green Light for No-News FM," *Broadcasting*, March 11, 1968, p. 66.

60 Alfred J. Jaffe, "Ted Bates Study Finds Impressive FM Growth," *Television/Radio Age*, March 8, 1971, pp. 21–23, 48–51.

61 "Ayer Study Underscores FM's Growing Stature," *Broadcasting*, December 11, 1972, p. 54.

62 Talk by Walter A. Schwartz, president, ABC Radio Network, before National Association of FM Broadcasters, March 21, 1969, Washington, D.C.

63 "Last Wall Falls as Top 40 Makes Its Mark on FM Radio," *Broadcasting*, September 24, 1973, p. 46.

64 "Program Formats—Top 10 Markets," *Broadcasting*, October 7, 1974, p. 41.

65 "National Radio Broadcasters Association, nee NAFMB, Strikes Out as All-Radio Trade Group," *Broadcasting*, September 22, 1975, p. 24. See also Lynn A. Christian and Christopher H. Sterling, "FM Trade Associations," in *Encyclopedia of Radio*, ed. Christopher H. Sterling (New York: Fitzroy Dearborn, 2004), pp. 609–10. In 1984 the NRBA merged with the National Association of Broadcasters, ending its history the same way earlier FM associations had—by folding affairs under the umbrella of the oldest and largest industry association.

66 Joseph S. Johnson and Kenneth K. Jones, *Modern Radio Station Practices*, 2nd ed. (Belmont, Calif.: Wadsworth, 1978), "Station Profiles," pp. 245–306. FM out-

lets included are WRFM in New York, WBAI (Pacifica) in New York, WFMT in Chicago, and KMET in Los Angeles.

67 National Association of Educational Broadcasters, *The Hidden Medium: A Status Report on Educational Radio in the United States* (Washington, D.C.: NAEB, April 1967).

68 While these focused on television, they also provided the framework for the system that developed. See *Public Television: The Report and Recommendations of the Carnegie Commission on Educational Television* (New York: Bantam, 1967).

69 U.S. Congress, *Communications Act of 1934*, 73rd Cong., June 18, 1934, as amended, provisions for the Corporation for Public Broadcasting, subpart D, sec. 396 (47 U.S.C. 396).

70 NPR website: <http://www.npr.org/about/growth> (accessed December 22, 2004).

71 Several books relate NPR history. This account is drawn largely from Michael P. McCauley, *NPR: The Trials and Triumphs of National Public Radio* (New York: Columbia University Press, 2005), chap. 2.

72 Ibid.

73 Faced with hundreds of existing stations and limited radio funding (most CPB money has gone to the more expensive television from the start), the corporation established minimal levels of full-time staffing and existing funding to make a station "CPB-qualified." Not to have done so would have spread too little money over far too many stations to the detriment of public radio's growth and impact. But the downside of this understandable policy decision was to leave hundreds (and eventually well more than a thousand) noncommercial FM stations totally outside the NPR system.

74 For more information, see the FCC website concerning these stations: <http://www.fcc.gov/mb/audio/translator.html#WHATIS>.

75 <http://www.nfcb.org/about/history.jsp> (accessed December 27, 2004).

76 Ibid.

77 NFCB website: <http://www.nfcb.org/about/history.jsp> (accessed May 16, 2007).

78 Allen Myers, FCC Mass Media Bureau, correspondence with authors, January 11, 2005.

79 <http://www.fcc.gov> (accessed January 2005). The proceeding was RM (rule making) 2493; it never progressed sufficiently to warrant a formal docket number.

80 "Quad—The New Sound in FM Stereo," *BM/E Magazine*, February 1970, pp. 20–21.

81 "The Battle over Quadraphonic Sound," *Broadcasting*, April 3, 1972, p. 128.

82 "Four-Channel FM: Standards Study to Begin," *Broadcasting*, May 8, 1972, p. 56.

83 "National Quadraphonic Radio Committee Submits Final Report to FCC" (press release from Electronic Industries Association, December 3, 1975);

and "EIA Group Says Go on Quadraphonic," *Broadcasting*, December 15, 1975, p. 61.

84 "Quad Consideration," *Broadcasting*, July 21, 1980, p. 34.

85 "FCC Fires Up Inquiry Machine Again for Quad," *Broadcasting*, January 15, 1979, p. 75.

86 This included the appearance of a brief-lived monthly newsletter, *The 4 Channel Scene*, in 1975. One book for audiophiles also appeared: Ken Sessions, *4-Channel Stereo: From Source to Sound* (Blue Ridge Summit, Pa.: TAB Books, 1973; rev. ed., 1974).

87 Based on figures provided by the Electronic Industries Association in various press releases and their annual marketbook.

88 "Are Car Radios Key to Future of FM Radio?," *Broadcasting*, April 2, 1973, pp. 87–88.

89 "All-Channel AM-FM Receiver Legislation," *NAFMB Washington Report*, April 1968.

90 U.S. Congress, Senate Commerce Committee, *All-Channel Radio Receivers: Hearings*, 93rd Cong., 2nd sess., April 1974.

91 U.S. Congress, House Small Business Committee, *AM/FM Stereo Radio Receivers in Automobiles: Hearing*, 95th Cong, 1st sess., September 1977.

92 James H. Duncan Jr., *American Radio: Tenth Anniversary Issue, 1976–1986* (Kalamazoo, Mich.: Duncan's American Radio, 1986), p. A-22 (citing Arbitron data).

93 "FM Radio Has to Change Its Tune," p. 173.

94 Mort Keshin, "FM Now a Mature Medium," *Media/Scope*, May 1967, p. 40.

95 CBS, *CBS Radio Network Affiliate Research/Promotion Reference Guide* (New York: CBS Radio, September 1972), pp. 9–12.

96 "The Rites of Passage Are All over for FM Radio: It's Out on Its Own," *Broadcasting*, September 24, 1973, p. 31.

97 "FM—Hope, Faith and No Charity," *Timebuyer*, December 1966, p. 52.

98 Todd Tolces and Andy Epstein, "FM Radio: Is There Life After Static?," *Bay Area Music*, May 19, 1978, p. 32.

CHAPTER 6

1 "Monitor," *Broadcasting*, May 28, 1979, p. 64. RADAR means the Radio All-Dimension Audience Research, a long-running program of commercial ratings research.

2 See, for just one example, "Can AM Radio Be Saved?," *Broadcasting*, July 3, 1989, p. 20.

3 "FM's Still Setting the Pace in Radio Trading, but AM's No Slouch," *Broadcasting*, August 25, 1980, p. 99.

4 "Record Price for FM: $44 million," *Broadcasting*, October 28, 1985, p. 41.

5 Alex Ben Block, "Signals Amid the Static," *Forbes*, March 14, 1986, p. 131.

6 Dorothy Gilliam, "The Sound of Progress," *Washington Post*, June 8, 1989.

7 "FCC Makes Firm Move to Adding FMs," *Broadcasting*, March 3, 1980, p. 30.

8 "Proposal to Alter FM Band Provokes Flood of Comments," *Broadcasting*, October 20, 1980, p. 34.

9 "NTIA Study Would Increase Number of Stations," *Broadcasting*, March 30, 1981, p. 57.

10 *Broadcasting*, May 4, 1987, p. 105.

11 "FCC Opens Up FM Spectrum—Wide," *Broadcasting*, May 30, 1983, p. 31.

12 "Top Secret" (editorial), *Broadcasting*, June 6, 1983, p. 114.

13 "Getting Ready for the Landrush on New FM Slots," *Broadcasting*, May 4, 1984, p. 39. What made this large allotment possible was the use of computer programming, which saved huge amounts of staff time and effort. See "FCC Computerizes FM Assignment," *Electronics*, April 5, 1984, p. 51.

14 "Guidelines for FM Landrush Suggested," *Broadcasting*, May 21, 1984, p. 90.

15 "FCC Grants AM Daytimers 80–90 Preference," *Broadcasting*, March 18, 1985, p. 27.

16 "Docket 80–90's 689 New FM Opportunities," *Broadcasting*, December 31, 1984, pp. 36–37. This lists the individual towns by state.

17 "FM Flood Control," *Broadcasting*, January 21, 1985, p. 7.

18 Dennis McDougal, "FCC Plans More FM Minority Stations," *Los Angeles Times*, December 11, 1989.

19 Lawrence Feinberg, "FCC Policy Aiding Women Overturned," *Washington Post*, August 24, 1985.

20 Reginald Stuart, "Court Kills F.C.C. Ruling Favoring Women as Owners of FM Stations," *New York Times*, August 24, 1985.

21 "FCC Ups Class A FM Power to 6kW—But Not for All," *Broadcasting*, July 17, 1989, p. 62.

22 Richard A. Shaffer, "New Rule May Let FM Radio Offer Paging, Electronic Mail," *Wall Street Journal*, August 6, 1982, p. 17.

23 "Lid's Off FM SCAs," *Broadcasting*, April 11, 1983, p. 35.

24 Penny Pagano, "FM Radio Plans a Growing Role as Pipeline for Data," *Los Angeles Times*, May 26, 1985.

25 One of the authors was long involved with Philadelphia's radio reading service for the blind, which provided hours of newspaper, magazine, and book-chapter reading directed at special receivers made available only to sight-impaired listeners. Copyright holders usually waived their rights for such services.

26 See, for example, Dennis P. Waters, "Surfacing: FM Radio Provides a New Alternative for Carrying Data," *Data Communications*, July 1985, pp. 173–81.

27 Daniel Minoli, "Making Use of Spare FM Band," *Computerworld*, June 16, 1986, p. 25.

28 "Simmering," *Broadcasting*, November 1, 1982, p. 7.

29 "FCC Says No to 'Low-Power' FM's," *Broadcasting*, March 12, 1990, p. 34.

30 "Official Lauds 'Mini' Radio Station Proposal," *St. Louis Globe-Democrat*, October 1, 1970.

31 Personal correspondence, May 22, 2007.

32 Jesse Walker, *Rebels on the Air: An Alternative History of Radio in America* (New York: New York University Press, 2001), p. 208.

33 Ibid., p. 208.

34 Ibid., p. 211.

35 Ibid., p. 208.

36 Ibid.

37 See Ted M. Coopman, "FCC Enforcement Difficulties with Unlicensed Micro-radio," *Journal of Broadcasting & Electronic Media* 43 (Fall 1999): 582–602.

38 Stephen Dunifer, "Free Radio: Liberating the Commons," *Context* 4 (Winter/ Spring 2006): 29.

39 Telephone interview, February 21, 2007.

40 Michael C. Keith, *Radio Programming: Consultancy and Formatics* (Boston: Focal Press, 1987), p. 78.

41 Michael C. Keith, *The Radio Station: Broadcast, Satellite, and Internet* (Boston: Focal Press, 2007), p. 354.

42 Monte Williams, "Frankie Crocker, a Champion of Black-Format Radio, Dies," *New York Times*, October 24, 2000.

43 Ibid.

44 David Stout, "Alison Steele, Disk Jockey, Dies: The Pioneer 'Nightbird' Was 58," *New York Times*, September 28, 1995.

45 "Oldies Action," *Broadcasting*, November 16, 1987, p. 140.

46 Pat Martin, "New FCC Rule Spurs AM/FM Combo Simulcasts," *Billboard*, May 24, 1986, pp. 10, 13–14.

47 This doctrine, initially developed in 1949 and revised regularly after the 1960s, held that stations (a) should cover controversial issues of public interest, and (b) present varied points of view on those issues. Stations were to select both issues and spokespersons. As the number of legal cases rose, the FCC became less sanguine with the constitutionality of its own policy, and in 1987 the Reagan-era commissioners voted to drop the doctrine completely. Stations would be free to cover (or not) any issues and select one side to the exclusion of others.

48 Vernon Stone, "News Operations at U.S. Radio Stations," provides an in-depth analysis of the situation in 1994 with an update to 2001. See <http://www .missouri.edu/~jourvs/graops.html> (accessed January 2005).

49 Reno Carlton, "Satellite Radio and Shock Jocks: Howard Stern? Bad Boy of the Airwaves," *Copyscope*, January 26, 2005, <http://www.satellite.info/idx/8/044/ satellite_radio/article/satellite_radio_shock_jocks_shoc>.

50 Nan Rubin, *Final Report on the Native American Training Project* (Washington, D.C.: NAPBC, 1987), p. 104.

51 Colleen Keane, "KSHI-FM Profile," *NFCB Community Radio News*, January 1991, p. 4.

52 Pam Shane, "Car Talk," in *Encyclopedia of Radio*, ed. Christopher H. Sterling (New York: Fitzroy Dearborn, 2004), pp. 301–2.

53 Corey Flintoff, "Fresh Air," in *Encyclopedia of Radio*, ed. Christopher H. Sterling, pp. 632–33.

54 "NPR's Growth During the Last 30 Years," <www.npr.org/About/growth.html> (January 2005).

55 Mark Braun, "Garrison Keillor," in *Encyclopedia of Radio*, ed. Christopher H. Sterling, pp. 806–9.

56 Corey Flintoff, "National Public Radio," in *Encyclopedia of Radio*, ed. Christopher H. Sterling, p. 1003.

57 The FCC's Allen Myers, in communication with the authors, told us:

The understanding at the time I came to the commission was that religious organizations didn't have an educational objective and, thus, did not comply with sections 73.503 and 73.612 of the rules to be licensed as noncommercial educational stations. As with a lot of things at the commission, standards slip over time and the exceptions become the rule. In the 1970s, the applicants were mainly churches which did not have education objectives. The churches could always form separate nonprofit educational corporations to be the licensee of their stations, but they were reluctant to do that because of the loss of control of a separate organization. However, as the nonreserved [commercial] frequencies became scarce, religious organizations were more willing to apply in the reserved [noncommercial] band, which still had some spectrum left. Once they began making showings as other educational organizations, albeit with religious education in mind, it was impossible for the commission to say no to them.

58 Myers, in communication with the authors.

59 Ibid.

60 See appendix Table B.6 for the trend.

61 "The Fortunate 501," *Broadcasting*, August 25, 1980, pp. 62, 66.

62 See appendix Table B.10.

63 "FM Share Nears 55 percent in Top 10 Markets," *Beyond the Ratings*, November 1981, p. 2.

64 "AM and FM Listeners Have a Lot in Common," *Broadcasting*, September 27, 1982, p. 81.

65 Communication from Lynn Christian, August 15, 2005.

66 FCC, *In the Matter of FM Quadraphonic Broadcasting, Memorandum Opinion and Order and Notice of Proposed Rule Making*, Docket 21310, July 1980.

67 See for example, letter from Radio Information Center for the Blind of Philadelphia to the FCC, October 29, 1980, which "appealed to you [the FCC] as humanitarians" not to harm similar services across the country.

68 For an excellent discussion of this proceeding and its larger importance, see Mark J. Braun, *AM Stereo and the FCC: Case Study of a Marketplace Shibboleth* (Norwood, N.J.: Ablex, 1994).

69 Michael Miller, "The History of Surround Sound," <http://www.informit.com/articles/article.asp?p=337317&seqNum=2> (accessed January 2005).

70 John D. Abel, Richard V. Ducey, and Mark R. Fratrik, *RadioOutlook: Forces Shaping the Radio Industry* (Washington, D.C.: National Association of Broadcasters, April 1988), p. 66.

71 Ibid., pp. 69–72.

72 Keith, *The Radio Station*, pp. 238–51.

73 "AM: Band on the Run," *Broadcasting*, November 11, 1985, p. 35.

CHAPTER 7

1 Lee Abrams, program chief of XM Radio, as interviewed by Michael C. Keith in *Journal of Radio Studies* 11 (December 2004): 222.

2 From 1977 to 1981, Congress grappled with several serious efforts to totally replace the law and, when the replacement notion failed, dramatically update it. Despite much time and struggle, and shelves of hearing-transcript volumes, nothing emerged from the effort save frustration. Only in the early 1990s, as communications technology changed ever more quickly, did the House and Senate once again take up the attempt to update the act to reflect current industry realities. Republican success in taking control of both houses of Congress in the 1994 midterm elections, however, delayed the effort as new members, committee chairs, and professional staff learned their way around. For a fuller discussion of the process that led up to the 1996 law, see Christopher H. Sterling and others, *Shaping American Telecommunications: A History of Technology, Policy, and Economics* (Mahwah, N.J.: Lawrence Erlbaum Associates, 2006), chap. 9.

3 Earlier substantial changes included the *Communications Satellite Act of 1962*, the public broadcasting provisions added in 1967, and the cable acts of 1984 and 1992.

4 This generally has been true in broadcasting history—which makes FM's decline in the early 1950s that much more striking.

5 Section 309 (k) of the *Communications Act of 1934*, as amended by the 1996 act.

6 Christopher H. Sterling, "Radio and the Telecommunications Act of 1996: An Initial Assessment," *Journal of Radio Studies* 4 (1997): 1–6.

7 David Foster Wallace, "Host," *Atlantic Monthly*, April 2005, p. 55.

8 R. Grover, "Deals: A Blare of Radio Mergers," *Business Week*, March 4, 1996, p. 42.

9 Todd Wirth, "Nationwide Format Oligopolies," *Journal of Radio Studies* 8 (Winter 2001): 249–70.

10 Anthony DeBarros, "Consolidation Changes Face of Radio," *USA Today* (July 7 1998), <www.radiodiversity.com/faceof radio.html> (January 2005).

11 "Mergers and Acquisitions," *Radio & Records*, September 24, 1999, p. 16.

12 DeBarros, "Consolidation Changes Face of Radio."

13 Ed Shane, "The State of the Industry," *Journal of Radio Studies* 5 (Summer 1998): 1–7.

14 James Lardner, "Radio: An Unexpected Hit in the Internet Age," *U.S. News and World Report*, October 18, 1999, p. 71.

15 Eric Boehlert, "Radio's Big Bully," <http://www.Salon.com>, April 30, 2001, <http://dir.salon.com/ent/feature/2001/04/30/clear_channel/index.html> (accessed January 2005).

16 Data provided to the authors from *Inside Radio*'s Cathy Devine, November 16, 2005.

17 *Texas Monthly* (October 27, 2001), <http://www.radiodiversity.com/archives/000736.shtml> (accessed January 2005).

18 Daren Fonda, "The Revolution in Radio," *Time*, April 19, 2004, p. 56.

19 Clear Channel Corporate Communications, November 16, 2006, <http://www.clearchannel.com/Corporate/PressRelease.aspx?PressReleaseID=1825>.

20 Radio newsletter editor Tom Taylor, personal communication, July 5, 2007.

21 DeBarros, "Consolidation Changes Face of Radio."

22 The estimate of a third is from Eric Rhoads, publisher of *Radio Ink*, in a communication with the authors, December 15, 2005. He readily admits there is no firm data and his guess is a "gut" reaction.

23 Eric Boehlert, "One Big Happy Channel," <http://www.Salon.com>, June 28, 2001, <http://dir.salon.com/tech/feature/2001/06/28/telecom_dereg/index.html> (accessed January 2005).

24 DeBarros, "Consolidation Changes Face of Radio."

25 Bill Snyder, "Take Back the Airwaves," *Twin Cities Revue*, June 10, 1999, <http://radiodiversity.com/tcrevue.html> (accessed January 2005).

26 Laura M. Holson, "Survey Shows Opposition to Radio Consolidation," *New York Times*, June 19, 2002.

27 Robert W. McChesney, "Digital Highway Robbery," *Nation* (April 1997), <http://www.thenation.com:80/issue/970421.0421mcch.htm> (accessed January 2005).

28 *Radio Ink*, January 28, 2005, <http://www.radioink.com/headlineentry.asp?hid=126980&pt=inkhead> (accessed January 2005).

29 Jennifer C. Kerr, "More Consolidation in Radio Business Could Hurt Free Expression, Senators Say," Associated Press, July 8, 2003, <http://sfgate.com/cgi-bin/article.cgi?file=/news/archive/2003/0> (accessed January 2005).

30 Matt Spangler, "Can't Find Nothin' on Radio?," *Radio & Records*, July 31, 1998, <http://www.radiodiversity.com/nothingonradio.html> (accessed January 2005).

31 DeBarros, "Consolidation Changes Face of Radio."

32 Marc Fisher, "The Great Radio Rebellion," *Washington Post*, June 2, 1998.

33 Todd L. Wirth, "Nationwide Format Oligopolies," *Journal of Radio Studies* 8 (Winter 2001): 249.

34 Todd Chambers, "Radio Programming Diversity in the Era of Consolidation," *Journal of Radio Studies* 10 (June 2003): 42–43.

35 Arbitron, *Radio Today* 2002 (2002).

36 *Barron's*, August 16, 2004, <http://online.barrons.com/documents/barrons2004 0816.htm>.

37 Marc Fisher, "On the FM Dial, Rock Is Sliding Away," *Washington Post*, November 27, 2005.

38 Joel Stein, "You Don't Know Jack," *Time*, August 15, 2005, p. 62.

39 Ibid.

40 Ben Sisaro, "Cousin Brucie Falls Victim to Changing Radio World," *New York Times*, June 6, 2005.

41 *Inside Radio*, December 16, 2005, p. 2.

42 Walter Sabo, "My FM Talk Diary," *Talkers Magazine*, April 2007, p. 10.

43 Michael Harrison, "Talk Media on the Front Lines of Reality," *Talkers Magazine*, January 2005, p. 8.

44 Kevin Casey, "The Coming Rise of FM Talk," *Talkers Magazine*, November 2005, p. 6.

45 Fisher, "On the FM Dial, Rock Is Sliding Away."

46 Joshua Green, "The Air America Plan," *Atlantic Monthly*, April 2005, p. 32.

47 Ibid., p. 8.

48 "Consultant Pins Radio's Hopes vs. Satellite on News/Talk," RAIN: *Radio and Internet Newsletter*, <http://www.kurthanson/archive/news/031405/index.asp> (accessed March 2005).

49 Admittedly, such ratings are largely found in markets with colleges and universities—or lots of people who are college alumni. See "Who's Got a 5.7 Share in San Fran., and a 4.1 in Boston?," *Inside Radio*, November 14, 2005, p. 2. (The 4.1 in Boston was for Boston University's WBUR, an NPR-programming station.)

50 Tom Taylor, "National Public Radio Says Listening Is Up," *Inside Radio*, March 29, 2005, <http://www.InsideRadio.com> (accessed March 2005).

51 Marc Fisher, "Beethoven's Revenge: Ratings Drop at Classical Music-less WETA," *Washington Post*, December 11, 2005.

52 James H. Duncan Jr., *An American Radio Trilogy, 1975 to 2004*, vol. 1, *The Markets* (Tesuque, N.Mex.: Duncan's American Radio, 2004), Los Angeles page 1.

53 The incident gave the language a new term: "wardrobe malfunction." Singers Janet Jackson and Justin Timberlake were performing a song when he (apparently inadvertently) undid part of her costume and her right breast was shown—for all of about 1.5 seconds. The impending furor, rapidly escalating to a white-hot political and social crisis during an election year, became the poster child for the whole argument about indecency on broadcast television and radio. Viacom was eventually stiffly fined by the FCC in a case still under court review as this book went to press.

54 Being subscription-based, satellite radio services (like cable TV) have traditionally been free of content limitations placed on freely available broadcasting. The fact that those who wish to listen have to purchase special receivers and pay a subscription fee makes listening a matter of choice, placing the process in a very different legal category than broadcast radio. Therefore, satellite radio offered shock jocks an opportunity to operate without restrictions.

55 *Inside Radio*, August 24, 2006, p. 2, citing <www.BridgeRatings.com>.

56 Ibid., p. 87.

57 *Inside Radio*, August 15, 2005, pp. 1–2.

58 "Host 'Bubba the Love Sponge' Fired," Reuters, February 24, 2004, <http://www.msnbc.msn.com/id/4362219> (accessed August 2005).

59 The courts have consistently held that services to which the audience must subscribe—such as satellite radio—are subject to much looser (if any) content control because such subscription clearly indicates a choice to listen.

60 FCC, "Broadcast Station Totals as of March 31, 2006," news release, May 26, 2006.

61 AM stations (all but about twenty-five of them commercial operations) totaled 4,978 in September 1990, 4,907 in mid-1995, and 4,685 in mid-2000. Their numbers increased slightly to 4,761 by early 2005. FCC official station totals, <http://www.fcc.gov/mb/audio/totals/index.html> (accessed August 2005).

62 This action was based on the 1997 decision by Congress to allow—if not actually encourage—the use of auctions for broadcasting stations, which had initially been exempted when spectrum auctions were first utilized for telecommunication services.

63 FCC, "FCC Announces Close to Unprecedented FM Auction: 110 Bidders Win 258 Construction Permits for New FM Stations," news release, November 24, 2004.

64 *Inside Radio*, August 11, 2006, p. 3.

65 Stephen Labaton, "F.C.C. Offers Low-Power FM Stations," *New York Times*, January 29, 1999.

66 Ibid.

67 Keith Brand, "The Rebirth of Low-Power FM Broadcasting in the U.S.," *Journal of Radio Studies* 11 (December 2004): 157.

68 FCC, *Creation of Low-Power Radio Service*, 15 FCC Record 19208 (2000).

69 The best survey of this whole period is found in Andy Opel, *Micro Radio and the FCC: Media Activism and the Struggle over Broadcast Policy* (Westport, Conn: Praeger, 2004).

70 Stephen Labaton, "Communications Lobby Puts Full-Court Press on Congress," *New York Times*, October 24, 2000.

71 FCC, "Report to the Congress on the Low-Power FM Interference Testing Program," February 19, 2004.

72 <http://www.fcc.gov/mb/audio/lpfm/index.html> (accessed January 2005). Emphasis added.

73 Brand, "The Rebirth of Low-Power FM Broadcasting in the U.S.," 153.

74 Allen Myers, FCC Mass Media Bureau, personal correspondence, January 18, 2005.

75 Brand, "The Rebirth of Low-Power FM Broadcasting in the U.S.," table 1, p. 163.

76 Personal correspondence with Michael Brown, January 4, 2005.

77 "NAB Urges Congress FCC Not to Remove LPFM Protections," *Radio Ink*, February 9, 2005, quoting NAB executive vice president of government relations

John S. Orlando, <http://www.radioink.com/headlineentry.asp?hid=127167& pt=inkhead> (accessed February 12, 2005).

78 "FCC Forces Radio Free Allston off Air; Station Weighs Options," *Boston Globe*, November 2, 1997.

79 "Activists Have Big Plans for Tiny Station," *Boston Globe*, March 9, 2000.

80 "Ruling Dooms Boston Webcaster," *Boston Globe*, July 18, 2002. The copyright payment ruling from the Library of Congress concerned music payments by webcasters. The AM station was off the air by 2005, according to communications with the authors from Donna Halper in Boston.

81 Heather Green et al., "The New Radio Revolution," *Business Week*, March 14, 2005, pp. 32–35. See also <http://www.businessweek.com/technology/content/ mar2005/tc2005> (accessed March 2005).

82 Fonda, "The Revolution in Radio," p. 55.

83 Arbitron, *Radio Today 2005* (2005).

84 Techtree news staff, "Sony Makes Walkman Mobile," February 15, 2005, <http://www.techtree.com/techtree/jsp/showstory.jsp?storyid=57639&s=ln> (accessed February 2005).

85 "Is Your Cell Phone the Future of Radio?," <http://www.about.com> (accessed February 2005).

86 Jon Fine, "Late to the Download Dance," *Business Week*, August 15, 2005, p. 24.

87 FCC, *Report and Order in General Docket 90-357 . . . Establishment and Regulation of New Digital Audio Radio Services*, January 12, 1995, paragraphs 2–5.

88 FCC, *Report and Order . . . Establishment of Rules and Policies for the Digital Audio Radio Satellite Service . . .* , 12 FCC rcd. 5754 (May 1997).

89 Michael C. Keith, interviewer, "Lee Abrams—From Broadcast to Satellite," *Journal of Radio Studies* 11 (December 2004): 221–22.

90 L. A. Lorek, "Changing the Way We People Listen," *San Antonio Express-News*, <http://www.insidebayarea.com/portlet/article/html/fragments/print_art> (accessed February 2005).

91 "Satellite Radio's Biggest Draw: No Commercials," *Radio Ink*, February 8, 2005, <http://radioink.com/headlineentry.asp?hid=127144&pt=inkhead> (accessed February 2005).

92 "Web Radio," as defined in Wikipedia, <http://en.wikipedia.org/wiki/web_ radio> (accessed January 2005).

93 Ibid.

94 Edison Media Research report for Arbitron as reported in Clea Simon, "The Web Catches and Reshapes Radio," *New York Times*, January 16, 2000.

95 Ibid.

96 See the survey of 365 randomly selected stations in Robert F. Potter, "Give the People What They Want: A Content Analysis of FM Radio Station Home Pages," *Journal of Broadcasting & Electronic Media* 46 (Fall 2002): 369–84.

97 They had argued similarly in the very early days of (AM) radio in the early 1920s, even before radio had adopted a commercial-advertising revenue model. In-

deed, the demands of ASCAP had led directly to the formation of the National Association of Broadcasters in 1923.

98 Public Law 104-39.

99 Public Law 105-304, 112 stat. 2860 (October 28, 1998).

100 67 Fed. Reg. 45239 (July 8, 2002).

101 Public Law 107-321; 116 Stat. 2780; 68 Fed. Reg. 35008 (June 11, 2003).

102 Michael Booth, "Denver Radio Stations Launch Battle to Win Back Listeners," *Denver Post*, December 5, 2004, <http://web.lexis-nexis.com/universe/document?_m=c302fc147c0e3f2> (accessed February 2005).

103 Fonda, "The Revolution in Radio," p. 55.

104 Hiawatha Bray, "Web 'radio' quickly finding niche markets," *Boston Globe* (March 28, 2005), pp. C1, C4.

105 "Tuning Out," *The Economist* (June 20, 2007), p. 74.

106 Olga Kharif, "The Last Days of Internet Radio?" <www.BusinessWeek.com> (March 7, 2007), <http://www.businessweek.com/print/technology/content/mar2007/tc>.

107 Fonda, "The Revolution in Radio," p. 55.

108 Shaun Assael, "Online and on the Edge," *New York Times*, September 23, 2007.

109 "FM Programming Adjusting to a World with Newer Media Options," *RAIN: Radio and Internet Newsletter*, January 6, 2005.

110 Andrew Keen, *The Cult of the Amateur: How Today's Internet Is Killing Our Culture* (New York: Doubleday, 2007), p. 126.

111 Gregory M. Lamb, "Radio Changes Its Tune," *Christian Science Monitor*, February 17, 2005, <http://www.csmonitor.com/2005/0217/p14s02-stct.html> (accessed February 2005).

112 "Clear Channel Radio Now Offering Digital Broadcast on 65 of Its Radio Stations," *Business Wire*, January 5, 2005, <http://www.businesswire.com> (accessed January 2005).

113 Stephen H. Wilstrom, "You Heard Right: HD Radio," *Business Week*, December 18, 2006, p. 28.

114 Richard Rudin and others, "Digital Audio Broadcasting," in *Encyclopedia of Radio*, ed. Christopher H. Sterling (New York: Fitzroy Dearborn, 2004), p. 456.

115 FCC, "Digital Audio Broadcasting (DAB)," <http://www.fcc.gov/mb/policy/dab.html> (accessed February 2005).

116 iBiquity Digital website, May 29, 2007, <http://www.ibiquity.com/hd_radio/hdradio_find_a_station>.

117 Charles Mann, "HD-Radio at a Glance," *Wired*, March 2005, p. 31.

118 *Inside Radio*, May 13, 2005, p. 2.

119 "Love of Radio Endures for Randy Michaels," <http://www.radioandrecords.com/Newsroom/2005_03_14/loveof.asp> (accessed March 2005).

120 *Inside Radio*, December 9, 2005, p. 3.

121 Michael Booth, "Stations Trying to Win Back Listeners," *Pittsburgh Post-Gazette*, December 6, 2004.

122 As quoted in "The Broadcasters Strike Back: 'Jack' and 'iPod-style' Radio,"

RAIN: *Radio and Internet Newsletter* (March 21, 2005), <http://www.kurthanson
.com/archive/news/031805/index.asp> (accessed March 2005).

123 "Wired: New Tech Will Not Kill, but 'Resurrect,' B'cast Radio," *Wired*, March
2005, <http://www.kurthanson.com/archive/news/022305/index.asp> (accessed March 2005).

124 Fine, "Late to the Download Dance."

EPILOGUE

1 Lawrence Lessing, *Man of High Fidelity: Edwin Howard Armstrong* (Philadelphia:
J. B. Lippincott, 1956; revised edition, Bantam Books, 1969), p. ix. A half
century after its original appearance in 1956, this remains the sole book-length
biography of the inventor.

2 Lynn Christian, in a fax communication with the authors, November 28,
2005.

3 W. Rupert Maclaurin, *Invention and Innovation in the Radio Industry* (New York:
Macmillan, 1949; repr. in "History of Broadcasting: Radio to Television" [New
York: Arno Press, 1971]).

4 Ibid., p. 190.

5 John Jewkes, David Sawers, and Richard Stillerman, *The Sources of Invention* (New
York: St. Martin's Press, 1958).

6 Ibid., p. 104.

7 Ibid., p. 354.

8 W. W. Rostow, *The Stages of Economic Growth: A Non-Communist Manifesto* (London:
Cambridge University Press, 1961; rev. ed., 1991).

9 Brian Winston, *Misunderstanding Media* (Cambridge, Mass: Harvard University
Press, 1986); revised as *Media Technology and Society: A History from the Telegraph to
the Internet* (London: Routledge, 1998). Neither title is very descriptive of Winston's selective approach. He focuses largely on the rise of four communication
technologies: telephone, television, computers, and communication satellites.
The revised edition provides more connecting glue among these four.

10 Everett M. Rogers, *Diffusion of Innovations*, 5th ed. (New York: Basic Books,
2003), appeared shortly before the author's death. Rogers provides a superior
survey of writing and research on the whole subject. The first edition appeared
in 1962, just a year after Rostow's work discussed above. Each edition became
more critical as the author sought to sift through and separate valid theories
from the crackpot schemes that inflict the subject.

11 Ibid., figure 6.1, p. 222.

12 Ibid., pp. 343–64.

13 The line (of more corporate than individual patents) was crossed in 1932, just
a year after the death of that consummate individual inventor, Thomas Edison.
A year later—just as Armstrong's patents were being granted—the U.S. Census Bureau dropped "inventor" as a career class. See Timothy L. O'Brien, "Not
Invented Here," *New York Times*, November 13, 2005.

14 Based on a dissertation (University of Illinois, 1969) and only to be read with

considerable care and caution is D. H. V. Erickson, *Armstrong's Fight for FM Broadcasting: One Man vs. Big Business and Bureaucracy* (University: University of Alabama Press, 1973).

15 Lessing, *Man of High Fidelity*. Lessing first wrote about Armstrong for *Fortune* magazine in 1939 and again in 1948. His book remains the best biography, but it is far from the scholarly analysis (with adequate documentation) that is still needed.

16 See Clayton Christensen, *The Innovator's Solution: Creating and Sustaining Successful Growth* (Cambridge, Mass.: Harvard Business School Press, 2003), for more on the role of the corporate "disruptor." For a useful brief summary of the central argument, see "The Blood of Incumbents," *The Economist*, October 30, 2004, pp. 23–24.

17 One of the authors of this history tunes to XM Radio while writing in his study—the disruption is closer than it may appear!

SELECTED BIBLIOGRAPHY

PUBLIC DOCUMENTS

Federal Communications Commission. *Annual Report.* Washington, D.C.: The
Commission, 1935–1997.

———. *Order No. 79.* Washington, D.C.: FCC mimeo 48496, March 20, 1941.

———. *Report on Docket 6651: FM Broadcast Service.* Washington, D.C.: FCC mimeo,
May 25, 1945.

———. *FCC Hearing on Docket No. 6768.* "Special Allocations Hearings" issue of
NAB Bulletin. Washington, D.C.: National Association of Broadcasters, August
24, 1945.

———. *Allocation Plan for FM Broadcast Stations.* FCC news release 87477, December
19, 1945.

———. *AM-FM Broadcast Financial Data.* FCC mimeo, 1956–81 (annual).

———. *Report and Order on Docket 12517: Technical Standards for Stereo Multiplex
Transmission.* FCC, April 20, 1961. Reprinted in *Broadcast Engineering* (May 1961).

———. *Report and Order on Docket 15084: . . . The Relationship between the AM and FM
Broadcast Services.* FCC mimeo 64-609, July 1, 1964.

———. *Memorandum Opinion and Order: Requests for Exemption from or Waiver of the
Provisions of Section 73.242 of the Commission's Rules (AM-FM Program Duplication).*
FCC mimeo 66-252, March 9, 1966.

———. *Report and Order: Creation of Low-Power Radio Service,* 15 FCC Record 19208
(2000).

———. *Report to Congress on the Low-Power FM Interference Testing Program.* February
19, 2004.

———. *Review of the Radio Industry* (2001, 2000, 1997). <http://fcc.gov/mb/policy/
radio.html>. July 2007.

U.S. Congress. *Communications Act of 1934.* 73rd Cong., June 18, 1934. Public Law
416. Washington, D.C.: Government Printing Office, 1934.

———. Senate Committee on Interstate and Foreign Commerce. *To Amend the
Communications Act of 1934: Hearings.* 78th Cong., 1st sess., November–December
1943. Washington, D.C.: Government Printing Office, 1943.

———. Senate Committee to Study Problems of American Small Business. *Small
Business Opportunities in FM Broadcasting: Report No. 4.* 79th Cong., 2nd sess., April
10, 1946. Washington, D.C.: Government Printing Office, 1946.

———. House Committee on Interstate and Foreign Commerce. *Radio Frequency
Modulation: Hearings.* 80th Cong., 2nd sess., February 1948. Washington, D.C.:
Government Printing Office, 1948.

———. Senate Committee on Interstate and Foreign Commerce. *Progress of FM Radio: Hearings.* 80th Cong., 2nd sess., March–May 1948. Washington, D.C.: Government Printing Office, 1948.

———. Senate Committee on the Judiciary, Subcommittee to Investigate the Administration of the Internal Security Act and other Internal Security Laws. *Pacifica Foundation: Hearings.* 88th Cong., 1st sess., January 1963. Washington, D.C.: Government Printing Office, 1963.

———. Library of Congress, Legislative Reference Service. "FM Programming," by Catherine S. Corry, June 30, 1965. Washington, D.C.: Government Printing Office, 1965.

———. *Public Broadcasting Act of 1967.* 90th Cong., November 7, 1967. Public Law 90-129. Washington, D.C.: Government Printing Office, 1967.

———. Senate Committee on Commerce, Subcommittee on Communications. *All-Channel Radio Receivers: Hearings.* 93rd Cong., 2nd sess., April 1974. Washington, D.C.: Government Printing Office, 1974.

———. House Committee on Small Business, Subcommittee on Antitrust, Consumers and Employment. *AM/FM/Stereo Radio Receivers in Automobiles: Hearings.* 95th Cong., 1st sess., September 1977. Washington, D.C.: Government Printing Office, 1977.

———. *Telecommunications Act of 1996.* 104th Cong., February 8, 1996. Public Law 104-104. Washington, D.C.: Government Printing Office, 1996.

———. House Energy and Commerce Committee. *FCC's Low-Power FM: A Review of the FCC's Spectrum Management Responsibilities: Hearing.* 106th Cong., 1st sess., February 2000.

U.S. Office of Education. *FM for Education.* Washington, D.C.: Government Printing Office, 1944; rev. ed., 1948.

BOOKS

All About Frequency Modulation. New York: Radcraft Publications (Radio-Craft Library no. 28), 1941.

Buzalski, Thomas J. "Field Tests of the Armstrong Wide-Band Frequency Modulation System from the Empire State Building." In *The Legacies of Edwin Howard Armstrong,* edited by John W. Morrisey, 245–50. New York: Radio Club of America, 1990.

Crowhurst, Norman H. *FM Stereo Multiplexing.* New York: Rider, 1961.

Davidson, Randall. *9XM Talking: WHA Radio and the Wisconsin Idea.* Madison: University of Wisconsin Press, 2006.

Dempsey, John Mark. *Sports-Talk Radio in America: Its Context and Culture.* Binghamton, N.Y.: Haworth Press, 2006.

Douglas, Susan J. *Listening In: Radio and the American Imagination.* New York: Times Books, 1999.

Duncan, James H., Jr. *American Radio: Tenth Anniversary Issue—A Prose and Statistical History.* Kalamazoo, Mich.: Duncan's American Radio, 1986.

———. *An American Radio Trilogy, 1975 to 2004.* 3 vols. Tesuque, N.Mex.: Duncan's American Radio, 2004–8.

Edelman, Murray. *The Licensing of Radio Services in the United States, 1927 to 1947.* Urbana: University of Illinois Press, 1950.

Elving, Bruce F. *FM Atlas and Station Directory.* Adolph, Minn.: FM Atlas, 1971–2007 (many editions).

Feldman, Leonard. *FM Multiplexing for Stereo.* 2nd ed. Indianapolis: Howard W. Sams, 1966

Fisher, Marc. *Something in the Air: Radio, Rock, and the Revolution That Shaped a Generation.* New York: Random House, 2007.

FM Station Operator's Handbook. Thurmont, Md.: TAB Books, 1966; rev. ed., 1973.

Fornatale, Peter, and Joshua E. Mills. *Radio in the Television Age.* New York: Overlook Press, 1980.

Foust, James C. *Big Voices on the Air: The Battle over Clear Channel Radio.* Ames: Iowa State University Press, 2000.

Halper, Donna L. *Invisible Stars: A Social History of Women in American Broadcasting.* Armonk, N.Y.: M. E. Sharpe, 2001.

Hill, Lewis. *Voluntary Listener-Sponsorship: A Report to Educational Broadcasters on the Experiment at KPFA, Berkeley, California.* Berkeley: Pacifica Foundation, 1958.

Hilliard, Robert L., and Michael C. Keith. *Dirty Discourse: Sex and Indecency in American Radio.* Ames: Iowa State Press, 2003.

———. *The Quieted Voice: The Rise and Demise of Localism in American Radio.* Carbondale: Southern Illinois University Press, 2005.

Hilmes, Michele. *Radio Voices: American Broadcasting, 1922–1952.* Minneapolis: University of Minnesota Press, 1997.

Hilmes, Michele, and Jason Loviglio, eds. *Radio Reader: Essays in the Cultural History of Radio.* New York: Routledge, 2002.

Hund, August. *Frequency Modulation.* New York: McGraw-Hill, 1942.

Inglis, Andrew F. "FM Radio Broadcasting." Chapter 3 of *Behind the Tube: A History of Broadcasting Technology and Business.* Stoneham, Mass.: Focal Press, 1990.

Johnson, Phylis A., and Michael C. Keith. *Queer Airwaves: The Story of Gay and Lesbian Broadcasting.* Armonk, N.Y.: M. E. Sharpe, 2001.

Keith, Michael C., ed. *Radio Cultures: The Sound Medium in American Life.* New York: Peter Lang Publishing, 2008.

———. *The Radio Station.* 5th ed. Boston: Focal Press, 2000.

———. *Signals in the Air: Native Broadcasting in America.* Westport, Conn.: Praeger, 1995.

———. *Sounds in the Dark: All-Night Radio in American Life.* Ames: Iowa State University Press, 2001.

———. *Talking Radio: An Oral History of American Radio in the Television Age.* Armonk, N.Y.: M. E. Sharpe, 2000.

———. *Voices in the Purple Haze: Underground Radio and the Sixties.* Westport, Conn.: Praeger, 1997.

Kiver, Stanley. *FM Simplified*. 3rd ed. Princeton, N.J.: Van Nostrand, 1960.

Kurtz, Howard. *Hot Air: All Talk All the Time*. New York: Times Books, 1996.

Ladd, Jim. *Radio Waves: Life and Revolution on the FM Dial*. New York: St. Martin's Press, 1991.

Land, Jeff. *Active Radio: Pacifica's Brash Experiment*. Minneapolis: University of Minnesota Press, 1999.

Lasar, Matthew. *Pacifica Radio: The Rise of an Alternative Network*. Philadelphia: Temple University Press, 1999.

Laufer, Peter. *Inside Talk Radio: America's Voice or Just Hot Air?* Secaucus, N.J.: Birch Lane Press, 1995.

Lessing, Lawrence. *Man of High Fidelity: Edwin Howard Armstrong*. Philadelphia: J. B. Lippincott, 1956; reissued with new introduction by Bantam Books, 1969.

Lewis, Tom. *Empire of the Air: The Men Who Made Radio*. New York: HarperCollins, 1991.

Looker, Thomas. *The Sound and the Story: NPR and the Art of Radio*. Boston: Houghton Mifflin, 1995.

Maclaurin, W. Rupert. *Invention and Innovation in the Radio Industry*. New York: Macmillan, 1949; reprinted in "History of Broadcasting: Radio to Television." New York: Arno Press, 1971.

Marchand, Nathan. *Frequency Modulation*. New York: Murray Hill Books, 1946.

McCauley, Michael. *NPR: The Trials and Triumphs of National Public Radio*. New York: Columbia University Press, 2005.

McCourt, Tom. *Conflicting Communication Interests in America: The Case of National Public Radio*. Westport, Conn.: Praeger, 1999.

Milam, Lorenzo. *Sex in Broadcasting: A Handbook on Starting a Radio Station for a Community*. Los Gatos, Calif: Dildo Press, 1975.

Morrisey, John W., ed. *The Legacies of Edwin Howard Armstrong*. New York: Radio Club of America, 1990.

Neer, Richard. *FM: The Rise and Fall of Rock Radio*. New York: Villard, 2001.

Olszewski, Mike. *Radio Daze: Stories from the Front in Cleveland's FM Air Wars*. Kent, Ohio: Kent State University Press, 2003.

Opel, Andy. *Micro Radio and the FCC: Media Activism and the Struggle over Broadcast Policy*. Westport, Conn.: Praeger, 2004.

Phillips, Lisa. *Public Radio: Behind the Voices*. New York: Perseus, 2006.

Post, Steve. *Playing in the FM Band*. New York: Viking Press, 1974.

Raymond, Dana M. "The Armstrong FM Litigation." In *The Legacies of Edwin Howard Armstrong*, edited by John W. Morrisey, 251–56. New York: Radio Club of America, 1990.

Rider, John F. *FM: An Introduction to Frequency Modulation*. New York: Rider, 1940.

Rogers, Everett M. *Diffusion of Innovations*. 5th ed. New York: Basic Books, 2003.

Rostow, W. W. *The Stages of Economic Growth—A Non-Communist Manifesto*. London: Cambridge University Press, 1961; rev. ed. 1991.

Ruggiero, G. *Microradio and Democracy: (Low) Power to the People*. New York: Seven Stories Press, 1999.

Sanger, Elliott. *Rebel in Radio: The Story of WQXR*. New York: Hastings House, 1973.

Siepmann, Charles A. *Radio's Second Chance*. Boston: Atlantic Little Brown, 1946.

Sleeper, Milton B., ed. *FM Radio Handbook: 1946 Edition*. Great Barrington, Mass.: FM Company, 1946.

Slotten, Hugh R. "'Rainbow in the Sky': FM Radio, Technical Superiority, and Regulatory Decision Making, 1936–1948." Chapter 4 of *Radio and Television Regulation: Broadcast Technology in the United States, 1920–1960*, 113–44. Baltimore: Johns Hopkins University Press, 2000.

Sterling, Christopher H. *Electronic Media: A Guide to Trends in Broadcasting and Newer Technologies, 1920–1983*. New York: Praeger, 1984.

——, ed. *Encyclopedia of Radio*. 3 vols. New York: Fitzroy-Dearborn, 2004.

——, ed. "Part C: FM Radio, 1940–1945." In *Regulating Radio*. Vol. 6 of *The Rise of American Radio*. London: Routledge, 2007.

Sterling, Christopher H., and John Michael Kittross. *Stay Tuned: A History of American Broadcasting*. 3rd ed. Mahwah, N.J.: Lawrence Erlbaum Associates, 2002.

Sunier, John. *The Story of Stereo, 1881–*. New York: Gernsback Library, 1960.

Walker, Jesse. *Rebels on the Air: An Alternative History of Radio in America*. New York: New York University Press, 2001.

Warner, Harry P. "Frequency Modulation." Chapter 6 of *Radio and Television Law*. Albany, N.Y.: Matthew Bender, 1948.

Winston, Brian. *Media Technology and Society: A History from the Telegraph to the Internet*. London: Routledge, 1998.

ARTICLES AND REPORTS

Advertisers Are Asking Questions about FM . . . New York: Radio Advertising Bureau, January 1961.

American Broadcasting Company. *FM Radio: A Report on Its Media and Market Characteristics*. New York: ABC, 1968.

Armstrong, Edwin Howard. "Evolution of Frequency Modulation." *Electronic Engineering* 59 (December 1940): 485–93.

——. "FM—Its Perspective in Radio History." *FM Business*, October 1946, pp. 11–13, 58.

——. "Future Uses of Frequency Modulation." *Annals of the American Academy of Political and Social Science* 213 (January 1941): 153–61.

——. "Mathematical Theory vs. Physical Concept." *FM and Television*, August 1944, pp. 11–13, 36.

——. "A Method of Reducing Disturbances in Radio Signaling by a System of Frequency Modulation." *Proceedings of the Institute of Radio Engineers* 24 (May 1936): 689–740.

——. "The New Radio Freedom." *Journal of the Franklin Institute* 232 (September 1941): 213–16.

"Armstrong of Radio." *Fortune*, February 1948, 88–91, 198–210.

"At Last—Admen Talk Real FM." *Sponsor*, July 9, 1962, pp. 32–35, 50.

"Automated Radio: It's Alive and Prospering." *Broadcasting*, June 9, 1969, pp. 54–65.

Beard, Richard L. "The Short Unhappy Life of Transit Radio." *Journal of Broadcasting* 12 (Fall 1968): 327–40.

Beson, Stanley M. "AM versus FM: The Battle of the Bands." *Industrial and Corporate Change* 1 (1992): 375–96.

Carson, John R. "Notes on the Theory of Modulation." *Proceedings of the Institute of Radio Engineers* 10 (February 1922): 57–64.

Conly, John. "FM to the Rescue." *Atlantic*, January 1951, 91–95.

———. "They Shall Have Music: Tuners, Aerials, and FM." *Atlantic*, September 1955, pp. 93–96.

Cox Looks at FM Radio Past, Present and Future. Atlanta: Cox Broadcasting, 1975.

DeMars, Paul A. "Frequency Modulation: History and Progress." *Broadcasting Yearbook 1940*. Washington, D.C.: Broadcasting, 1940, p. 372.

Denny, Charles. "FM: A Progress Report." *Frequency Modulation Business* 1 (May 1946): 7–10, 32–33.

Dick, Stephen J., and W. McDowell. "From Pirates, Pranksters, and Prophets: Understanding America's Unlicensed 'Free' Radio Movement." *Journal of Radio Studies* 7 (2000): 329–41.

[Dorrance, Dick]. *Broadcasting's Better Mousetrap*. New York: FM Broadcasters, Inc., n.d. [1940?].

———. *FM Bulletin of the FMBI*. New York and Washington, D.C.: FM Broadcasters, Inc., 1940–44 (biweekly).

Dreher, Carl. "E. H. Armstrong: The Hero as Inventor," *Harper's*, April 1956, pp. 58–66.

"Earliest FM Radio Stations." <http://members.aol.com/jeff560/fmfirst.html>. August 2005.

Eshelman, David. "The Emergence of Educational FM." *NAEB Journal* 26 (March–April 1967): 53–64.

"FM Broadcasting Chronology." <http://members.aol.com/jeff560/chronofm.html>. August 2005.

"FM Is Ready to Hit." *Mediascope*, January 1966, pp. 83–94.

"FM Radio Has to Change Its Tune." *Business Week*, September 24, 1966, pp. 173–76.

"FM Reaches for the Honey." *U.S. Radio*, July 1960, pp. 25–54.

Godley, Paul F. "Prof. Armstrong's System—What It Means." *Broadcasting*, July 1, 1936, pp. 72, 84.

Hoefer, P. B. "Facts on FM Station Ownership." *Radio News*, June 1945, pp. 36–37, 120–24.

Jaffe, Alfred J. "Ted Bates Study Finds Impressive FM Growth." *Television/Radio Age*, March 8, 1971, pp. 21–23, 48–50.

Keith, George W. "Sic Gloria Transit Radio." *Public Utilities Fornightly*, September 28, 1950, pp. 5–10.

Keston, Paul. *Post-War Shortwave, FM, and Television*. New York: CBS, 1944.

Konecky, Paul. "The People's Radio Foundation: A Plan to Foster the Establishment of Community FM Stations in the UAW-CIO-PAC Pattern." *FM and Television*, March 1945, pp. 33, 63–68.

Lapica, Ray. "The FCC: Protector or Censor: Part I—The FM Program Duplication Rule." *Southern California Law Review* 38 (Summer 1965): 634–71.

[Lessing, Lawrence]. "Revolution in Radio." *Fortune*, October 1939, pp. 86–88, 116–121.

Lewis, William B. "The Possibility of a Fifth Network: Why the American Network Was Dissolved, and Why the Newspapers May Form a New FM Net." *FM and Television*, November 1944, 18–20.

Liftgate, Tony, and Gil Faggen. "FM . . . Gold in Them Thar Hills?," *Timebuyer*, August 1966, pp. 16–19, 38–39.

Longley, Lawrence D. "The FM Shift in 1945." *Journal of Broadcasting* 12 (Fall 1968): 353–65.

Lubell, Samuel. "Comes the Radio Revolution." *Saturday Evening Post*, July 6, 1940, pp. 18–19, 36–39.

Maynard, Harry E. "A New Look at FM." *Audio*, February 1965, pp. 36–40.

National Association of Broadcasters. *FMphasis!* Washington, D.C.: NAB, 1959–72 (monthly).

National Association of Educational Broadcasters. *The Hidden Medium: A Status Report on Educational Radio in the United States*. Washington, D.C.: NAEB, April 1967.

National Association of FM Broadcasters. *National FM Programming Trends: 1967*. New York: NAFMB, 1967.

———. *National FM Programming Trends: 1968*. New York: NAFMB, 1968.

National Broadcasting Company. *FM: A Statement of NBC's FM Policy*. New York: NBC, 1944.

"A New Head of Steam for FM." *Sponsor*, June 13, 1959, 34–36, 70.

"New Radio Marvel Revealed in Test." *New York Times*, March 24, 1939, p. 24.

Parker, Lorne. *SCA—A New Medium*. Madison: University of Wisconsin Extension, 1967.

Radio Corporation of America. *FM Broadcasting*. New York: RCA, n.d. [1944?].

Sleeper, Milton B. "What's behind the AM vs. FM Battle?" *FM and Television*, August 1945, pp. 27–28, 80–85.

"Special Report: A Dramatic Spurt in FM Development." *Broadcasting*, February 20, 1961, pp. 78–96.

"Special Report: And Now FM Will Have the Numbers, Too." *Broadcasting*, July 29, 1963, pp. 51–66.

"Special Report: FM, At Long Last, Is Making Its Move." *Broadcasting*, February 23, 1970, pp. 47–58.

"Special Report: FM Sniffs Sweet Smell of Success." *Broadcasting*, July 31, 1967, pp. 55–100.

"Special Report: FM—The Great Leaps Forward." *Broadcasting*, January 22, 1979, pp. 32–49.

"Special Report: Have Audience, Can Sell—FM." *Broadcasting*, February 9, 1959, pp. 124–35.

"Special Report: The Rights of Passage Are All over for FM Radio; It's out on Its Own." *Broadcasting*, September 24, 1973, pp. 31–53.

Stanton, Frank. *FM—The Key to Future Radio Allocations*. New York: CBS, 1946.

"Staticless Radio." *Scientific American*, May 1939, 291.

Stavitsky, Alan G., Robert K. Avery, and Helena Vanhala. "From Class D to LPFM: The High-Powered Politics of Low-Power Radio." *Journalism & Mass Communication Quarterly* 78 (Summer 2001): 340–54.

"Stereo Broadcasting: What Does It Mean to Advertising?" *Printer's Ink*, October 24, 1958, pp. 21–24.

Sterling, Christopher H. "Newspaper Ownership of Broadcast Stations, 1920–1969." *Journalism Quarterly* 46 (Summer 1969): 227–36, 254.

———. "Second Service: Some Keys to the Development of FM Broadcasting." *Journal of Broadcasting* 15 (Spring 1971): 181–94.

———. "WTMJ-FM: A Case Study in the Development of FM Broadcasting." *Journal of Broadcasting* 12 (Fall 1968): 341–52.

Sulzer, Elmer G., and Jean C. Halterman. *Frequency Modulation Broadcasting in Indiana*. Bloomington: Indiana University School of Business, Indiana Business Information Bulletin No. 34, 1959.

"The 'Quality' Medium Is Not Strained." *Sponsor*, October 3, 1966, pp. 31–38, 56.

Toombs, Alfred. "The Radio Battle of 1941: FM vs. AM." *Radio News*, March 1941, pp. 7, 43–45.

What AM-FM Station Managers Say about Their FM Operations. New York: Radio Advertising Bureau, 1962.

Williams, Martin. "Networks for FM." *Saturday Review of Literature*, January 26, 1963, pp. 55–56, 93.

UNPUBLISHED MATERIALS

Allen, Lyman. "What Makes FM Succeed." South Lincoln, Mass.: Privately distributed, n.d. [February 1959?].

Dillard, Everett L. "The FM Facts of Life." Speech to the FM Association Sales Clinic, New York, April 1, 1949.

Fenz, Roland Edgar. "Building an Audience for an FM Radio Station." Master's thesis, University of Wisconsin, Madison, 1949.

Hardenstein, Phyllis M. "FM—Radio's Riddle." Master's thesis, University of Wisconsin, Madison, 1951.

Hastings, T. Mitchell. "The Future Is FM." Speech before the Fourth Annual Convention of the National Association of FM Broadcasters, Chicago, March 30, 1963.

Hogan, Mary Ellen. "The Innovation of FM Radio: Armstrong vs. the Radio Corporation of America." Master's thesis, Temple University, 1972.

Jansky, C. M., Jr. "FM—Educational Radio's Second Chance—Will Educators

Grasp It?" Remarks before the Public Service Radio Institute, Madison, Wis., August 5, 1946.

———. "The Demonstrated Potentialities of Frequency Modulation Broadcasting on Very High Frequencies." Remarks before delegates to the International Telecommunication Conference, Atlantic City, N.J., August 6, 1947.

Maxon, Inc. "FM Radio: The Frustrated Medium." New York: Maxon, March 30, 1956.

National Broadcasting Company, Division of Corporate Planning. "Frequency Modulation." New York, 1959.

Price, Glenn W. "The Resurgence of Commercial FM Broadcasting in Metropolitan Kansas City." Master's thesis, University of Wisconsin, Madison, 1959.

Radio Technical Planning Board. "Brief on Behalf of Panel 5, FM Broadcasting, of the Radio Technical Planning Board." Washington, D.C.: RTPB (before the FCC), February 21, 1945.

Saettler, L. Paul. "A Comparative Study of Frequency Modulation Programs in Los Angeles." Master's thesis, University of Southern California, 1949.

Salak, Ronald K. "The Development and Growth of FM Stereophonic Broadcasting: A History." Master's thesis, Michigan State University, 1965.

Schwartz, Walter. "FM Radio Is Dead." Speech before the Annual Convention of the National Association of FM Broadcasters, Washington, D.C., March 21, 1969.

Sterling, Christopher H. "WTMJ-FM: The Milwaukee Journal FM Station, 1939–1966." Master's thesis, University of Wisconsin, Madison, 1966.

———. "Second Service: A History of Commercial FM Broadcasting to 1969." Ph.D. diss., University of Wisconsin, Madison, 1969.

"10 Market Composite Three Media Study." New York: The Pulse, Inc., April 1964.

of (1940), 32–34. *See also* Licenses; Stations

Communications Act of 1934, 9, 87, 178–80, 266 (n. 84)

Communism, 116–17

Community stations: classification of, 62–63, 75–76; in developing countries, xii–xiii; development of, 147–48, 219; innovation on, 154; LPFM, 195; postwar growth in, lack of, 75–76

Compact discs (CDs), 175–76, 197

Competition: between AM and FM, 51; from digital technology, 178, 196–204, 213; from LPFM, 194–96; ownership consolidation and, 180, 187; and program diversity, 187; between public stations, 170–71; from satellite radio, 198–200; from television, 37, 56, 70–71, 102; from Web stations, 200

Concert Network, 112–13

Congress, U.S.: on AM stereo, 174; on auctions, 284 (n. 62); 1994 elections in, 281 (n. 2); on indecency, 192, 193; on LPFM, 195; on Pacifica Foundation, 116–17; postwar report on FM by, 72, 261 (n. 12); on public radio, 144; on receivers, 151; on simulcasting, 87; in spectrum allocation, 60, 62, 63, 64–65; Telecommunications Act by, 178–80; on webcasting, 201–3

Connecticut, 25, 138

Conservative talk radio, 4, 168

Consolidation of stations, 179–87

Construction, during World War II, 41, 43, 60

Construction permits (CPs), 39, 43, 74, 193. *See also* Licenses

Contemporary hit radio (CHR), 164, 187

Continental Network, 79–81

Cooke, Holland, 190

Cooperative Analysis of Broadcasting, 16

Copps, Michael, 186

Copyright issues, 201–3

Copyright Royalty Board, 202

Corporate control: academic study of, 5; as cost of success, 153–54; of patents, 211, 217, 287 (n. 13); and program diversity, 185

Corporation for Public Broadcasting (CPB), xii, 136, 144–48, 171, 206, 276 (n. 73)

Costas, Bob, 267 (n. 114)

Coughlin, Charles, 15

Counterculture, 11, 129–33

Counterfactual history, 221–22

Country music, 71, 166, 188

Countrypolitan, 166

Coverage expansion for FM, 77, 242–45

Cox Broadcasting, 152

Coy, Wayne, 72

Craig, Douglas, 6

Craven, T. A. M., 57, 62

Critical mass, 216

Critical studies movement, 5

Crocker, Frankie, 165

Crosby Laboratories, 109

Crystal, 173–74

Cue magazine, 114

Culbert, David, 6

Culture, FM in, 3, 4, 11, 135, 169–70

Cumia, Anthony, 192, 199

Cumulus, 186

Czitrom, Daniel, 5–6

Dallas, Tex., 70–71, 138

Damm, Walter, 43, 54, 57, 115–16

Daniels, Yvonne, 134

Daytime broadcasts, 71, 143, 158

Dees, Rick, 134

De Forest, Lee, 18

Electronic Industries Association, 110,
    111, 123
Empire of the Air (Lewis), 217
Empire State Building, 20, 28, 252
    (n. 27)
Engel, Harold, 95
Entertainment programs, 6–7
Ethics, in advertising, 190
Ethnic stations, xii
Eureka-147 digital-radio system, 205
European radio, 2, 247 (n. 1)
Evansville, Ind., 39, 51
Experimental FM stations: decline in,
    153; first stations as, 23, 27, 28–
    29; transition to commercial, 38;
    underground, 129–33

Facsimile, 14, 60
Fairness Doctrine, 168, 171, 279 (n. 47)
Fan magazines, 15, 251 (n. 5)
Fass, Bob, 131, 134
FCC. *See* Federal Communications
    Commission
Featherbedding, 87, 266 (n. 82)
Federal Communications Commission
    (FCC): academic study of, 10;
    on AM as standard radio, 251
    (n. 12); AM stations limited by,
    69; annual reports of, 105, 106,
    256 (n. 28); auctions by, 193,
    284 (n. 62); authorization of FM
    by, 28–29; on call letters, 40; in
    counterfactual history, 221–22; in
    development of FM, 212, 219–20;
    on drug-related content, 130; on
    educational stations, xi, 33, 94–95;
    on educational television, 97; on
    experimental FM stations, 23, 27,
    28–29, 38; Fairness Doctrine of, 168,
    171, 279 (n. 47); on four-channel
    sound, 150, 174; on HD, 205–6;
    on indecency, 191–93; on LPFM,
    159–60, 194–96; and pirate stations,

162; and postwar growth, 74–75; on
    religious radio, 148–49; rise of FM
    predicted by, 72, 106; on satellite
    radio, 198; on SCAs, 89, 90, 102,
    159; on station closures, 82–83; on
    station ownership, 33, 42, 63, 156,
    179–80; on stereo, 110–11, 174; on
    storecasting, 89; on subscription
    radio, 51–52; on transformation
    in 1958, 105; in World War II, 43.
    See also Allotments; Classification;
    Licenses; Simulcasting; Spectrum
    allocation
Federal Communications Commission
    (FCC) hearings: on newspaper
    ownership, 42; on spectrum
    allocation, 28, 55–60, 62, 63–64;
    on status of FM in 1940, 30–34
Federal Radio Commission, 9
Feedback circuit, 18
Films, promotional, 39–40
Film studies, 3, 247 (n. 6)
Fine-arts stations, 85, 86
Fine-music stations, xi, xii
Fireside chats, 6, 15
Fisher, Marc, 187
Florida, 138
Fly, James Lawrence, 42, 53, 62, 72,
    256 (n. 27)
FM (periodical), 39, 255 (n. 8)
FM and Television (periodical), 255 (n. 8)
FM Association (FMA), 74, 84
FM Broadcasters, Inc. (FMBI): on call
    letters, 40; conventions held by, 43,
    45; during decline of 1950s, 84; at
    FCC hearings, 31; mission of, 29;
    newsletters of, 29, 255 (n. 6); on
    newspaper ownership, 42; on press
    coverage, 39; on program guides, 52;
    on receivers in use, 54; on spectrum
    allocation, 56–57, 59; during World
    War II, 43, 54
FM Broadcasting Service, 113

in, 162–68, 187–89; syndicated,
138–39; television's influence
on, 70; transcribed, 23, 49; in
transformation of 1958, 113–16;
on underground stations, 130–31;
during World War II, 49, 50. *See also*
specific types of music
Mutual Broadcasting System, 15, 24,
45, 48, 159
Muzak, ix, 51–52
Myers, Allen, 148, 171, 280 (n. 57)

N. W. Ayer agency, 143
NAB. *See* National Association of
Broadcasters
Nadel, Roger, 204
NAFMB. *See* National Association of
FM Broadcasters
Narrowcasting, 167
Nashville, Tenn., 40, 51
National Association of Broadcasters
(NAB): on automation systems, 163;
Clear Channel in, 182; conventions
held by, 105, 142; during decline
of 1950s, 84; establishment of, 24,
286 (n. 97); on interference, 157;
on LPFM, 194, 195–96; merger with
other groups, 84, 275 (n. 65); on
pirate stations, 162; on simulcasting,
119, 128; on spectrum allocation, 59;
on Telecommunications Act, 179
National Association of Educational
Broadcasters, 144
National Association of FM
Broadcasters (NAFMB), 105, 119,
142, 143–44
National Association of Manufacturers,
83
National Bureau of Standards (NBS),
57
National Educational Radio (NER), 144
National Federation of Community
Broadcasters (NFCB), 148, 170
Nationalism, 8

National Public Radio (NPR): on
allotments, 157; audience size
for, 170; classical music on, 167;
creation of, xii, 145–46; expansion
in 1980s, 170; funding for, 171; HD
adopted by, 206; innovation on,
170, 215; membership criteria for,
146, 276 (n. 73); mission of, 145–
46; mistakes by, 170–71; news on,
191; personalities on, 134; on pirate
stations, 162; programming on,
145–46, 154, 170–71
National Quadraphonic Radio
Committee (NQRC), 150
National Radio Broadcasters
Association (NRBA), 144, 275
(n. 65)
National Stereophonic Radio
Committee (NSRC), 110
National Telecommunications and
Information Administration (NTIA),
136, 157
Native American radio, 8, 11, 135–36,
169–70
NBC: establishment of, 15; at FCC
hearings, 57; first FM station of,
28; FM network of, 45–48, 49, 113,
139–40; internal report on FM, 104;
news programs of, 15; simulcasting
by, 50, 119; stereo broadcasts by,
109
Nebraska, 70–71
Networks: AT&T links for, 77, 112, 140,
175, 263 (n. 41); development of,
45–49; national, 15, 48–49, 58, 77–
81; regional, 48, 58, 77–81, 112–13;
statewide educational, 53, 95–97. *See
also* specific networks
Newark, N.J., 51
New England, 62, 112–13
New Hampshire, 25, 51
New Jersey, 23, 49, 51, 73, 77, 79, 138
Newman, Kathy, 9
Newsletters, FMBI, 29, 255 (n. 6)

16; for digital technologies, 196–97;
first FM stations registering in,
124–25; FM surpassing AM in, 152,
155, 172; Hooper, 16, 125; separate,
for FM and AM, 125; and station
sale prices, 141; for underground
stations, 136; for Web stations, 202,
203

RCA. *See* Radio Corporation of America

Readus, DeWayne. *See* Kantako,
M'banna

Reagan, Ronald, 161

Real Audio Player software, 200

Receivers, FM: vs. AM, 229; and
audience size, 91, 122; booklets
promoting, 39, 54; cost of, 1, 28, 50,
54, 92, 123, 218; after FCC approval
of FM, 34; first, 23, 28; HD, 206;
imported, 151; stereo, 110–11, 149;
technological improvements to, 157;
transition to higher frequencies, 73,
76, 91; after World War II, 92–93;
during World War II, 53–55

Receiver sales and penetration: in
1930s, 14–15; in 1940s, 54; in 1950s,
91–94, 103, 122–23; in 1960s, 123–
24, 151; in 1970s, 152; in 1980s, 172;
historical statistics on, 234, 238–39

Record format, 85

Recording Industry Association of
America (RIAA), 201, 202

Regenerative circuit, 18

Regulation: academic study of, 8–10;
counterfactual history of, 221–22;
in development of FM, 212, 219–20.
See also Federal Communications
Commission

Relays, 77–80

Religious radio: development of, 148–
49, 219; LPFM, 195; noncommercial,
171–72, 280 (n. 57)

Research. *See* Academic research

Revenue: of ABC network, 141;
from functional-music services,

88–90; from multiplexing, 90,
98, 108; from satellite radio, 199–
200; from station consolidation,
180–82; from talk format, 189;
Telecommunications Act and, 180–
82; from underground stations, 136;
during World War II, 51–52

Rhoads, Eric, 282 (n. 22)

Rice, Condoleezza, 192

Rock music: development of, 71; and
DJs, 133–34; formats of, 136–37,
164–65, 188; in Top 40, 71, 164; on
underground stations, 130

Roger, Everett, 216, 287 (n. 10)

Roosevelt, Franklin D., 6, 15, 37–38

Rostow, W. W., 211–13, 216, 219

Roszak, Theodore, 103

Rotations, fast, 164

Royal, John, 50

Royalties, 202

Runyon, Carmine R. "Randy," 21–22,
23, 28

Rural Network, 77

Rural stations, 62–63, 75

Saddenwater, Harry, 20

St. Louis, Mo., 160

Salem Communications Corporation,
182

San Antonio Broadcasting Company,
182

San Francisco, Calif., 52, 113, 129, 131–
32, 133, 138, 174

San Francisco Bay Reporter, 117

Santayana, George, 3

Sarnoff, David, 16, 19–21, 47, 68, 217,
220

Satellite(s), 175, 197–98

Satellite CD Radio, 198

Satellite radio, 188, 189, 192, 197–200,
205, 283 (n. 54), 284 (n. 59)

SCA. *See* Subsidiary Communications
Authorization

Scelsa, Vin, 134

public, 190–91; revenue from, 189; shock jocks in, 168–69

Taped programs: in automation systems, 137–39; on Continental Network, 81; regional networks sharing, 112; on underground stations, 136

Taylor, Marlin, 139

Taylor, Tom, 191

Technology: academic study of, 5, 10, 248 (n. 16); evolution of, 157, 174–76; stages of development of, 213–16. *See also* specific types

Telecommunications Act of 1996, 178–80, 180, 183–85, 281 (n. 2)

Telephones, 14, 197

Television: in competition with radio, 37, 56, 70–71, 102; development of, vs. FM, 217–18; educational, 97; in FCC hearings, 31; growth of, 1, 68–70, 103; indecency on, 191; innovations in, 14, 217–18; as RCA focus, 20–21, 28, 31–32, 68; satellite, 199; stereo in, 109

Television sets, 69, 93, 151, 217

Television stations: allotments for, 107; low-power, 194; number of, 1, 69, 103; spectrum allocation for, 28, 31–32, 55–58, 61

Tennessee, 40, 51, 52, 78

Terkel, Studs, 115

Texas, ix–x, 70–71, 111, 112, 138

Texas Monthly, 183

Thomas, Jay, 134

Thomas, Tom, 148

Timberlake, Justin, 283 (n. 53)

Tipping point, 216

Tobey, Charles, 64

Top 40 radio, 70–71, 102, 113–14, 129, 143, 164, 166

Torick, Emil, 175

Totenberg, Nina, 134

Trade groups, 84, 105. *See also* specific groups

Transcriptions, 23, 49, 253 (n. 36)

Transistor radios, 123

Transit radio, 88, 89

Translators, 54, 147, 160

Transmitters: first, 23–25, 27–28; FM-translator, 147; improvements to, 157; transition to higher frequencies, 73, 76

Triple-A radio, 167, 188

Truman, Harry, 87

Two-channel sound, 149

UC108, 165

UHF television, 14, 151, 217–18

Ullman, Debbie, 132

Underground stations, 129–33, 136

United States Department of Agriculture (USDA), 71

University of Houston, 97

University of Illinois, 52

University of Wisconsin, xi, 95, 97

Urban areas. *See* Cities

Urban-contemporary (UC) stations, 165–66

U.S. FM (magazine), 125, 273 (n. 98)

U.S. *Radio* (periodical), 125, 273 (n. 98)

USA Today, 181, 183–84

Vancouver (Canada), 189

Vermont, 25

Veterans, 68, 69, 76

VHF spectrum, 31, 32, 217

Viacom, 283 (n. 53)

Vietnam War, 154

Volunteers, station, xii–xiii

W1XIR, 24–25

W1XOJ, 24, 253 (n. 42)

W2XDG, 20

W2XMN, 23, 48, 79, 161

W2XOR, 51

W2XQR, 27

W2XWG, 28

W39B, 51